FutureFish in Century 21:

The North Pacific Fisheries Handle Coming Trends, Radical Environmentalism and Digital Cyberspace (1991-92, 1994-97)

C.D. Bay-Hansen

Illustrations by Charles A. Rondeau

Printed in Victoria, Canada

Canadian Cataloguing in Publication Data

Bay-Hansen, C. D., 1944-
   FutureFish 2000

   Includes bibliographical references and index.
   ISBN 1-55212-411-8

   1. Fisheries--Pacific Coast (B.C.)   2. Fisheries--Pacific
Coast (U.S.)
   3. Fishery management--Pacific Coast (B.C.)   4. Fishery
management--Pacific Coast (U.S.)   I. Rondeau, Charles A.   II.
Title.

SH214.4.B39 2000   338.3'727'091643   C00-910699-5

TRAFFORD

This book was published *on-demand* in cooperation with Trafford Publishing.
On-demand publishing is a unique process and service of making a book available for retail
sale to the public taking advantage of on-demand manufacturing and Internet marketing.
On-demand publishing includes promotions, retail sales, manufacturing, order fulfilment, accounting and collecting royalties on behalf of the author.

Suite 6E, 2333 Government St., Victoria, B.C. V8T 4P4, CANADA
Phone   250-383-6864   Toll-free 1-888-232-4444 (Canada & US)
Fax   250-383-6804   E-mail   sales@trafford.com
Web site   www.trafford.com TRAFFORD PUBLISHING IS A DIVISION OF TRAFFORD HOLDINGS LTD.
Trafford Catalogue #00-0075   www.trafford.com/robots/00-0075.html

10   9   8   7   6   5   4   3   2   1

Original title:

<u>FutureFish in the Coming Conservative Century</u>

A Complete Social, Political, and Economic Analysis
of the North Pacific Seafood Industry
throughout the 1990s

...”The Coming ‘Conservative Century’”

–Irving Kristol, <u>Wall Street Journal</u>
1 February 1993

Cover painting: "Return of the Fall Chum"
(Chuck Rondeau, December 1999)

In Memoriam

James A. McEwen
(died 11 March, 1996, Petersburg, Alaska)

FOREWORD

The original title of this work was to be <u>Fisheries of the Pacific Northwest Coast,</u> <u>Volume III</u>. Volumes I and II, published by Vantage Press in 1991 and 1994 respectively, are history books and have had limited success in reaching members of today's fishing and seafood industry. I would have to employ a new marketing stratagem to interest potential readers, or end my days as road-kill on the global Information Superhighway!

Therefore, as a start, Volume III has become <u>FutureFish in the Coming Conservative</u> <u>Century</u>. Like Volumes I and II, this work also covers history, diplomacy, policies and analysis of the North Pacific fisheries. But <u>FutureFish</u> is concerned with the 1990s and beyond, rather than the 1980s and the past. These chapters are topical rather than descriptive, and view the forests rather than examine the trees. Entire fish markets and whole fisheries are analysed rather than individual fish species and single fisheries.

Chapter 2, 'Irrational Ecologism vs. Wise-Use Fisheries,' is a case in point. Parts I and II deal with environmentalism as a New Age religion with a world-view and political agenda. Fish and fishing are not even mentioned until Part III. I feel that it is vitally important to understand how Big Green thinks and acts and why. Only then can the fishing and seafood industry of the North Pacific take the steps necessary to protect their livelihood, while continuing to feed a hungry world.

Another topical chapter, in this cumulative collection, will examine the relationship between the Confucian work-ethic and the predominance of Japan and the Four Tigers (South Korea, Taiwan, Hong Kong, Singapore) in the new Far West Pacific technological, economic and cultural ecology. Except for Singapore, their success has manifested itself in the Pacific Basin fisheries. Catching up fast are the fishing nations of ASEAN (Association of South-East Asian Nations): Thailand, Malaysia, Indonesia and the Philippines. It is only a matter of time, during the "Coming Conservative Century", that Confucian-influenced Viet-Nam, North Korea and China itself ("Enter the Dragon") are part and parcel of the new Far West Pacific ecology. This includes seafood production. Mainland China at present, after an American jump-start, is a world primary producer of aquacultured bay scallops (now called "China bays").

And, finally, why North Pacific fishing? Because the vast fishery resource of the Pacific Ocean is located in the far North Pacific in a sweeping arc from northern Japan to the U.S. Pacific Northwest, the great bulk off Alaska and the Russian Far East. As a Master of Arts in Pacific history (University of Hawaii at Manoa, 1981), I am well aware of the significance of South Pacific fisheries; especially those of Australia, New Zealand, Chile, Peru and Ecuador. South Pacific, as well as the mid-Pacific Islands, fisheries were to be the focus of my doctoral dissertation at the University of Adelaide commencing in 1982. But as a Pacific Northwesterner by choice, I have concentrated my time and energy, for a decade and more, researching and writing about the North Pacific fisheries. It is my hope that these studies in "fisheriography" bear forth good fruit.

C.D. Bay-Hansen
Port Angeles, Wn.
August 1994

Author's Update 2000

It was bound to happen. The original, finished FutureFish filled 657 word-processed pages. Not only is such a voluminous manuscript very difficult to sell to (at best) a select readership, it would be nearly impossible to peddle so large a book to a fast [mind] food public. Not just this, but a "perfect-bound" volume (in publishing parlance) ought not exceed 500 pages. At the close of 1999, I was--pardon the pun-- in a bind.

What to do? Looking again at the greater FutureFish, I discovered a natural divide; out of one large manuscript two lesser books could be created. I am a hopelessly "Second Wave" type of fellow barely able to type but, with some inspired cutting, pasting, and juxtaposing, I have been able to produce (i.e., extract) one volume ready for immediate publication **FutureFish in Century 21: The North Pacific Fisheries Handle Coming Trends, Radical Environmentalism, and Digital Cyberspace (1991-1992, 1994-1997)**.

FutureFish in Century 21 deals with the three main topics contained in the subtitle, but also discusses Scandinavian fishermen of north Seattle and Southeast Alaska; the new physics and the New Age; evolution, scientism, and Christian apologetics. A second volume, gleaned from the second half of the parent FutureFish--plus an addended chapter on Micronesian seas--will be completed by 2001. It will feature Asian markets, the Can -Am Salmon Treaty, and more Norwegian Americana.

Lastly, I thank Mr. Francis E. Caldwell of Port Angeles, Wash.,for bringing to my attention Trafford Publishing of Victoria, B.C., and their on-demand self-publishing service. What an opportunity for those of us who have for years literally laboured in obscurity! A method of publishing, promoting, and distributing which avoids the terrible tyranny of The New York Times, Kirkus Reviews, and the sorry sight of 25,000 hard-cover copies gathering dust in a Fun City warehouse.........is truly millennial and "Third Wave"!

C.D.B-H.
Port Angeles, Wash.
March 2000

Table of Contents

Chapter 1

THE 1990's: FUTURE TRENDS IN THE NORTH

PACIFIC FISHERIES AND SEAFOOD INDUSTRY

Part I: "Pacific Shift"
Part II: The Fight for Fish in the North Pacific
Part III: (A) Fish for All Seasons

"The Mediterranean is the ocean of the past, the Atlantic the ocean of the present, the Pacific the ocean of the future."

--John Hay, U.S. Secretary of State at turn of last century

"The United States borders two oceans, one facing Europe, the other facing Asia: California, Oregon, Washington, Alaska, and Hawaii are all part of the Pacific Rim and even now are participating in the Asian boom. Our nation has a choice of following the sterile decline of post-Christian Europe or the long range future of a booming Asia."

--Evangelist Pat Robertson in The New Millennium

"Once we enter the next millennium we will feel the impact of more of the countries in the Pacific Rim--Mexico, Ecuador, North Korea, Vietnam, and all the others--but today the focus is on Asia."

--John Naisbitt and Patricia Aburdene

Introduction: 'Pacific Shift'

California futurist, William Irwin Thompson, wrote a thought-provoking book during the mid-1980s which he entitled Pacific Shift. In it he subdivided the Western World into four cultural ecologies. These are:

	Cultural ecology:	Time:	Place:
I.	Riverine	Ancient]	Egypt/Mesopotamia
II.	Mediterranean	World]	Greece/Rome
III.	Atlantic	476 A.D. Fall of Rome	W. Europe/East Coast N. America
IV.	Pacific-Aerospace	1945 - (End WWII)	Pacific Rim/West Coast N. America/Japan[1]

TABLE 1

The reader is compelled to wade through much New Age nonsense, both semantic and psychic, but the central theme of the world "cultural ecology" shifting to the Pacific Basic is, I feel, a valid one. That shift, wrote Thompson, is from Paris, London and New York to Tokyo, Sydney and Los Angeles, The shift is from Harvard, Princeton, Yale and M.I.T. to Berkeley, Stanford, U.C.L.A. and Cal. Tech. Thompson even went as far as to apply his theory to economic and communications systems, and pollution forms, to the four cultural ecologies:

	Economy (Marx)	Communications (McLuhan)	Forms of pollution
I.	Asiatic	Script	Soil loss
II.	Feudal	Alphabetic	Deforestation
III.	Capitalistic	Print	Atmospheric pollution
IV.	Socialistic[2]	Electronic	Noise, paranoia[3]

TABLE 2

The Pacific cultural ecology, then, is today's aerospace one, characterised by increasingly interdependent economies; an electronic communications system; and atmospheric pollution gradually being replaced by that of "noise and paranoia". Love or loathe William Irwin Thompson, we can have little doubt that the present cultural ecology of the world is shifting to the Pacific Rim. This Pacific Rim is composed of countries and political units ranging from Alaska to Chile, and from New Zealand to the Soviet Far East. The Pacific Rim includes the economic/technological giant, Japan, and the fast-developing Four Tigers: South Korea, Taiwan, Hong Kong and Singapore. These nations all have the Confucian work-ethic as a commonality, as well as being part of the Chinese cultural realm. Not far behind them in development potential are the South-East Asian nations of Thailand, Malaysia, Indonesia and the Philippines. And it is only a matter of time before the remainder of South-East Asia, North Korea and mainland China itself join the economic and cultural ecology of the new Far West Pacific Shift.

As this study will be concerned with trends in the North Pacific fisheries and seafood industry, the vast oceanic area south of the equator will not be examined. Australia, New Zealand, Chile, Peru and Ecuador are major seafood-producing nations of the Pacific Rim that are significant enough to merit a separate study. These southern hemisphere nations are very much part of Thompson's Pacific cultural ecology. The main players on the Pacific Rim stage, whether north or south, are the United States and Japan. These are also the leading fishing and seafood-producing nations of the Pacific. To accurately predict future trends in these North Pacific industries, means understanding past history and current events in the United States and Japan.

But first permit me a further forecast by another futurologist. John Naisbitt and his wife, Patricia Aburdene, are the authors of Megatrends 2000. Colorado-based Naisbitt considers himself the world's No. 1 hitchhiker on " 'the global information highway' "[4]. Utilising the most advanced information-gathering technology, citizens Naisbitt and Aburdene garner knowledge that was previously available only to human society's best educated or most powerful. Among the Naisbitts' ten millennial megatrends are predictions of a booming global economy for the 1990s, and the emergence of the Pacific Rim as an economic force.[5]

Today, in 1991, the United States economically dominates the eastern edge of the Pacific Rim as Japan does the western edge. The old Far East has become the new Far West, with Japan being ever more perceived as Number One --Ichiban-- economic power of the Pacific; indeed of the world. But the United States economy is more than twice that of Japan, and despite a rapidly closing gap in technology, is still the predominant partner in the present Pacific-Aerospace cultural ecology. Just about everything within the Pacific Basin revolves around the United States and Japan, but it is still America that makes the difference. Henry Luce, the founder of Time - Life, Inc, has called the Twentieth century the American Century[6]. But Naohiro Amaya, the Japanese economist and political theorist, has dubbed this century an Oil Century or an Oil Culture[7]. Nonetheless, Japan is steadily making up for its lack of oil in technological excellence.

Of the fishing nations of the world in volume of fish landed, Japan is number one. The Soviet Union is number two, and China is number three. Competing for number four spot are Chile, Peru and the United States[8]. All six nations are Pacific Rim nations. Advancing fast in hightech progress are the Asian "Four Tigers" of South Korea, Taiwan, Hong Kong and Singapore. The two former nations are already primary producers in the North Pacific fisheries and seafood industry. Along with Japan, South Korea (R.O.K.) and Taiwan (R.O.C., the Republic of China) have received much negative attention during the last few years due to driftnet fishing. What is ironic, however, is that the two smaller nations, until recently considered "undeveloped" and both under fifty years of age, are today international pariahs, feared and hated by global naturalists, ecologists, and concerned members of the Pacific fishing industry. Usually such intense emotion and ensuing political action is reserved for nations of significance...such as Japan. What it means, of course, is that South Korea and Taiwan are important players on the Pacific Rim -- hence the world-stage. They have "arrived", technologically speaking, even though in this sense it is a dubious distinction. More on "The curtains of death" will be examined later, as the question of driftnet fishing has ecological economic and political ramifications for the entire Pacific Basin, as well as Japan, South Korea and Taiwan.

The Pacific has been referred to as a new Mediterranean. Technologically and culturally the shift has been from the Atlantic Littoral to the Pacific Rim since 1945. Futurist Alvin Toffler has written that "Ideologically and intellectually, Western Europe's prime post-war exports have been a quasi-Marxist leftism and for a time, existentialism, followed by structuralism and, more recently, semiology. These are now waning in the world intellectual market."[9]

In stark contrast to the defeatism and self-doubt of post-Christian Europe, is the dynamism and "can do" attitude of Japan and the little Asian Tigers. Alot of this work ethic has to do with what Canadian author Eric Dowton has called "The Confucius Connection"[10]. It is not by accident that the five post-1945 hypergrowth Asian states are within the Chinese (i.e., Confucian) cultural sphere. Indeed, beneath the trappings of Communism in China, North Korea and Vietnam, the heritage of Confucianism is still a powerful influence[11]. An eventual Sino-Japanese axis, along with a Communism-free East Asia, could be a devastating political as well as economic force. Eric Downton has concluded:

> "...Behind those victories ... is ... a cultural coherence as significant as the Christianity factor was in the Atlantic nations' rise to world supremacy....
>
> "If the dynamic ... Confucians of the second industrial revolution come to believe that the West is trying to hold on to the global industrial supremacy it established with the first, Atlantic - based industrial revolution, then they might close ranks and launch trade war. From there it would be a short step to kulturkampf and political antagonism."[12]

If the Pacific is the new Mediterranean, the United States is the new Rome. If this parallel holds true, then Japan is the new Carthage. Like Carthage, Japan was destroyed by the U.S. (Rome) and then rebuilt. Later, Carthage would be the capital of Roman Africa. Just five years after its devastating defeat, Japan was the U.S. East Asian headquarters for the United Nation's shooting war with the Korean and Chinese communists. By 1952, Japan had regained its sovereignty. By 1953, Japan's economy was already well on its way to recovery, in large part due to American post-war aid and military expenditure during the Korean War (1950-1953). Today, in 1991, Japan is the other power in the Pacific-Aerospace cultural ecology.

Beside the Four Tigers, there are the non-Communist ASEAN[13] nations of Thailand, Malaysia, Singapore, Philippines, Indonesia and (now) Brunei. Singapore is the odd fellow, as it is part of the Confucian cultural realm, and one of the Four Tigers. All the other nations, save Brunei, are major fishing and seafood-producing nations of the Pacific Rim.

And so, finally, we come to our side of the Pacific Rim, the side which we North Americans are familiar with. There is the Mexican Pacific Coast, the American Pacific Coast and British Columbia, Canada. Then there are the U.S. non-contiguous states of Alaska and Hawaii; two political units that are cultural, social and economic entities in themselves. The Californias, both Mexican and American, and Hawaii have proud fishing and seafood-producing traditions of their own, mostly of pelagic finfish and shellfish. But it is farther north that the vast marine resources of the North Pacific Ocean are to be found -- in a great arc from Hokkaido, Japan, to northern California. This is salmon country, with the mighty rivers of the Russian Far East, Alaska, British Columbia and the Pacific Northwest emptying into the North Pacific Ocean. Under these seas and in these rivers are king salmon and king crab, giant sturgeon and giant halibut, huge shoals of whitefish such as hake and pollock.

As we approach the end of the twentieth century, even the least valued species of the North Pacific marine resource are being perceived as finite in number. But the Pacific Ocean, both north and south, is still the globe's richest repository of potential seafood. The far northern reaches of the Pacific Ocean -- the Sea of Okhotsk, Bering Sea, and the Gulf of Alaska -- have seen ships of many nations harvest their waters. The fishing vessels have been mainly from neighbouring Japan, U.S.S.R., U.S.A. and Canada. With extended 200-mile limits and a diminishing marine resource, the fight for fish will intensify during the 1990s. All four fishing nations are high-tech, but the U.S.S.R.[14] and Canada for obvious reasons, both socio-economic and demo-geographic, are more oriented to the Atlantic Littoral. With great natural resources both on land and at sea astride the Pacific Rim, both nations will increasingly become important members of the Pacific-Aerospace cultural ecology.

Recently (October, 1991) I was in a Victoria, B.C., bookshop. There, on a shelf in the travel section, was an 800-plus page book entitled <u>The Pacific Rim Almanac</u>. The subtitle struck me as revealing: 'A Complete Guide to the New Center of the Economic World.'[15] A "Pacific Shift" indeed.

NOTES

1. William Irwin Thompson, Pacific Shift (San Francisco: Sierra Club Books, 1985) p. 142.

2. In light of what transpired during the historic month of August 1991 in the U.S.S.R., Thompson might have wished to change Marxian Socialism to his own view of New Age Cosmic Commune-ism. No matter what, Thompson's definition of "catastrophe" certainly is applicable here.

3. Ibid., p. 142. Thompson also included polity and mathematical mode categories within his cultural ecology idea:

	Polity	Mathematical mode
I.	City-State	Enumeration
II.	Empire	Geometrizing
III.	Industrial nation-state	Equations of motion, dynamics
IV.	Enantiomorphic	Catastrophe theory

TABLE 3

4. Adele Malott, 'Trends of the Times', Friendly Exchange, Vol. 11, No. 3, Fall 1991, p. 31.

5. Ibid., p. 31. See John Naisbitt and Patricia Aburdene, Megatrends 2000 (New York: Avon Books, 1990); Ch.6, 'The Rise of the Pacific Rim'.

6. David Halberstam, The Next Century (New York: William Morrow and Co., Inc., 1991) p. 58.

7. Ibid., p. 67.

8. William McCloskey, 'Gringo Schmidt: An Alaskan fisherman tries his hand in Chile', Pacific Fishing, Fish Expo Issue, November 1991, p. 99.

9. Alvin Toffler, Powershift (New York: Bantam Books, 1990) p. 444.

10. Eric Downton, Pacific Challenge (Toronto: Stoddart Publishing Co. Ltd., 1986) p. 68 ff.

11. Ibid., p. 73.

12. Op. cit., Downton, p. 85.

13. Association of South-East Asian Nations.

14. In October, 1991, it is hardly clear whether the Soviet Far East will remain such, or become the Russian Maritime Territory.

15. Alexander Besher, The Pacific Rim Almanac (New York: Harper Collins, 1991).

Bibliography for Part I

1. Downton, Eric. Pacific Challenge. Stoddart Publishing Co., Ltd., Toronto, 1986.

2. Halberstam, David. The Next Century. William Morrow and Co., Inc., New York, 1991.

3. Robertson, Pat. The New Millennium. Word Publishing, Dallas, 1990.

4. Solzhenitsyn, Aleksandr. Rebuilding Russia. Farrar, Straus and Giraux, New York, 1991.

5. Thompson, William Irwin. Pacific Shift. Sierra Club Books, San Francisco, 1985.

6. Yutang, Lin, ed. The Wisdom of Confucius. Random House, Inc., New York, 1966.

PART II: THE FIGHT FOR FISH IN THE NORTH PACIFIC

Commencing 1 March 1977, the enforcement of the Magnuson Fishery Management and Conservation Act has changed the nature of American commercial fishing forever. Under the Magnuson Act (MFCMA), the United States took unilateral control of most finfish and shellfish within a 200 nautical mile zone (371 km) off the U.S. coasts. Management was required to be based on optimum yield (OY), which is maximum sustainable yield (MSY) modified by . . . "certain economic, social, and ecological considerations."[16] This initially had two consequences:

First, the Magnuson Act has "Americanized" the Alaska fisheries. The 200-mile economic zone (MEZ) has changed the relationship between the U.S. and Canada. Since 1976-77, B.C. salmon-trollers and halibut long-liners have no longer been welcome in Alaskan waters[17]. These are the two neighbouring Pacific nations that have done so much to conserve the salmon and halibut. The special relationship in the fisheries is gone, and Canada has been relegated to the same alien status as the (former) Soviet Union and Japan.

Second, is that for years American and Canadian fishermen blamed offshore fleets of Soviet, Japanese and other factory ships for depleting the salmon resource. This was done while scooping up tons of low-value bottomfish. These same pollock and other whitefish were deemed virtually worthless by the North Americans[18]. Real fishermen, the ethos seemed to say, fished for real fish . . . like Pacific salmon and halibut. By the late 1970s, of course, the true value of the bottomfish resource was comprehended by all sectors of the North American fishing and processing industry. The Magnuson Act, initially put through congress to Save Our Salmon, has ended up "Americanizing" one of the globe's largest foodfish reserves.

During the peak years of foreign fishing (1971-1974), the eastern Bering Sea and Aleutian Islands regions produced marine animal catches in the range of 2.2 to 2.5 million tons. With the enactment of the 1976-7 Magnuson Act, the enormous resources of this region came under exclusive U.S. jurisdiction.[19] To protect Pacific salmon and halibut, the United States, Canada and Japan had signed the International Pacific Fisheries Convention in 1953, which was renegotiated in 1978 due to the Magnuson Act. As stated above, Americanisation has also ended a relationship . . . "unique in international diplomacy".[20]

The United States and Canada have officially coöperated on several occasions during this century to protect and conserve the Pacific salmon and halibut stocks, and have become the jealous guardians -- as well as takers -- of these two great fishes. Now that both North American nations have control of their waters to the 200-mile limit, immature halibut have been better shielded from the intense trawling fleets of East Asian and East European nations. But salmon are still vulnerable. Several important species of salmon swim far out into the vast Pacific -- away beyond the projected 200-mile limits. The salmon are easily caught at sea by the foreign fleets.[21] Driftnet fishing by Japan, South Korea and Taiwan, which has devastated marine resources besides salmon during the 1980s, will be examined at the conclusion of Part II.

During the 1980s, with the bottomfish resource having been Americanised off the coasts of Alaska, the U.S. fleet grew faster than expected. Simultaneous to the expansion of the fleet was the building of shoreside processing plants in towns such as Dutch Harbor and Kodiak. Today, in the 1990s, the combined capacity of both fishing and processing has surpassed the supply of (even) bottomfish. Now that overharvesting and overproduction of Pacific cod and pollock threatened their numbers, the next steps are allocation and allotment. This means U.S. fishermen against U.S. fishermen and U.S. fishermen against U.S. processors. Just last June, 1991, the Anchorage-based North Pacific Fishery Management Council approved of a plan to award 45% of the fishery to the Alaska shoreside plants, and 55% to the Seattle-based factory trawlers.[22]

The NPFMC's decision has met with a storm of protest by the factory trawlers, who would face a cut of the Bering Sea pollock resource, re-allocated to the shoreside processors, from 80% in 1992 to 55% by 1994 . . . a reduction of 25%.[23] A heated response, in turn, has come from the Alaska processors, especially to an article headlining a Seattle Sunday newspaper.[24] The article has been perceived as biased and heavily in favour of the Seattle trawlers.[25] The latter, represented by the Alaska Factory Trawlers Association (AFTA), has accused certain NPFMC members of acting in their own local, special interests. All of four of eleven Council members own businesses in the Alaskan fishing industry, and two more are industry - group employees.[26] To further inflame already-strong feelings in the factory trawlers vs. shoreside plants debate, a dreadful element of "Japan - bashing" has been introduced. Robert F. Morgan, president of the AFTA has stated:

"In America's Aleutian Islands, the world's two largest seafood companies, both Japanese, have built shoreside processing plants representing a staggering 80% of the total on-shore processing capacity. To reach that output . . . these companies are angling for a significant percentage of the catch in the Bering Sea and the Gulf of Alaska. A guaranteed percentage. Neither American factory trawlers, nor any other segment of the U.S. seafood industry has asked for such protection.

" . . . The U.S. Department of Commerce is considering regulations that would ultimately guarantee nearly one-half of the North Pacific bottomfish resource to the Japanese-controlled shoreside processing plants . . . We are urging everyone concerned to write the Department of Commerce and urge them to reject this ill-conceived fisheries management plan."[27]

Legislation is pending, and the National Marine Fisheries Service (the NMFS is part of the U.S. Dept of Commerce) has its hands full refereeing a war of attrition between the factory trawlers and the shoreside processors. I should write a _civil_ war of attrition, as the Japan-bashing element has been brought in by the AFTA to cover the sad fact of Seattle trawlers versus Alaska processors. In other words, all the rhetoric boils down to work and money: Factory trawlers, and ". . . Washington state residents who rely on them for jobs and revenue -- are being aced out of Alaskan ground fisheries by special interests in Alaska."[28]

Even if it were not just the big Seattle newspapers that fishermen and processors read, the figures of Japanese ownership in Alaska would seem to clinch the argument in favour of the AFTA. It was, after all, the factory trawlers that learned how to efficiently catch and process bottomfish in Alaska seas, thus replacing the Japanese fleets with those of the U.S.A. By making the trawler vs. processor issue one of nationalism with Japan-bashing in there for good measure, the AFTA's position appears waterproof.

Robert F. Morgan has put the case well for the AFTA, but the opposing side has an articulate champion in Clement V. Tillion. "Clem" Tillion has helped negotiate several important North Pacific fisheries treaties involving Canada, the U.S.S.R., Japan and Korea during the last quarter century. He has been a charter member as well as chairman of the NPFMC, and in 1990 was appointed Special Assistant for Fisheries by Alaska Governor Wally Hickel. Tillion's position as "fish czar" is to last through 1994. Wayne Lee, managing editor of Seafood Leader magazine, interviewed Tillion last July (1991) at the latter's home in Halibut Cove, Alaska. When asked by Lee about Japanese investment and ownership in the Alaskan seafood industry, Tillion had some thoughtful answers:

"The disadvantage is that the Alaska seafood industry has become almost totally dependent on a single market . . . .

"Do I like having my market dependent on Japan? No, I don't . . . I'd rather require that 50 percent of our salmon be sold in the United States. But the fishermen would have to take less to do that and the packers would have to take less, and that's kind of un-American, too . . . .

"The factory trawlers scream because the surimi plants have Japanese investment; I haven't figured out yet why it's so wrong for the Japanese to invest and so right for the Christiania Bank of Norway to finance a factory trawler:

"The thing that's interesting to me is the Jap-bashing, when they pay the highest price of anybody in the world for our product . . . .

"Do you hear Tennessee crying because Toyota built a plant in their state? If the Japanese are willing to pay a higher price, we'd be very foolish not to accept it.

"The Japanese ownership in the United States is considerably less than that of Holland. So get off my case!"[29]

But Americanisation of the high seas fisheries in Bering Sea and the Gulf of Alaska hasn't made much of a difference farther south. Washington State and British Columbia are still within sight of each other across the Straits of Juan de Fuca. (And spawning Pacific salmon head up rivers that are Alaskan at their entrances but Canadian farther upstream). There have been several attempts at sharing the salmon resource between Canada and the U.S. -- in 1937, in 1956 and most recently in 1984-5.[30] But before a new treaty can be negotiated with Canada, user groups in Washington have to come to an agreement with each other. In this case, the Washington sport fishing group TRC ("The Recreation Coalition") sees the U.S. commercial catch of Fraser River sockeye as a great bargaining chip with the Canadians; i.e., your fish for their fish![31]

The author remembers, while living in Victoria, B.C., during the mid-1980s, the really vituperative meetings between the various salmon-user groups -- seiners, gillnetters, trollers, Natives and recreational fishermen. Cooler heads in B.C. then, were saying pretty much what the executive director for Salmon for Washington said in November, 1991:

". . . It is, however, going to take work. Work that cannot begin until we all have come to realize that mutual self-destruction is in nobody's best interests and that 'easy' answers like torpedoing the commercial fleet just aren't going to succeed. The sooner that realization occurs, the sooner we can all get started on the really important work of creating unified public support . . .

"Let's hope those among the sports fishing community who still resist the idea of working with the commercial industry can be convinced to see the light in time."[32]

If the United States has trouble talking fish with good, stable neighbour Canada, imagine the trouble ahead with (formerly) bad, unstable neighbour Russia![33]

There was serious talk last summer (1991) between the United States and (then) Soviet Union about plugging the "Donut Hole". The latter is a stretch of international waters between the American and Russian sectors of Bering Sea. A joint U.S. - Soviet trawl survey had been undertaken from the Kamchatka Peninsula, through the Donut Hole, and on to the eastern Bering Sea shelf. The tow results indicated a yield of 30 to 50 tons of fish per hour on the American and Russian sides, but a mere .6 tons per hour in the Donut Hole itself.[34]

The targeted species in these waters is Alaska, Pacific or walleye pollock (Theragra chalcogramma), which I wrote about in another work. But since that was written almost a decade ago, there are no more "acres" of Alaska pollock. No, indeed -- they have been overfished by the foreign factory-trawler fleets during the 1990s, as Pacific salmon and halibut were taken incidentally during the 1980s. The U.S. - Soviet catch survey of pollock was so low, in fact, that both countries called for a total closure of fishing in the Donut Hole. Japan was willing to comply, but not Poland, China or South Korea for various reasons.[35]

But the Donut Hole is closing. A little-known boundary dispute in Bering Sea has resurfaced after more than a century, and been amicably settled by the Russians and Americans. The dispute goes back the U.S. purchase of Alaska in 1867. Cartographers on both sides used different methods, getting different results, and nobody noticed until the establishment of 200-mile economic zones during the late 1970s. Senator Frank Murkowski (R-Alaska), who has done so much to stop high-seas driftnetting, helped work out the details of the argument with the Russians. The settlement gives the Americans jurisdiction over an extra 13,200 square miles of Bering Sea waters, including a piece of the Donut Hole. A unique feature of the agreement is that each country will be enforcing fishing regulations within areas of the other's zone. Thus the Donut Hole is being closed, thereby safeguarding the Bogoslof Island pollock stock -- the U.S. source from which migrate adult pollock into the Donut Hole for spawning. According to the NMFS, the Bogoslof Island pollock stock has declined 75 percent in the last two years; this stock is responsible for 15 percent of the Alaska pollock catch.[36]

It is absolutely imperative that the United States cultivate relations based on trust and cooperation with the fledgling Russian Republic. For Alaskans, Siberia is as virtually near a neighbour as Canada. Joint policing of the areas around the Donut Hole has been a good start. Despite disagreements within the Alaska fishing/seafood industry sectors, the Soviet salmon lift of 1991 has been generally seen as a good thing. The first of up to 40,000 cases of canned pink salmon was airlifted to the (then) Soviet Union in late August, 1991. The pink salmon run, arriving en masse two weeks late, clogged the Prince William Sound hatchery terminals. The Exxon Corporation (guilt for the oil spill of 1989?) made a $2 million donation for canning and transport of the fish to the U.S.S.R.. Worries concerned (1) wasted fish -- four times as many pinks were dumped as canned -- and (2) donated salmon ending up as competition on the international market, or as hard currency in the cash-strapped U.S.S.R. But the labels pasted on the cases proudly proclaimed in Russian and English: "Gift to the people of the USSR from the people of Alaska". All external and internal politics aside, this was surely a gesture of American good faith.[37]

As mentioned earlier, the U.S.A. and the U.S.S.R. have expressed serious ideas about plugging the Donut Hole. They brought up these concerns at the July (1991) meeting in Tokyo, where both countries pressed for a 1992 fishing moratorium. As stated, they were rebuffed by Poland, China and South Korea, the main Donut Hole fishing nations besides Japan. Only the latter showed interest. The United States would like the proposed moratorium to continue no matter how chaotic the domestic situation becomes in the former Soviet Union.[38]

At present, February 1992, the Soviet Ministry of Fisheries has become the Russian Ministry of Fisheries with staffing reduced by half to 300. The slack is supposed to be taken up by the fleets themselves, combines, co-ops and joint ventures.[39] The Yeltsin government feels that the Russian industry no longer needs a central bureaucratic body for planning and administration, but has not had time since the failed coup to fill the void. Voices within the Russian industry, however, have called for compromises between the old system and the free market to ease the transition.[40]

The new Russia has been included in a new four-party North Pacific salmon spawning states accord that has replaced the almost - 40 year old INPFC (International North Pacific Fisheries Convention).[41] In early November 1991, U.S., Canadian and Japanese delegations met in Tokyo to officially end a treaty that began in 1953 as a post-World War II plan to rebuild Japan's (fishing) industry. After this final INPFC meeting, the Americans were optimistic that real progress has been made in Pacific salmon conservation. The new agreement has also given skeptics in the U.S. industry hope that two holes in the leaking North Pacific fish-bucket will be finally plugged: The trawlers in the Donut Hole, and the high-seas driftnets everywhere else.[42]

The Japanese fleets have been in full retreat since Americanisation (the Magnuson Act) was passed in 1976, and have been pushed even farther back toward Asia by the Russians, who have discontinued permission for Japanese high-seas fishing after the 1991 season. Alaska Fisherman's Journal writer Harold Sparck has commented:

> "In its last years, the reduced Japanese fleet took less than 15,000 metric tons of salmon. Near the end, Japan initiated joint-venture aquaculture programs with the Soviets in Sakhalin and Kamchatka that will provide Russian territorial sea harvest by Japanese nationals for years to come."[43]

Another problem that has resurfaced (February 1992) has been a case involving the Commercial Vessel Anti-Reflagging Act of 1987. That law requires corporations owning boats fishing in U.S. waters to have a majority U.S. ownership, and those boats must be built or rebuilt in U.S. shipyards. The resurfacing problem has been a loophole in the law which permitted exemptions for boats already licensed when it was passed, and for other boats being rebuilt or under contract to be. The U.S. Coast Guard had decided that the loophole applied to the boat not the owner -- meaning a boat could be repeatedly bought and sold without losing its fishing privileges.[44]

This case, like the Seattle trawlers versus the Alaska processors, involves foreign ownership. But the complaint and challenge, this time, come from three Seattle fishing companies and two shipbuilding trade groups which contend that the U.S. Coast Guard has permitted a large number of foreign-owned vessels to fish within the U.S. 200-mile limit. A U.S. District judge ruled on 5 February (1992) that the Coast Guard should not allow the loophole to be used, and it would be up to the Coast Guard to appeal or enforce the ruling. The ruling, enforced or not, will affect 60% of the capacity of the present fleet. And the present fleet involves Norwegian, Korean and Japanese-owned vessels which tend to be newer and bigger with more production capacity. A Coast Guard spokesman has said that further litigation is to be expected.[45]

A big problem that has been legally solved is driftnet fishing. On 6 December 1991, the Second Committee of the United Nations approved a resolution that would ban the worldwide use of high-seas driftnets by 1993. (The Committee vote essentially guarantees passage by the General Assembly). The United Nations ban was first proposed by the United States and 20 other signatories in 1989. One crucial difference in the current agreement is that high-seas driftnetting, even by nations with conservation programs, is totally prohibited. The three main driftnetting offenders -- Japan, South Korea and Taiwan -- have at this writing relented to a 50% reduction in fishing effort by 30 June 1992, and the moratorium date of 31 December 1992. Obviously, such restrictions are meaningless to the outlaw pirate fleets.[46]

Much has been said and done about "the curtains of death" since this writer penned an essay on driftnetting in 1989.[47] I related then the brave efforts of the U.S. Secretary of Commerce Robert Mosbacher, Senator Frank Murkowski (R-Ak.), Representatives W.J. Tauzin (D-La.), John Miller (R-Wn.) and Jolene Unsoeld (D-Wn.) to ban driftnet fishing.[48] Three years later, I am happy to write, the ban is now the law of the sea. For the hue and the cry about high-seas driftnetting went beyond the habitual whine of Greenpeace and eco-freaks. By the late 1980s, the shrill keen of the Rainbow Warriors had become a full-throated roar from all sectors of the entire world. This included the fisheries and seafood industry of the Pacific Northwest Coast. Driftnetting had become more than just high-seas poaching of Pacific salmon -- it had become a global threat to the marine environment. The Pacific Rim Almanac has described "the wall of death" thusly:

> "High-seas driftnets are large-scale monofilament plastic gillnets deployed in the open ocean. A standard gillnet is a panel of strong plastic webbing suspended vertically in the water by floats attached at the top of the panel and weights attached at the bottom. The nets -- used to catch salmon, squid, marlin, and other species -- are so sheer that they cannot be seen by diving birds or detected by dolphin sonar. Marine creatures in search of food and lured by fish already caught in the nets, swim or dive into the plastic web, where they become entangled and drown . . .

> "In the Pacific Ocean, the nations of Japan, Taiwan, and the Republic of Korea have over 1500 ships that use driftnets. In the north, Japan operates over 200 salmon-fishing vessels, setting nine-mile-long nets.

> In the central North Pacific, Japan and Taiwan operate at least 600 driftnet
> vessels for fishing on billfish, primarily marlin and sailfish. In the North
> Pacific, the 700 squid driftnet boats of Japan, Taiwan and the Republic of
> Korea use nets up to 30 miles long . . . . During the fishing season, vessels
> set more than 20,000 miles of net each day -- more than one million miles
> each year. And unlike the salmon fishery, the squid and billfish fisheries are
> not even regulated by an international fisheries convention."[49]

Driftnets are a death trap for seabirds, a killer of marine mammals, and the squid over-harvest is threatening the food chain itself. Here, on the Pacific Northwest Coast, we have been most concerned with the poaching of our salmon stocks. A corollary of driftnets have been "ghost nets" -- threats to both wildlife and navigation. A ghost net is a lost or abandoned driftnet, sometimes many miles long, which combined with floating débris, entangles and kills many thousands of seals, cetaceans, seabirds, marine turtles and fish every year. There have been documented cases of propeller shafts and engine intakes ruined by floating ghost nets. Sailboats have been entangled in them, and they are a hazard to vessels at sea. According to Japanese data, the driftnet fleets shed about 500-600 miles (1,000 km) of ghost net into the North Pacific per year. If this fishing rate continues, there will enough ghost net in the Pacific to stretch a third of the way around the world.[50]

Actual figures of the toll taken by driftnet fishing are staggering. A definitive joint study was undertaken by the United States, Canada and Japan in 1990 to assess the effects of the Japanese squid and large-mesh driftnets on North Pacific marine life. From late May to December, 35 American, 10 Canadian and 29 Japanese observers were aboard 75 Japanese squid driftnet vessels collecting scientific information. The highly-trained observers then handed over their data to an aggregate of scientists from the three nations. The scientists were from the U.S. National Marine Fisheries Service (NMFS), the U.S. Fish and Wildlife Service, the Canadian Department of Fisheries and Oceans (DFO), and the Fisheries Agency of Japan. The meeting was held in Tokyo during February, 1991, to review the 1990 observations, correct known errors in the data, resolve differences, and to agree on content, format and timing for completion of the report. The ca. 200 page-record showed that over 3 million pomfret, 253,288 tuna, 81,956 blue sharks, 30,464 seabirds, and 1,758 whales and dolphins were killed incidentally in the sampled Japanese squid driftnets. Data collection included the recording of all bycatch species, rather than a specified list of species.[51]

The U.S. reaction was to initiate negotiations which led to bilateral agreements with Japan, South Korea and Taiwan which called for scientific monitoring of driftnet fishing in the North Pacific, requiring the vessels to be equipped with transmitters monitored by NMFS enforcement agents. The devices tell when driftnet boats are poaching in prohibited areas. And, said the NMFS, "The U.S. . . . .continues to strongly support the United Nations (UN) resolution calling for a moratorium on the use of this gear on the high seas by June 30, 1992."[52]

By August, 1991, the Bush administration had warned France, Japan, South Korea and Taiwan that they would be required to certify that fish products sold to the United States were not caught with driftnets. A month later, the Commerce Department banned U.S. import of any fish product caught by driftnet after 30 June 1992. The U.S. government also urged the U.N. to permanently ban all international driftnet fishing, closing loopholes in previous resolutions.[53] By early October, 1991, the Commerce Department's measure was unanimously approved by the House Merchant Marine and Fisheries Committee, and would be extended to include mandatory sanctions on all fishing tackle, lures and equipment from nations using driftnets. The extended measure would also close U.S. ports to driftnet vessels. Now that the frightful numbers of the birds, animals and fish incidentally caught in the observed Japanese driftnet fishery of 1990 had been made public, the reaction was predictable . . .especially when considering that a mere 10% of the fleet was monitored.[54]

By late October, 1991, it was the turn of South Korea and Taiwan to take the heat as well as Japan. The NMFS released figures suggesting that a fraction of the South Korean and Taiwanese driftnet fleets snagged at least 30,000 sharks, 200,000 tuna and 250,000 "other creatures" as a by-catch to squid fishing in the North Pacific the previous year. The raw numbers were estimated by U.S. and other observers on board South Korean and Taiwanese driftnet vessels. The Bush administration had put both countries on notice that summer of possible trade sanctions if they continued driftnet fishing, but later gave them an additional 90 days to show why they should not suffer retaliation.[55] Taiwan, in particular, has been accused by U.S. Representative Jolene Unsoeld (D-Wn.) as having had a "history of saying one thing on driftnets and then doing the exact opposite".[56]

On the evening of 25 November 1991, Secretary of State James Baker and Japanese officials agreed to jointly sponsor a U.N. resolution outlawing driftnets, without exception, by the end of 1992. Acceptance of the unconditional ban was an abrupt about-face for Japan, the globe's leader in driftnet fishing. The ever-pragmatic Japanese agreed to the ban as a result of growing American and international pressure. Republican Senators Slade Gorton (Wn.) and Bob Packwood (Ore.) said Japan's sudden change in policy was in part due to legislation they had helped push through the Senate, calling for trade sanctions against countries continuing to use driftnets. Senator Packwood remarked: "They saw the handwriting on the wall ... They wanted to get out of the business graciously rather than appear they were forced out. They thought they might as well get out and look good."[57]

As noted previously in this report, a Committee vote in the United Nations usually certifies passage by the General Assembly. And so it was on 20 December, 1991, that the Committee vote to ban worldwide use of driftnets by 1993 was approved by the General Assembly. The resolution had taken a mere fortnight for passage within the U.N.. The agreement has already been hailed as a great environmental victory. Officially speaking, all vessels that continue to ply the seas with driftnets will be considered pirate vessels. But Rep. Jolene Unsoeld (D-Wn.), among others, has expressed concern over enforcement of the law; international sanctions and naval policing have been suggested as means. Either way, the world will be looking to "leadership from the United States and Canada in stopping driftnet ships."[58]

Unlike previous moratorium language, this U.N. resolution has real teeth. Despite the pirate ships that will (always) be out there, the outlawing of driftnets is a great victory for the world's fishing and seafood industries as well as for the marine ecosystem. Growing international outrage at the high-seas "wall of death" translated itself, during the 1980s, to "unrelenting pressure from a coalition of environmental groups; sport, commercial and subsistence fishermen; and a few dedicated public servants ..."[59] It will mostly be up to the United States and Canada to make sure that the "curtains of death" stay furled in the North Pacific.

And so this chapter concludes with a resounding triumph. Except for the poaching pirate boats, high-seas driftnetting by Japan, South Korea and Taiwan will no longer be a problem. For the United States, good relations with these nations plus Canada, the Russian Republic, North Korea and China will be of utmost concern during the 1990s. The future welfare of the North Pacific fisheries depends on it. Good relations within the United States of fishing user-groups and other sectors of the industry are also crucial. Now that the far reaches of the North Pacific Ocean have been Americanised, the United States must exercise discretion in harvesting this rich area. Wise U.S. stewardship will ensure continuance of the resource, so that the future fight for fish in the North Pacific will mean cooperation rather than confrontation, both with other nations and within all sectors of the domestic industry.

NOTES

16. Roy E. Martin and George J. Flick, eds., <u>The Seafood Industry</u> (New York: Van Nostrand Reinhold, 1990) p. 11.

17. C.D. Bay-Hansen, <u>Fisheries of the North Pacific Coast, Vol. 1,</u> (New York: Vantage Press, 1991) pp. 207-208.

18. Ross Anderson, 'Fishy Business', <u>The Seattle Times/Seattle Post-Intelligencer,</u> pp. E-1, E-3.

19. Roy E. Martin and George J. Flick, pp. 11, 59. The MFCMA was passed in 1976 and enacted in 1977. The exact language describes a "200-mile-limit (371 km) law".

20. Op. cit., Bay-Hansen, p. 74.

21. <u>Ibid.,</u> p. 34.

22. Ross Anderson, 'Fishy Business', pp. E-1, E-3. Cf. 'Lawmakers seek review of fishery', <u>Peninsula Daily News,</u> 1 November 1991, p. A-6.

23. Donna Parker, <u>Pacific Fishing,</u> September 1991, p. 21.

24. Duff Wilson, 'A Fishy Situation', <u>The Seattle Times/Seattle Post-Intelligencer,</u> pp. A-1, A-18,19.

25. See 'Letters', <u>Pacific Fishing,</u> February 1992, pp. 8-10.

26. Duff Wilson, p. A-1.

27. Robert F. Morgan, president AFTA, 'Groundfish industry needs protection from Japan', <u>Peninsula Daily News,</u> 21 January 1992, p. A-9.

28. Joel Gay, 'Inshore/Offshore Goes to Washington, D.C.', <u>Pacific Fishing,</u> January 1992, p. 17.

29. Wayne Lee, 'The Oracle of Halibut Cove: An Interview with Alaska "Fish Czar" Clem Tillion', <u>Seafood Leader,</u> September/October 1991, pp. 153-154.

30. See C.D. Bay-Hansen, Vol. 1, Chapter V, 'Canadian-American Relations and the Pacific Salmon, 1937-1983'.

31. Donald D. Stuart, exec. dir Salmon for Washington, 'The Pacific Salmon Treaty: It's not just about fish; it's about creating a national agenda', <u>The Fishermen's News,</u> November 1991, p. 17.

32. Op. cit., Donald D. Stuart, p. 19.

NOTES (continued)

33.   The U.S.S.R. officially ceased to exist at midnight, 31 December 1991. The former Soviet Far East is now the Russian Maritime Territory.

34.   Donna Parker, 'U.S. and Soviets Seek Plug for Donut Hole', <u>Pacific Fishing</u>, October 1991, p. 37.

35.   <u>Ibid.</u>, p. 37. Poland needed the pollock, China had a fleet of trawlers to pay for, and South Korea said there was nowhere else to fish.

36.   'Bering Sea Boundary Redrawn', <u>Seafood Leader</u>, January/February 1992, p. 20.

37.   Bob Tkacz, 'Pinks for Reds: Hickel sends salmon to celebrate Soviet democracy', <u>Alaska Fisherman's Journal</u>, October 1991, pp. 14, 16.

38.   Harold Sparck, 'Soviet Turmoil Puts Donut Hole Moratorium On Hold', <u>Alaska Fisherman's Journal</u>, October 1991, p. 30. Cf. 'World Watch', <u>Pacific Fishing</u>, February 1992, p. 19.

39.   The author telephoned Steve Shapiro, editor of <u>Pacific Fishing</u>, on 5 December 1991. According to Shapiro, there were no JVs left in Alaska...although there was a Pacific hake fishing JV off Oregon.

40.   'World Watch', <u>Pacific Fishing</u>, February 1992, p. 19.

41.   The INPFC is not to be confused with the IPFSC (the International Pacific Salmon Fisheries Commission), the Canadian-American body that managed the Freaser River sockeye (and from 1956, pinks). See C.D. Bay-Hansen, Vol. 1, Ch. V, pp. 109-123; and Ch. X, pp. 201-213.

42.   Harold Sparck, 'And the Walls Came Tumbling Down', <u>Alaska Fisherman's Journal</u>, Yearbook '91, January 1992, p. 78.

43.   Op. cit., Harold Sparck, p. 78. The Russo-Japanese relationship will be a prominent feature, I predict, during the 1990s. Cash-poor Russia needs cash-rich Japan's investment and loans. Japan needs Russian fish, and wants her "Northern Territories" back: The Soviet-held islands of Kunashiri, Etorofu, Shikotan and Habbomai to the north of Hokkaido, occupied since World War II.

44.   'Judge bars foreign boats from waters', <u>Peninsula Daily News</u>, 9 February 1992, p. D-3. Cf. Donna Parker, 'Anti-Reflagging Decision Reaffirmed', <u>Pacific Fishing</u>, March 1992, pp. 28-29.

45.   <u>Ibid.</u> Quoted is U.S.C.G. Lt. Cmdr. Mike Lapinski.

46.   'U.S. Moves to Ban Driftnets', <u>Alaska Fisherman's Journal</u>, Year Book '91, January 1992, p. 12.

NOTES (continued)

47. See C.D. Bay-Hansen, Vol. 2, Ch XI, 'The Driftnet Fleets and High-Seas Pacific Salmon Interception'.

48. Rep. Tauzin of Louisiana was chairman of the House Merchant Marine and Fisheries Committee, of which Reps. Miller (R) and Unsoeld (D), both of Washington State, were members in 1989. This House subcommittee has jurisdiction over the U.S. Coast Guard.

49. Alexander Besher, The Pacific Rim Almanac (New York: Harper Collins, 1991), p. 432.

50. 'High-Seas Driftnets', Greenpeace Pacific Campaign pamphlet, 1991.

51. Int. North Pac. Fish Comm. 1991. Final report of 1990 observations of the Japanese high seas driftnet fisheries in the North Pacific Ocean. Joint report by the National Sections of Canada, Japan and the United States. NB. These figures were for 10% of total driftnet fleet.

52. Dr. William W. Fox, Jr., Assistant Administrator for NMFS. Quoted in NOAA Release Report on Driftnets, U.S. Department of 'COMMERCE NEWS', 14 June 1991.

53. 'Bush to ask U.N. for a total ban on driftnets', Peninsula Daily News, 23 September 1991, p. A-5.

54. 'Tough drift-net bill goes to full House', Peninsula Daily News, 4 October 1991, p. A-6.

55. 'Taiwan, S. Korea fish-net toll climbs', Peninsula Daily News, 25 October 1992, p. A-6.

56. Quoted in 'Taiwan "Promises" To Comply with U.N. Driftnet Ban', Seafood Leader, November/December 1991, p. 26.

57. Quoted in 'Japan to give up drift-nets by '93', Peninsula Daily News, 26 November 1991, pp. A-1, A-2. Cf. 'Japan to Ban Driftnets, Korea to Follow', Pacific Fishing, February 1992, p. 25.

58. 'UN adopts global drift-net fishing ban', Peninsula Daily News, 22 December 1991, p. A-12. Cf. 'Japan to Ban Driftnets, Korea to Follow', Pacific Fishing, February 1992, p. 60. The indirect quote is from Jerry Leape, a spokesman for Greenpeace International in Washington, D.C..

59. John van Amerogen, 'Say Good-bye to Driftnets', Alaska Fisherman's Journal, January 1992, p. 6.

PART III: (A) FISH FOR ALL SEASONS

In 1992, a good and plentiful supply of fresh seafood may be bought by the average North American consumer at any time of year.[60] Fishing methods and gear have become so advanced and effective that the harvesting of the resource is no longer a problem of technology. The problems of the 1990s, as this writer sees them, are five-fold: (1) Marketing fish that are readily available; (2) conservation and enhancement of fish stocks that show poor recruitment; (3) progress in methods of processing, preservation and packaging; (4) safe and viable new developments in mari-/aquaculture; and (5) the fishing and seafood industry's relationship with the "Ecotopia Lobby." The ultimate goal for the New Millennium should be the ongoing solution of these problems by the North Pacific industry. With the vast resource of fish technology and hands-on experience available in the United States, Canada, the Russian Republic and Japan, it will be up to these nations to set positive trends throughout the Pacific in the countdown to A.D. 2000.

Problem (1) is marketing fish that are readily available. A perfect example is the present (1991/1992) glut of Alaska pink salmon. As mentioned in Part II of this chapter, 40,000 cases of canned pink salmon were donated by the people of Alaska to the former Soviet Union. Four times that amount of salmon were destroyed, given the "deep six." This was in late August, 1991. By November 1991, the Alaska salmon industry had been told by the frozen seafood marketers that to sell its pinks ... "it will have to produce a high-quality, consistently priced, boneless fillet with a shelf life of at least 12 months. Neither current technology nor fishing practices meet those criteria."[61]

If the Alaska industry cannot be blamed for lack of current technology, the fishing and processing sectors can do a lot to improve fish handling, price disagreements, and general lack of cordiality within the industry. There exists not only the present glut of pinks, but the availability of farmed salmon makes Alaska wild salmon far less desirable on the world market ... especially the Japanese market. These markets now have year-'round choice of farmed fish from Norway, British Columbia and Chile.[62] One way to better market

Alaska salmon domestically is to stress Buy American; another way is to emphasise the superior quality of natural, wild salmon over the pellet-fed farmed fish. U.S. retailers can be won back with a lower price, and consumers with a finer product. That product's marketability is enhanced from the outset by careful handling -- even pink salmon, which is considered a garbage fish by some Alaska fishermen and treated accordingly.[63]

By February 1992, Valdez (Alaska) representative Gene Kubina had a pending marketing bill that will receive much attention when the legislature reconvenes for the year. This bill would assess all Alaska fishermen one percent of their gross to be set aside for domestic marketing of all salmon species. Questions have been asked by fishermen regarding the need for this added expense for a function already provided by the Alaska Seafood Marketing Institute (ASMI). Furthermore, the ASMI is perceived by many fishermen as hand-in-glove with processors. Again there exists a potential confrontation between fishermen and processors. The more pragmatic in the Alaska industry think that besides advertising, development of new product forms is essential in broadening the domestic market appeal of salmon. Putting thought into action, the Kodiak-based Fisheries Industrial Technical Center has appealed to both Alaska fishermen and processors for help in developing new salmon products and new processing techniques.[64]

We hope that good common sense will prevail in the Alaska industry, for there is much that may be done with the pink salmon. O. gorbuscha, the lowly and plentiful "humpie", is the common canned salmon found on market shelves. It is also the salmon frozen stiff, headed and gutted (H&G), found in the frozen-foods section of the same market, that is affordable to the average North American consumer. (If a frozen H&G pink is of good quality and cooked right, it can make an excellent fish dinner.) Other pink salmon products have potential. Minced pinks can be made into salmon patties and nuggets for the fast-food trade. Post '80s "yuppies" and single, career persons would accept "light/low fat" pink salmon entrées which are microwaveable. The Alaska industry should be aggressive about marketing Pacific salmon. Kate Troll, the executive director of SE Salmon Seiners has summed it up:

> "If Californians can convince Russians to buy volumes of almonds, certainly Alaskans should be able to convince them to buy protein for their meat-rationed population."[65]

Problem (2) is, and will be, the conservation and enhancement of fish stocks that show poor recruitment. The example that first comes to mind is easing fishing pressure. A way of doing so is being attempted at this writing (February 1992) in the British Columbia halibut fishery. Last summer and early autumn (1991), B.C. fishermen voted to try the Individual Vessel Quota (IVQ) system. The IVQ plan, approved by the Fisheries Minister, would benefit fishermen by the "promise of a safer and more profitable fishery, and the prospect of acquiring a valuable fixed asset that they could later sell."[66] The plan could be safer both for fishermen and the Pacific halibut as it would eliminate derby openings. Fishermen would no longer have to set their gear on opening day, weather permitting or not. The plan might mean higher profits as fishermen could schedule halibut fishing around other fishery seasons, with the slower pace translated into more care of fish and less crew. For the Pacific halibut, the plan promises a steadier and saner fishing pressure; surely a welcome relief from the hectic hysteria of one-day "derby daze." Time will tell how well the halibut will fare if and when Alaska fishermen enter the race under the Individual Fishing Quota (IFQ) program in 1994.[67]

Relieving fishing pressure on a favoured flatfish species has been taken a step further in Japan. There the flatfish is the California (or bastard) halibut (Paralichthys maculosus), rather than the grander Pacific halibut (Hippoglossus stenolepis). The more modest halibut is not being merely protected by the Japanese, its stocks are being actively enhanced. There are several reasons for this. As noted, Japan's distant-water fleets have been in full retreat all around the globe. Nations of the world are exerting increased control over their off-shore 200-mile Exclusive Economic Zones, and the seafood-loving Japanese are procuring less fish. To compensate for the deficit and to lessen dependence on imports, Japan has recently cultured the economically valuable California halibut, known as hirame, which has shown signs of commercial potential. While pen-reared hirame are still only a future possibility, Japanese fisheries scientists are presently ocean-ranching the species to rebuild inshore stock numbers for harvest. Even if the Hokkaido hirame program doesn't make big yen, its value signifies more than monetary profits for the Japanese. As John Sproul of Pacific Fishing magazine has written:

"...High social worth is placed on sustaining domestic inshore fisheries and their communities..."
"In Japan, the incentive to continue biological research in applied fisheries advancement is further motivated by the desire to compete with the foreign operators exporting those goods to Japan. In the coming years, as increasing numbers of stocked fish begin entering the fishery, stock enhancement programs will be responsible for allowing Japan to be aggressive about recapturing domestic seafood market share lost to foreign countries."[68]

Problem (3) is progress in methods of processing, preservation and packaging. Surimi, a whitefish paste that is treated, moulded, and sculpted to look and taste like crab legs and other seafood is the prime example. Now that the surimi market has become better established outside Japan, raw material for the product is getting harder to find. Alaska pollock (T. chalcogramma) has been the raw material, and Alaska exported 140,000 tons of pollock surimi to Japan in 1990. But, as mentioned in Part II, Alaska pollock has been overfished by the foreign factory trawler fleets during the early 1990s. Once the Donut Hole in the Bering Sea is closed, it must remain so until pollock recruitment improves to former levels. Until then, another raw material for surimi must be found.[69]

Two of the leading contenders to take the place of Alaska pollock are the Pacific whiting or hake (Merluccius productus), and the arrowtooth flounder or turbot (Atheresthes stomias). Both of these soft-fleshed fish have been examined in a previous work. Written during the mid-1980s, these sections raised tough questions about the use and marketability of the whiting and turbot. Diminished pollock stocks, the success of surimi, and advances in processing are providing answers in the 1990s. As for numbers, 200,000 tons a year of whiting are landed off the U.S. West Coast.[70] The turbot virtually "blankets the North Pacific; biomass estimated run as high as 500,000 tons."[71] The turbot resource in Alaska has been estimated at 3 billion; the guess is that 38 out of 100 fish in the Gulf of Alaska are turbots.[72] That both whiting and turbot are plentiful has been known for a long time...the difference today is the common solution to the problem of both fishes: Enzyme inhibitors.

As stated above, pollock has been the favoured fish processed into raw surimi material, and in its production the four cryo-protectants of sorbitol, sugar, phosphates and salt are used. But whiting surimi requires additional enzyme inhibitors, as its flesh breaks down more rapidly. Today's processor has a choice of five inhibitors: "Beef Plasma Protein; egg white (albumen), dehydrated potato derivative, whey protein concentrate and various inorganic salts."[73] These prevent myosin degradation.

The same applies to turbot. This fish, which is infamous for turning into "'a bag of jelly'" shortly after harvest, may be saved by rapid cooking and/or utilising enzyme inhibitors.[74] An NMFS researcher has said that turbot surimi was comparable to pollock surimi in colour, texture and length of shelf life. Indeed, turbot surimi actually became firmer after three months in cold storage, unlike other fish surimi. As the diminished Alaska pollock resource is trawled for the more valuable fillet market, Pacific whiting and turbot will be in growing demand for surimi production.[74]

The demand now (1992) exceeds production. It wasn't too long ago that U.S. surimi producers were desperately seeking markets. With the current cutback in pollock quotas, U.S. factory trawlers are targeting Pacific whiting. Other species besides turbot, being considered by industry researchers are menhaden and catfish. Scientists at the new joint NMFS/Mississippi State University laboratory at Pascagoula, Mississippi, recently mixed a 50/50 catfish-pollock crab-legs analog, and gave it an "A" for colour, flavour and gel strength. Meanwhile, the Japanese are producing surimi from New Zealand hoki...and the director of NMFS utilisation/research lab in Kodiak, Alaska, asks --and answers-- the question: "Can you make surimi out of pink salmon, if it comes to that? Of course you can."[75] Today, March 26, 1992, pink salmon is cheaper than catfish -- incredible but true.[76]

Another example of progress in processing is fish hydrolysate. The Alaska Fisheries Development Foundation (AFDF) is investigating a method of making seafood processing wastes into protein powders, supplements, feeds and other products. The AFDF is sanguine that hydrolysis technology will cut down on processing waste and its pollution, as well as create new and useful products. And in preserving seafood, Sea Grant publications is talking about a new method involving ultraviolet light. Previous attempts employing ultraviolet lights have killed bacteria but increased seafood rancidity; new progress, however, is said to preserve seafood flavour and enhance shelf life as well.[77]

There are current advancements even in packaging -- which might seem simple and straight forward -- that boggle the mind of even those in the industry. These range from crystallised polyester to polystyrene to plastics. Cans are tin no longer, paper is made from plastic, and packaging is entering a whole new era of innovation and invention, to keep pace with the advancements is seafood processing and preservation.[78]

An example of this is the recently-introduced tapered can. The newer and safer two-piece can has only one seam, on the lid, whereas the old can had three: on top, bottom and side. When traveling, the empty lidless cans are snugly nestled inside one another. This permits more cans to be shipped per pallet, and their tapering shape allows for easier stacking on retail shelves. To keep up with packaging proliferation, labeling is also undergoing change through computer technology. A Seattle-based production firm has teamed up with a national label manufacturer to ..."develop an exclusive, high-tech process that saves time and money..." which will ..."revolutionize the label conversion process..."[79]

Before moving on to the problems and prospects in aquaculture, I feel there is yet a development deserving mention in the processing category. The uncertainties about shellfish safety have become intensified, commensurate with fears of pollution, during the last quarter century. The fears could eventually endanger the seafood industry's future prosperity. North American ingenuity has come to the rescue. In September 1990, one Ed Millerstrom, owner of Unique Seafoods, Ltd. of San Francisco, envisioned a solution to the problem. Enlisting the aid of several shellfish depuration experts including the Canadian DFO, Millerstrom set up a depuration facility at Nanaimo, B.C.[80] By November 1991, Millerstrom had a plant that is the first closed marine depuration system for manila clams (Venerupis japonica) in all North America.[81]

(This) "...system circulates constantly purified water through the clams to cleanse them of any harmful micro-organisms, sand, grit, and digestive tract particulate matter. The bivalves are laboratory-tested at the beginning, middle and end of each 48-hour depuration cycle to ensure the absence of harmful bacteria and viral agents. The depuration plant can clean 7,344 pounds of clams every two days -- about 120,000 pounds a month."[82]

As the clams are mostly from restricted or new areas, the depuration plant at Nanaimo will greatly expand the B.C. manila clam industry as a whole. The process, concedes Millerstrom, adds up to 25% to product price, but the quality controlled result is fresh, clean, and certifiably safe. As the plant manager has said, "The success of this facility will determine the direction the industry takes in the years to come."[83]

Problem (4) is safe and viable new developments in mari-/aquaculture. Mariculture may be translated as "ocean ranching", or the sea itself as a farm. An example of this has been the hirame stock enhancement in Japan. Another example is the many salmon hatcheries on the Pacific Northwest Coast. Aquaculture may be defined as mariculture, and the cultivation, in any body of water, of aquatic animals and plants. To the people of our area, aquaculture means rainbow trout from Buhl, Idaho; Penn Cove mussels and Hood Canal oysters from Washington State; and farmed salmon from B.C.'s Sunshine Coast. But the most spectacular example of aquaculture here --and overseas-- has been that of Norwegian Atlantic salmon farming. It's rise during the 1980s was meteoric; its collapse during the 1990s catastrophic.

There are many reasons for the fall of an industry which, just a few years ago, showed such promise. Indeed, this writer has also called aquaculture "the way of the future."[84] But not all aquaculture, and certainly not Atlantic salmon farming, is the way of the present. On 13 November 1991, the Norwegian Fish Farmers' Sales Association filed for bankruptcy, with debts of 2 billion N.Kroner -- more than $300 million U.S. The reasons for the fall, according to the editor of Seafood Leader magazine, include overproduction and undermarketing. Aquaculture in general, and salmon farming in particular, was the industry's exciting new gospel of the 1980s, and if it was successful preached to usually hard-headed investors. But the visionary entrepreneurs did their job too well; by the 1990s, Norwegian salmon farming has gone from its boom to bust phase.[85]

The Old Country banks, which had so liberally backed the salmon farmers, went bust too. Kreditkassen, the largest creditor, was taken over by the Norwegian government in October 1991. The trouble from overproduction started as early as the mid-1980s. The Norwegian government loosened its (usually) tight grip on the industry, permitting more salmon farms. The recently deregulated banks eagerly financed the newcomers into Norway's hot new money-maker. "Norwegian salmon" became the standard of the industry, and production during 1988 had soared from 47,000 to 80,000 tons. European and U.S. markets had been able to handle the increase, but by autumn 1989, the flow of Norwegian farmed salmon had gone up almost 50% to 115,000 tons. Along with farmed salmon from the U.K., Canada, and Chile, world production had become a flood on international markets totaling 223,000 tons: "The flood of Norwegian salmon in 1989 became a tidal wave in 1990, when official production hit 160,000 tons."[86]

Overproduction and continued low prices in Norway caused resentment and then charges of dumping, first in the European Community and then in the United States. After carefully developing the American market and taking it for granted, the Norwegians were shocked when they were charged with an anti-dumping suit brought by a few (but determined) Maine salmon farmers in February 1990. Shock turned to dismay in March, 1991, when the U.S. International Trade Commission found the Norwegians guilty, and put a 24% duty on fresh, whole Norwegian salmon.[87] There is a whole lot more to this story, but the upshot is that the Norwegian Fish Farmers' Sales Association filed for bankruptcy, as noted, in November 1991, and the government is stuck with a "salmon mountain" of frozen product measuring "more than 37,000 tonnes." At last look, the State had agreed to buy the stored surplus salmon, and a BP company, Aqua Star, has been assigned to sell it ..."outside the traditional markets" (i.e., Eastern Europe).[88] But don't count the Norwegians out yet. As Seafood Leader's Peter Redmayne has concluded:

> "It may be in chaos now, but the Norwegian farmed salmon industry, which employs 15,000 people is too important to the country to let die. There will be considerable pain and confusion in the short term, but order will be restored, industry analysts believe. And then, hopefully, the industry can start growing again."[89]

There are, however, several reasons for not wanting salmon farms on the Pacific Northwest Coast. The first reason is that this is salmon country -- from western Alaska to northern California. The feeling is that there is an abundance of wild salmon here and plenty of employable fishermen to harvest it. Rather than importing Atlantic salmon eggs and raising the fish in net-pens on pellet-feed, local money would be better spent enhancing Pacific salmon habitat. There are five Pacific salmons[90] that spawn in the rivers of the Raincoast; surely natural propagation of these species makes more sense than artificially rearing the alien Atlantic salmon. Besides, wild fish is tastier....

The second reason transcends aesthetics and personal choice: Genetic and health risks associated with the transferral of Atlantic salmon (S. salar) smolts and eggs from Europe to North America. Genetic risks include intermingling of escaped farm fish with beleaguered native stocks, producing a hybrid salmon; which would further interbreed with wild fish, affecting their distinctive genetic make-up. Health hazards include damage to the fish, the environment and human beings. For the fish, unknown strains of disease could enter the U.S. and Canada from overseas; tough regulations notwithstanding. Also, a virus benign to Atlantic salmon could be devastating to Pacific salmon. A Canadian study has found that farming activity itself has spread a parasite into several B.C. rivers, resulting in the total loss of some wild stocks.[91]

Another health risk is that the use of toxicants and drugs in farm operations affect the environment and human beings. Residents on B.C.'s Sunshine Coast learned in 1986 that the average 2-hectare salmon farm produced sewage equal to a town of 2,000 population. Hundreds of tons of fish faeces being deposited from net-pens onto the sea-floor below has eradicated marine life. Canadian labour author Geoff Meggs has written: "The use of antibiotics in fish feed was linked to the production of new strains of bacteria in the food chain which could cause human illnesses ranging from gastroenteritis to cholera."[92] Additional concerns were --and are -- the proximity of farm-pens to river-runs, inspection standards at private hatcheries, proliferation of farming sites on foreshores abutting against private property, etc... the list seems endless.[93]

As if all the above were not enough, there is the triploid king salmon -- or "no-nookie chinookie" -- to worry about. And this time the blame cannot be placed on Atlantic intruders. After three years of R&D, fish culturists at Deer Mountain Hatchery in Ketchikan, Alaska, are in the final stages of creating chinook salmon (O. tshawytscha) that could eventually weigh more than 100 lb. The end product of the genetic research program is a sterile salmon that puts its growth energy into meat rather than mating. The biologists at Ketchikan have been genetically altering chinooks employing an easy heat-shock method: Immersion of normally fertilised eggs in warm water for about ten minutes. The result is a triploid salmon; one with three sets of chromosomes rather than the usual two (diploids).[94]

These sterile "steers of the sea" will not sexually mature and die, as do regular diploid Pacific salmon. Therefore, triploid fish grow bigger simply because they live longer. Some fifteen years ago, British scientists found out that certain fish were naturally triploid. Rivals in the growing European rainbow trout farming industry tried to find synthetic control of the process. The heat-shock method worked best. This is now applied mostly in private fish farms. The State of Alaska has the only official program in the world. The experimentation at Deer Mountain Hatchery is betting that triploid chinooks won't return to Ketchikan Creek to spawn. Instead, the "no-nookie" chinooks will swim around, from five to seven years or until taken by Southeast trollers.[95]

Questions concerning the Ketchikan kings include non-spawning: The triploids might return to their native stream, but cannot spawn. But sterile males could disrupt natural spawning by exhibiting spawning behaviour. The non-spawning triploids, however, would be valuable to sport fishermen looking to catch trophy kings. Commercial fishermen would also like triploid salmon for their bright, non-spawning colour.[96] Writer Laine Welch of Alaska Fisherman's Journal has added a humorous twist:

"Just when you thought it was safe to drag a herring behind your boat, genetic engineers get a hold of a few king salmon eggs, scramble their coding and create a race of sterile superfish.

"Now you're alone on the ocean, surrounded by giant king salmon with only one thing on their minds.

That's right, an entire race of "no-nookie chinookie" with nothing better to nibble on than your bait, your arm, or maybe your transom."[97]

Whether we like it or not, there will be evermore genetic engineering of marine animals and plants in the years ahead. There are, moreover, forms of aquaculture on the Pacific Rim other than salmon net-pens. A local example of this is the Pacific oyster (C. gigas), originally from Japan, grown in Washington. But the real masters of aquaculture are our neighbours to the west -- the East and South-East Asians. With long-established and high density populations, Asia has had to farm fish -- along with animals and plants -- just to survive over the centuries. Well-watered and part of the monsoon/typhoon cycles, southern East and South-East Asia took to aquaculture as a natural consequence of climate and biological need. Jennifer Brennan, who authored The Original Thai Cookbook, has expressed this well:

"The arteries of Thailand are inland waterways, nearly two thousand miles of superb fishing. If all this plenitude were not enough, fish are found in every flooded rice paddy, swamp, ditch, canal and pond. Bangkok itself is a spider's web of canals or klongs and, being at sea level or slightly lower, the city floods during the rainy season when the tides are high. The quiet little soi, or lane, where we lived would become a rushing river six inches deep when the rains came; with the flood would come the fish wiggling down the roadbed and playing tag with the vehicles."[98]

It is no surprise that 1989 was dubbed "the Year of the Tiger" -- the giant tiger prawn,[99] that is. Cultured shrimp production in South-East Asia boiled over, saturating the marketplace. U.S. imports from Thailand, Malaysia, Indonesia, and the Philippines nearly doubled in 1989 to more than 45,000 tons.[100] A year later, world shrimp farmers harvested a record 633,000 tons of whole shrimp; a 12% increase from 1989. Aquacultured shrimp now comprise circa 26% of the world supply, up 24% from a decade ago. Some industry observers believe that aquacultured shrimp will comprise fully half of the world supply by A.D. 2000.[101]

There appears to be none of the gastronomic stigma attached to farmed shrimp as is to farmed salmon. The seafood-loving but fastidious Japanese imported approximately 283,448 tons of shrimp during 1990; of which 48% were aquacultured. This was up 12.1% from 1989. Giant tiger prawns made up 101,837 tons of that total; white shrimp accounted for 30,752 tons. Indonesia (again) was the top shrimp exporter to Japan, supplying 53,162 tons, followed by China, Thailand, India and Vietnam, in that order.[102]

The problem of and prognosis for aquaculture are contained in both examples: Salmon farming in the Pacific Northwest and shrimp farming in South-East Asia. Like the industry observers who believe that a half of the world shrimp supply will be cultured by the year 2000, this writer believes --still-- that aqua-/mariculture is the wave of the future. Not all finfish or shellfish species lend themselves to being farmed, for various reasons. There is the question of salmon farming with marketing, environmental and biological problems. But on this side of the Pacific Rim, cultured rainbow trout and oysters have been very successful, and cultured shrimp are doing well in Mexico, Central America and Ecuador. With all the emotions and mystique surrounding the lordly salmon, perhaps it was not destined to be farmed in the Pacific Northwest ...just left to swim -- and spawn -- free. But aquaculture is here to stay.

Last, and certainly not least, is the relationship of the North Pacific fishing and seafood industry with the environmentalist lobby. In the opening paragraph to Part III, I have called the environmentalists the "Ecotopia Lobby." The reason is simple. About ten years ago a Washington Post editor named Joel Garreau wrote a book entitled The Nine Nations of North America. He argues convincingly that the original state, provincial and national boundaries bear no relation to the geographic, economic or cultural realities of the continental regions. Garreau draws borders that make some sense, and envisions our Pacific Northwest coastal area as part of "Ecotopia." This would include northern California, coastal Oregon and Washington State, western British Columbia and southeast Alaska. Ecotopia's shared interests include an almost religious dedication to "lifestyle", ecology, leisure and a fearful suspicion of development.[103]

So eco-(ecology)-topia(utopia) it has become.[104] The relationship between the fishing/seafood industry and the Ecotopia Lobby will be Problem (5) during the 1990s. There have already been many indications that confrontations will escalate. The environmentalist movement has ebbed and flowed since Earth Day, 1970.

It is beyond the scope of this presentation to study environmentalism in depth, but there must be some dishonourable mention. Like many well intended sociopolitical movements that have captured the popular imagination, the idealistic environmental movement of the 1960s/1970s has evolved into the militant and powerful environmentalist lobby of the 1980s/1990s.

This writer respectfully uses journalist Garreau's "ecotopia" idea with humorous irony. There is nothing funny, however, about the extreme positions of the Ecotopia Lobby regarding the Pacific Northwest Coast. The rhetoric has changed from slow-growth to no-growth. There has been desultory talk and sporadic attempts, via political initiative, to turn huge areas of Washington State and British Columbia into eco-Disneylands. No one, it seems, would be welcome to live in these areas except for the environmentally correct ex-urban post-yuppies, safely into arts, crafts and computer software. Commercial fishing and logging could be out as both are environment-unfriendly. The well-heeled sport fishing lobby, as exclusive as the Ecotopians, would go along with the eco-Disneyland concept for their own gain: A tourist-caught salmon is worth far more money than a commercially caught one. As there would be no growth, development or industry, the Pacific Northwest Coast could become an exclusive Ectopia indeed... with nobody to mar the landscape except for environment-friendly ectomorphs who bike, hike and jog, and don't smoke, drink or eat "chee-tos."

The National Fisheries Institute (NFI) held its annual convention at New Orleans last year, 30 October - 2 November 1991. NFI Executive Vice-President, Lee Weddig, had a somber warning for fellow members: "Mainstream, large, well financed environmental groups are turning to the fisheries as their next field of play in efforts to shape the world in the image they envision."[105]

To counter these "green" groups, the NFI has established the World Ocean Fund. The industry-wide non-profit organisation, according to Lee Weddig, will... "work with the marine community and the other ocean industries to conduct education and research that promotes reasonable access and rational use of ocean resources, and protects the ecological balance and diversity of the marine environment for mankind."[106]

The key phrase here is "reasonable access and rational use of ocean resources." Weddig's statement opened the multi-year, $2-$3 million fund-raising drive that will at first target the industry, then outside sources. As Weddig has concluded: "The seafood industry has a responsibility to look after the environment in order to supply future generations of mankind with supplies of fish and shellfish."[107]

The Alaska theatre, site of the present fight for fish in the North Pacific (see Part II), might soon become the stage for a real war between the combined industry versus government/environmentalists. This time the battle is being fought over a bottomfish-user group, whose feed is being inhibited, rather than the resource itself. This user group is neither fishermen nor processors -- it is the Steller sea lion. Even though the North Pacific Fishery Management Council (NPFMC) has recommended placing 10-mile buffer zones around sea lion rookeries in the Gulf of Alaska, Bering Sea and the Aleutians, the NMFS has drawn up regulations that would double the no-trawl zones around five major rookeries. Areas would be closed where large harvests of Alaska pollock and Pacific cod have been taken in recent years.[108]

The last minute closure by the NMFS has caught both trawlers and processors by surprise, without opportunity for public comment, and will hurt both industry sectors. The hapless NMFS, wanting to please the industry and mollify Greenpeace, has had to juggle fishing quotas while simultaneously keeping the Steller sea lion off the endangered species list. As John Iani, director of Pacific Seafood Processor's Association, wryly observed: "Somebody in the marine mammal office decided at the last minute we've go to do something... It's just goofy."[109]

It is my considered opinion that everyone in this beautiful area is aware of man-made dangers to our ecosystem. To be environmentally correct has become as socially significant as being politically correct. Entertainers and athletes describe themselves as environmental activists in the same breath as being AIDS fund-raisers. If all this trendy rectitude makes us ordinary folks more environmentally conscious... so be it for the better. But if the pendulum swings back from environmental abuse, to misuse, beyond use, back to no use... human welfare will be adversely affected.

As a fish-loving denizen of the Olympic Peninsula, this writer is well aware of problems relating to the terrestrial (i.e., logging, spotted owls) and marine (i.e., fishing, salmon) ecosystems. In an earlier work, I did a brief study on the lingcod (O. elongatus), written in ca. late 1985. I ended the essay with: "Let us of southern Vancouver Island and the Northern Olympic Peninsula be careful not to overfish the lingcod in the Strait of Juan de Fuca."[111] Imagine my surprise when just six years later, I read in a local newspaper: 'Fishermen agree to save the lings.' In 1985, the lingcod was considered a toothsome food-fish that was readily available.[112]

And so it goes. The environmental pendulum must swing back from abuse, stopping at use -- "Wise Use." Again the key phrase is "reasonable access and rational use of ocean resources," spoken by Lee Weddig of the NFI. It is my hope that these sentiments are shared by the vast majority of those in the fisheries and seafood industry. For assuredly if "Wise Use" is not practised, the Ectopia Lobby will wax in power while expanding its political platform. Most members of the environment movement are exactly what they profess to be: Concerned about the environment in which we all have to live.

There are some, however, that use the environmental movement as a vehicle to further their own radical agenda, ranging from sexist politics to New Age spiritualism. These other groups appear to be growing in influence, and one hears disturbing mention of eco-feminism, Mother (Earth) Goddess, Gaia, etc. Aging cause-hungry yippies of my generation might have to ultimately choose between Trade Unionism versus Environmentalism, as future economic realities will certainly unite all sectors of the industry. There will be no more room for the senseless business-bashing of the past. The realities are fishing, processing, and producing quality seafood from the waters of the Pacific Northwest Coast to feed North America and the world.

Ten years ago, in 1982, a survey was undertaken where it was estimated that a mere eight of the world's 173 nation-states consistently produced more food than they consumed. These were The United States,

Canada, Australia, New Zealand, South Africa, Argentina, France and Thailand. The Unites States alone has more of a monopoly on world food than does OPEC on the global petroleum supply.[113] The far reaches of the North Pacific Ocean, dominated by the U.S.A. and the Russian Republic, is one of the last seafood cornucopias remaining on earth. With the Cold War ended and a virtual Pax Americana in effect, it will be up to the United States to see to "Wise Use" of the vast marine resource stored therein. The present disagreement over which user group gets to fish Pacific pollock, human or sea lion, could escalate into eventual confrontation between the industry and the environmentalists. It is a prototype example of marine resource-use conflicts with which the 1990s will be fraught.

To conclude this study, allow me to take a literal page out of our local newspaper, The Peninsula Daily News. The page is D-3 from the Sunday business section, 17 November 1991. On this single page are three articles that have to do with both the fishing/seafood industry and the Pacific Rim.

The first article is entitled, 'Oregon port tries new fish industry':

"A Newport, Oregon fish plant has announced a $2 million joint venture investment to build the West Coast's first Pacific whiting surimi plant.
"The plant will allow Newport Shrimp Inc. to make surimi from Pacific whiting. Surimi is a fish paste used in artificial fish products such as imitation crab.
"The plant's partner is Talbot Investment Co. of Bellingham.
"A second Washington company, Arctic Alaska Fisheries Corp. is working with the Port of Newport to locate a $5 million plant on Yaquina Bay to turn fish wastes into fish meal."

The second article, 'Shrimp industry: A sinking feeling,' tells of duty free shrimp imports causing pain:

"The nation's shrimping industry is being battered by competition from farm-raised imports and listless consumer demand.
"... Some of the industry's problems may be outside its control -- pollution that affects estuaries, the loss of coastal wetlands, economic woes that have cut back on dining out, and imports that arrive duty-free from China, the Far East, Ecuador and Mexico."
"The president of Seafood Management Corp., a Falmouth, Maine, management consulting company has said:
"'Domestic producers are not able to catch the quantities of shrimp per day or per night that would bring their costs down. They're going to have more and more trouble competing with farm-raised shrimp.'"

The third article informs us that 'Alaska Airlines wants to add route to historic Russian port':

"Alaska Airlines, which began flying between Alaska and Siberia this year (1991) has applied to the U.S. Department of Transportation for an extension to serve the Russian port city of Vladivostok... "Alaska became the lone U.S. carrier to offer regular service between the West Coast and the Soviet Union in June (1991) with three flights a week using Boeing 727s between Anchorage, Alaska, and Magadan and Khabarovsk."[114]

A "Pacific Shift" indeed. This three-part study has attempted to describe the Pacific Rim's emerging role as the new centre of the economic world, and the part the North Pacific Fisheries and seafood industry will play -- during the 1990s and beyond 2000 -- in the Pacific-Aerospace cultural ecology. Who can accurately predict what the future might bring? Tomorrow's politically incorrect people might be live fish-eating Asian females, rather than today's dead meat-eating European males! For a closing thought on the future Pacific Rim, I quote from James A. Michener's Return to Paradise, written in 1951, a half century ago:

"I can foresee the day when the passage of goods and people and ideas across the Pacific will be of far greater importance to America than the similar exchange across the Atlantic. Asia must inevitably become more important to the United States than Europe."

Michener's thought applies to fish, too. In our own area of the Pacific Northwest Coast, not every Joe Six Pack has the leisure time, enough money or wherewithal for sportfishing. The trappings -- boat, gear, licenses, petroleum -- are expensive. It costs to angle in the forest of fibreglass poles. A sport-caught fish is shared by family and friends, and is not available on the open market. Only in keeping our North Pacific fisheries and seafood industry healthy and competitive, may North Americans be assured of a steady supply of fresh fish. Throughout my previous works, I have preached the basic gospel of the need for using underutilised finfish and shellfish species. Solving all five problems -- as perceived and listed above -- will make up future trends in the North Pacific fisheries and seafood industry.

NOTES

60.   Deleted, after same thought by author, is the prepositional phrase..."for a low price".

61.   Donna Parker, 'Sizing Up New Salmon Markets', <u>Pacific Fishing</u>, November 1991, p. 121.

62.   <u>Ibid.</u>, p. 124, Cf. <u>Salmon 2000</u>, a report published by the Alaska Seafood Marketing Institute (ASMI) in June, 1991.

63.   <u>Ibid.</u>, p. 130.

64.   Donna Parker, 'Prying Open the Salmon Market', <u>Alaska Fisherman's Journal</u>, February 1991, p. 5. Cf. <u>Ibid.</u>, Chuck Crapo, 'Adding Value to Alaska's Pink Salmon', p. 34.

65.   Kate Troll, executive director, SE Alaska Seiners, 'Pondering the Pinks', <u>Alaska Fisherman's Journal</u>, February 1992, p. 19.

66.   T.J. Doherty, 'B.C. Halibut Quotas: Benefit to Shareholders Despite a Few Bugs', <u>Pacific Fishing</u>, February 1992, p. 29.

67.   <u>Ibid.</u>, pp. 29, 35. Cf. Donna Parker, 'At Long Last AK Gets IFQS', <u>Pacific Fishing</u>, February 1992, pp. 21, 57.

68.   John Sproul, 'Hirame Enhancement: Efforts to Increase Inshore Halibut', <u>Pacific Fishing</u>, November 1991, pp. 104-110.

69.   "Surimi", 'WHOLE SEAFOOD CATALOG', <u>Seafood Leader</u>, Vol. 11, No. 5, September/October 1991, p. 128.

70.   <u>Ibid.</u>, "Fish Futures", p. 30.

71.   <u>Ibid.</u>, "Solving the Arrowtooth Enigma", p. 132.

72.   C. Horton, 'Arrowtooth Surimi?', <u>Alaska Fisherman's Journal</u>, October 1991, p. 21.

73.   "Fish Futures", 'WHOLE SEAFOOD CATALOG', p. 30.

74.   <u>Ibid.</u>, "Solving the Arrowtooth Enigma", p. 132.

75.   <u>Ibid.</u>, "Meeting the Surimi Demand", p. 130.

76.   <u>Seafood Leader</u>, '1992 BUYERS' GUIDE', Vol. 12, No. 2, March/April, 1992, p. 115.

77.   "Fish Futures", and "Ultraviolet, Man", 'WHOLE SEAFOOD CATALOG', p. 176.

78.   <u>Ibid.</u>, "Equipment: Packaging and Labeling", p. 182.

79.   <u>Ibid.</u>, "The Shape of Things to Come", p. 186.

80.   There is the official Pacific Biological Station at Nanaimo, B.C.

81. "S.F. Firm Cleans up B.C. Clams", 'Aquaculture', <u>Seafood Leader</u>, January/February 1992, p. 34.

82. <u>Ibid.</u>, p. 35.

83. <u>Ibid.</u>, Quoted is plant manager Bill McCarthy.

84. See C.D. Bay-Hansen, Vol.2, 'Mariculture and Aquaculture'.

85. Peter Redmayne, ed., "All Together Now", 'Aquaculture', <u>Seafood Leader</u>, January/February, 1992, p. 3.

86. <u>Ibid.</u>, Peter Redmayne, 'Norway's Salmon Industry Shatters Into Chaos', pp. 75, 78.

87. <u>Ibid.</u>, pp. 78, 82. Cf. 'Seafood Report', <u>Pacific Fishing</u>, February 1992, p. 13.

88. 'State and Banks in Fish Farming Rescue Bid', <u>Western Viking</u>, Vol. 103, No. 4, 24 January, 1992, p. 1.

89. Op. cif., Peter Redmayne, "Norway's Salmon Industry Shatters Into Chaos", <u>Seafood Leader</u>, January/February 1992, p. 82.

90. Six, if you count steelhead trout. The latter appears to have undergone a scientific metamorphosis, ca. 1990, from <u>S. gairdneri</u> to <u>O. mykiss</u>.

91. Geoff Meggs, <u>Salmon: The Decline of the British Columbia Fishery</u>, (Vancouver/Toronto: Douglas & McIntyre, 1991) p. 238.

92. Op. cif., Geoff Meggs, p. 235.

93. <u>Ibid.</u>, pp. 232-245.

94. Laine Welch, 'Genetic Engineers Seek Huge Sexless Chinook', <u>Alaska Fisherman's Journal</u>, December 1991, p. 50.

95. <u>Ibid.</u>, p. 50.

96. <u>Ibid.</u>, p. 50.

97. <u>Ibid.</u>, Laine Welch, 'The Day of the Triploids', p. 49.

98. "Thai Waterways", 'WHOLE SEAFOOD CATALOG', <u>Seafood Leader</u>, Vol. 11, No. 5, September/October 1991, p. 74. NB. This writer was in Thailand during September 1971, and noticed the prevalence of fish in the local diet.

99. <u>Penaeus monodon.</u>

100. <u>Ibid.</u>, 'WHOLE SEAFOOD CATALOG', p. 84. This figure includes the South Asian country of Bangladesh.

101. <u>Ibid.</u>, "Farmed Shrimp Hit 1990 High", p. 86.

102.   Ibid., "Japanese Eat More Farmed Shrimp", p. 94.

103.   Ric Dolphin, 'Reborn in the USA', Western Living, Vol. 22, No. 1, January 1992, pp. 40-41. Cf. Joel Garreau, The Nine Nations of North America, (New York: Avon Books, 1981) pp. 245-287.

104.   Ecology or oecology: Relationship of organisms to their environment. Utopia is derived from Greek u = not, and topos = place. I.e., Utopia is "nowhere."

105.   "NFI Goes Green With New Fund", 'Heads & Tails', Seafood Leader, January/February 1992, p. 30.

106.   Ibid., Op. cit., Lee Weddig, p. 30.

107.   Ibid., Op. cit., Lee Weddig, p. 30.

108.   John van Amerongen, 'That's far enough... or is it?', Alaska Fisherman's Journal, Vol. 15, No. 2, February 1992, p. 1.

109.   Ibid., John van Amerongen, 'Sea Lion Buffers Getting Bigger', p. 10.

110.   'Fishing to be most restrictive in history', Peninsula Daily News, 22 March, 1991, p. B-2.

111.   See C.D. Bay-Hansen, Vol.2, Ch.V, "Groundfishes': Section II.

112.   'Fishermen agree to save the lings', Peninsula Daily News, 19 November 1991, pp. B-1, B-3.

113.   Lowell Ponte, 'Food: America's Secret Weapon', Reader's Digest, May 1982, pp. 66-68. NB. The reader will note that five of the eight countries are on the Pacific Rim.

114.   At this writing, March 1992, Japanese companies already predominate in Khabarovsk.

BIBLIOGRAPHY FOR PART III

7.   Callenbach, Ernest. <u>Ecotopia: The Notebooks and Reports of William Weston</u>. Bantam Books, New York, 1990.

8.   Garreau, Joel. <u>The Nine Nations of North America</u>. Avon Books, New York, 1981.

NOTES ON SOURCES

The historian has no sources to work with when researching the future. Primary sources are word-of-mouth, and main references are secondary and even tertiary. In Part II I made wide use of <u>Alaska Fisherman's Journal</u> and <u>Pacific Fishing</u> magazines. And where would I have been in Part III without <u>Seafood Leader's</u> 'WHOLE SEAFOOD CATALOG' issue?

ACKNOWLEDGEMENTS

Part III of this study was presented 23 April 1992 at a 'Studium Generale' lecture, Peninsula College, Port Angeles, Washington. My thanks to Dr. Werner Quast for the opportunity.

I am grateful also to Mr. Scott McEntire of the NMFS for a copy of 'Final Report of 1990'... (driftnet observations); the editors of <u>Pacific Fishing</u> and <u>Seafood Leader</u> magazines; and Mr. Francis Caldwell of Port Angeles for loan of his slides.

AFTERWORD: "FISHERIOGRAPHY"

Joel Garreau's idea of Ecotopia was itself taken from <u>Ecotopia: The Notebooks And Reports of</u> <u>William Weston,</u> by Ernest Callenbach (Berkeley, Calif.: Banyan Tree Books, 1975). Although <u>The Nine</u> <u>Nations of North America</u> proved to be fascinating reading, Garreau mentions Pacific fishing only once: "Huge self-sufficient Japanese trawlers ply the Bering Sea, catching bottom fish North Americans are not used to eating, and not even landing in Alaska to pick up provisions, much less to generate cannery jobs" (p.281).

As for Ecotopia as a movement, no less a personage than Clifton Fadiman, writing for the San Francisco-based Foundation for National Progress ("A Technological Culture?" <u>Center</u> magazine, March/April 1977), has implied that Ecotopianism is doomed. Fadiman has listed...and quoted...in his report ("Technology: Over The Invisible Line?") many "new thinkers" and their concepts of the "new culture phase", which has been characterised as: "Post-Industrial, Technological (Jacques Ellul), Nuclear, Supranational, Space, Megalopolitan, Behavior-Controlled, 'Epoch B' (Jonas Salk), Bio-Engineering, Sensate (Herman Kahn), Post-Humanist (Lionel Trilling), and so forth".

Fadiman's observations, however astute, were made before the ascendancy of today's powerful New Age/Ecofeminist Movement. For every point there's a counterpoint, and this writer ventures that William Irwin Thompson's Pacific Aerospace cultural ecology will include the Gaia Hypothesis on the way to A.D.2000 and beyond. Far from being mutually exclusive, technology and environmentalism could mesh and form a left brain-right brain combination of technoecology; a potentially awesome union which might result in the Paradigm Shift sought by the New Agers. The Pacific Aerospace cultural ecology is hardly the smokestack industrial complex of the obsolescent "Rustbelt" Foundry, and a natural wedding of high-technocracy and the Ecotopians would occur. The ensuing marriage of these mega-forces will forever change the fundamental character of the North Pacific fisheries and seafood industry.

The New Age world view has even influenced the writing about the industry. A perfect example is the second-to-last book I read as a secondary source for this report. This book was published by an Alaskan company in a posh Seattle suburb, rather than at the usual Anchorage site. Although excellently written and beautifully illustrated by a famous Alaska artist, the book's admonitory and condescending tone was infuriating. The author, Pacific editor of a U.S. national fishing magazine, has made no secret of his eco-Evolutionary Humanist philosophy.

The former world-view was in stark contrast to that expressed in the very last work I read as a secondary source. The last work was written by a Canadian labour writer, describing the decline of the B.C. salmon fishery...a book richly rife with all the predictable stereotypes of greedy canners and/or implacable Americans, being bravely resisted throughout the years by the good and true UFAWU (the Communist-inspired United Fishermen and Allied Workers' Union). Here I was on familiar ground; Karl Marx being far easier to understand than Julian Huxley.

Shall, then, the two biases eventually meet and fuse, as might technology and environmentalism? Or will one evolve into the other, as NY Print Culture has evolved into LA Visual Culture? Let us hope that there are always "fisheriographers" out there, who venerate enough the resource and the men and women that harvest and process it, to write reports of the industry that are true, fair and free of prejudice.

APRIL 1992

BIBLIOGRAPHY

9.   Meggs, Geoff. <u>Salmon: The Decline of the British Columbia Fishery</u>. Douglas & McIntyre, Vancouver/Toronto, 1991.

10. Troll, Ray and Brad Matsen. <u>Ray Troll's Shocking Fish Tales</u>. Alaska Northwest Books, Bothell, Wa., 1991.

Chapter 2

Irrational Ecologism vs. Wise-Use Fisheries

Part I: Environmentalism -- A New Age Religion?

Part II: Shrinking the Big Green Agenda

Part III: North Pacific Rim Fishing, 2001 A.D.

"... Finally we got up and returned to bath house, Marissa pausing as we left the tree, mumbling something I couldn't catch. Dawned on me that it was a prayer of some kind and that this incredible woman is a goddam druid or something -- a tree-worshipper!"   - Ernest Callenbach in Ecotopia, 1975

"... Or we could end up in some visionary New Age with a Green government in a sci-fi intradimensional, dolphin-torn, whale-sounded, galactic music polity of extraterrestrial consciousness."
                    - William Irwin Thompson in The American Replacement of Nature, 1991

"We are different from other environmental groups, because we believe in seeking solutions to environmental and resource problems based on science rather than emotion."
                    - Thor Lassen, executive vp of Ocean Trust

Introduction: Is Environmentalism a New Age Religion?

"... I sprang out and after her, down a forest path. She's damn fast, and also good at dodging around trees. We got into deeper forest. Suddenly, ducking around a particularly huge redwood tree, she disappeared into a hollow at its base. Springing in after her, I found myself in some kind of shrine. She was lying there on a bed of needles, taking deep, gasping breaths. Dimly visible, suspended on the charred inside of the tree, were charms and pendants made of bone and teeth and feathers, gleaming polished stones. It was (as) if I was being sucked into the tree, into some powerful spirit....

"Finally we got up and returned to bath house, Marissa pausing as we left the tree, mumbling something I couldn't catch. Dawned on me that it was a prayer of some kind and that this incredible woman is a goddam druid or something -- a tree-worshipper!"[1]

The above is part of a seduction scene depicted in Ernest Callenbach's Ecotopia: The Notebook and

Reports of William Weston. Although written tongue-in-cheek during the 1970s for a hip, mostly West Coast

readership, Ecotopia is already twenty years old. And most of the ideas and attitudes expressed therein by

Callenbach, both good and bad, are embedded in 1990s mainstream environmentalist thought and speech.

Callenbach's book seems almost old by today's time-staggered standards, but it was contemporaneous with the

"Gaia Hypothesis" of Lyn Margolis and James E. Lovelock.[2]

Even though the Gaia Hypothesis has been around for about two decades, and is cloyingly familiar in academic and New Age circles, the average Joe Camel in the West Coast fishing and seafood industry has never heard of the Gaia Hypothesis; let alone Gaia. To put it simply, in the words of William Irwin Thompson, the hypothesis of Lyn Margolis and James E. Lovelock states that ..."the earth's atmosphere is not simply a gaseous fluid into which substances are dumped by animals, plants, and factories, but the metabolism of a complex organism..."[3] Thompson has concluded that the Gaia Hypothesis is an "extended animism", akin to the Taoist geomancy or feng-shui of ancient China.[4]

The key word here is animism, which is in the realm of religion. There are disagreements on whether Gaia is a religion or a scientific theory. According to Fr. Robert A. Sirico, in a recent article in National Review magazine, the Gaia Institute (yes, there is one) has commissioned a complete choral Mass entitled 'Missa Gaia.' Gaia begins to sound like a religion to me. Fr. Sirico has commented: ...."Certainly its religious aspect has found followers in spiritual feminist circles attracted to the idea of Mother Earth or an Earth goddess...."[6]

Animism, spiritual feminism, Gaia -- what do they all mean? To get to the heart of environmentalism one has to reach the soul of the New Age religion(s); the answer is there. Animism is defined in Webster's Dictionary as ..."the belief, widely held ... that souls are quasi-physical and can exist outside the body (in dreams and visions), can be transformed from one body to another and persist after the death of the body (ghosts and reincarnation)."[7]

But the "extended animism" of the Gaia Hypothesis, as coined by William Irwin Thompson, is aeons away from the basic animism of Central Africa and some Pacific Islands. The extended animism of Margolis and Lovelock is an amalgam of creeds, gleaned from many spiritual sources since the 1960s, and may be collectively termed ecotheology. Georgetown University professor Victor Ferkiss says that ecotheology "...starts with the premise that the Universe is God and that this belief will ... prevent the environmental exploitation of the Universe."[8]

Christian writers Dave Hunt and T.A. McMahon have labeled ecotheology as "neopantheism of academia," also as "scientism."[9] Ecotheology is academic neo-pantheism, and is also the scientism of Carl Sagan accompanied by the "nature spirits" of William Irwin Thompson "running the universe."[10] Put them all together and what we have is not a mere environmentalist ethos, but an entire New Age nature religion which has flared up from the low fires of several timeless ones.[11]

It is at this juncture that the question should be answered: Who or what is Gaia? Gaia (Gaea) in classical Greek mythology was the primordial goddess of the earth. Her consort, Uranus, was the primordial god of the heavens.[12] Children of Gaea and Uranus included the twelve Titans, among them Cronos, Oceanus, Mnemosyne and Hyperion. Gaea mated with Poseidon, her grandson through Cronos, and produced the sea monster, Charybdis. Gaea had Oedipal relations with her son, Oceanus, and bore Nereus, the Old Man of the Sea. (Nereus would eventually sire the Nereids through Doris).[13]

Gaea's further offspring, fathered by Uranus, were the Giants and the one-eyed Cyclopes, headed by Polyphemus. Cronos, Gaea's Titan son, through Rhea begot Zeus, Hera, Hades, Demeter, Poseidon, Hestia. Another Titan, Hyperion, who coupled with Thea, gave the cosmos Helios the sun, Selene the moon, and Eos the dawn. Mnemosyne, a Titaness and the goddess of memory, was consort -- and aunt -- of the god Zeus, and the result of their union was the nine Muses. Yet another Titaness, Tethys, committed incest with her brother, Oceanus, and the Oceanids were their progeny. From the loins of Uranus and the womb of Gaea issued forth the entire pantheon of Hellenic deities.[14]

But the Earth Mother/Goddess, the modern Gaia, has appeared in many cultures under many guises. The theme of sky-cult father and earth-cult mother was a common one in the ancient world. Regarding the nature of earth-cult mother, cultural historian Camille Paglia has observed: "The mother goddess gives life but takes it away.... She is morally ambivalent, violent as well as benevolent. The sanitized pacific goddess promoted by feminism is wishful thinking. From prehistory to the end of the Roman Empire, the Great Mother never lost her barbarism. She is the ever-changing face of chthonian nature, now savage, now smiling. The medieval Madonna, a direct descendant of Isis, is a Great Mother with chthonian terror removed. She has lost her roots in pagan nature, because it is pagan nature that Christianity rose to oppose."[15]

Today, Great Mother worship is alive and very well despite some determined opposition in Christendom. Although Margolis and Lovelock chose to call the Great Mother/Goddess Gaia, after the Greek ge (the earth), she was a divinity with many names and faces. These identities ranged in time and space from

Near Eastern mystery religions, where she was known as Inanna in Sumer, as Ishtar in Babylon, and Ashtoreth in Canaan; to West Africa where she was known as Ala, as Kali in India, and Frigg in Scandinavia. Behind all the varying personae, however, the Goddess represented a single belief system. From current South Asian Hinduism to North American shamanism, Mother Earth is regarded as one and the same.[16] James Lovelock has portrayed the Goddess for us:

"Gaia is Mother Earth. Gaia is immortal. She is the eternal source of life. She does not need to reproduce herself as she is immortal. She is certainly the mother of us all, including Jesus... Gaia is not a tolerant mother. She is rigid and inflexible, ruthless in the destruction of whoever transgresses. Her unconscious objective is that of maintaining a world adapted to life. If we men hinder this objective we will be eliminated without pity....[17]

"....At the same time not more than a few thousand years ago, the concept of a remote master God (the Judeo-Christian God), an overseer of Gaia, took root ... [As these people moved west] they brought a sky god, a warrior cult, and a patriarchal social order.... The evolution of these [people] to the modern men who ride their infinitely more powerful machines of destruction over the habitats of our partners in Gaia, seems only a small step."[18]

With the two short paragraphs of James Lovelock cited above is a whole cosmology containing a resurrected nature religion. The resistance in certain Christian (and Jewish) circles is readily understood as "the Judeo-Christian God" is specifically named. According to Lovelock, the Judaeo-Christian Gods' "people" [i.e., the Christians] brought with them [in their religious and cultural baggage] a "...sky god, a warrior cult, and a patriarchal social order."[19] But here Gaia is merely an excuse for a lot of Lovelockian Jehovah-bashing. For the sky-cult Judaeo-Christian God is the perennial and implacable enemy of the earth-cult Mother Goddess. He, not She, created nature rather than the other way around. The earth was made as a suitable dwelling place for mankind by a Father not a Mother, and a Maker perceived as distinctly outside and separate from His creation. Author Camille Paglia has remarked on this essential distinction:

"The book of Genesis is a male declaration of independence from the ancient mother-cults. Its challenge to nature, so sexist to modern ears, marks one of the crucial moments in western history.... The mother-cults, by reconciling man to nature, entrapped him in matter. Everything great in western civilization has come from struggle against our origins. Genesis is rigid and unjust, but it gave man hope as a man. It remade the world by male dynasty, canceling the power of mothers."[20]

Goddess worship has brought a disturbing new element into the resuscitated earth-cult -- feminism, or ecofeminism, with its rejection of the (male) Judaeo-Christian God. Western civilisation, despite the Christian imprint, has always had a plethora of pagan female divinities ready and waiting in its spiritual wings.

Gaia, Gaea, Ge, has been carefully selected from the Hellenic pantheon by modern earth-worshippers to do battle with the Hebraic patrimony of Christendom.

The ecofeminism, then, of the "spiritual feminist circles" referred to earlier by Fr. Robert Sirico[21], is the first disturbing element in the new ecotheology, the New Age nature religion. In 1991 a certain Tom Williams, priest of the Church of All Worlds, called the Christian Era the "Christian Interlude."[22] The Christian Interlude, in the mind of New Age astrology, is the Age of Pisces (from the fish, symbol of Christianity) soon to be eclipsed by the Age of Aquarius. The Age of Pisces, "fueled by masculine yang energy, is now at an end. It is being superseded by the feminine yin energy of the Age of Aquarius."[23]

The New Age astrologers have reckoned the Piscean (old) Age (of the fish) to have commenced in A.D.1, and will be replaced by the (new) Aquarian Age (of the water-bearer) in A.D. 1997.[24] The disturbing element previously mentioned is two-fold: A surging ecofeminism pits the earth-cult Mother Goddess against the sky-cult Father God, with feminine yin energy versus masculine yang strength. The much-vaunted Age of Aquarius will be ushered in by a psychic gender war to augment religious/spiritual conflict.

On first examination little of the New Age nature religion appears to owe its origins to Western classical tradition, save for the name of the Goddess Gaia. After all, so much of New Age thought and theology is derived from Eastern religions and primal cultures. Hip newspeak, starting with the Beats during the 1950s, has been fraught with cool, exotic words like Zen, karma and satori. Although mostly used in an off-hand manner, such words nonetheless have manifested a persistent interest in Hinduism and Buddhism that has lasted. The ecofeminism of the 1990s, however, derives many of its core beliefs from the familiar taproot of Mediterranean civilisation. Consciously or not, the offshoot chosen by the ecofeminists turned out to be an early Christian counterculture known as Gnosticism.

In a fine recent work on neo-Gnosticism by Christian writer Peter Jones, the old un-Christian heresy is shown to be here and now preaching the gospel of a hemaphroditic Father-God/Mother-Goddess. In the Gnostic God/Goddess, "...there is a dyad of masculine and feminine elements, a dynamic relationship of opposites like the yin and the yang.[25] Peter Jones refers to certain Gnostic texts where ..."God the Creator is castigated by a higher, feminine power, Sophia...."[25] Sophia-worship has become popular in American main-line churches during the 1990s.

But the feminisation of God to an androgynous God/Goddess in the Gnostic scriptures, has devolved in neo-Gnosticism as gender inversion and role reversal of the Creator. This dislocates Judaeo-Christian doctrinal orthodoxy as well as causing sexual confusion. The Fall, in neo-Gnostic eyes, is the way to salvation. The Woman and the Serpent (Satan-kundalini) in the Garden have become the teachers of truth. The evil Creator and the foolish Adam are male entities, therefore true (neo) Gnostic divinity is androgynous/female.[27] It is easy to understand why neo-Gnostic concepts are so dear to ecofeminism!

Combine neo-Gnosticism with Gaia/Goddess worship and the result is a dove-tailed cosmology for the "spiritual feminist circles" of Fr. Robert Sirico. The first commandment of the new ecotheology is for the immediate excommunication of the Judaeo-Christian God. For renegade Dominican Matthew Fox, now a New Age geologian, the "God of Guilt ... a phallic, vengeful, sadistic Deity ... has to go."[28] Thus in the absence of the Creator [or a Creatrix], the world -- indeed the universe and creation itself -- is merely a sum of all things, understood in pantheistic terminology, without a creation account. As Peter Jones has commented, a creation account is irrelevant to New Age thinking anyway. The very idea of a Creator, separate and apart from His creation, making an entire cosmos from absolutely nothing, is abhorrent."[29]

Another author who has effectively contrasted Gaia-worship to traditional Christianity is Berit Kjos. In her Under the Spell of Mother Earth are a series of charts describing the differences. Berit Kjos delineates earth-based spirituality as:

"Earth (Gaia, goddess) is... a living, feminine force... divine source of power and wisdom... in all (Pantheism)... one with all (Monism)....

"We are... part of Gaia, connected to all her other parts... naturally good, sacred... perfect when in harmony with nature... in control of ourselves....

"We have harmony... with earth, her rhythms through TM [transcendental meditation], visualization, guided imagery... to teach others....

"Faith means choosing to... grow in consciousness... trust natural thoughts, spirits, dreams, images... follow dreams and desires....

"We triumph by... connecting with the Earth... empowering ourselves for today... rebirth and reincarnation....

"We speak and project mental images, do magic...."[30]

Before continuing on to "magick" and witchcraft, two seminal ingredients in feminist ecotheology, I ask the reader to let me counter two contemporary cultural myths. In reference, two women writers are quoted -- the Christian Berit Kjos, and the chthonian Camille Paglia. Berit Kjos has identified these complementary myths as: (1) "Prehistoric cultures, led by Mother Goddesses, enjoyed perfect harmony"; and (2) "male god(s) brought war, exploitation."[31]

Camille Paglia has challenged both myths:

.... "A fantasy dogging feminist writing is that there was once a peacable matriarchy overthrown by warmongering men, founders of patriarchal society.... Not a shred of evidence supports the existence of matriarchy anywhere in the world at any time. Matriarchy, political rule by women, must not be confused with matrilineage, passive transmission of property or authority through the female side. The matriarchy hypothesis, revived by American feminism, continues to flourish outside the university."[32]

Although these myths were never more than that for most of us, they are very real in the mind of ecofeminism. The idyllic matriarchal society, it is averred by these "spiritual feminist circles," must be reinstated and shall be through Goddess worship. Until that time, our present patriarchal society -- dominated by war-like males worshipping the Judaeo-Christian God -- will continue to be plagued by crime, drugs, immorality, greed, violence, and pollution of planet Gaia.[33] With Woman as Redemtrix, terrestrial and human salvation shall be completed with nothing less than ultimate deicide itself: The termination [with extreme prejudice] of God Himself.[34]

A method that ecofeminism employs to promote its ecotheology is through popularised witchcraft, the "old religion." As the Goddess is the earth herself, feminist witchcraft is a nature religion in itself.[35] Witchcraft in British-descended North America is usually practised by Druids and wiccans, increasingly regarded as matrifocal earth-worshippers. Druids and priestesses of the wiccan church are often featured on television talk shows, and are therefore somewhat familiar figures to mainstream North America. As environmentalists and feminists come generally from the affluent and educated upper-middle-classes, ecofeminism as such seems not to have yet affected more tradition-bound African and Latin American witchcraft (Santería, Palo Mayombe, et al.). But this is changing too, especially in syncretised North America native cultures.

An environmentalist goal, pointed out by Berit Kjos, is to "rewrite earth's story based on wisdom from primal societies."[36] The First Nations of North America are home-made primal societies, ripe and ready to be used in the rewriting of earth's story. Natives, few in number and largely living on rural reservations, are perceived more sympathetically and as less threatening than urban Africans or Latins by majority North Americans. The Indian has undergone two incarnations as Noble Redman; during the 1970s as political freedom-fighter, and again in the 1990s as proto-environmentalist. And then there is ..."the wisdom from primal societies" -- in this case a North American form of home-grown shamanism. Webster's Dictionary defines shamanism as:

> "The religion practiced by a shaman.... a priest or witchdoctor among some Ural-Altaic peoples. He uses magic to propitiate gods and spirits, foretell the future, heal etc.... a similar religion eg. among North American Indians."[37]

Shamanism is the epitome of nature religion. Rather than being anti-God like neo-Gnosticism, shamanism is without God, replacing His function with the "nature spirits" of William Irwin Thompson. The ecofeminists have taken the Grecian Gaia and coronated her Earth Goddess over the shamanic nature spirits. This has been quite a feat of spiritual and cultural synthesis where classical Western mythology and cosmology have been skilfully blended with Third World magic and spiritism. The resultant symbiosis is a near-perfectly suited ecotheology for the New Age, bringing together the disturbing element(s) of the rejection of the male Judaeo-Christian God by an androgynous God/Goddess, along with gender ecofeminism.

Shamanism brings to the fray a second disturbing element of race and ethnicity, to add to the first composite element of God versus Goddess, of male yang against female yin. Furthermore, shamanism is hardly some obscure, localised heresy like Gnosticism, which has been revivified by feminist intellectuals. Shamanism is as old as humankind and is of world-wide consistency. Truly stated by Michael Harner, author of The Way of the Shaman, is that tribes separated by thousands of miles of land and sea, as well as millennia and cultural variations -- practise the same form of shamanic earth-spirit worship.[38]

What makes environmentalists happy in general, is that including shamanism into the hotch-potch of ecotheology means spiritual alliance with the world's indigenous peoples [i.e., of colour, peaceable]. There are UN-style politics here, with a gratuitous slap at the Judaeo-Christian God [i.e., white, bellicose]. There has occurred a global revival of shamanism throughout the 1990s, from Lappland in northern Scandinavia to the Hopi Nation in the American Southwest. What pleases ecofeminists in particular is that shamanism is much like their favourite "old religion" of wiccan witchcraft, that they associate with female empowerment. Unknown perhaps to ecofeminists is a bizarre, androgynous factor in traditional shamanism. Camille Paglia explains:

"....This phenomenon called shamanism migrated northward to Central Asia and has been reported in North and South America and Polynesia. Frazer describes the shaman's stages of sexual transformation, which resemble those of our candidates for sex-reassignment surgery. The religious call may come as a dream in which the man is 'possessed by a female spirit.'[39] He adopts female speech, hair style, and clothing and finally takes a husband. The Siberian shaman, who wears a woman's caftan sewn with large, round discs as female breasts is ...an example of 'ritual androgyny'[40], symbolizing the ...reconciliation of opposites. Inspired, the shaman goes into a trance and falls unconscious. He may disappear either to fly over distant lands or to die and be resurrected...."[41]

Granted that lengthy reference to traditional shamanism may appear risible in this otherwise serious essay, but there is nothing amusing about the unholy coupling of old spiritism with new scientism. It signifies far more than cultural patronising of native peoples by the ecosophists for social or political gains. No indeed; the unholy coupling is the scientism of Carl Sagan married to the "nature spirits" [updated and bleached shamanism] of William Irwin Thompson. It is not so incongruous an alliance as it might at first appear. After all, shamanism in its diverse forms and diffuse places, has historically attempted in its pre-scientific role to understand, explain, and then control the unknown forces of nature.[42] The scientist later fulfilled this function, but the shaman would never be entirely supplanted. Throughout the centuries he/she would practise earth spiritism peripheral to -- and not necessarily in opposition to -- technological society.

What scientism and shamanism continued to share over time were knowledge and power ... without the Judaeo-Christian God. Today's New Age movement, built on a foundation of Eastern mysticism derived from Hindu-Buddhist matrices, seeks to awaken the godhood dormant in human beings. The goal of materialistic science is for man to be ultimately in complete control of nature and the universe. In Millennium, Harvard theologian Harvey Cox has written:

"The magical impulse is the desire to control and direct nature, to use it for human ends, to tame its sometimes malevolent side.... This impulse developed through the centuries not into religion but into empirical science. The true successors to the sorcerers and alchemists are not the priests and theologians but the physicists and the computer engineers."[43]

Thus the shaman-magician may be viewed in the same light as the [naturalistic rather than supernaturalistic] empirical scientist. Their common roots are the knowledge of and power over natural forces, alluded to earlier. Moreover, as science fiction writer Arthur C. Clarke has remarked, people in "less developed societies" see little difference between scientifically-advanced technology and magic.[44] An archetypal shaman/scientist for our time is U Cal Berkeley physicist Fri tjof Capra. This New Age technocrat will conduct an experiment in quantum physics, then go home and cast I Ching wooden sticks as fortune-telling lots. Former New Ager Tal Brooke has commented:

"It is truly a picture out of C.S. Lewis' prophetic novel That Hideous Strength, where a postmodern agnostic science synthesizes with the occult -- a strange grafting indeed. Former enemies of belief are now allies."[45]

During a 1986 interview Fri tjof Capra was recorded as saying, "I knew with absolute certainty that the parallels between modern physics and Eastern mysticism would someday be common knowledge ... as part of a much larger movement [involving] ... a profound cultural transformation."[46] Influential psychologist Carl Rogers has even predicted that the movement of New Age paradigm shift[47] would spawn a new science ... "resembling the views of the Eastern mystic, rather than Newtonian mechanics."[48]

I have previously mentioned the potential mix of scientific technology and New Age ecologism into a technoecology. Thirty months after writing the Afterword to Part I, this writer beholds a synthesised fusion of the scientific/sorcerer's blend that is the present environmentalism; both as a political force and New Age nature religion. To amend one of my own quotes: "The ensuing marriage of these mega-forces (i.e., technocracy and ecologism) has already changed (rather than "will forever change...") the fundamental character of the North Pacific fisheries and seafood industry."[49] Just how much will be analysed in Part III.

Is environmentalism a New Age religion? The answer must be Yes. Environmentalism is an amalgamated ecotheology made up of the ten components discussed, practisioned by an élitist technocracy with a neo-Marxist ideology. (The Big Green political agenda will be examined in Part II). As Phillip Johnson, professor of law, Boalt Hall, U Cal Berkeley, has said:

"Once theology was the queen of the sciences.... Lately it has been replaced by physics, but there are signs that the physicists want to become theologians.... Ambitions like this have important consequences."[50]

There is more to the conflict than the current struggle with weird science and irrational ecologism; it is the age-old war waged by "the Great Mother, the dark nature-goddess whom St. Augustine condemns as the most formidable enemy of Christianity."[51]   But the topic of New Age ecotheology is best left to the

theologians. Before concluding Part I, I must emphasise how far and wide environmentalism has reached, even

penetrating the psyches of world leaders. Prime Minister Brundtland of Norway and Vice-President Gore of

the United States are two such examples. Religion writer Franz Cumont, referring to the decline and fall of

Greece and Rome, has noted:

"In the declining days of antiquity the common creed of all pagans came to be a scientific pantheism, in which the infinite power of the divinity that pervaded the universe was revealed by all the elements of nature....

"Preached on the one hand by men of letters and by men of science in centers of culture, diffused on the other hand among the bulk of the people ... it is finally patronized by the emperors...."[52]

NOTES

1.   Ernest Callenbach, Ecotopia: The Notebook and Reports of William Weston (New York: Bantam Books, 1990), p.58.

2.   Lyn Margolis and James E. Lovelock, 'The Gaia Hypothesis', Co-Evolution Quarterly, Summer 1975, pp.30-40. Quoted in William Irwin Thompson, Darkness and Scattered Light (Garden City, N.Y. Anchor Press/Doubleday, 1978), p.189.

3.   Op.cit., Thompson, pp.136-137.

4.   Ibid., p.137.

5.   Fr. Robert A. Sirico, 'The Greening of American Faith', National Review, 29 August 1994, p.43.

6.   Ibid., p.43.

7.   The New Lexicon Webster's Dictionary of the English Language, (New York:Lexicon Publications, Inc., 1989), p.36.

8.   Science Digest, November 1981, Mary Long, 'Visions of a New Faith', p.39. Quoted in Dave Hunt and T.A. McMahon, The New Spirituality (Eugene, Ore.:Harvest House Publishers, 1988), p.77.

9.   Op.cit., Dave Hunt and T.A. McMahon, p.77.

10. William Irwin Thompson, Passages about Earth (Harper & Row, 1973), pp.160-183. In Hunt and McMahon, p.77.

11. Op.cit., Hunt and McMahon, p.80.

12. A favourite New Age scripture is The Urantia Book.

13. Abraham H. Lass et al., The Dictionary of Classical, Biblical, and Literary Allusions (New York:Ballantine Books, 1987), passim.

14. Ibid., ff.

15. Camille Paglia, Sexual Personae (New York:Vintage Books, 1991), p.43.

16. Berit Kjos, Under the Spell of Mother Earth (Wheaton, Ill.:Victor Books, 1992), pp.82-83.

17. James Lovelock, Orion Quest Quart 8, no. 1 (1989):58. Quoted in Michael S. Coffman, Saviors of the Earth? (Chicago:Northfield Publishing, 1994), p.145.

18. James Lovelock, The Ages of Gaia: A Biography of our Living Earth (New York:Bantam Books, 1990), p.204. Quoted in Michael S. Coffman, p.147.

19. Op.cit., Lovelock, The Ages of Gaia..., p.204. Quoted in Michael S. Coffman, p.147. The Judaeo-Christian God is also, of course, the God of modern Jewry. Would Lovelock dare to appear anti-Semitic?

NOTES (cont'd)

20.   Op.cit., Camille Paglia, p.40.

21.   Op.cit., Robert A. Sirico, p.43.

22.   Cited in Dave Bass, 'Drawing Down the Moon', Christianity Today, April 1991, p.17. Quoted in Peter Jones, The Gnostic Empire Strikes Back (Phillipsburg, N.J.:P&R Publishing, 1992), p.13.

23.   Op.cit., Peter Jones, p.13. Cf. Shirley Maclaine, Going Within: A Guide for Inner Transformation (New York:Bantam Books, 1989), p.189. For more on this subject, see Appendix 'B'.

24.   Mitchell Pacwa, S.J., 'Catholicism for the New Age', Christian Research Journal, Fall 1992, pp.14-19, 29-31.

25.   Op.cit., Peter Jones, p.29.

26.   Ibid., p.29. Cf. Elaine Pagels, The Gnostic Gospels (New York:Random House, 1980), passim. NB. Sophia and gnosis are Greek words for "wisdom" and "knowledge."

27.   Ibid., pp.32-33.

28.   Quoted by Peter Jones, p.46.

29.   Ibid., p.46.

30.   Op.cit., Berit Kjos, p.42. See chart 2: 'The Armor of God.'

31.   Op.cit., Berit Kjos, p.55. See chart 3: 'Truths that Counter Myths'.

32.   Op.cit., Camille Paglia, p.42.

33.   Peter Jones, p.49.

34.   Ibid., p.54. For more myths of loving matriarchies overturned by hateful patriarchies, see Monica Sjöö and Barbara Mor, The Great Cosmic Mother (San Francisco:Harper & Row, 1987); Rosalind Miles, The Women's History of the World (New York:HarperCollins, 1990); and Riane Eisler, The Chalice and the Blade (San Francisco:Harper Collins, 1988).

35.   Peter Jones, p.46.

36.   Op.cit., Berit Kjos, p.55. See chart 3: 'Truths that Counter Myths.'

37.   The New Lexicon Webster's Dictionary..., p.914. The word shaman is Russian of Tungusic origin.

38.   Michael Harner, The Way of the Shaman: A Guide to Power and Healing (Harper & Row, 1980), p. xi; from Dave Hunt and T.A. McMahon, p.81.

39.   Sir James George Frazer, The Golden Bough, 3rd ed. (New York, 1935), 6:255-257. Quoted in Camille Paglia, p.45.

NOTES (cont'd)

40. Mircea Eliade, <u>Shamanism: Archaic Techniques of Ecstasy</u>, trans. Willard R. Trask (New York, 1964), 149,352. Quoted in Camille Paglia, p.45.

41. Op.cit., Camille Paglia, p.45.

42. Dave Hunt and T.A. McMahon, p.81.

43. <u>Science Digest</u>, November 1981, op.cit., p.39. Quoted in Hunt and McMahon, p.82.

44. <u>Ibid.</u>, p.82.

45. Tal Brooke, <u>When the World Will Be as One</u> (Eugene, Ore.:Harvest House Publishers, Inc., 1989), p.168.

46. <u>The Harmonist</u>, Vol.1, No.2, 1986, 'Interview:Fri tjof Capra', p.22. Quoted in Hunt and McMahon, p.84.

47. From Thomas Kuhn, historian of science: "People make models -- paradigms -- of the universe to direct their interpretations of events." Paraphrased from Mitchell Pacwa, S.J., 'Catholicism for the New Age', <u>Christian Research Journal</u>, Fall 1992, pp.14-19, 29-31.

48. <u>Life Times: Forum for a New Age</u>, Number 3, p.48, originally published in South African magazine, <u>Odyssey</u>, n.d. Quoted in Hunt and McMahon, p.84. For more of "newtonian mechanics", cf. Appendix B.

49. See p.47, 'AFTERWORD:FISHERIOGRAPHY' in this volume.

50. <u>Wall Street Journal</u>, 10 May 1993. Quoted by Cal Thomas, <u>The Things that Matter Most</u> (New York:HarperCollins, 1994), p.103.

51. Op.cit., Camille Paglia, p.230.

52. Franz Cumont, <u>Astrology and Religion Among the Greeks and Romans</u> (Dover Publications, 1960), p.56. In Hunt and McMahon, p.88.

Bibliography for Part I

1. Hunt, Dave and T.A. McMahon. The New Spirituality. Harvest House Publishers, Eugene, Ore., 1988.

2. Jones, Peter. The Gnostic Empire Strikes Back. P&R Publishing, Phillipsburg, N.J. 1992.

3. Kjos, Berit. Under the Spell of Mother Earth. Victor Books, Wheaton, Ill. 1992.

4. Lass, Abraham H. et al. The Dictionary of Classical, Biblical and Literary Allusions. Ballantine Books, N.Y. 1987.

5. Paglia, Camille. Sexual Personae. Vintage Books, N.Y. 1991.

6. Thompson, William Irwin. Darkness and Scattered Light. Anchor Press/Doubleday, Garden City, N.Y. 1978.

7. _____. The American Replacement of Nature. Doubleday/Currency, New York, 1991.

Author's note: For a lexicon of New Age religions, see Appendix A.

Part II: Shrinking the Big Green Agenda

This writer lives in Port Angeles, Washington, a "main street" all-American city. Port Angeles is centrally located at the northern end of the Olympic Peninsula, and on U.S. Highway 101, 52 miles west of Hood Canal Floating Bridge. Port Angeles is also situated 18 miles across the Strait of Juan de Fuca from Victoria, British Columbia; arguably Canada's most beautiful provincial capital city. A ferry, the M.V. Coho, sails to and from Victoria every day except for a few weeks in mid-winter. Port Angeles is also served by William R. Fairchild International Airport. Although a small city of some 18,310 souls (1995), tucked into the extreme northwest corner of the contiguous United States, Port Angeles is the industrial hub of Washington State's Olympic Peninsula. With a mild, marine climate and great natural beauty, the Olympic Peninsula is a pleasant and convenient place to live. This writer came for the fish, but stayed for the eagles and herons, dabbling and diving ducks, sea-lions and orcas.

Port Angeles has most of the small-city amenities without big-city perils. It is a mere 25-minute commute via air to Seattle-Tacoma International Airport (SEA-TAC), whence one can fly to any place in the world. The local Safeway daily stocks issues of The Seattle Times, The Seattle Post-Intelligencer, The New York Times, and The Wall Street Journal. This being the Information [Communications] Age, the local Northland cable television company offers on its ultra-basic programming the ABC, NBC, PBS, CBS, CBN, CBC, CTV, CKVU, KVOS, KSTW, and KCPQ networks and affiliates. Along with Ted Turner's Cable News Network (CNN) are his TBS, TNT, and TCM superstation outlets. There are also country music channels (TNN and CMT), a rock music channel (MTV), and channels for education, arts and entertainment, politics, cartoons, "sci-fi" and feminism. The list seems endless. All this printed and televised communication/information is received -- from the outside -- into a single small city on the Olympic Peninsula of Washington State.

Thus living in Port Angeles can be a temporary safe-haven from ever-advancing urban disaffinity and decay, but there is no escaping the print and video Culture. ("Culture" here is capitalised and used in the modern sense of Pop[ular] Culture. Today's mainstream is yesterday's "Counter-Culture".) For an ex-urban former New Yorker as the writer is, a wide choice of reading materials and television stations would appear advantageous to such a fellow living in a far corner. But the 1990s North American [Pop] Culture, so transcended and updated by the 1960s belief system, makes the very availability of mass communications of questionable value. Whether within arts and entertainment, environmentalism, journalism, politics, religion or music, the New Age of Aquarius is both pervasive and immanent. There is literally no place to hide.

The visitor to Port Angeles, in search of local journals, maps and information, will invariably end up at Port Book and News on East First Street downtown. Even a cursory examination of the environmental section on the magazine racks manifests the contemporary sorcerer's blend of ecologism and religion. There is Green Egg, "A Journal of the Awakening Earth." Purportedly representative of 21st century Judaism, the journal's lead article is entitled 'The Golden Asherah'. The writer recalls that this goddess was a heathen Canaanite deity whose worship was strictly proscribed under Mosaic Law. Right next to Green Egg is The Green Man... "A magazine for Pagan Men." Farther down the row is Lilith, "The Independent Jewish Women's Magazine." The writer remembers that Lilith, in kabbalic lore, was Adam's other, evil wife. Near Lilith is Lotus -- a "Journal for Personal Transformation."

Being a bookworm and omnivorous reader, the writer often stops by and browses at Port Book and News; both knows and likes the owner. Adjacent to the steadily ringing cash register is a rack of gratis newspapers and periodicals. One day in February 1995 the writer picked up a free copy of The New Times on leaving Port Book and News. What had attracted the writer's attention was the lead article -- 'The Way of the White Rabbit: Shamanism with Michael Harner', by Zaralaya G. Heartwood.[53] The writer recognised Michael Harner's name from a definitive modern work on the subject, The Way of the Shaman (Harper&Row, 1980). Ms. Heartwood's dramatically-titled article, combining recollections of Lewis Carroll and Grace Slick, envisioned the White Rabbit of Alice in Wonderland as a spirit guide/power animal on a shamanic journey:

"When the White Rabbit rushed past Alice muttering, 'I'm late, I'm late,' and then disappeared into a hole in the earth, she was compelled to follow, tumbling through darkness, the unknown, into the lower world .... Alice pursues her curiousity through the void after the White Rabbit. Her journey takes her into the lower world which is populated by strange animals who mystify and help her."[54]

In Michael Harner's shamanic workshop, Ms. Heartwood was told that "there are many doors into other realities," and psychedelic drug use was recommended for would-be shamans who "can't access the other world any other way." According to Harner, "Shamanic systems have used drugs, starvation, sensory deprivation, and self-mutilation, but drumming or rattling is the safest and easiest way into the other world."[55]

Ms. Heartwood concluded her shamanic journey in Harner's workshop with the White Rabbit-Alice motif:

"Our instructions were: go through a cave, hole, or root system to the lower world. Ask that an animal be waiting for you outside the tunnel. This would be a helping or power animal. See, touch, smell, hear as fully as possible. Hang out with the animal until called back by the drum.

".... I went to the foot of a huge maple tree.... I bowed and asked permission to enter .... I was sucked down into the roots through a concave area at the base of the trunk.

"The tree's roots were brightly lit with the gold life force energy. While travelling along a root, I spotted a rabbit burrow and headed down it...."[56]

Godspeed, Ms. Heartwood! Meanwhile, for those readers of The New Times whose shamanic journey has not yet commenced or has already gone off track, there are always other workshops or lecture-series to aid the novice or faltering pilgrim. An advertisement on page 15 promises:

"Experience the power of ritual to heal and transform your life. Mask making, shamanic journeys, and ecstatic dance prepare us to enter the ritual space together. Step through this door of initiation -- the ego death. Experience the rebirth of your passion and commitment to live out the life of your Spirit's intention and bring your gifts to the world."[57]

All these miraculous "power[s], signs and lying wonders" (2 Thess.2:9) are possible if the New Age pilgrim attends the "Masks of Illusion and the Authentic Self" at Breitenbush Hot Springs, Oregon, during five days in July 1995. Facilitating the healing and transformation will be a certain Christina Pratt, "shamanic healer, ritual artist, author, dancer." For those not able to wait until July, the "Last mask center for shamanic healing and counseling" moves to Seattle, March 1995. There the initiate may learn .... "Soul retrieval, soul part integration, training in shamanic methods, death and dying skills, dream tools, shamanic counseling."[58]

It was, of course, the writer's intention to read about the shamanism of Michael Harner in The New Times. But the New Age religions and cultural beliefs permeate the print culture, and are readily discerned in mainstream publications. The New Age input is quite naturally as diffused throughout the visual culture. One only has to watch Saturday morning cartoons to notice how widespread this has become. Themes of witches, warlocks, wizards and thinly disguised Western occultism and Eastern mysticism are standard fare. Somewhere in The American Replacement of Nature, New Age author William Irwin Thompson wrote that "Disneyism" is a form of religion. Thompson confided that watching Walt Disney's animated film "Fantasia" had a profound effect upon him as a child. One can only speculate how responsible the early viewing of "Fantasia" was for Thompson's later philosophy. Today's Disney Channel (DISN), with its benefit rock concerts, "awareness" award shows, and Shirley Maclaine-inspired movies, along with the Discovery Channel (DSC), are this writer's main televised sources of New Age religions, philosophical and political thought and practices. The programmes Magical Worlds and The Mysterious Universe of Arthur C. Clarke, both on DSC, have been a treasure trove of subjects ranging from psychic phenomena to shamanic rituals.

One memorable TV special deifying the New Age was an electronic apotheosis of the Cathedral of St. John the Divine in New York City. Sometime during 1992, California's Michael Huffington funded and had filmed a video, "The Living Cathedral", which this writer saw in early January 1995, on the Arts and Entertainment Channel (A&E). "The Living Cathedral", viewers were told in the pompous, treacly tones of actor James Earl Jones, is the largest Gothic cathedral on the planet and is still under construction. As a former New Yorker, the writer has followed with interest the Episcopal cathedral's theological devolution over the years. The church on Morningside Heights has, with time, devolved into little more than a well-heeled New Age ekklesia. The ultra-élite Smithsonian magazine featured an article on St. John the Divine last year (1994), but this writer was hardly prepared for the televised version of "The Living Cathedral." A radically chic coven, acting as the church hierarchy, has fashioned an institution that is all things to religiously correct people. Known as "The Valley" to neighbourhood African-American and Latin-American teenagers, the cathedral grounds are a safe haven and place to "hang out." Also on cathedral grounds is a model "bio-shelter", exhibiting the church's Concern for the Environment. Next on the programme was the Blessing of the Animals. Men and Women, absurdly dressed in full priestly regalia, ludicrously wearing the episcopal mitre and bearing the shepherd's crook, "blessed" the carefully selected assortment of domestic and exotic beasts crowding the church naves up to the chancel. All this spiritual tomfoolery was presided over by Dean James Park Morton, the same politically correct individual who had co-chaired the initial gathering of the Global Forum in April 1988.[59] Thus an epicentre of world ecumenism offers somethings to all living things -- ethnic minorities, children, animals, the environment -- something for everything and everybody; but nothing for (the sky) God.

"The Living Cathedral" video reminded the writer of what had transpired at Chicago, Illinois, from

28 August through 6 September 1993. This was the convening of the Parliament of the World's Religions, exactly a century after a similar gathering had taken place at Chicago for the identical reason: The establishment of a single world church. At this convocation in 1993, one hundred thirty of the earth's religions came together in the Parliament of the World's Religions to become One. Christian writer Dwight L. Kinman has described some of those in attendance:

"The Dalai Lama was there who believes that he is a man god. Joan Campbell, the feminist and director of the Marxist-slanted National Council of Churches, was there. The Lucis Trust representatives of the New Age religion were there. Voodoo, high priests, and wicka (sic) groups and witchcraft were all there.... Serpent charmers and druids and Satan worshippers, liberal Baptists, Zoroastrians to Zen Buddhists were all represented. The World Council of churches (sic) and the powerful church of Rome were highly represented. They met to celebrate 'unity in diversity.'"[60]

And The Los Angeles Times reported:

"Priests in Roman collars talked with saffron-robed Buddhist monks, and Rastafarians engaged in animated discussions with turbaned Sikhs.... On one night, followers of the neo-pagan Wicca [witchcraft] religion performed a full-moon ritual."[61]

Environmentalism in ecclesiastical vestments was very evident at the 1993 Parliament of the World's Religions. Dr. Gerald Barney of the Millennium Institute summarised current ecotheology by stating, from his 'Global Problematique', that cosmic urgency as "current world megacrisis ... is of an evolutionary order -- the crisis is actually the birth of a new, living planetary system (i.e., a global being, or Gaia)."[62]

There were also religious, philosophical, and political aspects to the UN-sponsored Earth Summit in June 1992 at Rio de Janeiro, Brazil. The Rio Summit was a high point in the fusion of religion with environmentalism, and Brazilian evangelicals were greatly responsible for the site and Summit itself.[63] A large delegation from the United Church of Christ, along with demonstrators from other denominations, opened with the gospel hymn, "Were You There When They Crucified My Lord?" -- substituting "Lord" with "Earth." Fr. Robert Sirico, in a National Review article, August 1994, made mention of Vice-President Al Gore's religious syncretism:

"Vice President Al Gore devoted an entire chapter in his book, Earth in the Balance, to 'Environmentalism of the Spirit,' in which he poses a sobering question, and answers it himself. 'When giving us dominion over the Earth, did God choose an appropriate technology?... The jury is still out.' The jury is still out on Whom?"[65]

Another Christian writer, Peter Jones, has commented on the Vice-President's chapter,

'Environmentalism of the Spirit', from <u>Earth in the Balance</u>:

".... Gore .... quotes favorably Pierre Teilhard de Chardin, the excommunicated Jesuit theologian, who is often cited by New Age authors. Gore attempts to mix Southern Baptist theology with New Age spirituality. While affirming that God is the Creator, Gore manages, in typical pantheistic fashion, to confuse the Creator with the creation. Using the example of the hologram, so dear to New Age philosophy, Gore proposes to show how God is manifest in the world. 'Each tiny portion of the hologram contains a tiny representation of the entire three-dimensional image. However ... when one looks ... at the entire hologram, these thousands of tiny faint images come together in the eye of the beholder as a single large vivid image.' God is thus the sum of all created things."[66]

Vice-President Gore has declared himself a Southern Baptist, but showed his true spiritist feelings when he wrote that goddess worship "... could offer us new insights into the nature of human experience,"[67] and praised the virtues of neo-pagan and New Age beliefs. The Christian (and Southern Baptist) dogma, which asserts that man is made in God's image, would fundamentally contradict Gore's statement that ... "the myriad slight strands from the earth's web of life ... that reflects the image of God."[68]

But Vice-President Gore, then Democratic Senator from Tennessee, was riding high in 1992 and moving in the most environmentally correct circles. He was in Rio de Janeiro at the Earth Summit and was, along with Norwegian Prime Minister Gro Harlem Brundtland, one of the shriller voices at what <u>National Review</u> magazine has called a "Carnival of Dunces". Gore proclaimed that ..."the environmental crisis is a spiritual crisis."[69] The peripatetic Senator was photographed for the <u>New Age Journal</u> (July/August 1992, p.70) along with leaders of the Joint Appeal by Religion and Science ..."a movement headquartered at the Cathedral of St. John the Divine in New York City...."[70]

Ostensibly, the Rio Earth Summit was to be an environmental summit. The conference, after all, was officially designated UNCED: The United Nations Conference [on] Environmental Development. But its New Age religious roots and philosophical bent could not be denied. One hundred seventy-seven nations of the world were represented, with (then) Senator Gore heading the American delegation. Besides the Dalai Lama, the man who would be god, there was Maurice Strong, chairperson of UNCED 1992.

Maurice F. Strong is the Canadian multi-millionaire whom <u>The New York Times</u> has called the "Custodian of the Planet."[71] He has been involved for many years with UN-mentored environmentalism, and also with the New Age movement. Mr. Strong and his wife are members of the Baha'i faith, pray for a one world religion, and dwell on a 160,000 acre spread in southern Colorado's San Luis Valley. The Strong residence, Boca Grande Ranch, has become (1994) a global New Age centre of significance. The ashrams of India are represented here, as well as an occult-channeling facility sponsored by Shirley MacLaine.[72] Also at the Strong ranch is a Sun Temple, built by the Lindisfarne Association.[73] Maurice Strong and associates have been financing the Sun Temple with millions of their own dollars, but probably expect to receive the remaining funds from the U.S. federal government and the United Nations.[74]

Christian author Michael S. Coffman has posed the question: "Is it any wonder that the Great Invocation was used at the Earth Summit?"[75] We regular folks have to refer to esoteric Theosophy to find out why. As simply put as possible, Maurice Strong and friends believe that all humanity, by visualising together in the collective conscious, will usher in the New Age of Aquarius through mystic power. According to the Plan of Theosophy, man (Aquarius) is evolving into a higher self where he unites with the cosmos and the web of life.[76] This shall occur when the mystic power is released by humanity's collective conscious. The preceding event is known as Harmonic Convergence, Omega, Fusion, The Turning Point, Mind Convergence. There's more Theosophical doubletalk and gobbletygook, but the desired result is that the Great Invocation will bring on the union of the sun (Shamballa) with the earth (Gaia); thereby at last ending cosmic evolution in universal peace and harmony .... the dawning of the Age of Aquarius.[77]

At present (March 1995) one doesn't have far to go to find religious syncretism. As stated before, the New Age is both pervasive and immanent. Back in the writer's hometown of Port Angeles, Washington (as microcosm), set high on a hill is Holy Trinity Lutheran Church. HTLC forsook its humbler downtown building sometime during the 1950s to move into its present location, a (Mad magazine's) Dave Berg-type vulgar structure, featuring a lot of concrete and parking space. HTLC is much like any other lukewarm Evangelical Lutheran Church in North America. Both pastors are warm and kindly, good-hearted and well-meaning. But the writer sees the senior pastor as a bona fide member of the Religious Left, an aspiring New Age (noetic) man.[78] The junior pastor is perceived, perhaps somewhat uncharitably, as a touchy-feely Boobus americanus. The pastors and parishioners exchange pleasantries and smiles -- some beatific, some saccharine -

- while pretending to ignore the pressing swarms of hyper-active MTV kids.

Adjoining the HTLC narthex is the fireside room, wherein the writer attended a weekly Bible class. It was here the writer heard the dreadful utterance, "The Bible means whatever you want it to mean." Among the clutter of cute coffee mugs on a side table, one was inscribed "The Cathedral of St. John The Divine, New York City." Since the conservative U.S. congressional victory in November 1994, the Pastor had of late been criticising private property rights as the politics of selfishness ... but please return those missing books to the relevant, pastoral lending library![79] Surely, the writer once ventured to a couple of fellow Bible class-mates, if Amos or Jeremiah came back today, they would return as fiery Pentecostals or literal Southern Baptists; not as tepid Laodicaean Lutherans. (But then neither would Martin Luther.)

Apart from the afore-mentioned empathetic couple, the HTLC Bible class was composed of various-stage agnostics; several middle-aged women searching for Spirituality and Meaning; a radical, retired Lutheran pastor and his witchy, old-crone wife; and an interesting gentleman who had once entertained notions of becoming a Jesuit priest. Once at a pregnant pause during Bible study, this individual dropped the name of Teilhard de Chardin, the famous (or notorious) French Jesuit, who has been called "The Father of the New Age." This writer reacted with a twinge of misgiving, remembering that the theory of the "noösphere" [hence noetic] of Teilhard de Chardin (also subscribed to by Aurelio Peccei, Club of Rome) was identical to the "Collective Unconsciousness" of Carl Gustav Jung. The idea of a collective unconscious-memory bank has been termed the "psi bank" by Jose Argüelles, and the "Akashic records" by Rudolf Steiner, Charles Bensinger and Edgar Cayce. Akash means "space" in Sanskrit, and the hypothesis is a Hindu version of the collective unconsciousness. As it was, Pastor could have erected a statue to the Great God of Lake Wobegon on the altar, and still gone unchallenged by his ovine flock. Almost needless to relate, this writer felt very much a contrary goat amidst compliant sheep and dropped out after thirteen sessions.

As for Homo noeticus, the New (noetic) Man, the writer first heard of him while researching the New Age movement vis-à-vis ecologism. Christian author Texe Marrs has remarked, "The age of the individual or homo sapiens (sic) is at an end, say the New World Order advocates. The age of homo noeticus (sic) -- The 'New Man', a superbeing inextricably tied to and interconnected with his/her fellow animals and the earth --

is at hand."[80] But it was an article in <u>Psychology Today</u> which rendered a more complete description:

"Winston Franklin, who as vice president for the Institute for Noetic Sciences in Sausalito, California, tracks new developments in spirituality.... It uses science, he says, not as the supreme rational goal for living, but as a tool to understand the larger mystery of experience.... It views personality as shaped by dynamic forces of the unconscious; it emphasizes multiple realities; it aims toward an understanding of extraordinary states of consciousness and expanded human potential. It promotes the paranormal as a reality of human functioning and takes seriously accounts of spirit communication on the after-death plane, dream images, personal symbols of one's destiny, and religious visions.

"With an intense attraction to the natural environment, the new awakening hints that there is some fundamental relationship between a return to nature and the recovery of basic values. What is divine shines through to us most clearly through nature. Hence, it spawns the imperative to save the earth.... And, because of a belief in the interconnectedness of all things, the new awakening seeks everywhere to create healing spiritual communities."[81] <u>Ecce Homo noeticus</u>! Behold the noetic Man!

As noted, Part II traces ecologism from its religious roots through its philosophical mind-set and on to its political goals. Mystic thinking based on elements of Hinduism and Buddhism, reinforced by Theosophy,[82] was quintessential to early conservationalist beliefs. The Counterculture of the 1960s brought these beliefs into the North American mainstream. Out of the ashes of the 1960s the ex-hippies and middle-aging yippies have arisen to become 1990s doctors, lawyers, politicians, movie moguls and environmentalist leaders.[83] The 1970s Gaia Hypothesis of Lovelock and Margolis was made-to-order for 1960s budding New Agers and nascent environmentalists. Two persons, both with Buddhist-influenced values, were to ignite the eventual "fierce green fire" [Philip Shabecoff, <u>A Fierce Green Fire: The American Environmental Movement</u> (New York:Hill and Wang, 1993)] of current ecologism. The first, David Brower, president of the Sierra Club from 1956-1971, brought radical ecologism to conservational activism.[84] The second, Rachel Carson, author of the informative <u>The Sea around Us</u> to the contentious <u>Silent Spring</u>, had been nurtured in the Buddhist "reverence of life" philosophy of Albert Schweitzer. Michael S. Coffman has commented that "....It was this book ... <u>Silent Spring</u> that ushered in environmental activism and hyperbole, with pseudoscience as its cornerstone. But these phenomena [Brower and Carson] were mere precursors to the main event."[85]

A main event, proving that countercultural ecologism had indeed come of (new) age, was staged during the 1990s in the U.S. Arizona desert. Biosphere 2, the over-hyped and grandiose eco-project, was accused of cheating, cutting corners, and corruption throughout its two-year history (1991-1993), and finished by posing ethical questions rather than by solving scientific problems. Funded by Texas billionaire Ed Bass,

Biosphere 2 was an enormous greenhouse with eight red jump-suited men and women inside, living within a closed, self-sustaining ecosystem for two years, cut off from the outside. The futuristic globus of Biosphere 2 was designed as a world in miniature, complete with varying terrestial geoforms and micro-climates -- even an aerated mini-ocean. Naturally, the inhabitants inside were to grow their own bio-food stuffs and breathe the oxygen liberated from their own plant photosynthesis. But, after only a few weeks, rumours were circulating that: Instead of subsisting on their own, home-grown foodstuffs, the "Biospherans" had stored up months' worth in advance; and fresh air was being pumped into the globus from outside. The supposedly balanced, closed ecosystem of Biosphere 2 wasn't self-sustaining at all.[86]

(Former Nixon aide and present Christian minister) Charles Colson has maintained that setbacks and scandals never deterred the Biospherans from their purpose, which was a two-fold agenda motivated as much by religion as by science:

"Biosphere 2 is the outgrowth of a philosophy concocted years ago in a countercultural commune of the 1970s. The leader of that commune used to preach that Western Civilization is dead, that the world is coming to an end, and that an elite group of people would flee to Mars, where they would evolve into a superior race. The commune eventually disbanded, but many of the members stayed together. They have now made a reappearance as the core group in Biosphere 2."[87]

According to Charles Colson, the Biospherans had gone so far as to bring back to life their old communal eschatology, and spread their gospel in literature available to wide-eyed tourists sight-seeing the green glass globus. In their literature, the Biospherans depicted themselves as a key link in a vast cosmological chain of being, poised in time and space to make a great leap upward, there to evolve into part of a super-race transformed ..."from localized planetary lifespans to cosmic immortality .... citizens of the world of science".[88]

In early April 1994, John Polk Allen sent a letter of resignation to Texas billionaire Ed Bass, the financial backer of Biosphere 2. John Polk Allen, a creator and mastermind of the U.S. $150 million Biosphere 2, was responding to a court order of 31 March (1994) suspending him from the private eco-project. Also suspended under the federal court order obtained by Ed Bass were five top managers. Allen's resignation culminated a series of mishaps besetting Biosphere 2. Earlier during the previous week, two Biospherans had been arrested for opening doors of the globus and letting in outside air. Both jump-suited denizens had been sacked the following day. Later during that week, another inhabitant had left the Biosphere due to an emergency involving his wife, who had also been involved with the eco-project. Prior to his resignation, Allen "... faxed a rambling four-page letter to drug-culture guru Timothy Leary, asking him to distribute it on a computer network.... In ... the fax ... Allen complained of poor pay, bemoaned the management shakeup, expressed safety concerns for the crew and called on Bass 'to negotiate' and 'to call off the seizure of assets, the playing with human lives.'"[89]

On 17 September 1994, seven Biospherans moved out of their green glass globus after a half-year habitation, effectively severing the eco-project's remaining ties to the ousted management team. The successful conclusion of the crew's stay (much to the relief of Ed Bass) finally dispersed much of the "... Biosphere's [overriding] image as a blend of fuzzy science and New Age philosophy and legitimize the glass dome as a research tool accepted by mainstream scientists."[90] The current Biospherans entered the globus on 6 March 1994, and as noted, Bass replaced the original managers of the eco-project with his own administrators the following month. The new regime subsequently set up a research consortium with scientists from Columbia University's Lamont-Doherty Earth Observatory. The Associated Press has reported that ".... A team of top scientific consultants has begun writing a series of papers to be the basis of a new scientific research plan...."[91] Perhaps an expectant world won't have long to wait for a possible Biosphere 3. What is certain is that the Biospherans -- in whatever guise or eco-project -- will be back.

Charles Colson averred in an above-quoted passage that ".... Biosphere 2 [was] the outgrowth of a philosophy concocted years ago in a countercultural commune of the 1970s." That philosophy, and the spiritual sources from which it was born, has been referred to often in these pages. But the Mind of Green was never better analysed than in The Greening of America by Charles A. Reich. First published in 1970 by Random House, The Greening of America turned out to be a seminal and pivotal work. Despite the title, The Greening of America was not concerned with saving the environment (despite the first Earth Day in April 1970); no indeed, Charles Reich laid down a highly organised and complete dialectic that would influence an entire generation of young Americans. Although dated in a darkly humourous, hindsight way in 1995, the slim Penguin paperback was a revered Little Mao Primer of the Pepsi Generation, a book feared and loathed by the 1970s Establishment.

The 1960s Counterculture was never more sympathetically noised abroad than by The Greening of America. It qualifies as a philosophical thesis, comparing and contrasting what Reich has labeled Consciousness I, II, III. Consciousness III, Reich's 1970s "artists, beatniks, Holden Caulfields", are the 1990s Aquarians, the New Age noetic men. [Amusing in light of contemporary gender correctness, Reich's Consciousness III characters were invariably male.] Consciousness II were categorised as "old-line leftists"; what this writer would dub Roosevelt Liberals -- a fast-dying breed in the 1990s. Finally, came the traditional conservatives, Reich's "just plain folks." If this designation appeared surprisingly mild, Reich further qualified Consciousness I by referring to them as:

"Farmers, owners of small businesses, immigrants who retain their sense of nationality, AMA-type doctors, many members of Congress, gangsters, Republicans.... In the second half of the twentieth century the beliefs of Consciousness I are drastically at variance with reality. But they are held in a stubborn, belligerent, opinionated way against all contrary evidence....."[92]

Reich's unkind assessment, however mild, was wholly predictable. What would surprise the 1970s reader was Reich's commensurate censure of Consciousness II, the "old-line leftists." Reich praised Consciousness II for combatting the "disastrous" consequences of a Consciousness I - ruled America which included "....[R]obber barons, business piracy, ruinous competition, unreliable products and false advertising, grotesque inequality and the chaos of excessive individualism and lack of coordination and planning, leading to a gangster world."[93] Reich, however, berated Consciousness II for not going far enough, and indirectly chastised them for selling out the Revolution:

".... Just as Consciousness I centres on the fiction of the American Adam, the competitive struggle and the triumph of the virtuous and strong individual, so Consciousness II rests on the fiction of logic and machinery; what it considers unreal is nature and subjective man. Consciousness II believes more in the automobile than in walking, more in the decision of an institution than in the feelings of an individual, more in a distant but rational goal than in the immediate present."[94]

The Consciousness II people identified by Reich were "... businessmen (new type), liberal intellectuals, the educated professionals and technicians, middle-class suburbanites, labour-union leaders, Gene McCarthy supporters, blue-collar workers with newly-purchased homes, old-line leftists and members of the Communist Party, U.S.A. ... the Kennedys and the editorial page of The New York Times. It is the consciousness of 'liberalism'....."[95] Much has changed since 1970, but surely nothing as much as the very definition of liberalism. Reich's Consciousness III political radicals were of a decidedly different stripe than" ... the Old Left, the communist, socialist or civil libertarian ready to dedicate himself and his life to the cause, puritanical, sour, righteous. To the New Consciousness, to make himself an object to serve the cause would be to subvert the cause."[96] In the mind of Consciousness II, political commitment translated itself into social reform -- more equality, better education -- a general direction in which society was heading anyway, with liberals visibly in the vanguard. The liberal commitment to reform had limits, too, with its proponents enjoying high living standards along with personal security, comfort, status, and at ease in elegant homes after a hard day on the political hustings. Consciousness III political radicals, on the other hand, felt that they must respond with themselves; by teaching in an inner-city school, for instance, which offered neither security nor status. But this job-experience would offer the inner fulfilment of personal interaction with ghetto youth. And Consciousness III would have to live on an extremely modest scale to retain the freedom and self-identity their commitment demanded.

Reich wrote with a somewhat perverse pride that Consciousness III were "... deeply suspicious of logic, rationality, analysis and of principles...." Consciousness III believed it "... essential to get free of what is now accepted as rational thought...."[97] Consciousness III started mostly with young people ["Holden Caulfields'] who were maladjusted and disenchanted with their lot in life. "But the new consciousness spread rapidly only when youth who had no special personal problems found models to emulate .... For the new converts ... could make that choice only by seeing it demonstrated by others ['artists, beatniks']."[98] Reich's brief, passing observation that ".... Consciousness III could have only come into existence given today's [1970] technology...."[99] is, in this writer's opinion, a crucial observation -- however offhand -- for understanding The Greening of America. Reich concluded his study of Consciousness III's mind-set and methodology with an impassioned call to a strangely prissy, anarchic hedonism:

> "The new consciousness [III] is always flexible, curious and ready to add something new to his character. At the same time, the new generation constantly tries to break away from the older, established forms which, in a changing society, must forever be obsolete. Authority, schedules, time, accepted customs, all are forms which must be questioned. Accepted patterns of thought must be broken; what is considered 'rational' thought must be opposed by 'non-rational' thought -- drug thought, mysticism, impulses. Of course, the latter kinds of thought are not really 'non-rational' at all; they merely introduce new elements into the sterile, rigid, outworn 'rationality' that prevails today [1970]."[100]

By now the reader will have recognised the 1970s Consciousness III as the 1990s Mind of Green. This writer has never approved of using block quotes in historiography, but The Greening of America is so archetypal a work, so clearly delineated, that Reich has been extensively quoted to be known by his own words. (Entire passages are reported verbatim in Appendix C.) This writer vividly remembers rooming with a Consciousness III individual (i.e., a proto-hippy) at Boston University during 1964-1965. Besides having vile and filthy personal habits, Consciousness III was inconsiderate, irresponsible, untrustworthy. Despite being brought up in an upper-middle class WASP family from the U.S. Northeast, Consciousness III was a true Holden Caulfield, a self-proclaimed existentialist and free spirit, eschewing all traditional and bourgeois values. Consciousness III would invite similar friends over to our dormitory room, where they would listen to Bob Dylan and Joan Baez recordings, and wonder from whom they could beg, borrow, or steal dope and drugs. The end of our room-mateship came when Consciousness III, after a particularly bad LSD "trip", endeavoured to achieve ultimate ananda ("bliss") by rectally adsorbing pomegranate pips while squatting in our common shower-bath. Three decades later, such Consciousness III persons have shed outer dirt and grime and grown up to become The Establishment ... with Consciousness III world-view intact.

During the early 1970s the academic cause of choice was the Vietnam War, with environmentalism still taking a back seat. Reich, ever on the alert for peaking social trends, tapped into that theme via Norman Mailer's Why Are We in Vietnam? (Weidenfeld&Nicolson, 1969) for an exemplar within a paradigm. In The Naked and the Dead, Mailer's much-acclaimed novel of the Pacific War (1941-1945), the unasked [and unanswered] question hanging like a pall over the men-at-war stories was: "What caused this senseless, meaningless, horrible war?" Reich felt that Mailer's answer in 1948 had been "... that the source of the war is in the barren, frustrated lives that are led in America: lives that lead men to aggression, force and power; lives that are so repressed that they can yield only anger and bitterness and evil; lives that deny the very possibility of a human community."[101] Twenty-one years later, Reich told us, Mailer's paraphrased answer remained unchanged:

"[W]e are in Vietnam because of the way of life of the American inhabitant of technology-land, a way of life so regimented, repressed and artificial that it has transmuted the brave and the good qualities of Americans into forces of destruction. The difference between the two books is this: The Naked and the Dead ends without hope while Why Are We in Vietnam? has a new character, D.J., the youthful son of [a] businessman-hunter; D.J. may find a way to live differently and thus offer a chance for redemption and renewal.[102]

".... Norman Mailer's hero, D.J., rids himself of the machine consciousness and, in the vastness of Alaska's remote Brooks Range, rediscovers a childlike, breathless sense of wonder; this is the quality that Consciousness III supremely treasures, to which it gives its ultimate sign of reverence, vulnerability and innocence, 'Oh wow!'"[103]

Consciousness III, Reich's exemplar within Mailer's paradigm, represents America's hope for the future. The Pacific War, waged by Consciousness I, [the Korean War pursued by Consciousness II] and the Vietnam War fought by Consciousness III, were both "the fault" of America. Reich's "Consciousness III, the hope for the future" ... could have only come into existence given today's [1970] technology.... "Yet America is "technology-land", the land that has transmuted ... "the good qualities of Americans into forces of destruction...." Somehow, the youthful Consciousness III D.J. has divested himself... "of the machine consciousness [and] ... rediscover[ed] a childlike, breathless sense of wonder... 'Oh wow!'" If inconsistencies are the hobgoblins of small minds, surely Reich's New Consciousness gets curiouser and curiouser.

Besides Norman Mailer, Reich acknowledged the written sources of Karl Marx, Herbert Marcuse, John Kenneth Galbraith, Ken Kesey et al., and "to long talks with" ... good and generous friends "Hugo L. Black, William O. Douglas and co. Reich concluded The Greening of America with the fuzzy-feely admission that "... [m]uch of the book was written in the Stiles-Morse dining halls at Yale, and the encouragement, the coffee, the warmth of all the people of the dining hall are part of it."[104] Oh, wow!

If the reader will permit the writer a brief digression: Let us return, twenty-five years later, to the Yale University campus, specifically Jonathan Edwards College, during the current tenure of Consciousness III:

"The properly acculturated historian of ideas will explain the 'evolution' of Yale by pointing out -- quite believably -- that the institution simply had to change when people stopped believing the old ideas, and started believing new ones. [But] an institution requires purpose, discipline, and a source of authority. These things are not recognized by the new institution, which is a result not any sort of institution at all and cannot begin to educate its 'students' out of their ignorance of institutions."[105]

Still at Yale, but over at Davenport College, a Julian Ku, a senior and departing editor-in-chief of the conservative Yale Free Press, was invited to participate in a panel discussion on eroticism during Bisexual, Gay, and Lesbian Awareness Days (BGLAD) in the spring of 1993. Before Ku could speak, he was denounced by a member of the Lesbian, Gay and Bisexual Co-op, who read a list of Ku's "crimes" inflicted on the gay community and demanded Ku's removal from the panel. As Ku has written:

"Had I been anywhere but Yale, the situation would have seemed ridiculous. The two men sitting next to me were representatives of the North American Man-Boy Love Association (NAMBLA), which supports the legalization of sexual intercourse between men and boys (some related encounters with 8-year-olds). Both admitted to engaging in pedophilic acts. And and the Co-op wanted to throw me out?

...."But the battle continues. Yale has institutionalized its major sources of campus leftism: the Women's Center, the cultural centers, and the Co-op. Even now, a new campus publication seeks to 'reclaim the margin' and revitalize leftism at Yale. Future generations of Yalies will likely embrace leftism as this one. The YFP [Yale Free Press] will always be just a gadfly in comparison to the continual sources of left-liberalism for Ivy League elites."[106]

Is this nightmare on campus, and on Capitol Hill, what Reich prophesied and wished for America in 1970 for 1995? The political correctness of the early 1990s has diffused into religious, philosophical, environmental and even healthful correctness of the mid-1990s. The political radical of the 1970s and 1980s was nurtured on books like The Greening of America and Why Are We in Vietnam?; the environmental equivalent of works such as Silent Spring. The inciteful ideas contained therein were a powerful and explosive blend.

Compared to the humourless Charles A. Reich, William Irwin Thompson was -- and is -- a happy countercultural warrior who observed rather than agonised. Unlike Reich, who perhaps thought the nomer undignified, Thompson has always called a "hippy" a hippy (or hippie). Thompson in 1971 described Conscientious III and their weltanschauung in typically glorious rhetoric:

".... The syncretic imagination of the hippies was ... planetary in its inclusiveness for Japanese Zen, Indian Yoga, Atlantean legends, Navaho myths, Plains Indian visions ... UFO's, and modern chemistry were all rolled into one joint. If the young of Jean-Luc Godards's Paris were the children of Marx and Coca-Cola, these were the children of McLuhan and DuPont living in a retribalized Global Village and achieving 'better things for better living through chemistry'. To encounter such an apocalyptic vision might be expected among the messianic cargo cults of Melanesia, but to find it in the dropout children of the California affluent upper middle-class, the most highly educated generation in history, was a blow to the liberal middle-class vision of progress."[107]

Thompson's use of the term "liberal" was employed as Reich's, to denote Consciousness II. The "L-word" has devolved considerably in meaning since the early 1970s. Thompson perceived the irony of Consciousness II liberals, having built the enormous U.Cal. education system for their Consciousness III progeny, of seeing their effective creation literally going up in (marijuana) smoke. In another essay, Thompson decried the present (1971) "union of science and nationalism controlled by secret police.... and the patriotic use of nuclear weapons [would] bring us to another Dark Age...."; [108] he foresaw, however, a "new medievalism, like the old, will be both angelic and demonic at once." [109] Thompson's projected new mediaevalism would come to pass from ending the "Protestant Ethic and the Spirit of Capitalism"; citing Roman Catholic thinkers Teilhard de Chardin (the end of middle-class democracies and industrial nation-states), Ivan Illich (the end of universal public education), and Marshall McLuhan (the end of the print age). [110] Whether or not these grim prophesies were wishful thinking by Teilhard, Illich and McLuhan as apologists for collectivisation, Thompson's new mediaevalism meant an elimination of the middle "... to achieve a new energized top and bottom: scientists and hippies, Pythagoreans and superstitious techno-peasants." [111] By the late 1970s, however, the ebullient Thompson was already celebrating the marriage of hip science/technology to hip religion/mysticism. He predicted that in computer science traditional Ahrimanic technologists would eventually compete with New Age Luciferian technologists. [112] This writer has gone to great lengths to prove this very point throughout this work. We leave Thompson in 1971 singing the praises of Consciousness III:

".... Eventually the progressive liberals will return to reinstitute the New Government of Youth. In their mod clothes and sensitivity-trained style, the new managers will understand the needs of a complex, post industrial culture: the last vestige of puritanical America will be swept away and in the new Empire they shall have psychedelic TV and legal pot." [113]

But Thompson's freak takeover of Western Civilisation is still encountering pockets of cultural resistance a near-quarter century later. In early April 1995, this writer read a book review of a just-published work by Gertrude Himmelfarb, The De-moralization of Society: From Victorian Virtues to Modern Values (New York: Alfred A. Knopf, 1995). In it are extolled the "traditional values" of "...work, thrift, self-reliance, self-respect, neighborliness, and patriotism .... sobriety, prudence, and frugality." [114] In 1995, the cultural citadel has yet to be captured. There are still signs, on the eve of 2000 A.D., that the forces of Irving Kristol's "Conservative Century" are still holding the American fort against William Irwin Thompson's New Millennial Managers.

Besides Holden Caulfield, the unsavoury anti-hero created by J.D. Salinger, this writer-as-schoolboy often heard the name of (and read the work of) Henry David Thoreau during the early 1960s. Both The Catcher in the Rye (1951) and Walden (1854) were de rigueur reading at the élite New England prep school attended by this writer. Adolescent memories were recently revived by reading <u>All the Trouble in the World</u> by social commentator P.J. O'Rourke, whose passages on Thoreau (and Ralph Waldo Emerson) are so amusing yet highly perceptive:

"Thoreau took the bad ideas and worse ideals of the primitivists, added the pitiful self-obsession of the romantics, and mixed all this into transcendentalism, that stew of bossy Brahmin spiritual hubris. The transcendentalists were much devoted to taking the most ordinary thoughts and ideas and investing them with preposterous spiritual gravity. They saw the divine in everything, even in long, boring lectures about how everything is divine. Any random peek into the essays of Ralph Waldo Emerson will show you how the method by which "Don't Litter" has been turned into an entire secular religion."[115]

Henry David Thoreau, like Jean-Jacques Rousseau before him, was a fervent believer in the myth of the Noble Savage. Perhaps the myth was perpetuated in Thoreau's mind as a result of living alone at Walden Pond, near Concord, Massachusetts, on land owned by fellow transcendentalist Ralph Waldo Emerson. There were no savages here, noble or ignoble, on land "...about as far out of town as the average modern driving range."[116] Thoreau emerged from his benign bower fully convinced that man is the implacable enemy of nature. Contemporary environmentalism's worship of nature has a corollary: The extreme denigration of man and all his works. Surely civilisation (as opposed to mere culture) is to protect man <u>and</u> nature, from each other, by ensuring "...an aesthetic and fructiferous harmony"[117] .... between them. Modern environmentalists have brushed the dust off the back-to-nature themes of Rousseau and Thoreau to challenge the very technological basis on which structural Western Civilisation is built. Behind the claims made from their occupied moral high grounds, modern environmentalists have been stifling scientific progress at every opportunity. As proof of their nay-saying, the ecological Cassandras cry "Acid rain!...Nuclear winter!...Ozone hole!...Greenhouse effect! to further strengthen their agenda, and to spread increasing anxiety amongst an already worried populace.[118]

An extreme example of the current environmentalist agenda was stated in the summer, 1991, issue of <u>Wild Earth</u> quarterly:

"If you haven't given voluntary human extinction much thought before, the idea of a world with no people in it may seem strange to you. But, if you give it a chance, I think you might agree that the extinction of Homo Sapiens would mean survival for millions, if not billions, of Earth-dwelling species.... Phasing out the human race will solve every problem on earth, social and environmental."[119]

Whose agenda? the reader might ask, cognisant of the multiplicity of Green organisations which have proliferated since Earth Day, 1970. The answer most often given is Deep Ecology. The next question might

be, Is there a "Shallow" Ecology? The reply would be Yes, there is a Shallow Ecology but it prefers to be

known as Social Green, or Humanist Green Activism. Christian author Berit Kjos has offered an enlightening

comparison chart, "Three views of the Earth", in her excellent book, Under the Spell of Mother Earth:

"Deep Ecology (Biocentric)	Humanist Green Activism (Anthropocentric)
Earth-centered	Human centered
Mother Earth evolved, and	Earth and man evolved
nurtures and organizes her parts	by chance
Human animals are conscious	Human animals are
expressions of Mother Earth	responsible for Earth
Wisdom from Nature	Wisdom for self
Connect with Gaia through ritual,	Connect with nature through
celebration, drugs, meditation, sex	human mind, emotions, experience
Help Earth save herself by	Save Earth by trusting
hearing her spirit and heeding	human nature.[120]
her wisdom (spiritism)	

All the environmentalist movements originated in sensible, back-to-basics conservation groups which

we could all support. These included the Audubon Society, the Nature Conservancy and the National Wildlife

Federation, although the latter recently reinvented itself by joining the New Ager John Denver's Windstar.[121]

The Shallow (Social) Greens are comprised of activist protest groups such as Greenpeace and Earth First!,

with roots deeply embedded in the 1960s counterculture. Their leftist political agenda goes beyond

environmentalism, extending to civil rights for minorities and homosexuals, global disarmament and economic

redistribution.[122] The Deep (Spiritual) Greens, on the other hand, have added an ecotheological dimension

to the Gaia Hypothesis. Not only is the Earth a living, breathing, self-sustaining organism, Gaia has actual

wisdom and the power to save herself. The heart of disagreement between Social and Spiritual Greens is over

the nature of environmentalism per se: Spiritual Greens blame Social Greens for wanting to save the earth

for humanity's sake -- a "shallow" motivation -- rather than for Gaia herself. Spokespersons for Spiritual

(Deep) Ecology number among them renegade Dominican priest Matthew Fox, and weird quantum physicist

Fritjof Capra, author of The Tao of Physics.[123] The term, "Deep Ecology", was coined by Norwegian

ecophilosopher Arne Naess in 1973. In a 1982 interview at the Los Angeles Zen Center, Arne Naess explained that Deep Ecology infers a "cultural shift from science to wisdom", and suggested that "necessary changes" were needed in society, education and religion which would be "beneficial for all life on the planet as a whole."[124]

Arne Naess was surely disingenuous in calling for a "cultural shift" during the 1982 interview at Los Angeles. In truth, he was calling for a paradigm shift; nothing less than a complete upheaval and restructuring of Western society, education and religion. Although he spoke at LA Zen Center, the personage who defined Deep Ecology had none of the touchy-feely, human-centred New Age pretensions and posturings of the Shallow Ecologists (Social Greens). For Arne Naess and like-minded Deep Ecologists (Spiritual Greens), biocentrism was their credo. In their eyes, Shallow Ecology was anthropocentric -- hence abusive -- "in a priestly garb'."[125] Shallow Ecologists were perceived as looking to their Aquarian future, whereas Deep Ecologists were seen as contemplating their [Earth's] perfect past.[126] Ecosophical lines between Deeps and Shallows have blurred considerably since 1982, but to us outsiders, a single combined agenda emanates from the Big Green monolith. In the 1990s, various political sanctions and government empowerments have given impetus to radical environmentalism, and spurred the movement on to further excesses of weird science and voodoo ecology. The power, wealth, arrogance, and abuses of the various environmental organisations and governmental agencies have been fully reported and well documented by the alert writers cited here, and many others. It is not within the scope of this work to ennumerate more of the same. Having examined some of the tenets of ecophilosophy[127], we must move on to how these principles are being applied to the environmentalist political agenda. For this, all roads lead to Rome ... and Rio.

The first real "Aquarian Conspiracy" (Marilyn Ferguson) on an official level was the advent of the Club of Rome in 1968. Italian industrialist Aurelio Peccei presided over the founding of this European "think tank", and he brought together the leaders of ten nations to formulate plans for the coming New World Order. From the outset, the Club of Rome has extolled the belief that earth's eventual salvation depends on all nations ultimately abandoning their sovereignty for a one-world government. Some of the Club of Rome's studies and reports include 'The Limits to Growth' and 'Mankind at the Turning Point.'[128] In 'The Limits of Growth', the Club of Rome's first report (1972), Christian author Hal Lindsey beheld "... a brave new world....

blueprint for today's bold new economic, military and political union in Europe. It stressed the negative consequences of unregulated economic growth and development and emphasized strict central governmental controls and regulations."[129]

Of interest to Christian readers is that founder Aurelio Peccei, in a 1973 study, divided the world into ten political and economical regions which were referred to as "kingdoms": Eg., Region 1, U.S.A., Canada, Mexico; Region 2, Western Europe (i.e. the EC/EU); Region 3, Japan ....[130] The Club of Rome, the reader will recall, started under ten national leaders.[131] Coincidentally, the American-inspired Trilateral Commission was formed during 1973, with its proposed political/economic axis of the United States, Western Europe and Japan. In recent years the Club of Rome has been in the forefront of calling for a single global government for the New World Order; at present meaning rule by the United Nations. The powers that be are fully aware that the voluntary transferral of sovereignty, of the earth's independent nations, shall be made much easier by eco-panic and environmental fear-mongering intentionally disseminated by international media and New Knowledge sectors. Current hysteria about the pollution crisis and population bomb is perfectly tailored for the awaited choral plea for a global power-shift: Only a one-world government will be able to solve the problems of industrial pollution and over-population, is the whine. Consider the cynical statement of intent to exaggerate environmental fears by the Club of Rome in 1991:

"The common enemy of humanity is man. In searching for a new enemy to unite us, we come up with the idea that pollution, the threat of global warning, water shortages, famine and the like would fill the bill. In their totality and in their interactions, these phenomenons [sic] do constitute a common threat which demands the solidarity of all peoples.... All these dangers are caused by human intervention.... The real enemy, then, is humanity itself.... The Club of Rome has, from its beginning, realized the need for such an approach."[132]

Echoing the call for unitary world government, seminal futurist Alvin Toffler has observed that "... the nation-state can no longer cope with the basic problems posed by the shift towards super-industrialism," and that "... what is happening, no more, no less, is the breakdown of industrial civilization on the planet and the first fragmentary appearance of a wholly new and dramatic different social order: a super-industrial civilization that will be technological, but no longer industrial."[133] Toffler recorded these thoughts in The Eco-Spasm Report (1975); five years later (1980) Toffler would write:

"The Third Wave [i.e., tidalwave of change in history] gives rise to groups with larger than national interests. These form the base of the emerging globalist ideology sometimes called 'planetary consciousness'. This consciousness is shared by multinational executives, long-haired environmental campaigners, financiers, revolutionaries, intellectuals, poets, and painters, not to mention members of the Trilateral Commission....

"....[P]recisely as nationalism claimed to speak for the whole nation, globalism claims to speak for the whole world .... [w]e are witnessing a devastating attack, from within and without, on that pillar of Second Wave civilization: the nation-state.[134]

There is, of course, at present only one international body which could meet the specifications of a projected single-world government... and that is the United Nations.[135] The UN has changed a lot since the halcyon high-minded years of Scandinavian secretaries-general Trygve Lie (1946-1953) and Dag Hammarskjöld (1953-1961). UN policy has fluctuated from resisting North Korean military aggression against South Korea in the 1950s, to standing by during the Communist invasion and conquest of South Vietnam in the 1960s and 1970s. The UN has officially equated Zionism with rascism, but in 1990-1991 approved the US-led expeditionary coalition to expel Saddam Hussein from Kuwait. The successful pursuit of the Persian Gulf War (thanks mainly to the Americans), and the non-recognition of Indonesia's annexation of formerly Portuguese East Timor (1975-1976), are in this writer's opinion the UN's sole acts of merit since the 1960s. Until just recently (June 1995) CNN's television programme, Diplomatic License, was one way to keep an [albeit uncritical] eye on the UN, although its sins of omission and commission are well known worldwide, to skeptics in general and political conservatives in particular. A waffling repository of the current wisdom (cw) and part-time enforcer of global political correctness (pc), the UN organisation would hardly appear to qualify as the people's choice for nerve-centre of future world government. But so it is for some. As an example, in his July 20, 2019: Life in the 21st Century, "weird science"-fiction writer, Arthur C. Clarke, wrote that the long-awaited Global Village is [1986] almost upon us. But before we come to realise that it is finally here, the Global Village will be replaced by the Global Family.... "And when we have the Global Family ['The United States of Earth'], we will no longer need the United Nations. But until then...."[136]

Former US President Jimmy (a/k/a James Earl, Jr.) Carter went even further. On 16 June 1977, then-President Carter -- after sending a recorded message of good will up into space -- quoth: "We cast this message into the cosmos.... [T]his is a present from a small, distant world .... We hope someday, having solved the problems we face, to join a community of galactic civilizations."[137] But until then....

Until then, we earthlings are to be subjected to UN-sponsored events like the Rio Earth Summit of 1992, a "worthy" environmental and political predecessor to the fatuous Parliament of the World's Religions held the following year at Chicago. The Rio Earth Summit was indeed a political as well as environmental convocation. Berit Kjos has written, "The feminist arm of the Earth Summit... blend[ed] all four pillars of the Green Colossus: Marxist idealism (and oppression), the illusion of peace, earth-centered spirituality, and feminist agenda."[138] Politics yes; as humourist P.J. O'Rourke has quipped:

"The specter of biosphere doom serves the mystical needs of people too sloppy and self-indulgent for regular religion. And it is a scary story to tell in the(energy-conserving) dark. But the ultimate appeal of environmental catastrophe has to do with politics rather than Yahweh or Rod Serling. Ecological utopias could be achieved only by massive political coercion."[139]

Politics yes; underneath all the razzmatazz, pajazz, and Carioca-style posturing, lurked the cold, hard realty of Agenda 21. The delegates to the United Nations Conference on Environment and Development (UNCED1980s, the official designation of the Rio Earth Summit) drafted Agenda 21, in its own words "... a comprehensive programme providing a blueprint for action in all areas relating to the sustainable development of the planet."[140] The original text of Agenda 21 was hardly a blueprint, running to more than 600 pages of ideologic and demagogic rhetoric. The ponderous tome would be boiled down to a 116-page Guide to Agenda 21, then further condensed to a still-factious 33-page 'Press Summary'.[141] But no matter how cooked and condensed, the messages emanating from Agenda 21, according to the Worldwatch Institute, were mixed but clear: (1) National sovereignty everywhere has been ceded to international governance as a result of solving otherwise unmanageable environmental problems; (2) therefore, to make environmental treaties more effective, they should be made less enforceable hence more acceptable to negotiators with national sovereignty in mind; (3) thus, "soft laws" would be enacted -- declarations, resolutions, "action plans" -- not legally binding, thereby inducing [i.e., lulling] negotiating nations to go along with an international consensus, laying a groundwork for truly binding treaties to be really enforced farther down the [one-world] road.[142]

Our old Canadian-Coloradan friend, Maurice Strong, was enthusiastically in accord. Agenda 21 , he said, will receive enough "high level political sanction [that its] potential for influencing and guiding the policies ... of governments will be substantial."[143]

The UN Earth Summit delegates were not the only Saviours of the Earth at Rio in June 1992. There was the Global Forum, a conclave of like-minded, privately-funded ecology groups. [This writer distinctly remembers at least one gathering of the Global Forum during the late 1980s, with the usual international cast of celebrity VIPs in attendance. Dean James Park Morton of New York City's Cathedral of St. John the Divine co-chaired the first Global Forum in April 1988.] As "private" seems to have become a non-word in UN newspeak, the groups convened under the auspices of the Global Forum were designated as NGOs, Non-Governmental Organisations. These ranged from the predictable to the zany: The Royal Swedish Academy of Sciences, Institute for Fusion of Law and Science, the Sierra Club Legal Defense Fund, Eco Tibet of California, and the World Council of Churches ... to name just a few in generally descending order of credibility.[144] Interested observer P.J. O'Rourke, in his hilarious <u>All the Trouble in the World</u>, has described the scene for posterity:

"Of all the people who sat inside the Global Forum's tents and listened to the gripes, about half were handsome, privileged young people groomed and dressed in that affectation of homely poverty which has been with us for more than a quarter of a century now.... All seemed confident in a sort of reverse astrology. Instead of believing that every aspect of their lives was affected by heavenly bodies, they believed that heavenly bodies were affected by every aspect of their lives."[145]

If there emerged a political eco-villain from the Rio Earth Summit, it was US President George Bush. First, President Bush insisted that "a global warming treaty contain something besides hot air".[146] Second, President Bush flatly refused to sign the biodiversity treaty. The biodiversity treaty, the climactic showpiece legislation of the entire eco-summit, declares that if any valuable flora, fauna, bacteria [or conceivably, virus] is discovered in a developing country, the government of that country is to be monetarily compensated. The biodiversity treaty further promises large financial donations to Third World national governments for environmental clean-up and protection. Some of these leaders have included Muammar Qaddafi, Idi Amin, Pol Pot, Kim Il Sung, Saddam Hussein and ... Fidel Castro.[147]

Yes; Fidel Castro. P.J. O'Rourke has expressed both an anger and amazement that have matched this writer's own:

"We throw these bastards out the door of human liberty and back they come through the window of ecological concern. Here is Old Bus[h]y Whiskers -- puffy, aging, abandoned at the altar of Marxism, a back-number tyrant and ideological bug case who has reduced the citizens of his own country to boiling stones for soup. And now he's a friend of the earth."[148]

Before returning to ecologism's enamourment of Third World and Communist dictators, it is time for us to leave the Rio Earth Summit of 1992. Meanwhile, readers should hang onto their hat [and Americans their Constitution] -- the Worldwatch Institute has noted that the next step down the one-world road is the "World Summit on Global Governance" in 1995 (this year), the 50th anniversary of the founding of the United Nations.[149]

The lionisation of the Rio Earth Summit of a morally and now politically toothless Fidel Castro came as no surprise. It has been going on ever since the early 1960s, when Castro was perceived by socialists everywhere as standing up to the Yankee (capitalist) Colossus. As long ago as 1985, with Castro backed by the USSR and exporting violent revolution, he was being praised by the environmentally enlightened. Helen Caldicott, Australian pediatrician speaking for the Union of Concerned Scientists said: ".... Free enterprise really means rich people get richer. And they have the freedom to exploit and psychologically rape their fellow human beings in the process .... Capitalism is destroying the earth. Cuba is a wonderful country. What Castro's done is superb."[150]

Late last year (November 1994), former Communist Party general secretary and Soviet president, Mikhail Gorbachev, was installed as head of Green Cross International by its board of directors. The board numbers among its "scientific experts" such luminaries as Carl Sagan, Ted Turner, Robert Redford, Olivia Newton-John, and Yoko Ono. President Gorbachev will go down in history as the ecologically-aware leader who permitted the nuclear meltdown at Chernobyl, the ongoing deterioration of the Caspian and Aral Seas and Lake Baikal, as well as the partial destruction of Afghanistan -- all on his watch. The grim after-effects of heavy Russian hands on the environment of neighbouring East Germany, Poland, Czechoslovakia, and Romania will be felt for decades to come. Nevertheless, Green Cross International chose Mr. Gorbachev to apply these same methods through "international ecological law."[151]

In All the Trouble in the World, political satirist P.J. O'Rourke used Czechoslovakia (before its break-up into the Czech lands and Slovakia) as an Eastern European environmental model. Czechoslovakia was not ruled by plutocrats for the profits of a few capitalists; it was run in a co-ordinated, collective way for the putative benefit of all Czechoslovaks. But, wrote O'Rourke, "The Communists had the same success creating workers' paradises as they had creating safe landfills.... [and they] are nearly indistinguishable.... [from each other!] The grand effects of Al Gore's dream of infinite government planning for the good of all mankind can be seen the moment you cross what used to be called the Iron (a recyclable material) Curtain."[152] A Dr. Mucha from Children of the Earth told O'Rourke that the ecological damage in the Czech lands was "'not a problem of the planned or open economy but a problem of ownership. Everything belonged to all of us and to nobody.'"[153] Therein, perhaps, lies the true "tragedy of the commons."

The tide seems to be finally turning against an eco-hysteria that has been at high-water mark since the 1960s. Futurist John Naisbitt has applied the brakes on eco-rhetoric in his recently-published Global Paradox. In a chapter titled 'New Rules', Naisbitt actually cites one Ronald Bailey, the environmentally-incorrect author of EcoScam (New York:St. Martin's Press, 1993), in reference to the eco-holocaust in Eastern Europe. Bailey had contended that the problem of environmental pollution is always understood as caused by industrial capitalism, whereas the problem is always understood as solved by international socialism. This simplistic formula played well in the liberal West until the collapse of Communism and the end of the Cold War. Naisbitt finds it ironic that "... whatever is deplorable in the environmental record of the industrial capitalists, the record pales in comparison to what was considered standard operating procedure by industry in the erstwhile Soviet Union and its former satellites. Compared to, say, the steel mills and coal mines of Copsa-Mica in Romania, U.S. Steel is a veritable Sierra Club."[154]

The afore-mentioned Ronald Bailey, along with writers like Michael Fumento [Science under Siege (New York:William Morrow, 1993)], have presented a more balanced and technically accurate portrayal of global ecological health than "the false prophets of ecological apocalypse" (Bailey). In EcoScam, Ronald Bailey depicted the outwardly hot protesters as inwardly cool salespersons, intentionally peddling eco-hysteria -- global warming, ozone holes, widespread famine; the population bomb, etc. -- to enrich themselves financially and for political empowerment as environmental custodians.[155] Bailey's book specifically drew comparisons between the gloomy forecasts of certain environmental "experts," and how these predictions have not come true. Bailey cited Paul Ehrlich, the Club of Rome, Barry Commoner, Carl Sagan, et al. who predicted (amongst other claims made during the 1960s and 1970s) that billions of people would starve to death by 1985; that the world would run out of oil, natural gas, and industrial metals in the 1980s; that an ice age was imminent; that global warming would overheat the earth, eventually endangering human life; and that atmospheric ozone depletion by chlorofluorocarbons would rob the planet of natural protection from ultra-violet light rays. Not one of the above prophesies, of course, was fulfilled during the 1980s. We are now (1995) halfway through the 1990s, and there still exists no evidence that human activity affects climate, or that fluctuations in temperature during the recent past occurred as a result of human industry.[156]

This writer clearly recalls the television appearances of Drs. Carl Sagan and Paul Ehrlich throughout the 1970s. Fawning talk-show hosts like Johnny Carson would never challenge their incredible numbers -- e.g., "millions and billions", and these weird scientists would be royally treated while announcing their fantastic projections unimpugned. And the underlying message of Paul Ehrlich, certainly, was that our free enterprise system was too much for the world to bear unless governments.... "following the recipes of 'scientists', create, in the words of Paul Ehrlich, a 'new civilization' which would strictly regulate all economic activity and redress 'the inequitable distribution of wealth and resources, racism and sexism'."[157] (Many was the wasted night this writer tossed and turned on his bed after hearing the dire projections of Paul Ehrlich, made in correspondingly sepulchral tones ... and none of which would come to pass.)

Presently it is mid-1995, half a year after the congressional Republican victory of November 1994. The air over North America is much cleaner than it was on Earth Day 1970. Forests have made a comeback, and the average price of food has dropped 70% over the last twenty-five years. As for global warming, temperatures have dropped during the past fifteen years. And except for the lung cancer caused by smoking, cancer rates have sunk, much farther down than the current wisdom about the dangers of synthetic chemical and pesticidal epidemics would have us believe.[158] In a recent review of Gregg Easterbrook's A Moment on the Earth,[159] Ronald Bailey (himself the author of EcoScam[160]) has quoted Easterbrook as writing:

"Contemporary doomsaying is hard to excuse, given that it comes at a time when most trends in developed countries are positive and most scientific findings suggest the biosphere is extremely robust.... Environmentalism remains mired in instant-doomsday thinking. Some of this fixation stems from a willful denial of progress made: an almost aching desire that news stay bad."[161]

Bailey, as reviewer, appears to agree with many of Easterbrooks's premises but few of his conclusions. Bailey cannot fathom why Easterbrook has suggested surrendering yet more of the environment and economy to politically-driven Big Green management. An EPA (Environmental Protection Agency) staff member is even purported to have told Easterbrook: "Everything the EPA does is driven by political considerations rather than scientific considerations. The science is always tailored to support whatever has already been concluded politically."[162] Bailey has concluded that Easterbrook sincerely anticipates "the coming age of environmental optimism", while not hearing Big Green beating the ecological drums for still more state/provincial-federal rules and regulations. "As a liberal", Easterbrook has gushed, "I eagerly await the moment when environmental progress is properly seen as the triumphal achievement of liberal political philosophy." Bailey ventures drily that Easterbrook will be stood-up for a long time. [163]

How financially and politically powerful is Big Green? There are two branches of Big Green in the United States -- the privately funded special-interest groups, and the governmental supervising agencies. The lack of accountability of an organisation such as Greenpeace has been noted in Forbes magazine:

"Outfits like Greenpeace attack big business as being faceless and responsible to no one. In fact, that description better fits Greenpeace than it does modern corporations that are regulated, patrolled and heavily taxed by governments, reported on by an adversarial press and carefully watched by their own shareholders. There [is] little accountability for outfits like Greenpeace."[164]

As for public Big Green, a Dr. John Isaacs, then director of the Institute of Marine Resources at the University of California, said it all right in 1978:

"Many of the great regulatory and enforcement agencies of the United States are beginning to adopt the pose of the medieval churches, with regard not for what is true and right, but rather for what defends their notions of the intent of regulatory laws or their established policies and for what supports their own delusions of power, omniscience, and infallibility! The beleaguered scientist with evidence of the fallibility of these agencies, or the triviality of a program that they regulate, or the underlying faults in their regulations can only recant his findings [if he wants any more research support]."[165]

Michael S. Coffman has remarked in Saviors of the Earth? that environmentalism is a tale of innocence lost. Like the Big Business it professes to despise, Big Green is most concerned with winning at any (body else's) cost; is least concerned with moral principle. The only major, and unfair, difference is that Big Business has to compete and survive in a real world of double standards, while being regulated and scrutinised by endless governmental agencies and hostile investigative reporters, hungry for eco-horror stories.[166] Public Big Green, of course, derives its financial and political power from the taxpayer and the government. Money magazine reported in December 1992 that privately-funded environmental groups took in U.S. $2.5 billion per annum ... whence flows all these funds? There are more than 3,000 [supposedly] non-profit environmental groups registered in the United States, and some of them, like the multi-million dollars-worth Nature Conservancy, are a law and fiefdom unto themselves. Another cornucopian source of revenue for these groups are the foundations. Ford, Rockefeller and dozens of other private foundations syphon hundreds of millions of dollars in tax-free grants to these eco-groups annually. To add insult to the injury of eco-scam, foundation money often doesn't appear on balance sheets as it is funneled through the parent environmental organisation, thence to a local Green front eco-group doing Gaia's work. ("Think globally, act locally.") One example of tax-free, private foundation largesse is the Earthwatch Institute, which played a leading eco-rôle at the Rio Earth Summit, was created from nothing by millions of Rockefeller dollars. Another example is the Environmental Defense Fund (EDF), spawned in 1969 by Ford and other foundation funds, which grew to be a monolithic activist agency, eventually pressuring the EPA and the State of California to do its bidding.[167]

This writer can speak from experience regarding the unholy coupling of private foundations with environmental groups. Briefly stated, this writer has sat since May 1992 on the directorial board of the Bay Foundation, so named after his deceased (1956) adoptive father Charles Ulrick Bay. Mr. Bay served as U.S. ambassador to post-World War II Norway, and worked as a New York-based investor and businessman. Also sitting on the Bay Foundation board are this writer's younger adoptive brother and former family attorney, both in senior positions. Although almost fifteen years apart in age, these two middle-aged men, respectively educated at Harvard and U. Michigan, are Charles A. Reich Consciousness III holdovers from the 1960s. [Today, superannuated counterculture types are The Establishment!] Several months into the writer's junior directorship, the two senior directors in question had concocted a scheme to confer Global Biodiversity Leadership Awards (of $180,000 each) ..."to three individuals whose work demonstrates problem-solving leadership in science or policy related to the loss of biological diversity. At least one of the awards will be granted to an individual working in a developing nation. [This last concession to political correctness is to allay any suspicion that the donors might be insensitive rich, white men.] The foundations have targeted three broadly-defined areas -- conservation biology [i.e., "biocentric nihilism"], environmental studies and conservation science advocacy for the award"....[168]

This writer's senior co-directors had their fantasies partially fulfilled during the early days of March 1995. On 7 March the Wildlife Conservation Society, in co-operation with Rockefeller University and the Fairfield Osborn Memorial Lectures in Environmental Science, presented its Centennial Lecture Series: 'CONSERVATION AT THE CROSSROADS: Man and Nature in the Twenty-first Century'. Serving on the Centennial Lecture Series Committee were honourary co-chairpersons Mrs. Vincent Astor and Laurence S. Rockefeller. Numbered among the Committee members were John Chancellor (NBC News) and George Plimpton (Paper Lion). The Centennial Lecture on that fateful evening was given by one Dr. Norman Myers of Oxford, England; his topic: "Save the Entire Biosphere!"

According to the WCS pamphlet proudly sent to this writer by the Bay Foundation, Dr. Norman Myers "... is an internationally-renowned scientist and independent consultant on environment and development issues, with an emphasis on sustainable development, systems ecology, resource economics, and tropical forests. He has provided advice to every major global agency with a natural resource agenda, including the United Nations, the World Bank, the European Union, the U.S. Department of State -- even NASA. He has won praise ... for his ... 'green' activism.... Dr. Myers is a winner of the 1992 Volvo Environment Prize.... A graduate of Oxford University and the University of California (Berkeley), Norman Myers is the author of hundreds of books and articles, including ... The Gaia Atlas of Plant Management (sic) and The Primary Source, his widely praised textbook on rain forests and their rapid disappearance.... He has recently advocated holistic, yet highly pragmatic strategies for protecting the planet's life-support systems, reflected in his aphorism, 'Our earth is one, our world is not!'"[169]

This writer has read the WCS pamphlet with a sinking heart, realising just from the list of usual suspects -- the U.N., the World Bank et al., added to the rather frivolously-titled topic, that Norman Myers was yet one more eco-doomsayer of the Paul Ehrlich variety. Less than three months later this suspicion would be somewhat confirmed. In an article in National Review, author Ronald Bailey analysed the newly-published book, A Moment on the Earth, by Gregg Easterbrook. In it, Easterbrook (a self-proclaimed liberal) expressed his opinion that numbers and predictions of species extinction rates have been greatly exaggerated. In his review Bailey wrote:

".... Environmental alarmists such as Norman Myers say that 150 human-caused extinctions occur each day. This would mean that roughly 1.2 million species should have died out since the Endangered Species Act was adopted in 1973. This extinction rate would imply 72,000 extinctions in the United States alone during the past 22 years. Yet only 7 actual extinctions in the U.S. have been confirmed."[170]

This writer felt a mounting sense of vindication after reading the above words. Having been trained as an historian, this writer is well aware that the above sources are secondary and tertiary, but the justified feeling has remained. For this writer to suggest to the senior directors that perhaps Dr. Myers and his eco-alarmist ilk should not be the recipients of Bay Foundation dollars ... would be fruitless. It would be the equivalent of explaining to Mormons or "Moonies" the theological error of their ways. For the fiftyish former Bay family attorney, and the writer's fortysomething younger adoptive brother, had swallowed Consciousness III philosophy whole during the late 1960s. These were individuals the writer had variously respected and loved his entire life. But now, grafted onto their Greening outlook during the preceding quarter century, were carefully-selected snippets of the environmentalist religion, a genteel PBS/NPR-type "watermelon" Marxism[171], and a radically chic Manhattan/Hollywood-style Green activism. In 1995 both men had fallen, along with like-minded cultural lemmings, into the bottomless pit of political (i.e., environmental) correctness. To ensure their ultimate one-world Ecotopia would be the United Nations blue-helmeted planeteers, armed and ready to enforce the environmental edicts of Agenda 21. This would be the perfect, unitary green-earth of grown-up Consciousness III ecosophists. To reiterate that 99.99% of North Americans are concerned about dirty drinking water, tainted meat, bad fish, polluted air and oceans, or in favour of recycling waste, reforestation and silviculture ... is to of no avail. The Big Green Agenda has long transcended the "Wise Use" of the land and seas for mankind's advantage while keeping ecosystems healthy. The environmental goals of Big Green don't really include mankind as a factor anyway. [Élitist Greens regard themselves as apart from the common, consuming herd.] In the meantime, the rest of us will be subjected to increased eco-scams, stepped up eco-hysteria, and further claims by weird science to soften up the laiety for the ever-expanding Big Green polity.

It is June Graduation Sunday 1995 at Holy Trinity Lutheran Church in Port Angeles, Washington. [During decidedly un-Christian lapses the writer has dubbed it the PC Church of JC Superstar at PA.] The altar guild today is made up of the flashiest, foxiest Senior girls being graduated from PA High School. There is no lingering modesty here, and they are wearing the briefest of mini-skirts. This is the six-month-old "New Song" service at 11 a.m., i.e., "contemporary worship," and there is no more hypocritical church gravitas either. [Extant narrow-minded fuddy-duddies can attend the 8:30 a.m. liturgical service.] At "New Song" there is a beatifically-smiling musical director, with thinning gray hair combed over his ears in a foetal-Beatle hairdo, cheerleading the celebration praise in the manner of a summer camp sing-along. Bill Moyers, PBS-enlightened Southern Baptist and cosmic Christian, would feel right at home here.

At this very moment the New Song being sung [none of the New Songs appear to have been composed before 1972] is 'The Butterfly Song' for the graduates: "If I were a Butterfly..." How utterly wet and weedy!, this writer was thinking, when the tall, gangly girl in front of him swooned away, sitting down hard on the pew. She was quickly revived but not before the writer noticed her frizzled orange hair, dead white face, opaque green eyes [designer-colour contact lenses?], and painted black lips and fingernails. She looked like a geeky teenage version of Annie Lennox of the Eurythmics. As the local cable TV company had very recently cancelled MTV [the kids "just don't get it" anymore], this girl had probably been up late last night at a pyjama party with friends watching "Cat's Eye" (starring James Woods and Drew Barrymore, 1985), a Stephen King-written horror movie. Then again it could have been that stifling church atmosphere and the hyper-excitement of graduation.

Be that as it may, it is now "Sharing & Prayer Time." This writer dutifully bows his head and thinks about an Augustinian quote brought to mind by Christian author Dave Hunt:

"Augustine lamented that those now inside the Church were ... 'drunkards, misers, tricksters, gamblers, adulterers, fornicators, people wearing amulets, assiduous clients of sorcerors, astrologers ... the same crowds that press into the churches on Christian festivals also fill the theatres on pagan holidays'."[172]

NOTES

53. Zaralaya G. Heartwood, 'The Way of the White Rabbit', The New Times, Vol. 10, No. 9, February 1995, p.1.

54. Op.cit., Heartwood, p.1.

55. Ibid. p.1. Heartwood paraphrases Harner.

56. Ibid. p.1.

57. Ibid. p.15.

58. Ibid. p. 15.

59. Peter Lalonde, One World under Anti-Christ (Eugene, Ore.:Harvest House Publishers, 1991), p.86. Author's note: Despite the lurid title (and cover) which so many Christian books seem to have, the above is an excellent and well-researched work. The same is true for those listed below.

60. Dwight L. Kinman, The World's Last Dictator (Woodburn, Ore.:Solid Rock Books, Inc., 1993), pp.97-98.

61. The Los Angeles Times, 5 September 1993, p.A-1. Cited in Dave Hunt, A Woman Rides the Beast (Eugene, Ore.:Harvest House Publishers, 1994), pp.427,540.

62. Elliot Miller, 'The 1993 Parliament of the World's Religions', Christian Research Journal, Vol. 16, No. 2, Fall 1993, p.14.

63. Robert A. Sirico, 'The Greening of American Faith, National Review, 29 August 1994, p.43. Fr. Sirico is president of the Acton Institute for the Study of Religion and Liberty in Grand Rapids, Michigan.

64. Ibid., pp.43,46.

65. Ibid., p.43. Reference is to Albert Gore, Earth in the Balance:Ecology and the Human Spirit (Boston:Houghton Mifflin, 1992).

66. Peter Jones, The Gnostic Empire Strikes Back (Phillipsburg, N.J.:P&R Publishing, 1992), p.109. References are to Albert Gore, Earth in the Balance, pp.258-260.

67. Op.cit., Albert Gore, p.260. Cited in Michael S. Coffman, Saviors of the Earth? The Politics and Religion of the Environmental Movement (Chicago, Ill.:Northfield Publishing, 1994), p.148.

68. Op.cit., Albert Gore, p.265. Cited by Michael S. Coffman, p.148.

69. Tom Heyden, 'Spirituality Infuses Hope for the Earth', The Los Angeles Times, 18 June 1992. Cited by Peter Jones, p.109.

70. Op.cit., Peter Jones, p.109.

NOTED (cont'd.)

71. Dwight L. Kinman, p.111. Author's note: Mr. Strong has been a man of many faces, wearing many hats. In <u>Trilateralism:The Trilateral Commission and Elite Planning for World Management</u> (Boston, Mass.:South End Press, 1980), editor Holly Sklar recorded Strong as serving on the Commission from 1976-1977. In the chapter 'Who's Who on the Trilateral Commission', Holly Sklar and Ros Everdell listed Strong's further achievements (p.110):

"Ch. Petro-Canada (76-); Pres. CIDA [Canadian International Development Agency] (66-); Exec. Dir. UN Environment Prog., (73-77); Tr.:Rockefeller Fund, Rockefeller U. Alt. gov.:Asian Dev. Bank."

As their source, Sklar and Everdell quoted from <u>Canadian Who's Who</u>, 1979 (Vol. XIV), Kieran Simpson, ed., U of Toronto Press.

72. <u>Ibid.</u>, p.111.

73. Op.cit., Michael S. Coffman, p.227. Author's note: Named in a mindlessly cruel irony for the "Holy Island" off the Northumberland coast where flourished 7th century Celtic Christianity, spreading missionary work onto the British mainland.

74. <u>Ibid.</u>, p.227.

75. Op.cit., Michael S. Coffman, p.226.

76. Alice Bailey, <u>Education in the New Age</u> (New York:Lucis, 1984), p.66. Cited in Michael S. Coffman, p.226.

77. Helena Blavatsky, <u>The Secret Doctrine:The Synthesis of Science, Religion and Philosophy</u>, 2 vols. (London:Theosophical Publishing, 1888; reprint by Theosophical Univ. Press, Pasadena,Calif., 1988), 1:71, 109, 481; 2:33, 65, 540. Cited in Michael S. Coffman, p.227.

78. See Appendix E for definition and details.

79. Religiously-correct books had insinuated themselves into the pastoral library.

80. Texe Marrs, <u>Big Sister Is Watching You</u> (Austin, Tex.:Living Truth Publishers, 1993), pp.110-111.

81. Eugene Taylor, Ph.D., 'Desperately Seeking Spirituality', <u>Psychology Today</u>, Vol.27, No.6, November/December 1994, p.62.

82. As exemplified and espoused by Helena Blavatsky, Annie Besant, Alice and Foster Bailey; the successive leading lights of Theosophy from its inception during the mid-1870s until the mid-20th century.

83. Michael S. Coffman, p.77.

84. Eventually Brower became too radical even for the Sierra Club, and went on to found Friends of the Earth. Michael S. Coffman, p.73.

NOTES (cont'd.)

85. Op.cit., Michael S. Coffman, p.73.

86. Charles Colson with Nancy R. Pearcey, 'Building Paradise --An Unscientific Experiment', <u>A Dance with Deception</u> (Dallas, Tex.:Word Publishing, 1993), p.228.

87. Op.cit., Charles Colson, pp.228-229.

88. <u>Ibid.</u>, p.229; Colson citing Biospheran literature. [Ie., "....You will be like God...." (Gen.3:5).]

89. 'Biosphere 2 mastermind resigns under pressure', <u>Peninsula Daily News</u>, 10 April 1994, p.A-6.

90. 'Biosphere crew ends project era', <u>Peninsula Daily News</u>, 18 September 1994, p.A-11.

91. <u>Ibid.</u>, p.A-11.

92. Charles A. Reich, <u>The Greening of America</u> (Harmondsworth, Mx.:Penguin Books Ltd., 1972), p.28.

93. <u>Ibid.</u>, p.56.

94. <u>Ibid.</u>, p.62.

95. <u>Ibid.</u>, pp.61-62.

96. <u>Ibid.</u>, p.195.

97. <u>Ibid.</u>, p.216.

98. <u>Ibid.</u>, p.224.

99. <u>Ibid.</u>, p.293.

100. <u>Ibid.</u>, p.301.

101. <u>Ibid.</u>, p.287.

102. <u>Ibid.</u>, p.288.

103. <u>Ibid.</u>, p.221.

104. <u>Ibid.</u>, p.332.

105. Joshua Hochschild, 'Corpus Yalensis', <u>Yale Free Press</u>, April 1994. Cited in 'How Does it Go for God and Man at Yale?', <u>National Review</u>, Vol. XLVII, No.6, 3 April 1995, p.18.

106. Julian Ku, 'Long Day's Journey to the Right', <u>Yale Free Press</u>, May 1994. Cited in <u>ibid.</u>, p.19.

107. William Irwin Thompson, 'Going Beyond It at Big Sur', <u>At the Edge of History</u> (New York:Harper Colophon Books, 1971) pp.45-46.

NOTES (cont'd.)

108. Op.cit., William Irwin Thompson, 'Values and Conflict through History', ibidem, p.141.

109. Op.cit., Thompson, p.140.

110. Ibid., p.140. Works referred to were: Pierre Teilhard de Chardin, The Future of Man (New York:1964), pp.130,132; Ivan Illich, The New York Review of Books, 9 October 1969, p.12; Marshall McLuhan, Understanding Media (New York:1965), p.34.

111. Op.cit., Thompson, p.140.

112. William Irwin Thompson, Darkness and Scattered Light (Garden City, N.Y.:Anchor Press/Doubleday, 1978), p.117,ff.

113. William Irwin Thompson, 'A.D.2000:The Millennium under New Management', At the Edge of History, p.169.

114. Christie Davis, 'What Made Them Moral?' National Review, Vol.XLVII, No.6, 3 April 1995, p.63.

115. P.J. O'Rourke, All the Trouble in the World (New York:Atlantic Monthly Press, 1994), p.129.

116. Ibid., p.129.

117. John Lucacs, 'To Hell with Culture', Chronicles, September 1994, p.18.

118. William A. Rusher, 'Forward, March!' National Review, 15 February 1993, pp.40-41.

119. Wild Earth, Summer 1991. Cited by Christian American, March 1993, p.21.

120. Berit Kjos, Under the Spell of Mother Earth (Wheaton, Ill.:Victor Books, 1992), p.28. Chart 1 shows "Three views of the Earth", with the third view being under Christian Stewardship (theocentric).

121. Ibid., pp.23-24. Windstar is an Aspen, Colorado-based organisation.

122. Ibid., p.23.

123. Ibid., p.23. Cf. Michael S. Coffman, p.92.

124. Op.cit., Berit Kjos, p.132, quoting Arne Naess.

125. Michael S. Coffman, p.92.

126. Ibid., p.92.

127. Please see Appendix D.

128. Grant R. Jeffrey, Prince of Darkness (Toronto:Frontier Research Publications, 1994), p.80.

NOTES (cont'd.)

129. Hal Lindsey, Planet Earth -- 2000A.D. (Palos Verdes, Calif.:Western Front, Ltd., 1994), p.221.

130. 'Ten Kingdoms with the Beast', Newswatch, March-April 1984 [sic], pp.12-15.

131. See Grant R. Jeffrey, p.80. Cf. Revelation 17:12.

132. Club of Rome, Alexander King and Bertrand Schneider, The First Global Revolution (New York:Pantheon Books, 1991), p.115. Quoted by Grant R. Jeffrey, p.88; and Dixie Lee Ray with Lou Guzzo, Environmental Overkill (Washington, D.C.:Regnery Gateway, 1993), p.205.

133. Alvin Toffler, The Eco-Spasm Report (New York:Bantam Books, 1975), pp.74,3. Cited by John Ankerberg and John Weldon, One World (Chicago:Moody Press, 1991), p.144.

134. Alvin Toffler, The Third Wave (New York:William Morrow, 1980), p.342. Cited by Ankerberg and Weldon, pp.145-146.

135. There also exists a stealth global government-in-waiting, the World Constitution and Parliament Association (WCPA), founded in 1959. As this self-appointed New World Order body has formulated some interesting plans for the earth's oceans and seas, the WCPA will be analysed (next) in Part III.

136. Arthur C. Clarke, July 20, 2019:Life in the 21st Century (New York:MacMillan, 1986), p.276. Cited by Ankerberg and Weldon, One World, p.146.

137. Quoted by Dave Hunt, ed., The Berean Call (Bend, Oregon), April 1995, p.1.

138. Berit Kjos, 'From the Counter-Culture to the Earth Summit', The Christian World Report, June-July 1992, p.19.

139. P.J. O'Rourke, p.172.

140. Quoted by P.J. O'Rourke, p.214.

141. Ibid., p.214.

142. Hilary French, After the Earth Summit: The Future of Environmental Governance (New York:Norton, 1992; Worldwatch paper #107); quoted in William Jasper, 'Launching Global Governance', The New American, June/August 1992, p.50. Cited in Michael S. Coffman, p.205.

143. Maurice Strong as quoted in 'Earth Summit to Forge Global Green Empire', Citizen Outlook 7, no. 3, May/June 1992, by CFACT, Washington, D.C. Cited in Michael S. Coffman.

144. P.J. O'Rourke, pp.215-216.

145. Op.cit., P.J. O'Rourke, p.219.

146. In the words of P.J. O'Rourke (p.221), not President Bush!

147. Ibid., p.221.

NOTES (cont'd.)

148. Op.cit., P.J. O'Rourke, pp.222-223.

149. Michael S. Coffman, p.206.

150. Helen Caldicott quoted in Elizabeth Whelan, Toxic Terror (Ottawa, Ill.:Jameson Books, 1985), pp.53-54.

151. National Review, 21 November 1994, p.12.

152. Op.cit., P.J. O'Rourke, p.176.

153. Ibid., p.188.

154. John Naisbitt, Global Paradox (New York:Avon Books, 1995), p.207.

155. Angelo M. Codevilla, 'Big Green', National Review, 12 April 1993, p.60.

156. Ibid., p.62.

157. Op.cit., Angelo M. Codevilla, quoting Dr. Paul Ehrlich, p.62.

158. Ronald Bailey, 'Earth to Easterbrook', National Review, Vol. XLVII, No.10, 29 May 1995, pp.59-60.

159. Subtitled: The Coming Age of Environmental Optimism (New York:Viking Press, 1995).

160. Subtitled: The False Prophets of Ecological Apocalypse (New York:St. Martin's Press, 1993).

161. Gregg Easterbrook quoted by Ronald Bailey in National Review, 29 May 1995, p.59.

162. Ibid., p.60.

163. Ibid., p.60.

164. Leslie Spenser et al., Forbes, 11 November 1991, p.176; cited by Michael S. Coffman.

165. Dr. John Isaacs in testimony given to the Water Resources Subcommittee of the House Committee on Public Works, 24-25 May 1978. Cited by Michael S. Coffman.

166. Ibid., p.166.

167. Ibid., p.101.

168. Introductory remarks, John Robinson, Wilderness Conservation Society (WCS:Founded in 1895 as the New York Zoölogical Society), at Centennial Lecture, 7 March 1995, Caspary Auditorium, Rockefeller University. (A John Denver Wildlife Concert was broadcast by the Arts and Entertainment Channel on 22 June 1995 for the WCS Centennial.)

169. 'CONSERVATION AT THE CROSSROADS:Man and Nature in the Twenty-first Century', 7 March 1995, Wildlife Conservation Society, New York City. WCS pamphlet, p.2.

NOTES (cont'd.)

170.   Ronald Bailey, 'Earth to Easterbrook', <u>National Review</u>, Vol. XLVII, No. 10, 29 May 1995, p.60.

171.   "Green on the outside, Red on the inside."

172.   Dave Hunt, <u>How Close Are We?</u> (Eugene, Ore.:Harvest House Publishers, 1993), p.97.

Bibliography for Part II

8.   Ankerberg, John and John Weldon. One World: Biblical Prophesy and the New World Order. Moody Press, Chicago, 1991.

9.   Coffman, Michael S. Saviors of the Earth? Northfield Publishing, Chicago, 1994.

10.   Kah, Gary. En Route to Global Occupation. Huntington House Publishers, Lafayette, La., 1992.

11.   Kinman, Dwight L. The World's Last Dictator. Solid Rock Books, Inc., Woodburn, Ore., 1993.

12.   O'Rourke, P.J. All the Trouble in the World. The Atlantic Monthly Press, New York, 1994.

13.   Ray, Dixie Lee with Lou Guzzo. Trashing the Planet. HarperCollins, New York, 1992.

14.   _____. Environmental Overkill. Regnery Gateway, Washington, D.C., 1993.

15.   Reich, Charles A. The Greening of America. The Penguin Press, Harmondsworth, Mx, England, 1972.

16.   Thompson, William Irwin. At the Edge of History. Harper Colophon Books, New York, 1972.

Part III: North Pacific Rim Fishing, 2001 A.D.

Prologue

    "So long, and thanks for all the fish"

                    - Douglas Adams, Hitchhiker's Guide

    This writer first learned of Galicia, Spain, during June of 1963 aboard the M/S Skauholt, a freighter that carried coal from Newport News, Virginia, to San Nicolás, Argentina. The Skauholt was owned by I.M. Skaugen A/S of Tvedestrand and Oslo, Norway. Among the ship's predominantly Norwegian crew were two Americans (myself included), an Argentine, a West German, and two Spaniards. The latter were from La Coruña, Spain, but they spoke a language to each other more akin to Portuguese than Castilian. By the time the writer disembarked from the Skauholt in late summer, he had crossed the equator into the South Atlantic, sailed up from Argentina past the Uruguayan littoral, and jettisoned all previous notions of Spain and Spaniards. By journey's end -- at summer's close -- ashore in Baltimore, Maryland, the writer had become good friends with both crewmen from La Coruña; admiring their superior seamanship as much as their industrious ways and sober habits. The writer learned that Galicia, the northwestern Spanish region above Portugal, was rainy, green, and Celtic. Instead of strumming Flamenco music on the guitar, Galicians (Gallegos) traditionally played the gaeta, a form of bagpipe, and often drank cider instead of wine. Due to the similarity of their language and culture to the Portuguese, many Gallegos chose to migrate to Brazil rather than to the Castellano-speaking countries of South America. And like the Portuguese, the Galicians have always fished the stormy North Atlantic seas for codfish.

    The writer decided to see Galicia for himself, and two years later, in 1965, booked passage on a Compañia Trasatlantica Española ship bound for La Coruña from New York. On board were Cuban emigrés, various Latin Americans, and, expectedly, homesick Spaniards. One of the writer's table-mates was an elderly man of Galician origin, now a naturalised U.S. citizen, retired after a life of fishing out of Bayonne, New Jersey. Brown and wrinkled as a nut, unsmiling and taciturn with the hard-bitten visage of an Inquisitor, the venerable Spanish-American allowed that his name was Al Freire and that he was going to visit his hometown of Sada. He had not been back since leaving for the States as a youth. Then Mr. Freire's thin-lipped mouth snapped shut like a trap and he said no more. This writer knew this was a tough breed -- (in)famous political strongmen of Galician roots ranged from Fascist Francisco Franco to Communist Fidel Castro.

But Galicia itself offered sparking fjord-like rías, verdant valleys, and a smiling countryside. Just north of La Coruña, past Sada on the way to the "Costa Verde" ("Green Coast"), lay El Ferrol, the birthplace of "El Caudillo" ("the Leader"), Francisco Franco himself. There was nothing in that bucolic landscape vaguely sinister, a land and seascape of fisherfolk and Celtas, to even remotely suggest a Spanish "Black Legend" ("Leyenda Negra").

Section A: The Collapse of the Atlantic Northeast Coast Fisheries

"Fisheries peaked in 1970, and now many traditional fishing areas of the ocean have essentially been 'fished out.'"
- Jeremy Rifkin, Entropy: A New World View, 1981

It is from the rías of Galicia and the jagged northwest coast of Spain that sail the powerful and feared Spanish fishing fleets. Along with their brother Portuguese, the Galician Spaniards have for centuries fished in their usual and accustomed places ... the turbulent and icy waters of the far northwestern Atlantic. In 1995, thirty years after the writer's journey to La Coruña, Francisco Franco has long lain in his grave. Spain today is a constitutional monarchy and a democratic member of the European Union. But there have been other changes since 1965 -- revised laws of the sea, extended maritime borders, and new international attitudes regarding the harvesting of fish.

During the first week of March 1995, Canada seized the Spanish trawler Estai in the Grand Banks off Newfoundland ostensibly to stop overfishing of endangered species. The Estai was arrested outside Canada's 200-mile territorial limit, and triumphantly escorted to St. John's, Newfoundland, like a captured Spanish man-'o'-war rather than a peaceful trawler. The captain was charged with unlawful fishing and other offenses under Canada's Coastal Fisheries Protection Act, then released on $8,000 bail. Canada's justification for the vessel's seizure resulted from the ongoing trans-Atlantic fishing dispute of the previous year, where Canada had implemented a law allowing her to stop ships in international waters suspected of overfishing. Canadian officials maintain that they must protect fish migrating from international to Canadian waters. The

Estai was believed to have been fishing for turbot.[173]

Before further discussing Spanish reaction to Canada's action off the Grand Banks, let us immediately establish what a "turbot" actually is and is not. This writer has called the arrowtooth flounder (Atheresthes stomias) a turbot in a chapter on North Pacific ground fishes.[174] The Atlantic turbot under analysis -- and contention -- is also known as the Greenland halibut, Greenland turbot, and black halibut. This writer empathises with U.S. fisheries expert F. Heward Bell's implication that the [lesser] Greenland halibut (Reinhardtius hippoglossoides) is misnamed: The mighty Pacific halibut (Hippoglossus stenolepis), sometimes weighing hundreds of pounds and fabled in Northwest Coast Native American myth and legend, should share the designation halibut with no other fish.[175] But for our purpose R. hippoglossoides is big enough. Of the family Pleuronectidae, the Greenland halibut weighs between ten and 25 lb., with an average adult weight of 22 lb. (10 kg.), and is of a median length of 40 inches (100 centimetres). The Greenland "turbot", unlike most flatfish, is solidly-coloured on both sides, of a usually brownish-blackish hue.[176]

The Greenland turbot is commonly found at depths of 136 to 875 fathoms (250 to 1600 metres) and is an active predator on the bottom, foraging in the mid-water column to the surface. This is behaviour quite unlike that of other flatfish -- the Greenland turbot quits the sea-bed to prey on prawns, shrimps, fishes, and squids. The hunting habits of the turbot are facilitated by the "...placing of [the] upper eye at [the] extreme edge of [the] head...",[177] thereby affording the species a greater angle of vision than is normal in flatfishes. This has been a brief, biological portrait of the Greenland halibut (R. hippoglossoides), a perhaps undistinguished species but nonetheless the fish of dispute embroiled in the Canada-Spain "turbot troubles."

Spanish diplomats responded predictably by calling Canada's arbitrary action a violation of international law. A Spanish foreign ministry spokesman said that Spain would protest Canada's seizure of the Estai before the World Court at the Hague, and would shortly send a second warship to protect Spanish boats and crews still fishing in the Grand Banks. The European Union (EU) as of 13 March 1995 suspended contacts with Canada ("the peacemongering North American good guy"), and Spain threatened to possibly sever diplomatic relations.[178] Enter now Canadian Fisheries Minister Brian Tobin onto the world stage, shortly to become a sorely-needed Maple Leaf national hero. Canada's options ranged, said Fisheries Minister

Tobin from Ottawa, "'from arrest to the use of warp-cutters to the use of techniques to prevent these vessels from having a successful day of fishing.'"[179]

Fisheries Minister Tobin backed tough talk with tough action: Before sending the Estai limping home to Spain, Canada had confiscated all the fish in her hold and forced the owners to post a $500,000 bond. But not all Canadians saw Fisheries Minister Tobin as "Admiral of the Fleet." Robert Lewis, editor of the magazine Maclean's (Canada's Time/Newsweek) cautioned:

"[Prime Minister] Chrétien and Tobin -- the only member[s] of the Liberal 'Rat Pack' to thrive in prime time -- pulled off a major coup. Having ignored the steady decline in fishing stocks, the Liberals now bask in congratulations from both coasts .... A nation that is a primary cause of the fish crisis in the Atlantic cast itself on troubled waters as the new savior of the stocks.... There was far too much strutting and posing and use of props last week, but Admiral Tobin's turbot tempest certainly suited the temper of the times."[180]

Indeed; there were other Canadian critics of Fisheries Minister Tobin's environmentalist stance as hypocritical, suspecting his political motives. There also surfaced the question of legality. Armand de Mestral, a McGill University professor of maritime law who helped negotiate the Law of the Sea Convention, remarked that Canada's dismal record of overfishing in her own 90% of the Grand Banks belied Fisheries Minister Tobin's eco-posturing. Professor Mestral surmised that the only area left to find fish off Canada's coasts was beyond the 200-mile limit.[181] The question of Canada's illegal action in turn has exhumed the perenially unanswered question: Just who owns the sea anyway? It is all the more ironic in light of the Canada-Spain fish fracas, that a UN-sponsored gathering of world maritime nations was scheduled to resume on 27 March 1995 and further debate that very question.[182]

No matter what is resolved at future UN conferences or the results are of the present Canada-Spain turbot imbroglio, the one option not on the table will be a return of the old high-seas fisheries in which any man with a boat and gear could participate. For better or worse those times are forever gone. Throughout history, coastal seafaring nations have jealously guarded freedom of the seas, restricting each other's attempts to impose limits or rule the waves. For the nearly four centuries since Netherlands scholar Hugo Grotius defined the three-mile offshore boundary, vessels beyond it could freely engage in any maritime pursuit so long as other shipping remained unimpeded and unimperiled. The premise remains in actual effect despite the many treaties and conventions which have attempted to impose some sort of legal structure on the earth's oceans. The most significant of them all has been the United Nations Convention on the Law of the Sea, a document negotiated during the 1970s but enforceable only since 16 November 1994, when Guyana became the 60th country to ratify the treaty.[183]

The Convention -- which Canada has not confirmed at this writing -- expanded the jurisdiction of coastal states from three to twelve nautical miles from their respective shores, with exclusive economic rights out to 200 miles. Beyond those limits, it is up to competing maritime nations like Canada and Spain, in this case jostling each other over fish, to appeal to agencies like the Northwest Atlantic Fisheries Organization (NAFO) for mediation -- and fair allocation -- in the disputed areas ("nose and tail") of the Grand Banks. If and when member nations disagree with NAFO pronouncements, they are technically free to reject quotas and set their own (invariably far) higher limits. Even when member nations do acknowledge NAFO rules, enforcement of regulations is toothless and fruitless as there is no penalty. Maclean's reporter Chris Woods has written:

".... In the case of the Estai, Canadian inspectors discovered that the mesh of the Spanish vessel's fishing net was 15mm smaller than the smallest size permitted by NAFO rules. More shocking still: the boat's crew had placed an even smaller-mesh net inside the first, ensuring that no fish escaped its nylon grasp."[184]

In Spanish eyes, net mesh size is almost a moot point. Spaniards from the Basque region (Vascongados) started fishing cod (bacalao) off the Grand Banks so long ago as the early 1500s. Fish tales travel fast, and John Cabot (Giovanni Caboto) had led an English expedition to the far northwestern Atlantic Ocean in 1497, and found the icy waters off the Grand Banks teeming with codfish. The intrepid Basque fishermen since then had sailed every spring in their small wooden ships across the uncharted ocean, for hundreds of nautical miles, spending the short boreal summer catching, salting and drying codfish (Gadus morhua callarias). As a Spanish editorial writer has commented: "For centuries before Canada existed, ships sailed by people of the [Spanish] coast have fished for cod. History supports our right to continue fishing."[185]

Today, Vigo is the fishing capital of Galicia -- and of all Spain; some say of all Europe. Galicia is composed of four political units: La Coruña, Lugo, Orense, and Pontevedra. Vigo is halfway between Pontevedra and the Portuguese border, at the head of the Ría de Vigo. It is only a few miles from where the Río Miño becomes the Minho. As Canadian reporter Bruce Wallace has observed, "Fishing is to Galicia what fishing is to Newfoundland: a pillar of the economy, the fabric of its history, inseparable from its soul."[186] Besides a common Celtic heritage, Galicians and Newfoundlanders share the anxiety that fishing for them is dying as a way of life. They are jointly blamed for overfishing the waters off the Grand Banks, and have a common scorn for politicians, at home and abroad, who would curtail their right to fish for a living. Last and not least, Gallegos and "Newfies" together fear and loathe those rapacious foreign fishing fleets.[187]

As might be predicted, the hue and cry from Canadian politicians and environmentalists have been loud and shrill. Newfoundland Premier Clyde Wells called the Estai's crew "environmental criminals."[188] Arthur Hanson, president of Winnipeg-based International Institute for Sustainable Development said, "The European Union is defending the indefensible."[189] And in Halifax, David Vander Zwaag, director of the marine environmental law programme at Dalhousie University, concluded that "Canada can't stand by and watch an important resource raped."[190] But Spain also had her side of the story. In fact an EU official sympathetic to Canada, during the pre-fish fracas negotiations, voiced the opinion that "Canada did some good organizing and pulled off a sort of coup d'état at NAFO.... But the final agreement was won on a knife-edge, a vote of 8 to 7 that carried no moral weight. We warned the Canadians that it was unsustainable, but [Fisheries Minister] Tobin wouldn't listen. He had rambunctious personal exchanges with other officials, and came across to a lot of people as simply aggressive."[191]

Finally, Spaniards are also concerned about the marine environment, all Anglophone rhetoric to the contrary. Sergio Iglasias Martínez, scientist at the Spanish Oceanography Institute at Vigo, grew up locally, remembers the tension that once existed between scientists and fishermen over fish stock recruitment and conservation. "But that has changed," Iglesias said in an interview with Bruce Wallace of Maclean's magazine:

"They [the fishermen] know they need the advice we [the scientists] give them, and they know that they must fish with care .... Those fish [off the Grand Banks] are so, so deep. This is a very technically driven fleet, and the fishermen feel that it was their expertise that found the grounds so the fish belong to them. Yet they let us do our work on board the ships, and they do care bout conservation."[192]

Meanwhile back at St. John's, the initial phase of the turbot tussle had ended. The Newfoundland Supreme Court, as previously noted, freed the Estai's captain and released the vessel after the owner put up a $500,000 bond. For the time being, Canada had forced the Spanish fleet out of the disputed fishing grounds ("nose and tail") off the Grand Banks. Moreover, following Canadian accusations of Spain's use of illegal nets and hiding fish in hard-to-find nooks and crannies aboard ship, the EU agreed to resume talks regarding the 27,000-ton Greenland halibut quota which NAFO had set for 1995. "There comes a time, when you've made your case in such a compelling fashion that you have to pause and give the other side a chance to catch its breath'", crowed Fisheries Minister Tobin.[193] The latter is a born-and-bred Newfoundlander, and there was a sense of triumph among the Fisheries Minister's fellow Newfies assembled at the St. John's waterfront to quietly watch the Estai slipping homeward through the harbour narrows. The Estai was escorted by the very Canadian fisheries patrol boat, the Cape Roger, that had fired four bursts of machine-gun bullets across her bow, after a high-speed chase on 9 March.[194] The Spanish crew members, proud and unashamed, boarded the Estai, flashing victory signs for the international television news cameras. These men would return another day to fish in their usual and accustomed places.[195]

To the one hundred or so staring Newfies gathered at the waterfront, the present crisis was the fault of the Spanish trawlers, huge factory ships that vacuumed fish from the Atlantic Ocean floor. It was also the fault of politicians at Ottawa, who hadn't cut quotas during the 1980s despite mounting evidence of fish stock depletion. But it was ultimately the fault of the hard-scrabble, extractive inshore fisheries of the Newfoundlanders themselves. Even local boy Brian Tobin has had to admit, "We are not without sin."[196]

On a day trip to Victoria, B.C., along with spouse in early spring 1995, the writer picked up a copy of The Vancouver Sun. The cartoonist, one Peterson, had drawn up an amusing recipe:

"Spanish Fish Mess Stew -

- Catch a mess of fish
- Gut the fishery, strip backbone from EU partners.
- Add ever-decreasing fish stock to Spanish Port.
- Poach over the Canadian 'nose & tail.'
- Turn up heat.
- Stir in cheap Spanish whine. Simmer.
- Mix in a whiff of Canadian grapeshot.
- Add more Spanish whine.
- Bring Fisheries Minister Brian Tobin to a rolling boil by reducing fish stock to depletion.
- Cover and let steam until everything gets flakey [sic].
- Prepare side dish. Eurocrat Relish: Combine jellied brains, mealy-mouthed stuffed shirts and bull whiz.
- Suck a lemon.
- Give peas a chance.
- Negotiate out of hot water.
- Garnish with stale rhetoric and stale capers."[197]

While the Estai was limping -- bloody but unbowed -- home to Spain, tense negotiations (i.e., furious accusations, recriminations) were going on between Canadian and Spanish representatives. The writer here specifies Spanish rather than EU negotiators as cracks were already appearing in the European "Union." Great Britain, true-blue to her daughter country, was quick to sink EU threats against Canada.[198] Although there were warning signs of Anglophone solidarity against Evil Spain (Inquisition, Armada, "Black Legend" Spain), Canada would be supported by Irish, Dutch, German, Swedish and Finnish politicos and fishermen nursing similar grievances.[199] By the latter days of March 1995, the Canada-Spain turbot tempest had become of international interest. On Monday evening, 27 March, the CBC Primetime news programme (aired locally on CBUT, Victoria) featured televised interviews with Spanish officials and Galician fishermen. Two days later, on 29 March, the PBS MacNeil-Lehrer Newshour had Greenpeace-type Professor Paul Burke of the University of Washington and Premier Clyde Wells of Newfoundland as "live" TV guests. Fisheries Minister Tobin, aware of his current celebrity status, took full advantage of his fifteen-minutes of fame as Canada's eco-hero. On Tuesday 28 March, Fisheries Minister Tobin took his act to UN headquarters in mid-town Manhattan. This was to be Brian Tobin's finest hour. As the Canadian Press reported:

"Tobin took a [show]boat full of journalists across the East River in New York City to show off the 5.5-tonne net with undersized mesh that he said was cut loose by the Spanish trawler Estai two weeks ago. He called the net 'an ecological monstrosity'...."

"'We're down now finally to one last, lonely, unloved, unattractive little turbot clinging on by its fingernails to the Grand Banks of Newfoundland,' Tobin told Canadian, American and international reporters."[200]

Brian Tobin had been awaiting this opportunity throughout his political life. Clenching a microphone and addressing the television cameras, the Canadian fisheries minister mock-quoted the very last Greenland halibut as saying, "Someone reach out and save me in this 11th hour as I'm about to go down to extinction."[201] And so it went.

Despite Fisheries Minister Tobin's hyperbole and histrionics, or because of them, letters to the editor in Canada were generally favourable.[202] Meanwhile, during the ongoing Canada-EU talkfests, Fisheries Minister Tobin stayed busy by equipping Canadian patrol boats with warp-cutters. This device would be towed behind the fisheries or coast guard vessel, and could sever the warps, or steel cables, of a wrong-sized mesh net being dragged by a trawler fishing unlawfully. Asserted Minister Tobin, "We retain all the options open to us that we've had since this conflict began. One way or another, there will be an effective enforcement regime. One way or another, Canada will get control of this zone."[203]

By the end of the first week of April 1995, Fisheries Minister Tobin's posing and posturing were paying off for Canada. The fiery fisheries minister enlisted the support of Great Britain's John Major, who told the (British) House of Commons that "Canada is quite right to take a tough line on enforcement."[204] At the UN, an agreement was taking shape that week which would allow for closer monitoring and enforcement of the Greenland halibut catch quota. These were to take place in the disputed areas of the "nose and tail", beyond Canadian jurisdiction outside the Grand Banks. If all went well, the pact would be a clear victory for Canada ... and for North Atlantic fish conservation. In return, Spain, Portugal and other EU nations would receive a larger share of the Greenland halibut harvest than previously allotted them by NAFO (Northwest Atlantic Fisheries Organization).[205]

John Crosbie, former Canadian fisheries minister during the previous Conservative administration, was asked by Maclean's about the waging of "Tobin's War." Crosbie replied, "I am damned sure this is happening despite all the effort [sic] of External Affairs [Canadian state department] to stop it, and Tobin is able to do it because he has [Prime Minister Jean] Chrétien backing him."[205] In another interview Crosbie said, "Canadians are pleased to see Canada using a little muscle to advance its own interests .... It's not just Canada being selfish."[206]

The consensus arrived at with the EU on 15 April 1995 was cause enough for celebration at Ottawa and St. John's, although it meant Canada's struggle to save the northwest Atlantic fish stocks would have to commence in earnest. The bargain awarded 6,000 tons of Canada's 1995 Greenland halibut quota to the EU. But a long-time Canadian proposal, now contained within the latest agreement, permitted the full-time presence of independent inspectors aboard all foreign (i.e., Spanish) fishing vessels. As this same proposal had been urged upon NAFO years previously and then rejected by the EU (i.e., Spain), Canada's victory wasn't entirely Pyrrhic. After all, Canada's actions against the Estai were technically illegal under the Law of the Sea -- even though area rules were still in hot dispute.[207]

There exists no doubt that Canada pinned Spain in the turbot tussle; an especially humiliating defeat for the proud Spanish who had been counting on support from their EU "partners." Moreover EU members United Kingdom and Ireland flew Maple Leaf flags to show solidarity with Canada, and the British House of Commons vocally declared for "Canada, conservation and common sense."[208] Great Britain chose to back her old war-time and Commonwealth allay over her fellow Europeans. "La Leyenda Negra" was once again alive and well in the Anglophone world, although Spain might well have the last laugh.

It is the end of summer 1995, and Spain has taken her turn at the helm of the European Union. One Snr. Esteruelas, fisheries and agriculture counselor at the Spanish Embassy in London, made some apologies and predictions concerning the state of fishing and the marine environment in the North Atlantic. Esteruelas conceded that the EU would soon look at new regulations on control, including monitoring by satellite. During the preceding decade, continued Esteruelas, the Spanish fishing fleet had endured rigourous monitoring of its activities, and, he concluded:

"[T]he inspection carried out by some member states limited itself solely to inspecting Spanish fishing vessels. As of January 1, 1996, the inspections will be extended to the fishing fleets of other member states, which, hopefully, will remove Spain from the headlines of both the British and Canadian press."[209]

Before fitting Fisheries Minister Tobin for an environmental crown of glory, or an Admiral of the Fleet tunic, Canadians should look well to their own seas and coasts. There can be no "wise use" of the marine resource if there is none left. As for Fisheries Minister Tobin, let him have his day in the sun. Consider him -- and Canada -- lucky that the (in)flammable Spanish temper was contained by the narrow constraints of the Eurocrats in Brussels. Brian Tobin will find the free-wheeling, ebullient Alaskans on Canada's other side a decidedly different kettle of fish. (So long, Mr. Tobin, we will meet again in these pages.) In the meanwhile, we North Americans wish the Newfoundlanders and Maritimers, wise in the ways of fish, the best of marine resource management ... with minimal interference from Ottawa.

Fish know no political borders. If the reader travels due south and west by sea from Newfoundland, he will cross the Cabot Strait to Nova Scotia, or the Gulf of St. Lawrence to Prince Edward Island and New Brunswick. The French presence is felt just south of Newfoundland; here are the islets of St. Pierre and Miquelon, an overseas territory of France. Farther west, off the western tip of Nova Scotia, lie the Îsles de la Madeleine. These constitute an integral part of Francophone Province Québec, whose long banks south of Labrador stand guard over the great seaway of the St. Lawrence River. Just below Québec, the two American states of Vermont and Maine reflect a French heritage in their name and population. The state of Maine, contiguous to the province of New Brunswick, is situated across the Bay of Fundy from Nova Scotia's western shore. Maine is by far the largest of the six New England states, and is blessed with an extensive irregular coastline. Along with Massachusetts, "the home of the bean and the cod," Maine is the only (other) New England state with a significant fishing and seafood processing industry. The men from these states, true Yankees and "Down Easters," are the fishing-lore peers of the Maritime "Bluenoses" north of the border. They also share a love of fish and concern for their traditional way of life.

It was during October 1994 at an emotionally-charged meeting in Danvers, Massachusetts, that the New England Fisheries Management Council voted unanimously to impose harsh new restrictions on area fishermen to conserve groundfish stocks. These restrictions would include fishing on fabled Georges Bank and in surrounding waters, once among the world's richest commercial fishing grounds. The Council was responding to the scientific findings of August 1994 which reported rock-bottom levels of Atlantic cod (Gadus morhua), haddock (Melanogrammus aeglefinus), and yellowtail flounder (Pleuronectes ferrugineus). The above-named species are the mainstay of the New England fishery, as the Greenland halibut is the fish of contention farther north. Some areas not liable to closure, such as southern New England waters, might (for the very first time) see a limited groundfish quota for additional species, including witch flounder (Glyptocephalus cynoglossus), American plaice (Hippoglossoides platessoides), and others.[210]

At the October 1994 meeting, angry fishermen attacked both the New England Fisheries Management Council and environmentalist groups for proposing the drastic actions. Inshore fishermen knew that, were Georges Bank grounds closed, offshore fishermen would move back into already-crowded inshore waters. The problem was the old one of too many boats chasing too few fish, although the actual number of vessels fishing has decreased two-thirds since the late 1970s. The loss to the industry has been estimated at about 14,000 jobs. There have already been loud calls by some for a $100 million buy-back programme; more muted voices have speculated that a bail-out would cost much more. Still others have remained hushed when regarding the new fiscal mood in Washington, D.C. $30 million have already been allocated to needy coastal communities; of these dollars some funds have been reserved for fishermen targeting underutilised species like the Atlantic [sea]herring (Clupea harengus).[211]

So exactly how did the Atlantic Northeast Coast fish stocks fall to such a sorry state of depletion? There are several possible answers; among them fleet overcapitalisation, aided and abetted by the U.S. government. Also, according to Ken Coons, executive director of the New England Fisheries Development Association, there was some weird science involved: Certain irregularities in year classes led scientists to miscalculate fish stock biomasses. To quote Ken Coons: "[They] presented a stronger impression of the biomass than was actually there .... [but] [t]here's plenty of blame to go around .... All the participants share in it [the decline] to some extent."[212]

Things have gotten so bad in fact in the Atlantic Northeast Coast fisheries, that two long news-stories on the New England industry were featured on American network television. There are often reports on fish and fishing (although most exclusively focusing on King salmon) broadcast on local Pacific Northwest and British Columbia stations or affiliates, but it is rare indeed that fish stories are transmitted on American network television. Both broadcasts were presented during November 1994.

The first fish news-story was aired on The MacNeil-Lehrer Newshour, 3 November 1994, with Business Correspondent Paul Solman of WGBH-Boston reporting. Mr. Solman interviewed at length several members of the industry in Gloucester, Massachusetts, but (like so many telejournalists) couldn't refrain from injecting his "own" environmentally-correct sophistry:

"Mr. Solman:.... 'In other words, there just might not be enough fish left to maintain the stock. And so we come to the classic economic problem, as true on land and sea and famously described in a 1968 article by Garret Hardin, "The Tragedy of the Commons".... The tragedy of the commons ... is in "the remorseless working of things," i.e., what makes sense for each individual spells ruin for the community as a whole.... [W]hat's true of the commons is just as true of the ocean.... [As] catches become smaller, fishermen work harder to maintain their income. Sonar and other technologies improve their efficiency, and it all just accelerates the remorseless working of things.'"[213]

These are obvious truths easily pronounced by Mr. Solman, but the big-city reporter would encounter some local fisherfolk not as convinced as he. One such individual was a Joe Salisbury, former lobsterman. In response to charges of overfishing the resource, Salisbury said, "It hasn't dropped dramatically, and I think

117

you'd be taking a lot of dollars out of people's pockets if you jump too soon."[214] Solman's counter-response

was typically condescending: "'You see, ... we were more concerned about today's profit than tomorrow's

potential problem, which ... is precisely the mindset the New England Fisheries Council has faced for years.'"[215]

The New England Fisheries Council was created by the Magnuson Act in 1976, to protect and

conserve the Atlantic Northeast Coast fisheries. (The Magnuson Act, dearly familiar to Pacific

Northwesterners and Alaskans, is best known for keeping foreign vessels outside the 200-mile limit.) The

Council itself has closed fishing grounds, set limits on catches and number of days boats may fish, and

increased net-mesh size for juvenile fish escapement. Despite all the steps taken by the Council, harvest

numbers have dwindled. Another individual to challenge the dire predictions of the marine biologists, and

confront Correspondent Solman, was Angela Sanfilippo of the Fishermen's Wives Association:

"'I'm not saying that they're making [it all] up, but ... marine science is an assumption.... We're
working with Mother Nature ... and ... biologists and scientists ... wan·t to take the place of Mother Nature,
it isn't like in the field, we plant the trees or we know how many trees we're cutting, and we can actually see
them, we cannot do that with the ocean.'"[216]

After a high-school teacher had spoken to Solman of proposed boat buy-back plans and stricter fish

allocations, the interviewer again turned to former lobsterman Joe Salisbury and asked, "What do you think?

You're the hard-nosed one here.'" Salisbury shot back, "It sounds like socialized fishing to me. It doesn't set

well.'" Now was the moment for Paul Solman to carpe diem (seize the opportunity), to show his honchos at

WGBH-Boston (as well as engaged public TV viewers) that he was an eco-reporter worth his green. He rose

to the former lobsterman's bait:

.... "And so, the remorseless working of short-term, self-interest continue[s] to take its toll....
[E]conomics does make for adaptation. The Gloucester fleet, running out of prime species like cod, has of
necessity diversified into such unlikely and unprepossessing creatures as the dogfish, a leading export to
England, where it's the secret ingredient in fish and chips. But even dogfish looks good compared to the latest
hot species in Gloucester, the slime eel, which feels about as pleasant as it looks. Koreans skin them and turn
them into wallets. They also eat these suckers, and while slime eel may sound unappetizing to you, remember,
tastes change.... As catches of cod ... have thinned, the price of fish has soared, keeping fishermen afloat...."[217]

The writer does not recall whether or not Mr. Solman paused for breath before his next, brief

interview-exchange. But there would be ample time for him to again pontificate, further disparaging various

sectors of the New England industry before the end of PBS 'Focus--A Fish Story.' And Paul Solman did just

that, summing up with:

"....[The industry's] norms emphasized self-gain, competition, and winning at all costs, rather than trust, shared sacrifice, and the good of the whole. Now, the orthodox, economic response to STUPID overexploitation is limiting access by, in effect, privatizing, granting exclusive fishing rights wherever possible ... because owners it is felt will husband their resources. But as long as people have to work together, the competitive instinct will have to be harnessed'...."[218]

But by whom, Correspondent Solman? Ah -- "the remorseless working of things"! The American or Canadian viewer might well expect such overdrawn n eo-Marxist analysis on a state-run television channel, but as Joe Salisbury (the erstwhile lobsterman) commented earlier in the PBS report, "It sounds like socialized fishing to me. it doesn't set well." No indeed.

The second fish news-story was on ABC News Nightline, 24 November 1994, with Chris Bury reporting on site from Cape Cod and New Bedford, Massachusetts. Like Paul Solman before him in the previous report, Chris Bury interviewed various members of the New England industry. The difference in tone and feel, though, was striking: Bury came out with the same basic, hard, unavoidable facts about a fishing industry in peril, but without pontificating or disparaging its various sectors. 'The Last Harvest' was broadcast on American Thanksgiving Day, so the lead-in by Chris Wallace (Mike Wallace, fils) was appropriately unctious:

"'As you sat down to your Thanksgiving dinner today, you may or may not have thought back to your school lessons about the first Thanksgiving feast, in 1621. After surviving a brutal winter, the Pilgrims of Plymouth Colony invited the Indians who had helped them to share in the riches of their new land, a meal that included not only wild turkeys, but also lobsters, clams and bass'"....[219]

Then came a (thankfully) short litany of woes afflicting the New England fisheries after almost four centuries of plenty: Supplies were almost exhausted, the federal government was expected to close off wide areas of Atlantic Northeast coastal waters to fishing for at least half a year, plus a moratorium loomed that threatened to last much longer. Before the TV cameras focused on Chris Bury up in Massachusetts, Chris Wallace signed off with, "'Tonight we have a Thanksgiving story from Nightline's Chris Bury about fishermen and a government that failed to heed some of the lessons learned by our forefathers centuries ago.'"[220]

But Chris Bury, ABC News, did not adopt a patronising tone or condescending manner with the local fisherfolk he interviewed:

"Chris Bury: (voice over) 'The Luce family[,] like most small hook-and-line fishermen, is bitterly opposed to the coming closures. They are demanding an exemption, blaming the bigger boats, with their giant nets, for wrecking the resource.'
"Jim Luce: 'When they tow on the bottom, they tear up the bottom, and they ruin the habitat that's

on the bottom, and they just tear up the bottom and turn it into a desert, and just vacuum everything right up off the bottom, anything that's alive....'

"Chris Bury: (voice-over) 'The collapse in Atlantic fishing, a long time coming, has been a case study in bungled policy. In the '60s, enormous Soviet and Japanese trawlers, floating factories, swept up tons of prime fish just off the East Coast. Under pressure from the American industry, Congress kicked the foreigners out by extending U.S. territorial waters. Then the government tried to prop up American fishermen by helping them to buy bigger, better boats.'

"Jim Luce: Government made it real easy when they had the Magnuson Act, I think it was in 1976, for anybody to go out and buy a boat, get a boat, low interest loan, the government gave them low interest loans, and so everybody just went out and bought a boat. And a lot of guys didn't just buy one, they bought five."[221]

Later on in Bury's report, still in the vicinity of Cape Cod, the talk turned to the rôle of the New England Fishery Council. Another fisherman, Bill Amarou, observed that fishery regulation by the Council was akin to "the fox guarding the henhouse,"[222] as vested fishing interests governed the Council. But Councilman Philip Haring disagreed, saying that the Council had "...operated within its policy of trying to manage the fishery with a minimum of government intervention, and that, many people think, is a desirable way to allow an industry to operate. That has failed, partly because of the inherent competitiveness of individuals who are all doing their best to catch fish, and together they are causing the decline."[223]

In New Bedford, Massachusetts, home port of the largest fishing fleet on the U.S. East Coast, views were every bit as pessimistic regarding the industry. Mayor Rose Tierney predicted that even a temporary ban on commercial fishing would affect from 2,000 to 8,000 persons dependent on the industry. These include jobs in restaurants, marine supply stores and welding shops, petrol stations, groceries, ice-houses etc. Whither the fishermen themselves? One Yankee skipper, who represented an association of 150 New Bedford skippers, told Nightline that "'We'll probably go down South, South Carolina, North Carolina, Virginia, and catch fluke [a flatfish], or summer flounder and winter flounder. We'll probably go up into the -- go up into Maine and try to catch fish in their -- off their shores.'"[224] This is, for once, a well-founded fear shared by government, marine biologists, environmentalists, and responsible members of the fishing industry: Displaced fleets will plunder away grounds where the fishing is no better.

Chris Bury, ABC News, finished up 'The Last Harvest': "'In the years it will take to rebuild the resource, the fishermen of New England face a stark and historic choice. They can protect the harvest for future generations or, like the American whalers here before them, become just another relic of a bygone era...."[225]

Decisively proving itself pro-fish, the New England Fishery Management Council in late November 1994 made an emergency request of the National Marine Fisheries Service (NMFS) to halt the continued decline of groundfish. The Council's emergency request called for the immediate closure of two groundfish spawning areas at Georges Bank, and points west around the Nantucket Lightship. These areas would also be placed strictly off limits to scallopers, who had hitherto continued to dredge the grounds despite juvenile fish by-catch. In addition, the nets used off southern New England and eastern Long Island (New York), would be increased from the required net-mesh size of 5 1/2 inches to six inches. Fishermen employing net-mesh of less than six inches -- for fish such as whiting, squid, shrimp and mackerel -- would be prohibited from taking groundfish species.[226]

There were further proposals for restrictions by the Council but none as draconian as Amendment 7, which would effectively close down entire sections of Georges Bank to fishing; far larger than the areas planned under the emergency action. The inevitable voices were raised that Amendment 7 be accompanied by a government-funded buy-back programme. The government's answer, in the person of the Commerce Department's director for sustainable development, was that no additional funds were ear-marked for a vessel buy-back programme... but that "$30 million had been made available in assistance to the fishing industry" ... the government would continue to seek out sources of funding via the "government, private sector, and foundation community."[227]

The preceding type of patronising talk by a government official is what a once-proud industry has to hear as insult added to the injury of a renewable resource missing in action. Poor marine resource stewardship and bad fish husbandry by various sectors mean that traditional Yankee fisherfolk will have to genuflect before Big Government, Big Business or "the foundation community" for a cash bail-out. It is the secular equivalent of Esau selling his patrimony to Jacob for a bowl of pottage (Genesis 27). Big Green has been quick to take advantage of the adverse circumstances facing the industry. During the spring of 1995, Greenpeace completed a six-day campaign through New England fishing towns to lobby against soon-to-come government-imposed fishing quotas. A Greenpeace spokesperson said their organisation was trying to save small fishermen from extinction: "'We've seen that whenever (quotas) come into play, corporations become very interested. It's a commodity. It's tradeable, it's saleable, it's leasable.'"[228]

Rhode Island lobsterman and New England Fishery Management Council member, Dick Allen, owns one boat and is for quotas on individual fishermen:

"'It [quotas] offers the best alternative for conserving fisheries' resources while allowing fishermen to continue to run fishing business....

"'Given the state many of our fisheries are in, it's pretty frustrating that people are trying to eliminate what appears to be the best option for the fish and the fisherman.'"[229]

Amen! The very idea that Greenpeace, Inc., is fighting to save small fishermen from extinction is laughable. On the Pacific Coast is an equivalent outfit, Save Our Sealife (SOS), a well-heeled sport lobby endeavouring to fool the fishing public by masquerading as environmentalists. Let us hope, pray and act now to insure that the North Pacific fisheries resource never sinks so low as that of New England. There already exists bad blood between Seattle-based trawlers and Alaska-based fishermen and processors, waiting to be overheated, with the situation exploited by outside sources both domestic and foreign. With good marine resource stewardship and wise [use of] fish husbandry by all industrial sectors, the tragedy of [the] New England [oceanic commons] can be avoided. This not only makes good economic sense, but will generate confidence and encourage independence in the North Pacific industry. Self-confidence and self-sufficiency, in turn, will keep rapacious outside corporations outside, intrusive government at bay, and Big Green from further empowering itself by driving eco-political wedges between the various industry sectors. Let us hope, pray, and act now so that the North Pacific industry learns from New England's tragic example, thereby avoiding the same pitfall - while there is still time.

Section B: Century 21 -- Time for Big Green Oceanic Regulation?

"[We are] planetary citizens in a global village."
- Dr. Werner Quast of Peninsula College, Port
Angeles, Washington

It has been the eco-fashion, since the late 1960s, to breathlessly invoke "the tragedy of the commons" whenever the subject of private property or freedom of the seas is brought up. In this chapter on environmentalism, the tragedy of the commons has already been name-dropped no less than three times. This writer first used the eco-phrase in Part II to illustrate a point satirist P.J. O'Rourke made in <u>All the Trouble in the World</u>. In the former Czechoslovakia, one Dr. Mucha, of Children of the Earth, told O'Rourke that ecological damage to the Czech landscape was "not a problem of the planned or open economy but a problem of ownership. Everything belonged to all of us and to nobody."[230] This writer had then noted that therein lay the true tragedy of the commons; meaning that privately-owned and tended cabbage gardens invariably produced more per hectare than state-run farms.

Fisheries Minister Brian Tobin of Canada was next to mention the tragedy of the commons, but in the way it was originally meant. In an interview with <u>Maclean's</u> magazine, Fisheries Minister Tobin blithely explicated the reason for [i.e., Spain's] lawlessness on the high seas: "No nation has authority to set the rules, and more importantly, no nation has authority to enforce the rules. Therefore there are no rules, and it's a free-for-all.... It's the tragedy of the commons."[231]

The "commons" in pre-Industrial Revolution Great Britain were the common lands on which "cotters and villeins" (villagers) were permitted to let their livestock freely graze. Over time the herds waxed fat and multiplied until the commons yielded no more pasturage. Some marine scientists maintain that, in a parallel manner, the commercial overexploitation of oceanic commons is the chief reason for [melo]dramatic declines in ten of the world's fourteen main food-fisheries. With a fast-diminishing fish resource being hunted and harvested by ever smarter and faster boats, the oceanic commons are literally becoming a battleground. Analyses have been made in this work of the destructive high-seas driftnets in the Pacific, and the turbot imbroglio between Canada and Spain in the Atlantic. In the South China Sea, China and Vietnam have exchanged gunfire over fishing rights surrounding the Spratl y Islands.[232] Pasturage in the oceanic commons is shrinking too; another tragedy of the commons.

Business correspondent Paul Solman of WGBH-Boston was the third person in this study to utter the dreaded T-phrase: "'The tragedy of the commons,'" he explained quoting Garret Hardin, "is in 'the remorseless working of things', i.e., what makes sense for each individual spells ruin for the community as a whole...."[233] Mr. Solman's version of the tragedy of the (oceanic) commons is naturally very similar to that of like-minded environmentalists and ecologists. Garret Hardin, Professor Emeritus of Human Ecology and an originator

of the T-phrase, declared in 1968:

"Likewise, the oceans of the world continue to suffer from the survival of the philosophy of the
commons. Maritime nations still respond automatically to the shibboleth of the 'freedom of the seas.'
Professing to believe in the 'inexhaustible resources of the oceans', they bring species after species of fish and
whales closer to extinction."[234]

The above is the human ecologist's Great Truth on the oceans in a clamshell.

Throughout 1991 when this writer was researching environmentalism, Garret Hadin and the T-phrase

kept reappearing. "The Tragedy of the Commons" sounded so eco-pessimistic -- yet so convincingly true --

that this writer (to read the seminal article) obtained Managing the Commons, edited by Garret Hardin and

John Baden, a collection of essays on environmental policy by various academicians. The compilation was

divided into three parts: The first contained Hardin's piece, along with lesser academic lights referring to Marx

and Malthus; in the second part the T-phrase became politicised in collegiate-rhetorical terms; Part III was

a flat-out Ivory Tower cheer for the Collective Action-Common Pool management of the commons, both

terrestrial and marine. What had begun as a set of verifiable premises, had ended as a series of nonsensical

conclusions. But Managing the Commons was assembled during the late 1970s, a time of disco, chicken

détente, Jimmy Carter, and (early pc) neo-Marxism at the universities. To prove the point, the reader may

experience the language of Colin W. Clark in "The Economics of Exploitation":

"A prerequisite for effective regulation is a clear understanding of the basic reasons for
overexploitation, and in this regard the outstanding article by Hardin on 'the tragedy of the commons' has been
a positive asset, even though economists have long been aware of the common property problem in the
fisheries. Indeed, in concentrating their attention on the problems of competitive overexploitation of fisheries,
economists appear to have largely overlooked the fact that a corporate owner of property rights in a biological
resource might actually prefer extermination to conservation, on the basis of maximization of profits. In this
article I argue that overexploitation, perhaps even to the point of actual extinction, is a definite possibility
under private management of renewable resources."[235]

After reading this kind of virtual eco-"hate speech", one wonders if Colin W. Clark had ever been to

Newfoundland or Alaska, had ever spoken to the fisherfolk or seafood processors of those places. Further

on in the essay, to assure academic readers and economic students of his political solidarity with "the

impoverished and the powerless," Clark commented: "....Yet the most spectacular and threatening

developments of today, such as the reduction of the whale stocks and of the demersal fisheries on the Grand

Banks, can by no means be attributed to impoverished local fishermen. On the contrary, it is the large, high-powered ships and the factory fleets of the wealthiest nations that are now the real danger...."[236]

Not all "impoverished local fishermen" would bite on Colin Clark's angle. Greenpeace tried trolling the same solidarity lure before fishermen like Rhode Island lobsterman and New England Fishery Management member Dick Allen and others recorded earlier in this report, and they weren't biting. The "us versus them" appeal didn't work in 1994 and shouldn't have worked in 1973. The world has been politically transformed since the 1970s -- the bloody massacre at Tiananmen Square, the tearing down of the Berlin Wall, the total disintegration of the Soviet Union -- with the utter, absolute discrediting of Marxism-Leninism as gospel and creed. Communist dictators such as Nicolae Ceauşescu of Romania and Todor Zhivkov of Bulgaria are now dead or gone; a few remnants of their failed philosophy are scattered among Western academicians and radical Greens. The latter, like the proverbial watermelon, are Green on the outside, Red on the inside. As a consequence, Colin Clark's final thoughts to his discourse on economic rent came as no surprise:

"There is no reason to suppose that the fishing corporations themselves desire regulations designed to conserve the world's fisheries. The governments of the world will fail in their responsibility to their citizens unless they succeed in formulating effective international conservation treaties in spite of pressures from these corporations."[237]

The surprise comes that such political trash-talk is still heeded by certain economists in 1995. It is more ironic still that some modern Greens still envision Big Government as having answers to solving today's environmental problems. After the rolling up of the 45 year-old Iron Curtain in Eastern Europe, the stark evidence of the devastated industrial landscape shocked spoiled Westerners, accustomed to whining about the ecological evils of Capitalism. As futurist John Naisbitt recently quipped, ".... Compared to, say the steel mills and coal mines of Copsa-Mica in Romania, U.S. Steel is a veritable Sierra Club."[238] Before returning to the topic of managing the (oceanic) commons, academic Greens and professional eco-activists should be often reminded that it is foundational and corporate funds which in large part finance their investigative studies and divisive works; often their daily bread and very sustenance.

The next essay specifically dealing with fisheries in Managing the Commons was contributed by James A. Wilson, "A Test of the Tragedy of the Commons." Wilson believed that oceanic fisheries particularly seemed to be subject to Hardin's hypothesis, due to the lack of control over the resource in the freedom of the seas tradition. Wilson chose as his paradigm the inshore lobster fishery off the state of Maine. There, Wilson appeared horrified to relate, small areas of the fishery had become "effectively appropriated by groups of fishermen for their own use...."[239] To Wilson, the lobstermen had accrued to themselves extralegal group property rights in the very midst of the oceanic commons. Furthermore, Wilson pursued, "In each case in which such property rights exist, the fishermen have chosen to exercise their rights of property through both the exclusion of other men from their property and controls on the fishing effort of the group itself."[240]

A fisheries advocate might have responded to Wilson by asking: If the first group of lobstermen were indeed pot-fishing in "oceanic common property", how then could they have been assuming "extra legal group property rights"? This writer, who grew up in a fiercely-competitive lobster fishing area of southeastern Norway, could answer that it is in the nature of the fishery itself; the early-bird fisherman traps the lobster. James Wilson went on to theorise: ...."[T]he common property nature of the resource creates a situation in which the individual fisherman has no incentive to conserve resources, since his inability to withhold the resource from others in the future means that he will not be able to reap the rewards of his conservationist (waiting) action."[241]

Once again an entire sector of the industry has been deprecated. Hitherto it has been the fishing company or seafood corporation which has incurred academic and environmentalist ire. In a former essay it was the "impoverished local fisherman" (Colin W. Clark) who was worthy, as victim, of our empathy. To bolster his argument, James Wilson illustrated the exact nature of the Maine lobster pot-fishery as exemplar:

"Inshore area lobsters are caught in wooden traps which are baited and left on the bottom for a period of one day to a week or more. Each trap, or sometimes a trawl of traps, is marked by buoys in the distinctive colors of each fisherman. These characteristics of the fishery -- almost daily access to the fishing area and the ready identification of gear -- have made possible the practice of a kind of territoriality by the fisherman."[242]

This writer has not personally experienced the Maine lobster pot-fishery, but remembers in the Norway of his youth the fists, oars, or threats thereof if a fishing group (usually a family) became too territorial. The fisherfolk in the Old Country would settle these affairs themselves, or in an absolute crisis call for outside mediation. (The autumn lobster pot-fishery in Hvaler, Norway, predates that of Maine by several centuries.) And surely this is the purpose of the New England Fisheries Management Council -- to settle fixed-gear conflicts and fishing ground disputes of the sort analysed, somewhat cynically, by James A. Wilson. This type of territorial strife may even be seen in the Bible, where the livestock herders of Abram and Lot fought for turf (Gen.13:6-11). The general answer then, as now, was to seperate the warring factions, and then to either divide extant -- or designate alternate - pasturage. If there were no additional green pastures left to graze, incoming herders had to move on with their flocks to lands able to sustain them. If controls on fishing are to be instituted on the inshore Maine lobster pot-fishery, which is limited to a specific marine commons, the "major cost will be in terms of the exclusion of potential entrants into the fishery."[243] A relevant answer to James Wilson's particular question was provided in June 1995 by Rhode Island lobsterman Dick Allen: The local enforcement of quotas on individual fishermen. Here, at last, was a modicum of agreement.

In Managing the Commons Part III, Robert L. Bish contributed the essay, "Environmental Resource Management: Public or Private?" To his credit, Bish tried transference: "....[E]ven if one has a right to fish in a common fishery forever, it might not be wise to limit one's own fishing in order to preserve the fishery if others do not do likewise. Even if all fishermen agree to limit their activities, a fisherman would come along in the future and negate the agreement by overfishing."[244] Again, the solution to overfishing and to assure wise management (and use) of a finite though renewable resource should lie with the local fisheries management council, run by and for fisherfolk and other industry sectors. A counter query to the academic authors of Managing the Commons could be: Why would members of the fishing and seafood industry willfully exterminate the very raw materials giving them sustenance?

And so we return full-circle to Garret Hardin, an originator of the T-phrase, who closed out Managing the Commons with the unoriginal and anticlimactic essay, "Living on a Lifeboat." In his summing up, Hardin issued dire warning to the fishing industry:

"The fish populations of the oceans are exploited as commons, and ruin lies ahead. No technological invention can prevent this fate: in fact, all improvements in the art of fishing merely hasten the day of complete ruin. Only the replacement of the system of the commons with a responsible system can save oceanic fisheries."[245]

When Garret Hardin, writing during the 1970s foresaw ultimate ruin for the fisheries, he also forecast technological inventions and innovations in the "art of fishing" ... but no improvements in the awareness or shifts in attitude of the industry regarding the finite marine resource. With typical academic arrogance, Hardin assumed that only a "replacement of the system of the commons" [i.e., government nationalisation with a "responsible system" of public waters] would be able to "save oceanic fisheries" for posterity. Only a powerful central bureaucracy, so beloved of neo-Marxist environmentalists, can exert the brute controls necessary to physically police the oceanic commons. Alaska fishermen, highly self-reliant and independent-minded, would be highly resistant to a federal oceanic force of armed planeteers telling them where, and where not, to fish. "Yet," Christian author Michael S. Coffman has written, "a central bureaucracy -- where they [the Greens] can exert tremendous influence -- is exactly what eco-leadership demands by passing increasingly restrictive laws."[246]

The aforenamed Coffman and other conservative commentators have linked the Tragedy of the Commons with the Law of the Commons,[247] but, although closely related, are not one and same concept. In the mind of Garret Hardin et al., unregulated economic activity in a terrestrial or oceanic commons spells doom for a public resource. Hence the tragedy of the commons concerns use, abuse, and resource regulation. The law of the commons, on the other hand, involves production and ownership. Under the law of the commons, no one owns anything as theoretically everything is owned in common. Therefore, in free-market thinking, there is no pride of ownership or motivation for excellence. The very vim-and-vigour, then, of free-for-all Alaska men fishing in the oceanic commons, is the exact reverse of listless Russian peasants toiling in communal fields. The apple-to-orange differences here are (1) pastoral or marine commons with readily available or harvestable produce and forage; and (2) agriculture or aquaculture, both of which entail human labour and nurture for yield in settled areas over specific time periods. As both agriculture and aquaculture have justifiably flourished best under private ownership, the questions of ownership and protection have been evidentially answered (although not to Western academicians). Coffman has observed:

"The collapse of the Soviet Empire has proven that the law of the commons is not only disastrous for its people, but also for the environment. Yet, our eco-leaders are bent on nationalizing all private land."[248] [Coffman should have added "...and open seas" to his sentiment.]

There remain the thorny problems of use, abuse, and regulation. During the 1970s, Garret Hardin and co. saw visions of the imminent catastrophe in the commons; unavoidable save for massive governmental regulation. The Ivory Towers of Académe felt that regulating the oceanic commons should not be entrusted to fishing and seafood industry members. In the 1970s of Jimmy Carter, the shared eco-belief was that U.S.

federal nationalisation alone could save the American (oceanic) commons from extinction. But standing in the U.S. government's path to federalisation of both lands and seas is the concept of Common Law, American property rights with deep roots in the English Magna Carta.[249] Although these rights are land-based, the common law concept may be applied to the seas as well: The freedom to fish the oceanic commons, without infringing on the rights of others to do so ... and wise use of the resource, without endangering the marine environment. As Michael Coffman has summarised, "Common law has been, and will continue to be, the best and cheapest protector of America's environment....[250] The principle behind free market environmentalism is exactly the same as the common law approach...[251] Common law and free market environmentalism are the only common ground on which all willing Americans can find solutions."[252]

As there has to be foodfish available for the consuming public, there has to be commercial fishermen to harvest the marine resource, and processors to manufacture seafood from the harvested resource. Wise use of the marine resource ensures a renewable harvest the next fishing season. One would expect that by the mid-1990s, in a post-Communist world, the lessons taught by both concepts of the Commons would have been learned by private and public sectors alike. The formerly free-wheeling Pacific Coast fisheries, so over-confident during the 1970s and '80s, now appear more cautious. Perhaps their Atlantic Coast counterparts have really learned their wise use lesson this time around. But the public sector hasn't changed. It still thinks, sounds, and acts in ways concerning regulation as it always has.

Was that "Fire and Rain" balding rock star, James Taylor, this writer saw on television the other night (25 September 1995)? If so, James Taylor appeared on behalf of the Center for Marine Conservation. If this was true, Elliott A. Norse, chief scientist and fundraiser for the CMC, has climbed high on the ladder-rungs of eco-High Society. This is one ecologist who personally interests the writer for several reasons, not the least being that Elliott Norse edited the thought-provoking and well-researched Global Marine Biological Diversity: A Strategy for Building Conservation into Decision Making.[253] A rough draught copy was presented for this writer's perusal by a Bay Foundation director in late 1992. This writer felt a strange, previously-experienced ambivalence on reading the draught -- agreement with all the premises but none of the conclusions. Ecologist Elliott Norse, author of Ancient Forests of the Pacific Northwest, had certainly done his homework well, thoroughly covering oceanic commons and private rights, national sovereignty and international jurisdiction, fishery treaties and the Law of the Sea. But the obligatory theme of impending eco-doom was always there, as was the tragedy of the commons. Norse smartly used Garret Hardin's dreaded T-phrase as an oceanic obversal of the pastoral commons. This writer recalls thumbing through Global Marine Biological Diversity with mounting exasperation at the obviously implied conclusion: Nothing less than complete internationalisation of the earth's oceans could save marine biological diversity.[254] But this was back in 1992, and this writer had merely filed away the Elliot Norse rough draft as just another environmentally-correct tract.

Two years later, in the waning months of 1994, this writer was sent a Bay Foundation folder for an upcoming biodiversity conference. The cover showed a fragile, acqua biosphere superimposed on a harsh cobalt background. Emblazoned in large white letters across the folder's top half was, 'THE LIVING PLANET IN CRISIS: BIODIVERSITY SCIENCE AND POLICY.' At the bottom, in far smaller letters, was printed: 'An International Conference -- Presented and Organized by American Museum of Natural History -- Center for Biodiversity and Conservation -- March 9 and 10, 1995.' Inside the folder, on (corresponding) page 3, was the line-up for Part II of 'THE LIVING PLANET IN CRISIS'. The scheduled topic was "What are the implications of biodiversity science for our global future?" The speakers included eco-alarmist Norman Myers of Oxford, England, and ... Elliott Norse of the Center for Marine Conservation. Elliott Norse had finally "arrived" in environmentalist High Society. Conference contributors to the Center for Biodiversity and Conservation numbered among them: The Bay Foundation, Condé Nast Publications, Origins Natural Resources, Inc. - Estee Lauder Companies, The Rockefeller Brothers Fund., Inc., and the Geraldine R. Dodge Foundation. Despite their radically-chic rhetoric, self-imaged eco-mavericks like Norman Myers and Elliott Norse are supported by mega-corporate foundation funds. Part III of the Conference, "The [r]elationship between biodiversity science, policy change and institutional decision making" featured speakers from heavyweight, usual-suspect organisations such as the Smithsonian Institution, United Nations, and World Bank.[255]

After reading Managing the Commons, the lasting impression made on this writer was a call by Garret Hardin and others to nationalise [i.e., replacement ... with a "responsible system"] American coastal waters, thereby controlling the fisheries and supervising the offshore environment. On looking again through Global Marine Biological Diversity, this writer beheld a rough blueprint to effectively internationalise the earth's oceans. To internationalise, in Elliott Norse's connotation, meant the exact opposite of freedom of the seas; it meant a global body [i.e., the United Nations] would have absolute jurisdiction over all the planet's waterways ... just part of a horrifying globalisation imagined in the prescient lyrics of Beatle John Lennon ("Imagine ... when the world is one"). On national sovereignty, Norse expressed his view that:

"[S]elf-government is one of the oldest, most entrenched, and most cherished concepts that humans have established.... In this century, as the global economy has pulled nations into a web of economic interdependence, international treaties have encroached on national sovereignty by regulating trade, human rights, and labor practices. To partake in the advantages of the global market, nations have been compelled to comply, lest they incur sanctions such as embargoes or other trade restrictions.

"Since the 1972 Stockholm Conference, increasing environmental degradation has stimulated growing awareness of the need for regional and global cooperation, and a new round of treaties have [sic] been proposed to regulate nations' environmental impacts on their neighbors and the rest of the biosphere. The Earth is increasingly seen as a finite, self-contained, interacting ecological and economic system."[256]

This writer was in his native Norway at the time of the 1972 Stockholm Conference, and is reminded of seeing Canadian-Coloradan Maurice F. Strong, the "Custodian of the Planet", chairing the Conference on Swedish TV (SR-1). Only two decades later, nations resisting environmental agreements are finding increased social, political, and economic sanctions imposed on them by world bodies.... "China's 'right' to burn its huge coal reserves, Japan's 'right' to kill whales, and many other sovereign 'rights' are challenged by other nations whose interests are affected by these activities."[257] As would be inferred by the gist of his preceding statements, Norse had high hopes for the future clout of the Law of the Sea: "The UN Convention on the Law of the Sea (UNCLOS III) is the current authority on what constitutes sovereignty over the marine environment. Although not in force yet [1992] largely because of opposition from [seabed] mining interests in the USA, most of UNCLOS III policies are now part of International Law.[258] But the Law of the Sea III became enforceable starting from 16 November 1994, when Guyana became the 60th nation to ratify the Treaty.[259] Time will tell how an enforceable UNCLOS III will affect American and Canadian national sovereignty over their coastal seas. Back in 1992, Norse expressed his aspirations for national sovereignty's pending demise:

"Slowly, haltingly, but unmistakably, nations are yielding sovereignty in some areas where they cannot afford to ignore the marine environmental commons of other nations. However, the world's need to acquire scientific knowledge is less obvious than the need to stop pollution or depletion of species, but like those needs, it will be more effectively fulfilled as nations emerge from the cover of nationalism."[260]

Eco-alarmist Dr. Norman Myers has lamented "Our earth is one, our world is not!"[261] Inventor of the communications satellite Arthur C. Clarke has pronounced his longing for... "[W]hen we have the global family [i.e., United Earth], we will no longer need the United Nations. But until then...."[262] Harvard Fellow Ronnie Dugger recently (June 1995) told The New York Times that the United Nations should form a military [blue-helmeted planeteer] force composed of volunteer peacekeepers, financed by dues-paying, card-carrying, global citizen-members. If that wouldn't work, Dugger suggested that members of non-governmental organisations (NGOs) like Greenpeace could become citizen-members of their own inter[supra]national agency, then [s]elect a [i.e., global] parliament to pass and enforce [environmental] laws through a voluntary military ["Rainbow Warrior"] force.[263] And why not? In the very words of U.N. Secretary-General Boutros Boutros-Ghali: "Underlying the rights of the individual and the rights of peoples is a dimension of universal sovereignty that resides in all humanity and provides all peoples with legitimate involvement in issues affecting the world as a whole."[264]

If the United Nations is unable to mobilise, or Greenpeace cannot muster, the eco-force de frappe necessary to impose the global authority called for by Harvard Fellow Dugger and the like-minded, there is a little-known world body that has been waiting in the wings since 1959. For that was the year during which the World Constitution and Parliamentary Association (WCPA) was founded in Lakewood, Colorado. According to Gary Kah, the author of En Route to Global Occupation, the main figures behind the WCPA's organisation and development have been one Philip Isely and his wife, Margaret.[266] In 1992, when Kah's exposé was published, Philip Isely (commencing 1966) held the position of secretary-general of the WCPA executive cabinet with Margaret Isely serving as treasurer.[267] From the time of its founding in 1959, the WCPA has assembled a Provisional World Parliament which, since 1982, has already held three sessions, adopting a number of World Legislative Acts. At the last session, held in 1987, a Provisional World Pr[a]esidium and World Cabinet were appointed to act as executive branch for the emerging global government. Despite all these activities, Kah wondered how "... the WCPA has found time to oversee the drafting of a world constitution and lobbying to get this constitution ratified by national parliaments and governments, many of which are already dominated or strongly influenced by members of these same groups."[268] The final campaign for ratifying the WCPA constitution was officially launched during the spring of 1991 at the World Constituent Assembly in Portugal.

Conspiracy theorist Kah's writing reflected some urgency at both the stealth tactics and membership affiliations of the WCPA. This writer, unlike Kah, readily admits to never having heard of the World Constitution and Parliamentary Association, much less been aware of its political actions. Author Kah attributed the WCPA's secrecy strategy for its low public profile -- the WCPA has preferred "collaborating" or "networking" for change rather than "conspiring" to describe its efforts. In the quiet meantime, the WCPA has accomplished getting its legislative acts and its global constitution copyrighted, thereby seeking protection under the U.S. Constitution. This is the exact document, Kah warned, the WCPA is trying to eventually supplant. Also in the WCPA's agenda were plans for a ten-region world-ruling system, a new international monetary system, environmental reasons for why global governance is required for planetary survival ... all proposals similarly propounded by the Club of Rome.[269]

The WCPA's rank and file membership and affiliates read as a global <u>Who's Who</u>. Kah named the Rt.Hon. Tony Benn, U.K. (MP, fmr. Cabinet Minister and Chm. Labour Party), and the Hon. Ramsey Clark, U.S.A. (lawyer, frm. Attorney General), as among thirteen co-vice presidents.[270] And several big-name back-up troops appeared in the form of "honorary sponsors": "Out of 150 Honorary Sponsors listed on one of the letterheads, a total of thirty-four were identified with the United Nations; fourteen came from the area of commerce, banking or finance; and eight were Nobel Laureates."[271] Many distinguished and well-known monnikers appeared on the WCPA letterhead, among them (some deceased by 1995) were: Mayor Wilson Goode, Dr. Glenn Seaborg, Archbishop Desmond Tutu, Dr. Linus Pauling, Edward Asner, Alexander Dubček, Dr. Anatoly Gromyko, Oliver Stone, and John Hersey.[272] The list of Honorary Sponsors was replete with religious, academic, political, professional and corporate élites.

Gary Kah became involved with the WCPA during the spring of 1987 through an acquaintance, whom had been invited to attend the third session of the Provisional World Parliament. This was to convene in June

1987 at Miami Beach. Kah filled out an application form, portraying himself "as a globalist with New Age leanings."[273] Although his registration was approved, Kah didn't attend for personal reasons but continued to receive WCPA print-outs. As a political conservative, Kah became increasingly concerned with the blatant One World propaganda contained in the documents. As an evangelical Christian, Kah was troubled by the WCPA's roster of "spiritual leaders" scheduled to speak at the Provisional World Parliament. Rather than being "reverends" or "fathers" from the Western tradition, they were all "yogis" or "swamis" from the Eastern. Indeed, Yogi Shanti Swaroop of India served (1992) as the WCPA's official "spiritual liaison."[274] Here, anyway, was proof of the WCPA's religious motivation and New Age connection.

To obtain additional literature Kah remained in contact with the WCPA, both by written correspondence and telephone, until the late winter of 1991. Still on the WCPA's mailing list, Kah received an information packet sent to everyone in the network. The accompanying letter requested that all WCPA members should help prepare for the coming meeting of the World Constituent Assembly (held later that year at Lisbon, Portugal), to launch the final ratification campaign for the world constitution.[275] The WCPA missive explained that this could be done in three ways:

"1) By getting the signatures of seven hundred or more people on election petitions approved by the Preparatory Committee, 2) by publishing advertisements that promoted the event in periodicals with a combined circulation of twenty-five thousand or more, or 3) by getting an organization of five thousand or more members to ratify the Call to the 1991 World Constituent Assembly and to accept the Constitution for the Federation of the Earth."[276]

In all good conscience Gary Kah believed, that both as a conservative and as evangelical, he could go no further without actually promoting the WCPA. And attending WCPA meetings would amount to two-fold hypocrisy. Kah considered telling all -- even Christian witnessing -- to WCPA founder and secretary-general, Philip Isely. Instead, he submitted a formal letter of resignation, and then sat down and wrote a complete account in En Route to Global Occupation.[277] What finally convinced Kah that the WCPA posed a political threat to national independence conceptually, was the association's interlocking with other powerful globalist societies. Otherwise the WCPA could be deemed a mere paper-tiger, a phantastical experiment in global government by Philip and Margaret Isely. For this reason Kah -- a conspiracy theorist vis-à-vis a New World Order -- felt compelled to bring to public light the "deception" of the WCPA.[278]

If the list of "honorary sponsors" were individually not impressive enough, the organisations collectively interconnected to the WCPA looked like a <u>Who's Who</u> of globalism: World Union, the World Council of Churches (WCC), the World Future Society served as an organisational triumvirate heading up a host of satellite bodies. World Union joined with World Goodwill in 1961. (World Goodwill, as every good conspiracy theorist knows, was a creation of Lucis [formerly Lucifer] Trust.) The president of the ultra-liberal, oecumenical WCC in 1992 had been a WCPA "honorary sponsor" since 1975. The World Future Society [a front for the WCPA] has long been a mentor for annual symposia, among them Worldview 84 in 1984, essentially a meeting for instigating global government.[279] The WCPA emerged from Worldview 84 as the head usher for the coming New World Order. According to Kah, "hundreds" of organisations were represented at Worldview 84, and therefore would have had to be aware of the WCPA's agenda. Some of these institutions included: Baha'i, the Brookings Institute, Club of Rome, Fellowship of Inner Light, Global 2000 Project, International Association of Educators for World Peace, Planetary Initiative, the International Monetary Fund, The World Bank, and other usual suspects. Corporations which have backed the World Future Society (i.e., the WCPA) are AT&T, GE Corp., GM Inc., IBM Ltd., Ortho Pharmaceutical Corp., Xerox Corp. and more of the like.[280] This reader might ask, With forces arrayed behind it such as these, how could the WCPA not win? Were Gary Kah's fears justified?

This writer is also a conservative and evangelical, although not a conspiracy theorist as Gary Kah. Never far out of touch from the church or the academy, the writer finds the networking between the New Age religious and academic élites with political and corporate globalists in high places to be truly worrisome. If Kah believed the WCPA to be just another potential UN, his book would be just another conspiracy-theory polemic scribbled by a wild-eyed Christian Rightist. But this writer is assuredly more open to heeding cautionary tales of globalist intentions, after sitting for more than three years on the board of a foundation with a multi-million dollar endowment. This writer, however, has not penned the preceding pages as a specific indictment of the WCPA per se, but as prime example of globalist thinking. If the nations of the earth are to be subjected to an eventual New World Order, they will be by the existing UN; armed blue-helmeted planeteers already in place. The United Nations would absorb the World Constitution and Parliamentary

Association as surely as Turner Broadcasting System was taken over earlier this year (1995) by itself-merged Time[-Life] Warner [Brothers]. It is globalist mind-set that is frightening, if not the WCPA in particular.

What has been most instructive about En Route to Global Occupation was the WCPA fine blueprint for global governance. The Provisional World Parliament could be described as the literal mouthpiece of the WCPA. Under the charter heading (Exhibit 01), 'Design and Action for a New World', the Provisional World Parliament spelled out "Eleven Major Bills Enacted into World Law...,"[281] two of which would have greatly interested all sectors of the North American fishing and seafood industry: "Bill #3, for the Ownership, Administration and Development of Oceans and Seabeds of Earth as the Common Heritage of the People of Earth.... Bill #9, to Protect Life and Nature on Planet Earth, and to Create a Global Ministry of Environment." Exhibit 02 of Gary Kah's primary sources showed a 'Partial List of World Problems'... (which require a world legislature and a world government to devise and implement adequate solutions). After the given calls for global disarmament [except, of course, for the global government] and global redistribution of wealth, this writer counted fully eighteen (nearly one third) of the forty-nine "world problems" as having to do with the environment -- atmospheric, terrestrial, and marine. For our purposes here, Problems 23 and 24 were most pertinent:

"23. Ocean pollution which threatens Earth's fish and oxygen supplies. Pollution of oceans from transport, drilling and pumping oil: How long can this go on before the death of the oceans?
"24. Claims by nations of 200 miles off shore (the exclusive economic zone under proposed law of seas) which contain most of easily accessible ocean resources."[282]

To preside over all this governance of the Federation of the Earth was the projected 28-tiered World Administration, with departments such as Genetics, Disarmament and War Prevention, Health and Nutrition. [World Problem 18: "Use of land to produce tobacco, alcoholic beverages ... sugar, and to satisfy meats diets...." (sic). There would surely ensue the absolute proscription of all tobacco and alcohol products. But if the New Millenial Managers of William Irwin Thompson were to take charge, "heavy grass" and recreational drugs would certainly be legalised for the New Élites ... with soma tablets possibly sanctioned for the compu-stupid lumpen-proletariat.] Also for our purposes here, there were envisioned departments of World Resources, Environment and Ecology, Oceans and Seabeds.[283] The WCPA, to this writer, is simply wishful-thinking UN encore, and as such poses no political threat to conceptual national sovereignty despite Gary Kah's thoughtful fears. But like Winston Smith in George Orwell's <u>1984</u>, this writer peers into the future searching for the Ministry of Love and the Thought Police but hasn't seen them ... yet.

It is Harvest Sunday 1995 at Holy Trinity Lutheran Church in Port Angeles, Washington. Boxes, bags, and tin-cans of mostly processed foods line the inner church walls, parallel to the outer pews up to the chancel. A box near this seated writer contains Betty Crocker's "Super Moist Devil's Food" -- damp, dark chthonian cake doesn't augur well for HTLC. There are five minutes left until show-and-tell time; the eleven a.m. "New Song" service. Upfront a weedy, hairy young man is bent over, plugging in an electric violin. (This is, after all, an Electric Church). A bright-blue huge-handled Afro-comb protrudes from the young man's back pocket, under the Levi Dockers' label. Hovering above the communion rail is the assistant pastor, his great, balding, down-covered head bobbing like a child's big pink balloon. In his own mind's-eye VCR, the writer fast-backs and fast-forwards to reverend <u>Doofus washingtonus,</u> at Pacific Lutheran University not so long ago, being hit on the noggin by a giant frisbee over and over again. The thirty-something assistant pastor is a big "Guns R Us" fetishist, his Jimmy Carter-peace and Habitat for Humanity love-talk notwithstanding. He had given the sermon on "relationships" last Sunday, with '90s psychobabble worthier of the Great Oprah rather than the Great God.

The "New Song" service commences with a New Song (ca. 1972) of praise with lyrics better suited to the mystic, sweet communion of gay men with the departed Judy Garland than of Christians with their Lord. At last it was time for the sermon ... What flaming foolishness would it be this week? The writer was not to be disappointed: "Repentance just means being found." The sermon's biblical text was the Parable of the Prodigal Son (Luke 15:11-32). But the senior pastor, as was his wont, got it all wrong. Forgiveness by father or God without correlative contrition on part of son or Man is wasted, and renders the repentance process valueless. The father must forgive his son; the son must repent of his sin. If the father doesn't forgive the son, the son might not repent and will possibly sin again. If the father forgives but the son doesn't truly repent, the son shall probably sin again. The mundane father in modern Wellness parlance has become "an enabler." But the celestial Father, by definition, can never be an enabler to sin.

Surely the senior pastor, a parent, knew this too? The writer himself had learned this lesson the hard way, as father of a once-lost now-found younger son. "Repentance just means being found" is the meaningless 1990s equivalent of the 1970s movie "Love Story"'s slogan: "Love means never having to say you're sorry." If moral decay starts in the church, the meaning of all the above is that there are no meanings.

SECTION C: Managing the North Pacific Commons

"Starting in the 1970s ... the environmental equation began to shift from 'wise use' of our resources to one of 'no use'.... [T]he demands for 'no use' policies began to be justified by pseudoscience grounded in emotion rather than science."

- Michael S. Coffman, Saviors of the Earth?

On 6 February 1992, the Greenpeace vessel Rainbow Warrior steamed into San Diego harbour with her customary self-importance. Greenpeace was there as a media show for a tough new law prohibiting the capture of dolphins (porpoises) at all, in any way. According to Greenpeace literature, the 100-boat American tuna fleet berthed at San Diego was responsible for incidentally-catching dolphins to near extinction. Dolphins (Phocaena Delphinidae) often swim alongside schools of mature yellowfin and are used by tuna fishermen to locate the schools. Unhappily for the dolphins, they have often become entangled in the tuna nets along with the fish. Although the California-based tuna fishery had gone to extraordinary lengths in time, personal expense, and catch-method technology to reduce dolphin mortality, the efforts involved did not sufficiently placate Greenpeace. But when the Rainbow Warrior so confidently arrived at San Diego, Greenpeace discovered that the American tuna fleet was gone ... maybe forever. Greenpeace and other environmentalist groups, having relentlessly and successfully pushed their "dolphin-safe" policy, had at last compelled the domestic yellowfin tuna fishery to either sell out, reflag, or regroup elsewhere. Instead, Greenpeace was met at the harbour by hundreds of angry, jeering protestors bearing ill-will and imprecatory placards. Greenpeace, Inc., was finally getting a dose of its own medicine.[284]

But the demonstrators at the docks, families and friends of American tuna fishermen, were not merely angry at industry members becoming unemployed: They were outraged because they knew the entire sanctimonious "dolphin-free" campaign had been a sham from start to finish. The environmental catalyst, which had convinced the U.S. Congress to pass the strict "dolphin-safe" laws, was a video clip showing the needless killing of a net full of dolphins, caught incidentally with (a lesser number of) yellowfin tuna. The video was supposed to have been secretly filmed by one Samuel La Budde, of Earth Island Institute, who had signed on a tuna-fishing boat as a mechanic and cook. But this Earth Island-produced video, like an earlier faked Greenpeace film of baby seals being skinned alive, was also a bogus. Among the protestors at San Diego that February day in 1992 was the wife of Angelo Souza, a California tuna boat skipper now forced to fish in the Western Pacific. She confronted Greenpeace concerning the La Budde video:

"I have been involved with the tuna industry for over thirty years. I have gone to sea with my captain husband. The vessel and crew in this video are not American[s]. This is not how Americans work. The whole film is a fraud. It is an old boat with a new owner and an inexperienced crew. Even the film was rigged, it was spliced from two different trips. It's common knowledge among fishermen that Samuel La Budde lied about that dolphin slaughter. It's not typical of anything. You're all a bunch of liars! And you've destroyed the jobs of thousands of innocent people with your lies!"[285]

After the initial shock of actually being demonstrated against had worn off, Greenpeace [this writer would educatedly guess] shrugged its collective denim-clad shoulders and sailed home. Lies and fraudulent statements are not uncommon ploys used by the environmentalists: They know what's best for Earth -- and us -- and the ends justify their means. Big Green agitation had resulted in U.S. federal legislation to protect a dubiously-endangered marine mammal (the dolphin), made anthropomorphic and wise beyond its kind by American television ("Flipper"). With the scuttling of the California tuna-fishing fleet, the Pacific yellowfin fishery now belongs to Japan and other nations. A renewable American marine resource is no longer available for Americans to fish, and American consumers must now pay more for an inferior product. Except for the immediate impact on tuna fishermen, processors, their families, and the local California economy, environmentalists can rationalise: Who really cares so long as all dolphins are safe forever?[286]

A related topic regarding fish nets versus marine life, and one which engenders as much emotion, has been high-seas driftnet fishing. This problem is referred to in Chapter 1 and extensively in an earlier work.[287] This writer (among others in 1989) expressed gratitude to a number of U.S. West Coast politicians for their contribution in the struggle to ban (specifically Pacific) driftnet fishing. By 1992, the United Nations had enacted a world-wide ban on high-seas driftnet fishing. Although no admirer of the UN, this writer nonetheless was greatly pleased that ridding the earth's oceans of the "curtains of death" had become law. The view in 1992 had been that the world would be looking to ..."leadership from the United States and Canada in stopping [i.e., pirate] driftnet ships."[288]

Many North Americans were part of a global consensus that eliminated the driftnet fleets of Japan, South Korea, and Taiwan. But by autumn 1994 a discordant study had been published, 'United Nations Resolutions on Driftnet Fishing: An Unsustainable Precedent for High-seas and Coastal Fisheries

Management.' Issued by the British journal <u>Ocean Development and International law</u>, the study was written by William T. Burke of the University of Washington School of Law, Mark Freeberg of Seattle's National Resource Consultants, and Edward L. Miles of the UW School of Marine Affairs.[289] The three authors of the study claimed that: (1) The UN resolutions which proscribed driftnet fishing were based on faulty by-catch and wrong waste-level statistics; and (2) the ban harbours bad presentiments for coastal (i.e., within national, sovereign EEZs) net fisheries, some with higher by-catch and waste-level rates than high-seas driftnets. William Burke of the UW Law School has stated their (his, Freeberg's, Miles') case:

"By whipping up moral indignation against ... high seas driftnets, [fishing nations] succeeded in using the U.N. General Assembly as the global forum to lay the basis for coercing three states into abandoning their exercise of legitimate high-seas rights.... Shrimp trawl fisheries [in the Gulf of Mexico] are already in some difficulty because of their turtle by-catch; and they are attracting attention because of their fin-fish by-catch, which is an order of magnitude higher than some high-seas driftnet by catch rates."[290]

Burke maintained that although the high-seas driftnets ranged from up to 50 kilometres in length, they were hardly the "wall of death" in popular imagination -- the high-seas driftnets were designed with regularly-spaced gaps for non-targeted species escapement. The world public mostly learned of driftnets through a video produced by the environmentalist group Earth Trust. Like the dolphin video of Earth Island Institute, the Earth Trust driftnet video inflamed world opinion. But the Earth Trust driftnet video was the genuine article, and clearly showed underwater scenes of fish, birds, and marine mammals -- by the scores -- entangled and strangled in miles of monofilament netting. There was no gainsaying the stark truth of those moving pictures. North American public opinion was especially ignited when U.S.and Canadian law officers released their own video tapes, proving that certain East Asian pirate vessels had been catching salmon illegally, and had been selling the fish at sub-market prices. It was well documented that a goodly portion of the East Asian neon flying squid-fishing fleets had become a front for poaching Pacific salmon originally from North American rivers.

By July 1989, representatives from Alaska, British Columbia, the Pacific Northwest, and Hawaii had had enough. They met together for the Pacific Driftnet Conference, calling for the U.S. and Canada to (1) monitor driftnet fishing, (2) reduce driftnet use, and (3) halt illegal salmon harvests. But things didn't stop there. By the autumn of 1989, the problem of driftnet fishing had entered the UN General Assembly itself.

A coalition of Pacific Island nations (bypassing the usually-consulted UN Food and Agriculture Organization [FAO]), headed by Australia and New Zealand, had demanded direct, immediate action. The petitioners, contended the report by Burke, Freeberg, and Miles, had intentionally gone over the FAO's head to the larger, more potent General Assembly to make their point ...thus paving the way for the UN to set "an unsustainable precedent for high-seas and coastal fisheries management."[291]

But here this writer half-way disagreed with the candid and gutsy authors of 'United Nations Resolutions on Driftnet Fishing'. High-seas driftnet fishing by the three East Asian nations is opposed by all sectors of the American and Canadian fishing and seafood industry. This writer was proud of the U.S. Commerce Department generally, and of U.S. politicos Frank Murkowski, Jolene Unsoeld, and Billy Tauzin in particular, when the UN officially banned during late 1991 the world-wide use of driftnets by 1993. This writer still thinks that the United States deserved the real credit, but at the time felt a seldom glow for the United Nations. Surely this was the primary function of a globally-empowered body? Although the Law of the Sea (UNCLOS III) established the 200 nautical mile (371-km) EEZ for coastal nations, approximately two thirds of the earth's oceans are not under national jurisdiction. A perfect example of this "jurisdictional gap"[292] is the marine area known as "The Donut Hole" in Bering Sea, completely surrounded by American and Russian EEZs but still outside their jurisdiction. Smack-dab in the middle of the Sea of Okhotsk is another such area of marine jurisdictional gap, totally within the Russian EEZ yet outside it. Under international law, these jurisdictional gaps are high-seas areas and thus heavily fished by Pacific Rim nations. As political and ecological boundaries rarely coincide, foreign fishing vessels deplete fish stocks which straddle the high seas/EEZ boundaries, thus undermining the national maritime efforts to effectively manage their fisheries.[293] Overlapping stocks of targeted marine species from adjacent EEZs are considered transboundary, shared or straddling stocks, so regional coöperation in marine resource management is imperative by the neighbouring sovereign nations.[294]

Thus it finally gets down to hypothetical analysis of marine geopolitics in a literal doughnut hole. Using the Russian-American "Donut Hole" in Bering Sea as perfect political model, the Liberal-Environmentalist view would be to declare the "Donut Hole" a "no use" marine area, to be administered directly by the UN as the remainder of the high seas. The Libertarian "free use" philosophy would regard all high-seas marine areas -- including jurisdictional gaps and overgaps -- as open to all commercial traffic and fishing. The Conservative "wise use" movement would envision an efficient but limited UN (or comparable world body!) policing of high-seas marine areas, without ever interfering in national sovereign waters. UNCLOS III should be seen as the Law of the Sea, not of the United Nations. The UN should act as arbiter between quarreling maritime nations, and as a watchdog forum for commonly perceived environmental problems affecting the earth's oceans (i.e., high-seas driftnet fishing). An all-powerful UN brings to mind the old Latin adage, Quis custodiet ipsos custodes? ("Who will guard the guards themselves?"). But a toothless General Assembly could have never ridded the high seas of the East Asian driftnet fleets. Conservatism (wise use) and conservation (wise management) both branch from the root stem "conserve", which means "to preserve in a sound state."[295] A conservancy (from the same stem word "conserve") is a committee with (common sense) authority to control (eg.) fishing rights.[296] There is a place both for national and international conservancies to ensure optimum yield (OY) of ocean harvests while conserving the marine resource.

In Garret Hardin's essay "Living on a Lifeboat", advanced future fishing technology was forecast as dooming fish and fisheries to extinction.[297] Twenty years after Hardin's grim prognostications, it is intimidating to stand at the bridge of a modern factory trawler. One would behold:

"Modern diesel-powered vessels ... can deploy vast trawler nets, some large enough to swallow a dozen 747s in a single gulp. The electronic gear on the boats' bridges ... often rivals that of the jumbo jets. Side-scan sonar reveals the presence of fish so accurately that in some instances operators can even identify the species. Global positioning satellites allow navigators to return to the most productive fishing grounds with a margin of error of less than 100 metres. At the same time, factory vessels that process fish at sea have allowed many nations to send their fleets thousands of kilometres from home in search of catches.... Against such sophistication, fish have little chance...."[298]

When one considers that advanced technology, plus the capacity of the world's fishing fleets, has expanded far beyond the ability of earth's oceans to regenerate fish...[299] one is prone to think as Garret Hardin. As this writer has previously observed, Hardin from his Ivory Tower prospect couldn't envision change in the attitude of the industry regarding the finite resource. Contemporary West Coast environmentalists make the same mistake, condescendingly believing that the Pacific industry is somehow unaware of the diminishing marine resource, and wouldn't change its attitude -- or adjust to changes -- if it did.

And changes are in the offing. On the West Coast, where most groundfish stocks are still in fairly good shape due to strictly enforced quota management, Pacific fishermen are still going broke. Seafood Leader magazine editor Peter Redmayne has written that since fishery managers have not put limits on entry in the enormous Alaska bottomfish and crab fisheries, boats are able to fish for only a few months per year. Tying up a $40-million factory trawler at the dock for half a year is no way to produce seafood at lowest possible price for the consumer.[300] In 1992, the North Pacific Council passed a moratorium on new boats entering the fisheries, but the National Marine Fisheries Service (NMFS), which had initially backed the moratorium, hemmed and hawed for two years before finally withdrawing support. Redmayne concluded his 1994 state-of-the-fisheries editorial with a challenge to both government and the industry:

"The Magnuson Act comes up for reauthorization in Congress next year [1995]. IT NEEDS TO BE CHANGED[!]. While self-policing, industry-led management councils were a good idea in theory, in reality they don't work. Technology has changed the fishing industry, and fisheries management these days requires a lot of hard choices like enacting limited entry and individually transferable quotas (ITQs). And that means putting some people out of business and making others mad. But it's got to be done. The question is: Does anybody in this industry -- or in the government -- have the guts to do it?"[301]

Redmayne's editorial interested this writer in three aspects. The first was that "[w]hile self-policing, industry-led management councils were a good idea in theory, in reality they didn't work." This is true only so long a fishery management allows it to be. The Pacific industry has already undergone a shift in attitude toward the diminishing marine resource. The second point was the change in fisheries technology, and the parallel adjustment by the industry to synchronise with that change. The third aspect was Redmayne's asking if anyone in the (U.S.) government had "the guts" to enact hard choices like limited entry and ITQs. It is hoped by many that government will play as diminutive a rôle as possible in the fisheries of 2001 A.D. and beyond; that the "self-policing, industry-led management councils" will be sufficiently competent to police themselves and manage the Pacific oceanic commons. But by merely posing the question, the Seafood Leader editor implied that the (U.S.) government is not omnipotent ... yet.

As government is not considered powerful enough to enforce the liberal environmentalist agenda, various "non-government organisations" (designated NGOs by the U.N.) have been nothing loath to step into the breach. The Marine Fish Conservation Network has recently set a trend of NGO activism; the eventual outcome of the reauthorised Magnuson (Fishery Conservation and Management) Act notwithstanding. In 1992, five national (U.S.) organisations formed the Marine Fish Conservation. The steering committee in 1994 still consisted of a number of the core founders: Center for Marine Conservation (Elliott A. Norse, James Taylor and co.), Greenpeace, National Audubon Society, National Coalition for Marine Conservation, and World Wildlife Fund.[302] By spring 1994, a coalition of more than 50 groups comprised the Marine Fish Conservation Network ... all ready to rumble over the Magnuson Act. The Network's avowed goal was "to shift the emphasis of fisheries management from short-term economic gain to long-term economic and ecological sustainability."[303] On the Network's agenda for amending the Magnuson Act were eliminating overfishing, reducing by-catch, and conserving large pelagic fishes. Ken Kelley, field editor of National Fisherman magazine, commented that.... "While the [N]etwork has been able to find common ground with the commercial industry on proposals like strengthening habitat-protection provisions in the law, other goals sought by the [N]etwork are contentious."[304]

The collapse of the New England fisheries has left Pacific industry-led fishery management councils vulnerable to flagging general confidence. Because of this wide-spread (mis)perception, Congress has been more open to special interest suggestions by eco-conglomerates like the Network. Network proposals might have a far-reaching impact on future Pacific fisheries management, if approved by Congress and amended to the Magnuson Act. The changes, already briefly alluded to, proposed by the Network (1994) were: (1) The prevention of over-fishing a priority; (2) adoption of a precautionary "risk averse" approach to fisheries management; (3) minimising by-catch, i.e., "clean fishing"; (4) domestic (U.S.) management of large pelagic fishes like bluefin tuna, marlin, and swordfish; (5) and the fortifying of habitat-protection regulations. Although there was accord on habitat protection between the Network and the industry, a yawning chasm remained unbridged on other aspects of fisheries management. National Fisherman's Ken Kelley explained why:

....."The [N]etwork charges that fishing interests now dominate the councils, preventing them from making tough management decisions. They've proposed overturning and restructuring the system, along with strict new rules to reduce conflicts-of-interest. In addition, they want non-user representatives on the councils."[305]

Even a bona fide (Network) member who represented commercial fishing interests worried about the

Network's conflict-of-interest stance. Linda Behnken of the Alaska Longline Fishermen's Association stated, "'While we feel it's best to work together with the [N]etwork and find common ground, fishermen feel it's very important to have actual fishermen on the councils, so you have people up there that know their fisheries.'"[306]

Dick Gutting, government affairs director of the pro-industry National Fisheries Institute (NFI), told National Fisherman that the NFI had decided not to join the Marine Fish Conservation Network. Gutting said, "If you look at the people who have joined, it's clear that the recreation people [the sport lobby] are involved in this over allocation issues. We feel that the environmental groups have been snookered by the recreational interests, and as long as that's true, we'd rather deal at arm's length with the [N]etwork."[307]

True enough, but perhaps Dick Gutting of NFI was in turn himself snookered by the environmentalists. Earlier in this essay, the writer referred to a report on the activities of Greenpeace in New England last summer (1995). Greenpeace, by loudly opposing limited-entry quotas, was ostensibly trying to save small fishermen form extinction. Greenpeace hoped that the ploy would set small fishermen against big fishing interests -- those hateful corporations which profit from quotas. One suspected, that in this case, the marine resource was of less concern to Greenpeace, Inc., than egging on internecine strife within the fishing industry. The rich and powerful West Coast sport lobby for years has attempted to achieve respectability by aligning itself with the environmentally-correct. When it comes to snookering the fishing public, the sport lobby and the environmentalists are equally culpable.

"Divide and conquer" has been a useful tactic since time immemorial. Recently this strategy has been used with devastating effect by environmentalists against industries they don't like. Big Green will instigate inter-industrial conflicts, like fishing against logging, and exascerbate intra-industrial hostilities, such as small fishermen versus big fishing companies. In Maine during 1991, the Conservation Law Foundation was paid $50,000 in private funds to agitate the U.S. Department of Commerce for a plan reversing the decline of Georges Bank food-fisheries. The plan would have thrown droves of Maine lobstermen out of business. Concurrently, the Maine Coast Heritage Trust was inciting local fishermen by telling them that fin-fish and scallop declines were caused by Penobscot River logging companies and paper mills. By 1993 the environmentalist ruse at Penobscot Bay was to openly confront the fishing industry through the Conservation

Law Foundation; at the same time the Maine Coast Heritage Trust guilefully diverted fishing industry wrath upriver toward the logging companies and paper mills. The good cop-bad cop trick works every time on the unsuspecting. Meanwhile, eco-outfits such as the Conservation Law Foundation and the Maine Coast Heritage Trust, in the sanctioned name of public property rights, continue to erode the public's sanctified private property rights.[308]

Down East members of the Atlantic fishing industry were aware, too, of the Marine Fish Conservation Network and its plans for the amended Magnuson Act. Jeff Kaelin of the Associated Fisheries of Maine was interviewed by National Fisherman about the Network's agenda. Kaelin, also executive director of the Maine Sardine Council, found areas of agreement with the Network; for instance supporting the elimination of TALFF (total allowable level of foreign fishing) for species like Atlantic mackerel. But Kaelin also told field editor Kelley that environmental groups blame "the fishermen and government [for not enough regulation?] for mismanagement, and now they've found a new issue and way to raise money by saying they're going to save the oceans."[309] An anonymous staff member of the House committee conceded to National Fisherman that the fishing industry ..."has never been very organized or effective when it comes to lobbying. But perhaps that's just due to the independent and diverse nature of the industry.... The [N]etwork has been very organized and effective in raising the awareness factor."[310]

At this writing, 18 October 1995, the House voted to extend an amended Magnuson Act, with new provisions to keep U.S. fishermen from exceeding maximum sustainable yield (MSY). The renewed bill, which passed 388-37, authorises $610-millon for continued fisheries management programmes over five years, and directs regional councils to minimise by-catch. Ever since the 1976 Magnuson Act extended the U.S. fishing zone to 200 miles offshore, foreign harvesting dropped from 3.8 billion lbs (77% of the total catch) in 1977 to zero from 1992 and on.[311] The American catch, moreover, has increased from 1.56 billion lbs in 1977 to 6.32 billion lbs in 1993.[312] The amended law will attempt to deal with domestic over-fishing rather than foreign harvesting. Don Young (R-Alaska), chairman of the House Resources Committee, said that the bill... "allows fishermen and processors to make a living from the sea, while also making them better stewards of the resource that they rely on for their livelihood."[313] Amen, and let's hope time proves Chairman Young right.

The amended bill, which has still to go through the Senate, includes a statement to the effect that the Secretary of Commerce must not approve foreign applications to fish Atlantic mackerel or Atlantic herring without the prior recommendation of the appropriate regional council [author's emphasis].[314] Provisions in the bill keeping domestic fishermen from over-fishing the resource might be regarded as ambivalent language. At present a crucial election looms in the writer's home state of Washington. On the November 1995 list of ballots is Initiative Measure 640 which places the trick question: "Shall state fishing regulations ensure certain survival rates for targeted catch, and commercial and recreational fisheries be prioritized?"[315] This leading, interrogatory statement would appear to demand a simple Yes vote, but those who fish for a living in Washington waters are passionately opposed to Initiative 640. Indeed, the measure threatens their very existence. Dig deeply behind 640, and one will find the well-heeled sport-fishing lobby wanting the state's remaining chinook and coho salmon, all to themselves. Similarly misleading semantic mind-games have been played by the Marine Fish Conservation Network. A Network agenda precedent has been domestic management of large pelagic fishes like bluefin tuna, marlin, and swordfish. Arguing that the International Commission for the Conservation of Atlantic Tunas (ICCAT) had failed to halt international over-fishing of these migratory species, the Network has called for stricter American management by the Atlantic councils [author's emphasis]. Despite their patriotic-sounding homeboy jive, Dick Gutting of NFI was not snookered by the Network. Said he, "We should not be saving fish so they can be caught by another country."[316]

Underneath the angry rhetoric of fish-user groups, government and environmentalists, there really is a danger of exhausting the oceanic commons through over-fishing. The collapse of the northwest Atlantic fisheries bears witness to this. The world wild-fish harvest in 1990 was 85 million tons; the projected catch for 2010 A.D. is 102 million tons -- a per capita change of -10%.[317] Lester Brown, Worldwatch Institute president, said during an interview in January 1994, that ...."Human demands are approaching the limits of oceanic fisheries to supply fish...."[318] A Worldwatch study reported that from 1950 to 1984 the earth's waterways yielded so much fish, that the seafood catch per person doubled..." '[b]ut in recent years these trends in [sea]food output per person have been reversed with unanticipated abruptness."[319] In another study, 'Net loss: Fish, Jobs and the Marine Environment,' released by Worldwatch in July 1994, author Peter Weber reported that an exploding world population has ... "'caused armed confrontations between fishing nations, gunfire between fishers and hunger in the developing world.... If current mismanagement continues, we can expect a future in which millions of fishers are out of work ... A future in which traditional fishing cultures from Nova Scotia to Malaysia disappear."[320]

Weber claimed that the total catch has declined by more than 30% in some areas, among them the Pacific's east-central region. Declining harvests have cost more than 100,000 jobs during recent years in the world fishing industry, according to Weber, but from 1970 to 1990 the world fishing fleet doubled.[321]

Are the warnings of the Worldwatch Institute worth heeding, or are they merely more words of eco-alarmism? The rantings and ravings of such doom-doctors as Paul Ehrlich and Norman Myers notwithstanding, there are undeniably threats to the world-wide marine resource. Figures and statistics handed down from the non-profit Worldwatch Institute tend to tally and make sense. The Pacific industry has no excuse for not learning the lesson of the Atlantic fisheries. Cutting waste is the best first step in any conservation programme, and, thanks mainly to NMFS service director Steve Pennoyer, this has already been underway in Alaska's Bering Sea. First publicised in November 1993, the National Marine Fisheries Service issued an experimental fishing permit to the non-profit group Terra Marine in time for the Bering Sea winter pollock and (true) cod trawl fisheries. The idea: All incidentally-caught salmon (and other species taken as catch averages) will be headed, gutted, individually frozen, packed in 50-lb. boxes, labeled "not for sale", and shipped from Dutch Harbor to Seattle in containers donated by SeaLand. From Seattle, after further processing at the Food Lifeline Warehouse, the otherwise-discarded fish is to be distributed by the Second Harvest national food-bank to the poor throughout Western Washington.[322]

Tuck Donnelly, the director of Terra Marine Research, an environmental organisation headquartered on Washington State's Bainbridge Island, has been quick to praise the NMFS and credit the North Pacific Fishery Management Council for their support. Fully twenty-one vessels are to participate in the programme, including all of Unisea's shore-based vessels; factory trawler Brown's Point owned by Golden Age Seafoods; and boats delivering to mothership Excellence, owned by Anchorage-based Supreme Alaska Seafoods.[323] Here is an extraordinary case of government (Steve Pennoyer and the NMFS), environmentalism (Tuck Donnelly and Terra Marine Research), and the industry (the North Pacific Fishery Management Council, the seafood companies and Alaska fishermen) working together to cut waste and feed the hungry too. A grateful Tuck Donnelly expressed deep satisfaction:

"The future of this is tremendous.... [the first delivery] is just the tip of the iceberg. This is a public resource so it is only logical to give it to the needy and this program is a means of protecting the resource and utilizing it for the public benefit.[324]

".... It's been the fishermen's idea from the beginning and I'm very proud that we've been able to bring agencies and the industry together to solve what we think should never have been a problem to begin with. The fact that discarding fish is used as a management tool just doesn't make sense to people any longer."[325]

Let us of the Pacific Northwest hope that after April 1994 when Terra Marine's experimental permit expires, that it will be renewed and the "Let 'em Eat By-catch" programme expanded. Concurrent to the "Let 'em Eat By-catch" programme, the National Fisheries Institute announced that Americans ate 3.94 billion lbs. of seafood in 1994, breaking the previous record of 3.9[0] billion lbs. in 1987.[326] NFI's executive vp Lee Weddig said that the increase "reflects consumers' desire to keep fish and shellfish as a regular part of their diets."[327] Although the numbers were good news for the national industry, the NFI supports further restrictions on fishing. Weddig has urged the new Congress to pass a tougher version of the Magnuson Act, and criticised attempts to dismantle the U.S. Department of Commerce. The Commerce Department is the federal parent of the National Oceanic and Atmospheric Administration (NOAA), which in turn oversees the National Marine Fisheries Service (NMFS). The NOAA federally regulates the fishing industry and is ultimately responsible for the condition of the American marine resource. NFI's Weddig has acted as a catalyst for keeping relations good and workable between the federal government and the fishing industry, and has suggested moving NOAA to another department if Commerce is closed. In an August 1995 interview, Weddig commented: "What is going to destroy progress is if the agency that has to provide the science and provide the regulations is torn apart."[328]

The American fishing and seafood industry is going to sorely miss Lee Weddig when he relinquishes his post as executive vice-president of NFI sometime in early 1996. Since joining the National Fisheries Institute in 1967, Weddig has been a tireless warrior for the industry and especially as a "balancing force" in fisheries management.[329] Weddig has predicted that challenges ahead for the industry will be making new seafood safety standards really work, and in "keeping fisheries intact while providing the public with a product that's a good value."[330] This writer will also miss Wedding as a strong spokesman for the American industry, particularly on environmental issues. (Readers have sampled Weddig's terse on-target remarks quoted in Chapter 1.)

In 1991 a fisheries-friendly non-profit environmental organisation, today named Ocean Trust, was founded having a mission with a twist: "...[T]o protect the ocean and its natural resources -- [but] as a source of food and livelihood to people worldwide."[331] On Ocean's Trust honourary board of directors in 1992 were rock musicians Billy Joel and Bruce Hornsby; art patroness Adelaide de Menil; author Peter Matthiessen; J. Roy Duggan, CEO, King & Prince Seafood Corp.; John Peterson, former CEO, Ocean Bounty; and ... Lee J. Weddig, NFI executive vice-president.[332]

This writer next saw Weddig's name in a Seafood Leader article in late 1994.[333] The NFI had petitioned the Court of International Trade to block a lawsuit filed by various environmental groups, headed by Earth Island Institute, which sought to ban the importation of $2-billion worth of shrimp from over 100 countries. The environmentalists claimed that the U.S. State Department should have imposed sea turtle regulations against every nation in the world which net-fished shrimp -- not just those in the Caribbean which already had to comply to avoid U.S. embargo. Weddig was quick to respond in usual fashion:

"Unless dismissed, this lawsuit could disrupt 25% of the volume of the entire U.S. seafood industry, causing business failures, processing plant shut downs, layoffs and sky-high prices for consumers. The drastic measures called for by the plaintiffs are contrary to international agreements and destroy the cooperative spirit needed to solve global environmental issues."[334]

In spite of the pro-resource pro-industry efforts made by organisations like Terra Marine and Ocean Trust, and individuals such as Tuck Donnelly and Lee Weddig, eco-groups like Greenpeace, Inc. still "don't get it." The U.S. fishing industry, in Greenpeaceful eyes, is still not trying hard enough to earn its global citizenship seal-of-approval. During the summer of 1995, Seattle Metro buses sported Greenpeace-sponsored cartoon-signs on their sides showing a factory trawler dragging a torn net, with dead fish spilling out, from her stern. The printed caption accused: "Factory trawlers are WASTING 500,000,000 pounds of fish a year. You Can Stop This. Call Greenpeace 632-4326.[335] When queried by Alaska Fisherman's Journal about the aggressive campaign against factory trawlers, Greenpeace spokesman Fred Munson replied, "It's time to call a spade a spade, and you guys [factory trawlers] are the biggest part of the problem.... [Your] measure of success is how cheaply [you] can take fish out of the ocean. For [you], as long as pollock are healthy, it doesn't matter whether the Steller sea lion goes extinct.... We're not against fishing, we're for sustainable fishing."[336]

But editor John van Amerongen wouldn't be put off, pressing Munson as to why Greenpeace had gone public with the issue of factory trawlers. Munson responded that public opinion was the Greenpeace method of countering the influence of paid lobbyists at Washington, D.C.: "They've got inside lobbyists, we've got public opinion."[337] Joe Blum, executive director of the American Factory Trawler Association (AFTA) contended that North Pacific stocks are not being overfished, despite the seemingly contrary evidence of discard rate (which is fully accounted for in the total allowable catch [TAC] annually set by the North Pacific Council and the Secretary of Commerce). Explained Blum:

"People get the impression that we go out there to catch bycatch, and we don't... We go out there to catch target species.... They're [Greenpeaceniks] using it [the trawling issue] to raise money, and the truth isn't going to get in the way.... We're going to every bycatch forum, two in Alaska, one here [Seattle] and one in D.C. We're out there, but they don't care. They're not interested in the truth. They're interested in theater that will raise money, and I suspect that some of them have an aversion to removing anything from the ecosystem."[338]

Editor Mark S. Lundsten wrote an outstanding "Fisherman's Forum" in the February 1995 issue of Alaska Fisherman's Journal. 'Environmental Politics: Don't cast your lot with a misinformed public' turned out to be an avowed clean bill of conservational health for the North Pacific fisheries. It was also a formal invitation to the environmentalists to coöperate with, instead of denigrating, a self-policing industry. The success of Pacific fishermen "speaking for the fish'" has been reflected in the strength of the traditionally targeted resources, salmon and halibut. Lundsten identified industry figures Harold Lokken, Gordon Jensen, and Jake Phillips as rôle models of integrity and responsibility. Yet no kudos have been forthcoming to the industry from the environmentalists. Lundsten believed that the Green" ... unspoken agenda of institutional survival has overtaken their stated agenda of conservation. Their need of a cause and to raise funds in order to survive often obviates their professed desire to protect the environment."[339]

Most frustrating to editor Lundsten has been environmentalism's attitude towards fishery waste and by-catch. When, for instance, the entire Seattle trawl fleet called for individual fishing quotas (IFQs) to solve both problems, environmentalism's response was "....'IFQs have no conservation benefits that we can ascertain.'"[340] (The same line was used against the Pacific halibut-sablefish IFQ programme.) In fact, expanded Lundsten, the lack of IFQs or the license limitation plan for the North Pacific as a whole remains the paramount conservation problem. Without a long-term allocation arrangement, every fishery management issue -- including discards and bycatch -- becomes a short-time allocation war in itself between user-groups and industry sectors. Lundsten summed up:

"It seems to be that environmental groups are simply taking advantage of that [industry] division and furthering it for their own cause. The phony environmental politics we are playing into now is not only [distracting] us from real conservation programs, but keep us from a pile of other problems that won't go away without industry consensus.

"The North Pacific fisheries have a history of conservation that needs to continue. Environmental groups, who have consistently played too dirty for me to trust them, need to establish accountability if they want to be an honest part of the process. I hope they sincerely collaborate with the fishing industry. We can use their help on a lot of issues...."[341]

Epilogue

"The North Pacific produces more than 60% of all U.S. seafood ... has 22% of the world's seafood resources."
- Pacific Fishing magazine, April 1994

It is a cold, clear All Saints Day 1995. The writer and his spouse are aboard the M.V. Coho headed across the Strait of Juan de Fuca for Victoria, B.C. In Canada, feisty premier Jacques Parizeau has just resigned after the Québec sovereignty referendum failed by barely a percentage point. But we are journeying to Canada's "Pacific Island" of Vancouver, where English is spoken and local marine waters are warmed by the Kuro Shio ("black current"). The North Pacific appears a dead, gunmetal gray under the wan, autumnal sun, but this stretch of ocean is nutrient-rich and is home to a vast marine resource. Because of the significance of this resource for the whole world, a jealous Rim watch is kept on how fish stocks are faring. As a retired Oregon State University professor has observed, studying the entire ecosystem of the North Pacific is an "'enormous undertaking.'"[342] The questions of how and why fish stocks rise and fall depend on the system of the near-shore environment, fish predation and escapement, water temperature, ocean currents with atmospheric influences, the intricate food chain-web from phytoplankton to whales, or a combination of the above forces. Scientists -- oceanographers, marine biologists et al -- are compelled to consider the entire North Pacific ecosystem as fish management problems are broadening in complexity. Fishing just isn't simply fishing anymore.[343]

Interest in marine ecosystems has greatly increased since the disastrous 1989 Exxon Valdez oil spill in Alaska's Prince William Sound. Millions of dollars -- both governmental and corporate, willing and coerced -- have been spent on research as a result. Pink salmon has been the principal species studied so far; pinks are visible one spring as fry and the following summer as adults, plus the lowly "humpie" has long been the dependable salmon of Prince William Sound fishermen. Although pink runs are predictable, they are also variable. The oil spill aside, an expected 20 million run in 1993 produced a return of a mere 4 million pinks. Scientists have speculated that during any given year fully 80% of emerging pink fry fall prey to birds, fish, and marine mammals even before leaving the Sound.[344] An unusual characteristic of Prince William Sound is its depth of up to 250 fathoms in some areas, just a nautical mile or so offshore. During some years, strong southeasterly winter gales blow into the Sound, pushing nutrient-poor Gulf (of Alaska) surface water into the Sound, displacing its nutrient-rich water. Scientists thus believe that when spring arrives there is less to eat throughout the Sound's food chain-web. As the injected Gulf water is colder, the pink fry don't grow so fast and are therefore vulnerable to predators for a longer time.[345]

North Pacific scientists are confident they have the method of determining exactly what is ingesting what in the food chain-web; a method known as "stable isotope" study. Instead of examining the stomach contents of each individual fish or animal, modern scientists are able to discover what ate what by ascertaining the unique ratio of carbon to nitrogen isotopes in zoöplankton. The ratio is unique in that it differs in the zoöplankton of any given area. Every fish or animal -- no matter its position in the food chain-web hierarchy -- which feeds on the zoöplankton of a specific area, will exhibit the same specific isotope ratio. When the fish or animal migrates, it moves with an internalised nutritional profile.[346] In the case of Prince William Sound pink salmon, scientists hope to use stable isotopes in identifying the predators of fry. A U.Alaska professor of chemical oceanography has predicted that when there is a goodly supply of zoöplankton "markers" from around the Pacific Basin, it may be possible to tell where a fish or animal has been, from what it has eaten.[347]

As noted, water temperature is vitally important to salmon and for other fishes too. Canadian studies have proven that, within the physical environment, ocean temperature is a key to the growth and health of fish stocks. Oceanographers learned that the northeastern Pacific entered a warm phase in 1977, with ocean temperature going up ca.1.5° above normal. The rise was unrelated to any "El Niño occurrence. The rise and fall of a single degree in ocean temperature can play havoc with a fishery. Marine biologists at Nanaimo, B.C., who have been measuring the effects of the warmer water from LaPerouse Bank off Vancouver Island, noticed a seldom-seen invasion of in-migrating chub mackerel (Scomber japonicus) from the south. The mackerel have been devouring huge numbers of out-migrating salmon smolts. This has happened before off British Columbia, and the Nanaimo biologists anxiously await the warming regime -- and mackerel invasion -- to cease; probably within five years.[348]

An Oregon State U. professor has agreed with meteorologists that air temperature, especially the Aleutian Low pressure cell, affects Pacific salmon stocks. The Aleutian Low is the major low-pressure zone over the North Pacific, influencing the north-south flow of the Pacific Current. Changes in the Aleutian Low affect weather patterns all along the Pacific Coast.[349] The Aleutian Low has shifted westward during the present warming regime (absent El Niño), inhibiting the southerly flow of the Pacific Current and southern upwelling. As a rule the southern upwelling pushes cool, nutrient-rich water to the surface all along the Pacific Coast. During the present warming regime, however, the inhibition of the southern upwelling has denied newly-emergent salmon fry the nutrients needed for their survival. Air and ocean temperatures rise and fall frequently, and with them marine temperatures. A U.Alaska marine ecologist has said to Pacific Fishing magazine that:

"It is possible precipitous declines in any species -- cod, salmon, even Steller sea lions -- happen regularly, and that the impact of commercial fishing on those species may be secondary to changes in the environment."[350]

Oh, wow! And all this time we have been told, again and again, by the environmentalists for decades now, that 99.9% of problems in Pacific marine ecosystems are caused by human industrial activity, with over-fishing a major culprit. Compounding the eco-disinformation dispersed by Big Green, is the confusing babble of bureaucratic language emanating from scientific research bodies. Recently, a U.S.-based organisation has been created to filter the gobbletygook and bridge the communications gap between science and the laity. The Pacific Marine Science Organization (PICES) was formed to stimulate meaningful discussion and coördination all around the Pacific Rim. The present (1994) chairman of PICES is retired Oregon State U. dean of oceanography, professor Warren Wooster. Chairman Wooster has said that PICES must analyse problems such as the North Pacific's "carrying capacity" (optimum [sustainable] yield) in Rim-oriented forums. And so it has been -- PICES has sponsored two international conferences prior to 1994, and another Rim forum was planned for Japan in November 1995.[351]

Alaska Governor Walter Hickel has proposed funding a North Pacific Research Institute, to be built at Seward, with $36-million in Exxon Valdez oil settlement money. The Institute is projected to incorporate the existent U.Alaska-Fairbanks (UAF) Institute of Marine Science, eventually expanding with laboratories, a shellfish hatchery, docks for research vessels, warehouses etc. Research scientists foresee a future where fisheries managers will have a clear-cut, all-encompassing view of the North Pacific marine ecosystem as an organic whole ... and base their everyday decisions on hard, empirically-proven data.[352]

This writer is highly optimistic that true science rather than weird science will rule North Pacific fishery management decisions of the coming (conservative) century. As Thor Lassen, executive vp of Ocean Trust, remarked in 1992, ..."[W]e believe in seeking solutions to environmental and resource problems based on science rather than emotion."[353] With organisations like PICES and North Pacific Research Institute "walking point", outfits such as Greenpeace, Inc. and Earth Island Institute shall become increasingly irrelevant. After the collapse of the North Atlantic fisheries, it will be up to American and Canadian fishermen of the North Pacific oceanic commons to replenish the dearth with wholesome, healthful seafood for the domestic and international marketplace. A parting word of advice to the fishing industry by outgoing NFI executive vp Lee J. Weddig is both instructive and appropriate:

"Finally, and probably most important, the industry needs to do some serious work on its [poor environmental] image. It must take the lead at correcting real and perceived problems. Industry leaders must be in the forefront of realistic, necessary conservation programs. They must lead the way in development of more selective, effective technology."[354]

NOTES

173. 'Canada faces sanctions over seizure,' <u>Peninsula Daily News</u>, 13 March 1995, p. A-10.

174. C.D. Bay-Hansen, <u>Fisheries of the Pacific Northwest Coast, Vol.2</u> (New York:Vantage Press, 1994), pp.44-47.

175. F. Heward Bell, <u>The Pacific Halibut: The Resource and the Fishery</u> (Anchorage:Alaska Northwest Publishing Company, 1981), <u>passim</u>.

176. <u>Webster's Third New International Dictionary</u> (Springfield, Mass.:G&C. Merriam Company Publishers, 1965), p.997.

177. Alwyne Wheeler, <u>Fishes of the World</u> (New York:MacMillan Publishing Co., Inc., 1975), p.308.

178. 'Canada faces sanctions over seizure,' <u>ibidem</u>, p.A-10.

179. 'Fishing talks,' <u>Peninsula Daily News</u>, 26 March 1995, p.A-11.

180. Robert Lewis, 'The Turbot Tempest,' <u>Maclean's</u>, Vol.108, No.13, 27 March 1995, p.2.

181. Chris Wood, 'Who Owns the Sea?', <u>ibidem</u>, p.16 (or last page).

182. <u>Ibid.</u>, p.14.

183. <u>Ibid.</u>, p.15. Law of the Sea conferences: "[I]nternational agreement[s] made in Geneva in 1958 and 1960 defining base lines for contiguous zones, innocent passage, recovery of food and resources from the seabed, and conservation of sea life." <u>The New Lexicon Webster's Dictionary of the English Language</u> (New York:Lexicon Publications, Inc., 1989 ed.), p.560.

184. Op.cit., Chris Wood, p.15.

185. <u>Ibid.</u>, p.15.

186. Bruce Wallace, 'Enemies--with Much in Common,' <u>Maclean's</u>, Vol.108, No.13, 27 march 1995, p.18 (or first page).

187. <u>Ibid.</u>, p.18 (or first page). Author's note: While visiting southeast Norway in 1994, this writer heard a childhood friend say that Norwegian fisherfolk would vote against EU membership mainly to keep the Spanish fishing fleet away from Norway's (west) coast, and out of the Barents Sea.

188. Chris Wood, 'Who Owns the Sea?' <u>ibidem</u>, p.14.

189. <u>Ibid.</u>, p.15.

190. <u>Ibid.</u>, p.16 (or last page).

191. Bruce Wallace, 'Enemies--with Much in Common,' <u>ibidem</u>, p.19.

192. <u>Ibid.</u>, p.19.

NOTES (cont'd)

193. John DeMont, 'Conflicting Emotions,' Maclean's, Vol.108, No.13, 27 March 1995, p.19.

194. Ibid., p.21.

195. Ibid., p.22.

196. Ibid., p.21.

197. 'Turbot Wars,' The Vancouver Sun, 31 March 1995, p. A-18.

198. Stephen Thorne, "'Spanish are Coming," Tobin tells Europeans,' ibidem, p.A-4.

199. Juliet O'Neill and Pamela Rolfe, 'Spain angry as Canada ducks sanctions over fishing dispute,' ibidem, p.A-4.

200. 'Spanish nets "ecological monstrosity"', Victoria Times-Colonist, 29 March 1995, p.A-3. ['Show''] author's word only.

201. Ibid., p.A-3.

202. 'Citizen's arrest,' Maclean's, Vol. 108, No.14, 3 April 1995, p.4.

203. 'A new tack in the fish war,' ibidem, p.25.

204. John DeMont, 'Tobin's War,' Maclean's, Vol.108, No.15, 10 April 1995, p.14.

205. Ibid., p.15.

206. Warren Caragata, 'No more Mr. Nice Guy,' ibidem, p.16.

207. John DeMont with E. Kay Fulton, 'A partial victory,' Maclean's, Vol.108, No.18, 1 May 1995, p.12. Author's note: Under the Law of the Sea, flag-of-convenience vessels fall under the jurisdiction of the state in which they are registered. Hence Belize-registered trawlers essentially operate ungoverned.

208. Bruce Wallace, 'Splitting Europe,' ibidem, p.14.

209. 'World Bites,' Pacific Fishing, Vol.XVI, No.9, September 1995, p.17.

210. 'Bad News for New England Fishermen,' Alaska Fisherman's Journal, Vol.18, No.1, January 1995, p.8. Cf. 'Georges Bank:Closed for Withdrawals', Seafood Leader, Vol.15, No.1, January/February 1995, p.16.

211. 'Bad News for New England Fishermen,' ibidem, p.8.

212. 'Georges Bank:Closed for Withdrawals,' ibidem, p.16.

213. Paul Solman, 'Focus--A Fish Story ("Fishing in Gloucester--Fishbanks Game"),' MacNeil/Lehrer Newshour, WNET New York, N.Y., 3 November 1994, p.9.

NOTES (cont'd)

214.   <u>Ibid.</u>, p.10.

215.   <u>Ibid.</u>, p.10.

216.   <u>Ibid.</u>, p.11.

217.   <u>Ibid.</u>, p.11.

218.   <u>Ibid.</u>, p.12.

219.   Chris Bury, 'The Last Harvest,' <u>ABC News Nightline</u>, 24 November 1994, p.1.

220.   <u>Ibid.</u>, p.1.

221.   <u>Ibid.</u>, p.2.

222.   <u>Ibid.</u>, p.3.

223.   <u>Ibid.</u>, p.3.

224.   <u>Ibid.</u>, p.3. Ie., summer flounder (<u>Paralichthys dentatus</u>) and winter flounder (<u>Pseudopleuronectes americanus</u>).

225.   <u>Ibid.</u>, p.4.

226.   Susan Pollack, 'Emergency restrictions loom for Northeast groundfishermen,' <u>National Fisherman</u>, Vol.75, No.9, p.14. Ie., Atlantic mackerel (<u>Scomber scombrus</u>).

227.   <u>Ibid.</u>, p.64.

228.   'Fish quota focuses on small boats,' <u>Peninsula Daily News</u>, 7 June 1995, p.A-1.

229.   <u>Ibid.</u>, p.A-1. Ie., American lobster (<u>Homarus americanus</u>).

230.   P.J. O'Rourke, <u>All the Trouble in the World</u> (New York:The Atlantic Monthly Press, 1994), p.188.

231.   Chris Wood, 'Who Owns the Sea?', <u>Maclean's</u>, Vol.18, No.13, 27 March 1995, p.14.

232.   <u>Ibid.</u>, p.14.

233.   Paul Solman, 'Focus--A Fish Story,' <u>MacNeil/Lehrer Newshour</u>, WNET New York, N.Y., 3 November 1994, p.9.

234.   Garret Hardin and John Baden, eds., <u>Managing the Commons</u> (New York:W.H. Freeman and Company, 1977). Garret Hardin, 3, "The Tragedy of the Commons" (1968), p.16ff. Interior quotes are from S. McVay, <u>Scientific American</u> 216 (No.8), 13 (1966).

NOTES (cont'd)

235. <u>Ibidem</u>. Colin W. Clark, 11, "The Economics of Overexploitation" (1973), p.83. Clark's sources are: G. Hardin, <u>Science</u> 162, 1243 (1968); H.S. Gordon, <u>Journal of Political Economy</u>, 62, 124 (1954); J. Crutchfield and A. Zellner, <u>Economic Aspects of the Pacific Halibut Fishery</u> (Government Printing Office, Washington, D.C., 1963), pp.19-20.

236. <u>Ibidem</u>. Op.cit., Colin W. Clark, p.87.

237. <u>Ibid.</u>, p.88.

238. John Naisbitt, <u>Global Paradox</u> (New York:Avon Books, 1995), p.207.

239. <u>Managing the Commons</u>. James A. Wilson, 12, "A Test of the Tragedy of the Commons" (n.d.), p.96.

240. <u>Ibid.</u>, p.97.

241. <u>Ibid.</u>, p.97.

242. <u>Ibid.</u>, p.100. Interior quotes: "A trawl is a number of connected traps, usually ten or more, marked by two buoys one on the first and one on the last trap.... Significantly, when lobster fishermen participate in the shrimp, scallop, or herring fisheries, none of which are fixed gear fisheries, they recognize no territorial boundaries whatsoever."
Op.cit., Wilson, p.110.

243. <u>Ibid.</u>, p.109.

244. <u>Ibidem</u>. Robert L. Bish, 21, "Environmental Resource Management: Public or Private?" (n.d.), p.219.

245. <u>Ibidem</u>. Garret Hardin, 25, "Living on a Lifeboat" (n.d.), p.265.

246. Michael S. Coffman, <u>Saviors of the Earth?</u> (Chicago:Northfield Publishing, 1994), p.273.

247. <u>Ibid.</u>, p.273. Cf. P.J. O'Rourke, p.188.

248. Op.cit., Michael S. Coffman, p.273.

249. <u>Ibid.</u>, p.275. These rights were pressed out of a reluctant King John at swordpoint, in Runnymede, England, 1215.

250. <u>Ibid.</u>, p.276.

251. <u>Ibid.</u>, p.277.

252. <u>Ibid.</u>, p.281.

253. Rough draught copy, 1992. Center for Marine Conservation, 15806 N.E. 47th Court, Redmond, Washington.

254. Elliott A. Norse, ed., <u>Global Marine Biological Diversity</u>, p.118ff.

NOTES (cont'd)

255. 'THE LIVING PLANET IN CRISIS: Biodiversity Science and Policy', 9/10 March 1995, Center for Biodiversity and Conservation, American Museum of Natural History, New York, N.Y. AMNH pamphlet, pp.3,4. N.B.: The reader will recall that Norman Myers, mentioned earlier in this chapter, gave a lecture ("Save the Entire Biosphere!") at the Wildlife Conservation Society, also in early March (1995), New York City. See endnote no. 169.

256. Elliott A. Norse, ed., Global Marine Biological Diversity, roughdraft copy, p.126.

257. Ibid., p.126.

258. Ibid., pp.126-127. "UNCLOS III [from 1973-1982] establishe[d] a comprehensive regulating framework for the oceans, with provisions governing jurisdiction, access to the seas, navigation, protection of the marine environment, exploitation of living resources, scientific research, seabed mining, and the settlement of disputes. It allows establishment of a territorial sea of up to 12 nautical miles (22 kilometers) over which the coastal state has sovereignty, subject to the right of innocent passage ....[N]ational laws apply to this space. There is another 12 nautical miles of contiguous zone over which a coastal state can exercise control necessary for public safety and order.

"Within the next space, the 200 mile (371 kilometer)-wide EEZ, Articles 61 to 68 set forth principles for the exploitation of the living resources...." Op.cit., Elliott A. Norse, ed., p.168.

259. Chris Wood, 'Who Owns the Sea?', Maclean's, Vol.108, No.13, 27 March 1995, p.15. Note: At this writing, Canada has not yet signed UNCLOS III.

260. Op.cit., Elliott A. Norse, ed., p.127.

261. 'CONSERVATION AT THE CROSSROADS,' 7 March 1995, NYC, Wildlife Conservation Society pamphlet, p.2.

262. Arthur C. Clarke, July 20, 2019: Life in the 21st Century (New York:MacMillan, 1986), p.276.

263. Gary L. Bauer and Robert L. Maginnis, 'Singing the U.N. Blues,' Chronicles, Vol.19, No.10, October 1995, p.42.

264. Ibid., p.42. Boutros-Ghali quoted by Bauer and Maginnis.

265. Gary Kah, 'Part Two--The WCPA,' En Route to Global Occupation (Lafayette, La.:Huntington House, 1992), p.77.

266. Ibid., pp.77-78.

267. Ibid., Exhibit A.

268. Op.cit., Gary Kah, p.78.

269. Ibid., pp.78,79.

270. Ibid., Exhibit A. Three WCPA co-presidents were listed; the only one familiar to this writer was Prof. Dr. Dennis Brutus, Africa and U.S.A. (poet, university Prof., USA and UK, organiser of Africa Network).

NOTES (cont'd)

271.	Ibid., Exhibit A.

272.	Ibid., WCPA "List of Honorary Sponsors," Exhibits N3-N6. Of interest to ichthyophiles, John Hersey (also) wrote Blues (New York:Random House, 1988 ed.).

273.	Op.cit., Gary Kah, p.79.

274.	Ibid., pp.79-80. See also Exhibit C.

275.	Ibid., p.80.

276.	Op.cit., Gary Kah, p.81.

277.	Ibid., p.82.

278.	Ibid., p.83.

279.	Ibid., pp.83-85. Note: 1984 was not an auspicious year for promoting world government, considering George Orwell.

280.	Ibid., pp.85,86.

281.	..."[A]t the First Three Sessions of the Provisional World Parliament." These three sessions were organised under Article XIX of the Constitution for the Federation of Earth, and were held respectively at Brighton, England (1982); New Delhi, India; and Miami Beach, Fla. (1987). Ibid., Exhibit 01.

282.	Ibid., Exhibit 02.

283.	Ibid., Exhibit 03. Note: The full text of the Constitution for the Federation of the Earth is available (for a small fee) from: The World Constitution and Parliament Association, 1480 Hoyt St., Ste. 31, Lakewood, CO 80215, U.S.A.

284.	Michael S. Coffman, pp.157-158. Quoted from Ron Arnold and Alan Gottlieb, Trashing the Economy: How Runaway Environmentalism is Wrecking America (Bellevue, Wash.:Free Enterprize [Merril Press], 1993), pp.179-181.

285.	Ibid., p.158. Dolphin release figures provided by observer records as analysed by Porpoise Rescue Foundation, as cited by Ron Arnold and Alan Gottlieb, 490.

286.	Ibid., pp.157-159.

287.	C.D. Bay-Hansen, 'Postscript: The Drift-Net Fleets and High Seas Pacific Salmon Interception' (Vol.2), pp.130-146. See note. no.174.

288.	Quote from Greenpeace spokesman Jerry Leape. Cf. 'Japan to Ban Driftnets, Korea to Follow,' Pacific Fishing, February 1992, p.25. See Ch.1, note 57.

289.	The ed[s], 'Study Criticizes U.N. Driftnet Ban,' Pacific Fishing, September 1994, p.26.

NOTES (cont'd)

290. Ibid., pp.26,73.

291. Ibid., p.73.

292. Op.cit., Elliott A. Norse, ed., Global Marine Biological Diversity, p.127.

293. Ibid., pp.127-128. Editor Norse actually seemed to support national sovereign powers regarding "jurisdictional overlap." [In the absence of an international government, a national government will have to do.]

294. Ibid., p.173.

295. The New Lexicon, Webster's Dictionary of the English Language, p.208.

296. Ibid., p.208.

297. Garret Hardin, "Living on a Lifeboat," Managing the Commons, p.265.

298. Chris Wood, 'Who Owns the Sea?', Maclean's, Vol.108, No.13,27 March 1995, p.16 (or final page).

299. Ibid., p.16 (or final page). By the late 1980s, according to Worldwatch Institute, the Nova Scotia trawler fleet was four times larger than necessary to harvest its annual groundfish quota.

300. Peter Redmayne, ed., 'Bad Management Makes Fish Expensive,' Seafood Leader, Vol. 14, No.6, November/December 1994, p.5.

301. Ibid., p.5.

302. Ken Kelley, field ed., 'The Marine Fish Conservation Network: Pressing for basic changes in how fisheries are managed,' National Fisherman, Vol.74, No.12, April 1994, p.57.

303. Ibid., p.56.

304. Ibid., p.56.

305. Ibid., p.56.

306. Ibid., p.56.

307. Ibid., p.56-57.

308. Michael S. Coffman, pp.116-117.

309. Ken Kelley, ed., 'The Marine Fish Conservation Network...," National Fisherman, p.57. ["For not enough regulation?"] author's words only.

310. Ibid., p.57.

311. 'House thrashes out fishing bill, Peninsula Daily News, 19 October 1995, p.A-7.

NOTES (cont'd)

312. Ibid., p.A-7.

313. Ibid., p.A-7.

314. Ibid., p.A-7.

315. Washington State Voters Pamphlet (Olympia:Office of the Secretary of State, 1995), p.4.

316. Ken Kelley, ed.,'The Marine Fish Conservation Network...,' National Fisherman, p.56.

317. 'Supplies of food peaking,' Peninsula Daily News, 16 January 1994, p.A-11. Associated Press source for figures: U.S. Bureau of the Census, Department of Commerce, U.N. Food and Agriculture Organization.

318. Ibid., p.A-11.

319. Ibid., p.A-11.

320. Scott Sonner, 'Report: Overfishing stresses world's oceans,' Peninsula Daily News, 24 July 1994, p.A-5.

321. Ibid., p.A-5.

322. Laine Welch, 'Let 'em Eat By-catch,' Pacific Fishing, November 1993, p.35.

323. Ibid., p.35.

324. 'Illegal fish will benefit food banks,' Peninsula Daily News, 7 November 1993, p.A-5.

325. Laine Welch, 'Let 'em Eat By-catch,' p.35.

326. 'Lovers of fish can't be stopped,' Peninsula Daily News, 30 August 1995, p.C-1.

327. Ibid., p.C-1.

328. Ibid., p.C-1.

329. 'Lee Weddig to Step Down from NFI,' Seafood Leader, Vol.15, No.4, July/August 1995, p.24.

330. Ibid., p.24.

331. 'In Neptune We Trust,' Seafood Leader Whole Seafood Catalog, Vol.12, No.5, September/October 1992, p.32.

332. Ibid., p.32. Ocean Trust was formerly known as World Oceans Fund.

333. 'NFI Jumps into Shrimp Suit,' Seafood Leader, November/December 1994, p.81.

334. Ibid., p.81.

NOTES (cont'd)

335. John van Amerongen, 'Bashing at the Bus Stop,' <u>Alaska Fisherman's Journal</u>, Vol.18, No.10, October 1995, p.10.

336. <u>Ibid.</u>, p.10.

337. <u>Ibid.</u>, p.10.

338. <u>Ibid.</u>, p.10. ["Greenpeaceniks"] author's term only.

339. Mark S. Lundsten, 'Environmental Politics,' <u>Alaska Fisherman's Journal</u>, Vol.18, No.2, p.15.

340. <u>Ibid.</u>, p.15.

341. <u>Ibid.</u>, p.15.

342. 'An Ocean of Uncertainty', <u>Pacific Fishing</u> Yearbook 1994, p.62.

343. <u>Ibid.</u>, pp.62-63.

344. <u>Ibid.</u>, p.63.

345. <u>Ibid.</u>, p.64.

346. <u>Ibid.</u>, p.64.

347. <u>Ibid.</u>, p.66.

348. <u>Ibid.</u>, pp.67-68. Cf. C.D. Bay-Hansen, <u>Fisheries of the Pacific Northwest Coast Vol.1</u> (New York:Vantage Press, 1991), pp.144-146.

349. <u>Ibid.</u>, p.68.

350. <u>Ibid.</u>, p.69.

351. <u>Ibid.</u>, pp.69-70.

352. <u>Ibid.</u>, p.70.

353. <u>Seafood Leader</u> Whole Seafood Catalog, Vol.12, No.5, September/October 1992, p.32.

354. Lee J. Weddig, 'Commercial Overview,' <u>Seafood Leader</u>, Vol.15, No.4, July/August 1995, p.46.

Bibliography for Part III

17. Hardin, Garret and John Baden. Managing the Commons. W.H. Freeman and Company, New York, 1977.

Major References

A. Norse, Elliot A., ed. Global Marine Biological Diversity. Island Press, Washington, D.C., and Covelo, Calif. 1993.

B. Our Living Oceans. NOAA Tech. Memo. NMFS-F/SPO-15. U.S. Dept. of Comm., Silver Spring, MD 1993.

Acknowledgements

I am grateful to Mr. James Meehan of the NMFS for a copy of Our Living Oceans. Thanks to Pastor Harald Petersen and Ms. Holly Knowles of Port Angeles for reading and commenting on Part I, "Is Environmentalism a Religion?"

Interword: En Fimbulvinter ("A Terrible Winter")

"When I was one - and - [fifty]
I heard a wise man say
'Give crowns and pounds and guineas
But not your heart away....
'Tis paid with sighs a plenty,
And sold for endless rue'.
.... And I['ll be] two - and - [fifty]
And oh, 'tis true 'tis true."

- from A.E. Housman, A Shropshire Lad (1896), paraphrased

"96 Tears" was a hit song performed by ? and the Mysterians, circa 1968. Around that time Jimi Hendrix sang and played his composition "51st Anniversary." Well, it's now March 1996 and this writer is presently fifty-one years old and could be described as chronologically-challenged, folically-impaired, (still) a slow-learner and late-starter. But life is good in Port Angeles, Washington. During early autumn 1995 a P.A. parking-lot sign had advertised: "Sweet Corn, Apples, Cider, Smoked Salmon, Yellow Potatoes." Yes, the North Olympic Peninsula is still a good place to live. There is no prospect from the windows of the writer's sturdy wood-frame house of either the (Olympic) Mountains to the south, or the Strait (of Juan de Fuca) to the north. But from a back-yard hot-tub -- the only concession to luxury -- the writer is afforded a nightly panorama of the glorious firmament above. So although denied a view of both landscape and seascape, the writer is treated to an ever-changing skyscape that has been greatly inspirational in writing this book (including the easily-observed [x-ray emitting] Hyakutake comet in late March 1996).

Whither FutureFish? Rough draughts have been scribbled on legal pads, Post-it notes, and candy-coloured notebook paper with cartooned ice cream cones decorating the sheets; the out-grown property of the writer's youngest child. It is amazing how long it takes, and how expensive it is, to produce a serious work without ghost writers, federal grants, or help of any kind. Chapter 1 was started from scratch during August 1991 and not completed until April 1992. Chapter 2 was just finished last December (1995); a full sixteen months after commencement. As for a unifying theme, this writer was determined to balance the "fisheriographical" scales, as stated in the Afterword to Chapter 1. From the almost five years spent in Victoria, B.C. (1982-1987), the writer can recall one fisheriography which sided with corporate management (salmon canners, i.e., B.C. Packers) versus unionised labour (i.e., the United Fishermen and Allied Workers

Union). And the work in question had been written by a long-time B.C. Packers employee, Cicely Lyons (Salmon: Our Heritage, Mitchell Press, Vancouver, B.C., 1969). Since the late 1980s, the trend has been fisheriography with less "Second Wave" rust-belt politicking and more of a "Third Wave" software feel and texture. One well-known U.S. fisheriographer, who is also Pacific editor of a national fisheries magazine, doubles as the commercial fishermen's staunch allay from his monthly column; all the while snuggling up to the environmentally-correct ecosophists through his slick-paged, lavishly-appointed coffee-table volumes ... a literary deceit worthy of a Dr. Jekyll/Mr. Hyde. How such persons of power and influence see humans, fishes, and marine biodiversity deeply affects the fishing and seafood industry. With this caveat in mind, the writer endeavours to expose such consistent hypocrisies without being himself tautological.

As to science .... Before the New Age diffused throughout the culture, Norman Mailer commented in 1969 that he "... could not regard science apart from technology" (Of a Fire on the Moon, Grove Press, Inc., New York, 1970, p.143). Since then science has devolved into pseudo, paradoxical, borderline, and weird science ... with technology solely collateral to true science. To further complicate the equation there are true scientists who are weird. They vary from New Age quantum physicist Fritjof Capra of Berkeley with his I-Ching fortune-sticks, to astronomer Carl Sagan of Cornell with his spiritless Scientism. Both physicists, however, appear to share a remarkably similar political outlook and cultural perspective. How such persons of power and influence view matter, life, energy, and the cosmos deeply affects the Church, the Academy, and the Culture at large.

As to religion .... By the 1990s, voodoo religions had coupled with orthodox religion and true science to spawn heterodox religion and weird science, which in turn have meshed and merged into the cultural mainstream. The classical Western religious tradition of Judaeo-Christianity was historically concerned with the world, the flesh, and the devil. How the Church regarded Creation affected us all. As the eclectic, Electric Church abandoned the evangelical battle for the hearts, minds, and souls of men, it became a sorcerer's apprentice to New Age syncretism. Never out of touch with each other, the Church and the Academy are increasingly interchangeable in philosophy. Such institutions of power and influence deeply affect ideologies in business and government, arts and entertainment, hence the culture at large.

The writer resigned from the New York-based Bay Foundation during the summer of 1995. As in many small American cities, most of the jobs available in Port Angeles are service oriented: Hair care and nail technology, car sales and autobody repairs, attending at nursing homes or waiting at fast-food franchises. So it was back to the Academy in January 1996 for this writer, as a Norwegian-language instructor at Peninsula College. Every freak, geek, gimp, and gump is entitled to an education at the local community college. And kids who were barely graduated from High School (but had indulgent parents) could now take courses on Inner Tennis or Grasshopper Theology for two years, before finally going on to Evergreen State College or Western Washington University. The very first evening the writer went to teach class he noticed violet signs on the Student Center walls which queried: "Gay or Lesbian?" The 1990s peculiarly Clintonesque answer to that question is: "Don't ask, don't tell." Otherwise the hallowed walls of académe hadn't changed much during the last decade. That aside, the writer was grateful to Peninsula College for the work and the Norwegian class for their interest.

March 1996

Bibliography

18.   Capra, Fritjof. The Turning Point. Bantam Books, New York, 1988 ed.

19.   Mailer, Norman. Of a Fire on the Moon. Grove Press, Inc., New York, 1970.

20.   Sagan, Carl. The Demon-Haunted World. Random House, New York, 1995.

FISH, BIRDS, AND MARINE ANIMALS OF THE OLYMPIC PENINSULA
Chuck Rondeau

"Chinook salmon"

"Rainbow trout"

CHUCK RONDEAU 97

"Halibut"

© CHUCK RONDEAU 97

"Herring"

"Lingcod"

CHUCK RONDEAU 97

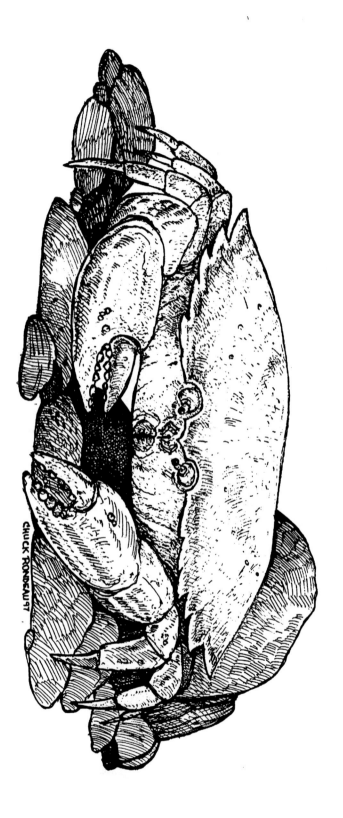

"Dungeness crab"

CHUCK RONDEAU '97

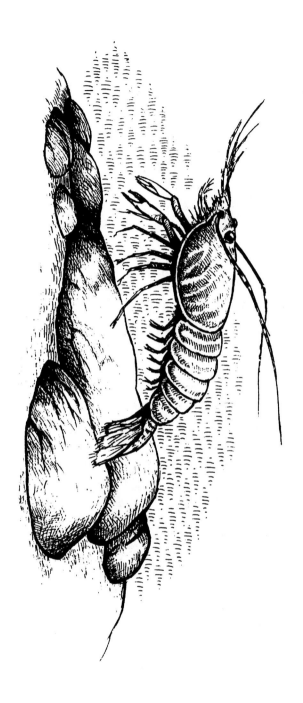

"Shrimp"

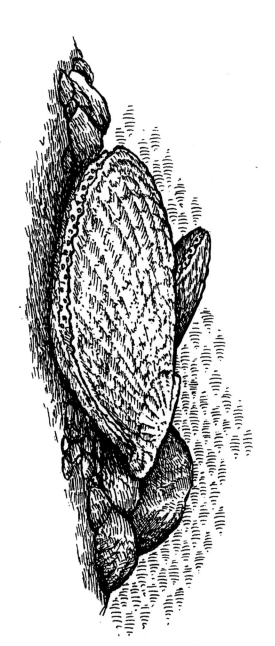

"Rock scallops"

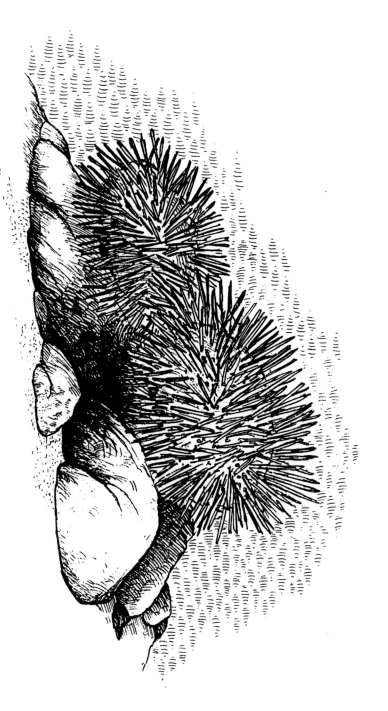

"Urchins"

"Bald eagle"

"Gull"

"Cormorant"

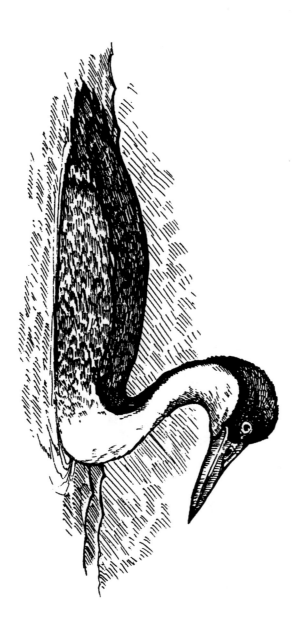

"Grebe"

"Orca"

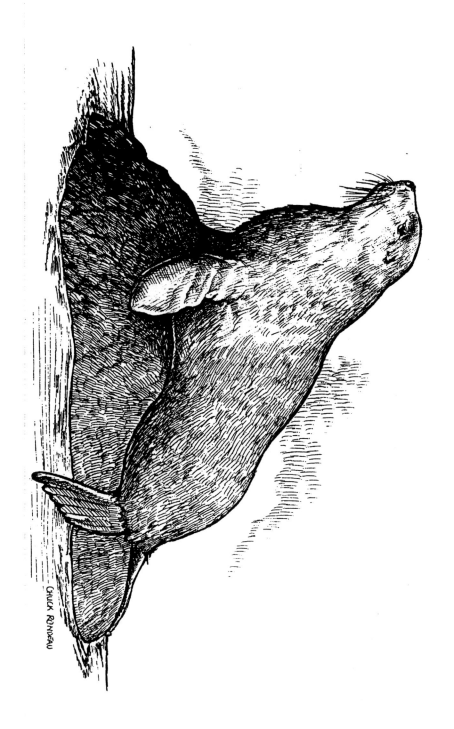

"Sea lion"

CHUCK RONDEAU

Chapter 3 The Pacific Industry Comes of New Age

Part I: "Alaska-menn", Fisherpersons, and Hippies with Guns
(A Norwegian-American View)

Part II: The Pacific Northwest Prepares for Cybercentury
(A Seattle, Washington Vision)

Part III: The Fish of Science and the Pisces of Magic (Scientific vs. Magickal Perspectives)

"The ... New Age Movement ... scarcely excites attention in the media these days not because it has declined, but because it has become commonplace and acceptable .... A movement succeeds when its essential features have become so integrated and established in the larger community that it is no longer recognizable as a movement."
-Elliot Miller, ed. Christian Research Journal[1]

Prelude: From the Electric Church -- Pass the Buck Here

"The New Age didn't crest, it soaked in."
-Terry Mattingly of Milligan College, Johnson, City, Tenn.[2]

It is Advent Sunday 1995 at Holy Trinity Lutheran Church in Port Angeles, Washington. As the months have rolled by since the "New Song" worship began, the musical director's (Praise Team leader) foetal Beatle hair-do has now grown into a full-fledged Rolling Stone hair-helmet. Someone at HTLC must have slipped up for the visiting children's choir is singing "Holy, Holy, Holy", that wonderful classic by hymnodist Reginald Heber (1783-1826). It is a magnificent bluebird of pure reverence, putting to shame the gilded starlings of shallow worship by current composers with first names like Judi, Randee, and Terrye. But the lovely old hymn is soon sung, and a brief moment of agapē passes into oblivion. We are back to being the Lutheran Lite Church wherein every soul is promised a post-mortem safe passage to, and an assured place in, the celestial Lake Wobegon. All are welcome in the Garrison Keillorised heaven except conservative right-wing extremists, and Christian-fundamentalist religious bigots.[3] The only real sinners left in today's all-tolerating Lutheran Church are modern Pharisees; the only remaining sins are guilt and feeling guilty about guilt. In the Lutheran Lite Eternity, there is no judgment and punishment, no wailings and gnashing of teeth in outer darkness.

A New Song finishes, sounding as if composed on amphetamines. The words are meaningless, maudlin, and the herky-jerky music is impossible to follow for ordinary parishioners. This writer sits down and looks up, waiting for the Praise Team show-off girls to be seated. The male musicians, usually clad in Nike sweat-suits or designer levis, are hunched over their amplified instruments. The senior pastor strides to the lectern, beaming with the priggish self-assurance of one embodying a religiously-correct clergyperson. He reminds this writer of Tom Wolfe's Modern Churchman in The Kandy-Kolored Tangerine-Flake Streamline Baby. In one chapter -- 'Old Faces, New Fashions' -- Wolfe cleverly sketched a 1963 portrait of "The Modern Churchman at the hootenanny, reaching the Urban Young People."[4] Wolfe's drawing depicted the Modern Churchman, complete with Evelyn Waugh thatched hair-style, singing and strumming a banjo. A clerical collar peeks up from out of his V-necked, thick-ribbed Arran Islander sweater. Tom Wolfe's 1963 model served as the spiritual forerunner of the Homo novus (Wolfe's New Man) now addressing the bemused HTLC congregation:

"Hold life-affirming values, including commitments to racial and gender equality, affirmation of cultural and religious diversity .... Advocate social and global change to bring about greater social justice ...."[5]

This is politically-correct speech down to the last jot and tittle, with all the fine-sounding buzz-phrases of the 1960s, once considered so cutting-edge, now so banally mainstream. Some social results of Homo novus thinking have been that political inequality and lack of cultural diversity are wrongs, but, in our Oprahesque "relationships", lying and cheating are relative behavioural patterns, always to be rationalised as up to individual choosing. Sin has evolved from personal failing to cosmic injury, just as God has been metamorphed from personal Lord into impersonal deity. The upshot has been for the No-Fault Church to advocate the weed-trimming of sins; though out of sight, the roots of the flowers of evil are still deeply planted. And they will sprout again, more luxuriantly than ever. This cosmetic mowing is a basic tenet of the Church of Convenience, run by religious apostates and rank amateurs.

Thus one can't really blame the wildly pagan, Darwinist libertarian types (numerous in the contemporary fishing industry) for eschewing as sappy the collectivist Peter, Paul and Mary atmosphere of the 1990s Amplified Church. But this writer deeply resents a commonly-held secular perception that Christianity itself is a repressive, passive "religion of losers." The preceding phrase was employed to describe Christianity by self-made, self-seen Alpha wolf Ted Turner of TBS (now surely a Beta after absorbtion by Time Warner). On second thought this writer cannot blame Ted Turner (Mr. Jane Fonda) either, for considering oecumenical Christianity a namby-pamby religion. The call for "affirmation of religious diversity" by liberal theologians is inconsistent with Church doctrine, and indeed negates the exclusive claims which lie at the very heart of evangelical Christianity. This writer can hardly imagine questioning the (also) exclusive claims of Judaism or Islam -- the other great monotheisms -- to a Chassidic rabbi or Shi'ite mullah in the name of "religious diversity."

The tall, solidly-built boobus of a junior pastor was reading the scripture lesson for today. His pink cheeks were covered with a three-day down of designer-stubble to atone for the dearth of hair on his bulbous head. This writer suspects that the thirtysomething junior pastor thought of himself as looking both adult and pretty "rad"(ical). Excepting for outward appearance, the junior pastor was a near-perfect Seventies imitation of the Sixties senior pastor. There was one other big difference: Mention guns to the junior pastor and his normally sheep-like eyes would immediately harden and glaze over like Charles Bronson's. He now read John 8:1-11 (The Woman Taken in Adultery) and then preached a pointless, follow-up sermonette. [Those hateful scribes and Pharisees were judgmental like today's conservatives.] The sermonette was pointless on purpose. In the reading, the junior pastor had slyly omitted the concluding sentence where Jesus admonishes the woman -- '[G]o and sin no more" -- without which the parable is incomplete. Jesus forgives -- "Neither do I condemn thee" -- in the previous sentence, when none of the woman's accusers could cast the first stone. But without the clincher of the finale, there is forgiveness but no admonishment. As the theme of admonishment is religiously incorrect in the Electric Church, it is avoided (along with atonement) wherever possible. After the service the writer accosted the junior pastor concerning his omission, but to no avail.

To leave the church building this writer had to go by the pastoral library. Last month's HTLC periodical had proudly announced a new [age] arrival to grace the pastoral bookshelf: "Old Turtle -- by Douglas Wood, Abby Book of the year 1993 Children's book [sic] Award. An enchanting fable for children and adults promotes a deeper understanding of the earth and our relationship with all the beings who inhabit it."[6] Perhaps the "E" in ELC (Evangelical Lutheran Church) should stand for Electric or [O]Ecumenical (universal). Perhaps by competing with Ted Turner's Captain Planet, the ELC's hip god of Lake Wobegon will qualify for New Age status.

For Lutherans of true faith, the Church year did not get off to a good start in 1996:

".... The Evangelical Lutheran Church in America (ELCA) considers it no longer essential to believe that Christ rose from the dead. A book recently published by the Augsburg-Fortress Press of the 5.6 million - member ELCA, by Professor Gerd Luedemann, comes to the conclusion that the body of Jesus decayed in the grave."[7]

Surely the Resurrection is the bedrock on which the Christian faith is built! For this Lutheran of good faith, the Church year got off to an especially bad start in 1996. The January HTLC pastoral newsletter featured a column by a canonical journeyperson; a wimpy, soppy cosmic New Christian who fancied himself a religiously-correct cut above the common pastoral flock. He archly promised that,

"As I go into the New Year I resolve to let the light of Christmas brighten those parts of the larger world that I can affect. The tree and the trains [the columnist's belovèd American Flyer choo-choos] will be put away and the light of the day will reveal opportunities to minister. I will remember that Jesus' ministry was marked by forgiveness, compassion, and acceptance, and I will pray that these values enlighten my actions...."[8]

Oh, wow! How utterly wet and weedy! This writer had seen Mr. New Christian at church, in Bible class, and around the neighbourhood "doing his thing" as male co-mother. He seemed to be in constant competition with his doctor-wife as to which Mom (Mrs. or Mr.) was the more child-carrying (in back pack), caring, nourishing, nurturing, touching, feeling and indulging parent. As a result their two young sons were always out of control -- bawling like calves, with protruded tongues, distended eyes, and contorted limbs. New [Age] Christians don't believe in fatherhood or discipline and it showed. Mr. New Christian wrote so easily of "acceptance." And one wonders how much "compassion" he would have for a pedophile who had sexually molested one -- or both -- of his precious young sons? And could Mr. New Christian forgive the predator?

May Martinus Luther rest in peace, the doughty Saxon who challenged Rome and once hurled an ink-well at the devil! Though the church that bears his name is a back-slidden church, there are thousands of latter-day Lutherans from Norway to New Zealand, in the fields and on the boats, who still truly worship the ..."[B]ulwark never failing."[9]

End Note:

"[T]he Church indulges our desire 'to feel good' instead of responding to our need to be spiritually challenged and fed through solid exposition of the Scriptures. The [E]lectronic Church in particular panders to our appetite for entertainment rather than authentic discipleship and maturity."
-Joyce Main Hanks,
In the Preface to The Humiliation of the Word
by Jacques Ellul
(Quoted in The Berean Call, (Bend, Ore.), March 1996, p.3.)

Part I: "Alaska-menn," Fisherpersons, and Hippies with Guns

(A Norwegian-American View)

"[I]t seems probable that the dolicho-blond type of European man is possessed of a greater facility for ... reversion to barbarism than the other ethnic elements with which that type is associated in the Western culture."
-Thorstein Veblen, The Theory of the Leisure Class (1899)

.... "I am one of the true conservatives, as are many of the old hippies from that [1960s] time. We want to be left alone. We don't want the government on our backs, telling us what we can and cannot do, when it is none of their business."
-Arlo Guthrie in a 1996 interview

.... "There are several guys online for every woman. But, like the outlook for women in Alaska, the odds are good, but the goods are odd."
-Clifford Stoll, from Silicon Snake Oil

A 1995 year-end subscription renewal advertisement for Pacific Fishing magazine shows two strong young men sitting on the beach at Waikiki. They are looking at an issue of Pacific Fishing, with luxury hotels and Diamond Head looming in the background. Underneath the inset photograph the advertisement reads:

".... Gunnar and Pete bought their tickets to Hawaii right after cashing in the season's settlement check.... A quick, free call updated their subscription for another year. Follow the lead of these two savvy fishermen....

"Whether you're heading out to fish or heading for vacation, you need to stay informed about prices, catches, regulations, new products and overall trends in commercial fishing...."

The Pacific Fisherman reader would guess that the fellow pictured on the left, the huskier of the two, would be "Gunnar." Although appearing very North American in his sleeveless T-shirt and baseball cap, Gunnar definitely has the look of a good Scandihoovian boy. Gunnar's parents (or more likely grandparents) were very possibly born in Norway or Sweden, and Gunnar himself is most probably a native of Western Washington, British Columbia, or Southeast Alaska. The Pacific Fishing editors know their demographics as a goodly portion of North Pacific fishermen, both American and Canadian, are of Scandinavian origin or descent. The social, political, and economic metro-centre of Norwegian America is Seattle, Washington. The Pacific Northwest and Alaska have long since displaced Minnesota and the north-central states of the Upper Midwest as the living repository of Nordic Americana.[10] North of downtown Seattle across the Ballard Bridge lies "Snoose Junction," the cultural hub of Scandinavian Seattle. (Burnaby, B.C., is Vancouver, Canada's opposite number.) This writer moved to Ballard with his family in late summer 1976.

The Ballard section of Seattle -- that general area north of Salmon Bay and east of Shilshole Bay -- had been touted as being the perfect urban setting for a Norwegian-American family to settle. Social satirist Tom Wolfe would have dubbed the 1970s residents of Ballard as ethnically an "Anglo-European ... ghetto-colonial population." But Ballard, fondly and defiantly called "Snoose [snus] Junction", was a ghetto first by chance and now by choice, has worked hard overtime maintaining Scandinavian roots and ties. The main reason Seattle generally, and Ballard particularly, remains ascendant as the heart of Norwegian America is the North Pacific fishing industry. A large part of the Old Country roots and ties is mutual economic interest. A constant stream of Norwegian fishermen, engineers, and technicians came and went during the mid-late 1970s -- and still are -- on their way to and from the lucrative fishing grounds in the Gulf of Alaska, Bristol Bay, Bering Sea, and Norton Sound. This writer would sometimes encounter these transient, but well-heeled, Alaska-menn at watering holes like the Vasa Grill on Ballard Avenue, or the Valhalla Tavern on Market Street; drink beer and speak Norwegian with them. These high-rollin', high-tech fellows were strictly here for the Big Bucks, and most regarded Seattleite-Scandinavian cultural aspirations as quaint, laughable, and strictly for old folks (gamlinger). The Alaska-menn found the prevalence of Norwegian language and institutions in Ballard pleasantly convenient, but felt no personal stake in keeping them. And as well-paid sockeye salmon highliners or king crabber-cowboys, they had the usual contempt for domestic society of rich, young unmarried men everywhere.

Another aggregate of Alaska-menn, far greater in number and older in age than the Norwegian nationals depicted above, were fishermen, engineers, and technicians of Norwegian origin who had become American citizens and permanently lived in the United States. Some of them as children had accompanied their immigrant parents to America during the 1950s, and had grown up in places like the Upper Midwest or on the East Coast. Although not an <u>Alaska-mann</u>, this writer identified with the latter social category of true Norwegian-Americans. It was the naturalised Norwegian-Americans who ran Ballard as a distinctly ethnic community, with power-nodes at Ballard First Lutheran Church, Sons of Norway, the Freemasonic Lodge, the University of Washington, and Fishermen's Terminal. Ballard had its own Norwegian-language weekly newspaper, <u>Western Viking</u>, and the BFLC pastor blessed the Alaska-bound fleet at the onset of every fishing season. Passions in Ballard ran high on "<u>Syttende mai</u>" (17 May 1814, Norwegian Constitution Day); yet higher on a rare visit by the King of Norway. Unlike the usually younger transients from the Old Country, these U.S. citizen-residents had a crucial stake in Ballard and indeed in Norwegian America.

This writer got to know one naturalised <u>Alaska-mann</u> quite well during 1975-1978, the three years spent in the Seattle-Tacoma area. He was six years my senior, born in Kvinesdal in southern Norway, and brought up in Bay Ridge, Brooklyn (New York City's version of Ballard). Although speaking English in a slight Vest-Agder accent, Gustav ("Gus") was virtually indistinguishable from his American-born peers. He followed Mariners baseball, drank Rainier beer and Mac Naughton's Canadian, favoured rare beef-steaks, and was doted on by his elderly mother "Back East." One couldn't appear to be a more localised product than Gus, and as an adopted Seattleite that was fine with him. It was the New York connection as much as the Norwegian commonality that related this writer to Gus. But he also had his down side: He was an <u>Alaska-mann</u> after all, and at age thirty-seven years had been twice married and divorced "Up North." The writer had once visited Gus at his sumptious two-storey home in Richmond Beach, north of Seattle. The huge, half-empty house was interiorly decorated in Las Vegas-style 1970s Lounge Elvisiana. Gus had a young son from one of his failed marriages staying with him that weekend. The boy was an attractive child with Irish first names and black Amerindian eyes. The writer recalls thinking that the entire sad situation was as especially All-American as Gus envisioned himself to be. His son had as little chance of learning Norwegian language, or appreciating Norwegian heritage, as he did of becoming close to his father and paternal grandmother. There was something tragically American about that too. But it was also the result of what made Gustav a restless, driven <u>Alaska-mann</u>.

Last and most numerous of the Alaska-menn, of all ages, were the Americans of largely Norwegian descent domiciled in Ballard and the greater Seattle-Tacoma area. This writer specifies "largely" as the majority of home-grown Alaska-menn were of mixed North European ancestry; (other) Scandinavian, Baltic, Germanic, Anglo-Saxon and Celtic. But superimposed on all the Caucasian denizens of greater Ballard was a common Americanised Scandihoovian cultural identity, constantly freshened by new arrivals from Norway, the Upper Midwest, and Southeast Alaska. To be sure there were Native Americans, Aleuts and Asians residing in greater Ballard, but the Snoose Junction of the 1970s was basically Tom Wolfe's "Anglo-European ... ghetto colonial population" with a self-imposed Scandinavian imprint.

A prototypal example of the American-born Alaska-mann was "Pinky," the Ballard real estate agent from whom this writer bought his house. Pinky, resplendent in chocolate double-knit leisure suit with matching saffron vinyl belt and loafers, was relaxed in his retirement after a hard life as Seattle bus-driver and Alaska fisherman. Pinky wore a diamond-studded Masonic ring alongside his wedding band, and seemed to enormously enjoy his late-life incarnation as realtor. A large, powerful man in his mid-sixties with work-worn hands, Pinky boostered the virtues of Ballard in his bull-horn voice, while endlessly puffing Pall Mall filters. The ashtray of his limousine-like 1973 Chrysler overflowed with cigarette butts, and these would spill onto the floor whenever Pinky brake-stopped for a frequent "fuel injection" at (many) a favourite tavern in greater Ballard. Once down in Ballard proper, preferably at the F.O.E. (Fraternal Order of Eagles), Pinky would get serious about his drinking and forsake Lucky Lager for Fleischmann's 90 Proof. It was at the Eagles that Pinky, his pale blue eyes getting all watery, would speak longingly of his dear, departed Swedish-born Mamma from Luleå; while cursing the memory of his Latvian first wife. Like Gus, the younger Alaska-mann, Pinky had been twice married with little influence on his only child. Both men had succumbed, in more ways than one, to a rough and distant fishery.

Despite the trials of life with Pinky, the writer learned valuable first lessons about the Alaska fisheries. It was through the unlikely Pinky that this writer developed an abiding interest in the North Pacific fisheries which has persisted to this day. Although earning a history degree in 1978 from Seattle Pacific University, this writer's most treasured textbook was Fisheries of the North Pacific by Robert J. Browning.[11] In time the oversized blue book became this writer's main reference -- a staple for the Pacific fisheries student, as the Bible is for the Christian or the "Big Book" of A.A. for the alcoholic. And it was through Pinky that the writer became acquainted with "halibut skippers from Sunset Hill" and other Alaska-menn resident in greater Ballard. The cocky and coarse Alaska Norwegians reminded the writer of the self-made Greek-Americans in Henry Miller's The Colossus of Maroussi. These Alaska-menn -- productive fishermen, pipeline technicians and the like -- had achieved great material success on the "Last Frontier" -- and felt fully deserving of the lionisation they were accorded. A preponderance of these Alaska-menn appeared to hail from Karmøy, in southwestern Norway between Stavanger and Haugesund. They served in Seattle as a fairly benign, Nordic-Masonic mafia, and did a lot of Aussie and Texas-style bragging. One could read the lavish praises heaped on them in Western Viking, Ballard's Norwegian weekly; and, if lucky, catch a glimpse of "storguttene" ("the big boys") in their big boats at the yearly blessing of the fleet.

The pastor of First Ballard Lutheran Church presided over the annual event at the onset of the spring fishing season. The Norwegian-descended pastor was a laid-back, Marlboro-smoking, former pharmacist from North Dakota. He looked surprised then amused, when this writer, a man of thirty-two years, requested to be instructed in the Catechism and confirmed as a Lutheran. Evidently, from the pastor's reaction, the American Lutheran Church (ALC), was similar to the Church of Norway: The parishioner was christened as a baby, confirmed as a teenager, married as an adult, and subsequently buried after shuffling off this mortal coil. Except for celebrating Christmas and sometimes Easter, the vast majority of nominal Norwegian Lutherans attended only "milestone" services for themselves, friends and relatives. This was certainly true in Norway; was it also true in America? The comfortable ALC pastor smiled at the writer's probing questions concerning Church canon and Lutheran doctrine. He sighed easily, knowing from long experience that the initial enthusiasm of most "born-again" Christians didn't last. The pastor could afford to be indulgent. People were searching everywhere these days (mid-1970s) for "spirituality"; from the Astara Foundation to Zen Buddhism. As it transpired, this writer was confirmed a short time after his infant daughter was baptised. But the casual Ballard First Lutheran Church pastor was wrong -- the new confirmand would, like the Bereans, diligently glean ".... the Scriptures ... to find out whether these things were so" (Acts 17:11).

This writer occasionally broached the topic of religious belief to Gus and Pinky, though suspecting that both were reluctant believers, if at all. It sufficed for Gus that his mother attended a Norwegian church back in Brooklyn, and prayed for him. As for Pinky, the Freemasonic Lodge was his church. Although not a member of Ballard First Lutheran Church, Pinky said, he had "Viking hår -- running big, speckled hands through thinning, pale-orange strands to prove his point and change the subject. Pinky always took pains to emphasize his Scandihoovian connections, even as he pronounced "Einar" as "Eener" (rhyming with "wiener"). Gus and Pinky were hardly equivalent to the Kiplingesque fishermen in Captain's Courageous; they were rather the hard-bitten characters in Bill McCloskey's Highliners.[12] In the words of this writer's wife, Alaska-menn were "... bein-harde, lut-fattige, barske og bause karer" (bone-hard, lye [i.e., dirt]-poor, fierce and reckless fellows"). It followed that neither Gus (now fairly rich) nor Pinky (now well-off) were the ideologically-motivated Nordic Alaskans of the future, as envisioned by Hjalmar Rutzebeck, Danish-American author and left-wing political activist of the 1920s.[13] Conversations with Gus seldom transcended beer or baseball; this writer never learned the Alaska-mann's politics. Off-handed remarks made by Gus indicated a vaguely Darwinistic libertarianism. But Pinky was politically involved, and true to his nick-name preached "wobbly" unionist syndicalist sermons. This didn't jive with Pinky's big V-8 Chrysler and assiduously cultivated persona of polyester-clad realtor. To indicate this obvious inconsistency to him would have engendered a blustery denial in fog-horn tones. Pinky was, after all, running for Seattle City Council.

By mid-1978, this writer was ready to move on. Post-graduate studies in Pacific history beckoned from the University of Hawaii at Manoa. The arch-liberal mayor of Seattle, Charles Royer, had spoken of city-wide "busing" of public school children to achieve racial parity in education. Both of the writer's young sons were happy and doing well at Adams, the Ballard neighbourhood primary school. And who were the Seattle City or Washington State social engineers to tell folks which school their children should, or should not, attend? Although the ominous threat of city-wide busing was never carried out, there remained the unsettled feeling of having been let down. There were other reasons for leaving Ballard. For this writer, still in his salad days at the time, young and green in judgment, there was the very real crisis of overdosing on Norwegian-American Scandihoovian culture. Just how many times could one hear the same old lutefisk jokes and still find them funny?[14]

And modern Norway, all chauvinist propaganda to the contrary, stood for nothing on the political world stage except U.N.-inspired globalist values. The Norwegian royal family -- loved and lauded by Norwegians everywhere -- since the death of the majestic Haakon VII in 1957, was a dull remnant of vulgar clods headed by Olav V, a monarch who made endless, meaningless speeches punctuated by a braying laugh. His son and heir, the weak and doltish Crown Prince Harald, had married a calculating commoner, "Crown Princess" Sonja, who had quickly assumed control at the royal palace. While in Norway some years ago, this writer had, in consternation, watched as King Olav gave the 1975 New Year address over the state-run television medium (NRK). The United Nations had officially designated 1975 as the Year of the [Feminist] Woman. Olav V had obediently read a prepared statement extolling the U.N. (FN) and the Year of the Woman (Kvinneåret). Crown Princess Sonja was seated directly behind the King, gazing on with a triumphant smirk. This was Her Highness' crowning achievement, and she savoured every moment of it.

Americans of Norwegian extraction, as well as Norwegian-Americans, dutifully bowed and scraped whenever and wherever His Majesty and Their Highnesses appeared. This writer felt no more love for the devolved Norwegian royal family than loyalty for the rigidly-Socialist Norwegian state. Views like these were considered anathema in the Old Country, Ballard, or Bay Ridge, Brooklyn. Well-intentioned, (usually) "seasoned [American] citizens" of Norwegian origin, wishing to share their enthusiasm for kongefamilien with this writer would be clearly told, "My King died in 1957."

This writer thus quit Ballard with some pangs of traitrous guilt but few regrets. Gus, as expected, would send no post; his efforts were spared for present and future gal-pals and for Mamma back in Bay Ridge. Pinky, though, turned out to be a voluminous correspondent. The writer could only wonder uncomprehendingly at the lengthy, scrawled letters signed "Pop." What Pinky wanted more than anything else was a proud and profane "highliner" for a son ... an Alaska-mann like Gus. The writer left for graduate study at U.H. Manoa, with his two most important textbooks being the King James Version (KJV) Bible, and Fisheries of the North Pacific by Robert J. Browning. In 1978 the writer had never heard of the New Age movement.

The writer returned to the Pacific Northwest with his family in 1982, having thoroughly digested both the Bible and Browning's book. After living four years in Honolulu, Hawaii, the writer knew of the New Age movement but dismissed it as a mere cultic fad among the many polyestrous haole women and surfer girls infesting the Islands. Hawaii Nei was a U.S.-extended California Ultima; a geographical cultural refuge for unstable Mainland Americans, many female. The sought Polynesian gods were there, promising mana (empowerment) and imparting aloha (peace, love, joy) to those paying them homage. Priapic Local men would surround these witless and vulnerable wahines like hyaenas hunting antelope. James A. Michener's leering portrayal of the ukelele-strumming beach-boy sexual stereotype in Hawaii was true-to-life ugly. This writer attributed the New Age ascendancy to a 1960s Judaeo-Christian "great falling away", which also resulted in the frenzied Jesus-freakery of the 1970s as a delayed reaction. Norman Mailer had prophetically commented on the eve of the 1970s: "[I] could see ... how new religions might crystallize in the Seventies, they could give life, for their view of God might be new...."[15] Those hot-house flowers of evil planted during the 1960s would bloom during the 1970s and on.

This writer once back on the Mainland soon forgot the weird, chanting, neo-pagan women in Hawaii. The New Age movement was again rationalised as a passing fancy, poisonous only to the lotus-eaters in Paradise and La-La Land. There was little sign of a portending New Age invasion of the Pacific Northwest. If anything, the opposite seemed true. In August 1982 the writer visited Pinky and spouse, who had moved from Ballard to Sequim, Washington. And the writer distinctly remembers a conversation at the Key Hole Tavern in nearby Carlsborg. The proprietor, an acquaintance of Pinky's, tried to offset his sour-faced mate by always smiling. The subject which eventually came under discussion -- over Olympia Pale Export beer -- was death and the afterlife. The publican's wife stated, emphatically, that human beings after death fared no better than sand dollars (phylum Echinodermata), from which we are no different. At this the writer balked, indignantly declaring "Hey! Everybody in this room is special!" In retrospect, if the writer had put down his glass of Oly and looked about him at the human flotsam and jetsam that mostly comprised the Key Hole clientele, he might not have spoken so hastily. In 1982 the writer was still in his thirties, but the contention had been valid: Surely death, and its aftermath, signified more for humankind than fertiliser production as ultimate eco-therapy? Perhaps not for the proprietress of the Key Hole Tavern.

By 1987, when the writer and his family settled in Port Angeles, the New Age movement had reached high-tide. At first glance, New Age ecosophy had merely promoted whales and dolphins to the mind and spirit level of man, rather than demoting man to the biological level of sand dollars, as had the neo-Darwinians. But like two bisecting lines the at-variance mind-sets would meet at some locus -- of this the writer was sure, but in the mid-late 1980s didn't know where. The main point of departure, as well as area of commonality, was eco-Evolution. That, and a hatred/denial of a Creator-God, was where the New Age and neo-Darwinism appeared to be in accord. It was while doing early research for FutureFish that the writer suddenly stumbled upon the New Age-cetacean connection. Ernest Callenbach had written in the mid-1970s of an ecological utopia, Ectopia, [supposedly] wherein...

"Special types of oceanographic research are highly advanced; a seaborne unit, for instance, has been at work for some years in an attempt to decode the 'speech' of dolphins and whales -- specially equipped divers live among dolphins at sea for long periods, just as ethnographers would do if they wished to learn the language of an unknown tribe...."[16]

Once the connection was made -- the dam was breached -- a whitewater tide of cetacean current wisdom (cw) flooded out. In The American Replacement of Nature (1991), William Irwin Thompson mused, "Now a planetary entity is evolving, and individual minds are being enclosed within a planetary lattice. New Age folk see is a bodhisattvaic ideal of empathy for all sentient beings, from whales and dolphins to starving nomads in the Sahel...."[17] Thompson also visualised a "dolphin-torn, whale-sounded, galactic music polity of extraterrestrial consciousness" as his personally projected New Age ecotopia.[18]

The language of dolphins and the music of whales have become a staple on televised nature programmes. Discovery Sunday (DSC) on 2 April 1995 featured 'Dolphins, Whales and Us', with "us" as a poor third. Background sound was provided by whale-singing and the given catecean eco-reproof. (Is the latter a form of mammalian species-ism?) No less an institution than the Cousteau Society publishes a monthly eco-newsmagazine, Dolphin Log. The lead article in the January 1995 issue featured a gushing letter from bland astronaut Steve Smith, that praised Captain Jacques to (presumably) young readers.[19] The élitiste Cousteau, like H.R.H. the Duke of Edinburgh, believes that millions of human beings should perish to make room on the Blue Planet ... so that more favoured life forms, such as cetaceans, may live. This eco-cleansing naturally does not apply to the Captain or His Grace. The 1970s Jacques Cousteau, the once-personable and informative skipper of the <u>Calypso</u>, has evolved into the distant eco-<u>Pontifex Maximus</u> of the 1990s New Age oceanography. Satirical writer P.J. O'Rourke has brought porpoise lore back to basic sea-level:

"Our friend and fellow intellectual the dolphin .... [w]ith the help of various activist groups ... has achieved everything except the vote and abortion rights. But out in blue water the dolphin is a fish thief and welfare cheat. A hooked game fish is an easy mugging, a finned food stamp to a dolphin....

"[A] dolphin makes one swipe at a king fish the size of a golf bag -- a king fish you've been fighting for half an hour -- and leaves nothing but the head. Anybody who's seen this will think again before getting into the Sea World swim tank with smiling, playful Flipper."[20]

Orcas -- killer whales --have been called "wolves of the sea" for good reason. In the hierarchical eco-pecking order of mammalia, cetaceans precede pinnipeds. Orcas hunt sea-lions and seals the way cats do rats and mice. The North American public has manifested an enormous interest in predator-prey "action scenes", a not-so-subtle form of animal "snuff movie." A video series widely advertised on TV has been <u>The Trials of Life</u>, Video One: 'Hunting and [precious little] Escaping'. One brief clip of this video (if memory serves) shows a seal pup, having been separated from its frantic mother, being tossed back and forth high in the air by a pod of "playful" orcas. That's entertainment! Although the general public today is especially aware of nature's beauty and brutality through TV nature programming, the eco-scam of animal anthropomorphism -- for fun and profit -- continues unabated. A Dr. Randall Eaton, along with his Orca Project volunteers, has been swimming for two decades with wild orcas and <u>feeling</u> the effects of their sounds. The good doctor has theorised:

"We don't know exactly what happens, but the orca sounds elevate moods. Some people say that they feel their hearts open. Others describe it as the most profound experience of their lives...

"... Orcas are giant dolphins. We suspect that the sounds they direct to people in the water with them are not unlike those used by dolphins with handicapped children in the Florida Keys."[21]

But there has never been an eco-con job so successful or so pervasive as Save the Whales. For the last quarter century and more, this aggregated lobby has influenced public opinion to the extent that the U.S., and other Western nations, have virtually banned whaling world-wide. Whales are far more cinematic than starving humans, and Hollywood along with a compliant press have disseminated eco-disinformation about both whales and whaling. The blue, gray, and humpback whales have indeed been endangered species, but all three whales were protected by international agreement long before Greenpeace or Sea Shepherd existed. The only species hunted by modern Norwegian whalers is the minke whale, which Norwegians eat as hvalbiff (whale-beef). In 1994, thirty-two Norwegian whaling ships harvested 279 minkes, from an estimated local population of 87,000 and a world population of 900,000.[22] In 1982, the International Whaling Commission (IWC) voted to adopt a five-year moratorium on commercial whaling (ostensibly to collect better data on whale populations), to commence in 1986. Norway, although complying voluntarily, nonetheless excused herself from the moratorium as the IWC treaty allowed. Other whaling nations were soon to find out that the IWC, including the U.S., had no intention of ever lifting the ban on commercial harvesting, whale numbers notwithstanding. Canada quit the Commission in 1982, Iceland left in 1992, and Norway ended her voluntary compliance in 1993. Also during 1993, the British chairman of the IWC's scientific committee resigned in protest at the Commission's attitude and actions as having ..."nothing to do with science."[23]

According to David Andrew Price, a writer and an attorney practising with the Washington (D.C.) Legal Foundation, New Age cetacean lore originated with physician and weird science exponent John Lilly. During the 1950s the (mad) doctor convinced himself that cetaceans were so brilliant and communicative, that they were able to orally pass down accumulated whale/dolphin knowledge of philosophy, history, and science to their progeny. (A grey whale cow in Scammon's Lagoon could, conceivably, "tell" her weaned calf of Maya brain-trepanning.) John Lilly's conclusions were based on his observations of dolphins at his Virgin Islands laboratory. By the late 1970s, the dotty Dr. Lilly foresaw the U.S. State Department actually negotiating treaties with cetacean civilisations![24] True scientists have also observed cetacean intelligence and arrived at different conclusions than Dr. Lilly. Margaret Klinowska of Cambridge University sees whale brain structures as more similar to those of bats or hedgehogs than of the higher primates. And the late David and Melba Campbell of U.Florida have flatly stated that "dolphins do not talk.... [D]olphins probably are just exceptionally amiable mammals with an intelligence now considered by most workers, on a subjective basis, to be comparable to that of a better-than-average dog."[25]

And as for the vaunted "whale-sounded, galactic music" of the New Age guru William Irwin Thompson, true science asserts that whale vocalisation is no different from that of other animals. Indeed, whale "singing" is done solely by males and only for half the year at that; more like random bird-song than deliberate human speech. Louis Herman, director of U.Hawaii's marine mammal laboratory, has studied captive dolphins since 1967 and whales in the wild since 1976. Herman says that he has found no evidence that cetacean vocalisation constitutes a language.[26] Another dolphin researcher, Kenneth Norris of U.Cal. Santa Cruz, and one of the first to study dolphins in the wild, has written that they have "a complicated animal communication system, yes, but for an abstract syntactic language like ours, no compelling evidence seemed, or seems, to exist."[27] (Louis Herman opposes whaling, and Kenneth Norris is responsible for much of the knowledge about dolphin sonar.)

So the current ban on whaling, related to the anthropomorphising of dolphins, has nothing to do with conservation. It boils down to the wistful wish of many North Americans and Western Europeans to impose their cetacean-sensibilities upon whaling peoples; the Norwegians, Icelanders, Russians, Japanese, American and Canadian Inuits. The Save-the-Whales aggregated lobby has convinced the Western World that whales are "endangered under-water Einsteins."[28] What has afforded this writer some especial amusement has been the political machinations of Gro Harlem Brundtland, Prime Minister of Norway. "Statsminister Gro", ecofeminist and shrillest voice at the 1992 Rio Earth Summit, has been of late on the horns of a literal dilemma: How to remain the global high-priestess of eco-correctness while simultaneously appearing to defend, in the international forum, the ancient tradition and honourable trade of Norwegian whaling.

On the Northwest Coast of North America it is the five species of Pacific salmon which have been anthropomorphised.[29] They are held in the same high-holy esteem that whales and dolphins are elsewhere. Much of the Salmon People mythology has been passed down by Native Northwest tribes as a rich, historical legacy to the present heterogeneous population. In Pacific Northwest waters the salmon is the only fish to achieve an ecologically-favoured niche. The difference, from cetaceans, is in the eating: The Pacific salmon is a fish, and sustains Northwest man by its timely spawning cycles, traditionally imparting to its consumers a local form of mana empowerment. The Makah of Cape Flattery have hunted the whale for centuries, but whales outrank humans -- even aboriginals -- in the ecologically-correct current wisdom. Somehow the Pacific salmon, though fished and canned, retains its special place in the hearts and minds of the Northwest Coast populace. Farther south the tunas are fished, canned, and consumed too, but remain unfavoured fishes in the lower echelons of eco-ichthyology. There is worry, certainly, concerning tuna migration patterns and recruitment numbers, but with none of that spiritual eco-fervour accorded the salmons. There are no Tuna People in Native West Coast legend, thus the tunas are relegated to being a piscine category of sea-lions and seals, mere pinnipeds, while salmons are regarded as the opposite number of the more beautiful, more intelligent cetaceans.

In a fairly recent British Columbia Farmed Salmon Institute advertisement, it stated: "Salmon thrive not only in our waters, but in our souls...."[30] And then, "There's no better place to farm salmon than where they've flourished for millions of years. And where today, it's not just a way to make a living, it's a way of life...."[31] Across the two-page advertising layout was the reproduced image of a Salish salmon carving, a purloined example of Native Northwest art. What the ad does not tell the reader is that B.C. farmed salmon are overwhelmingly Atlantic salmon (Salmo salar), biological intruders in Pacific Northwest waters. The ad may be shrugged off by the politically-correct as the stereotypical dishonesty of the corporate mind-set, but the language -- "our waters", "our souls", "flourished for millions of years" -- is instructive; for it is the very language of the eco-con artists themselves when evoking public emotion to save the threatened Pacific salmon.[32]

This writer first noticed the New Age eco-speak while doing research for his own fisheriography. There weren't many sources immediately available to the writer on the Olympic Peninsula anadromous fish ecology, so Bruce Brown's Mountain in the Clouds: A Search for the Wild Salmon was a good place to start.[33] But, unlike the biological and historical books this writer had read prior to 1987, Bruce Brown's work contained a mild but pure environmental agendum:

".... I spotted a six-pound pink male lying between two boulders the color of rotten ice. He had a high, knife-edged hump flying like a burgundy banner above the water, hooked snout and a rainbow across his tail that caught fire as the sun cleared the opposite ridge, charging the river with color and revealing thousands of diaphanous dew-covered cobwebs on the branches of the trees....

"During the course of my three years' wandering around the Olympic Peninsula, I saw wild salmon of every Pacific species, as well as the two anadromous trout, the steelhead, and the sea-run cutthroat. Many were beautiful fish, and occasionally the massed display was stunning..., but nowhere did I find the old glory, or the life it supported. To see relatively unsullied salmon runs and a yeomanry of subsistence salmon fishermen today, one must travel to Alaska, the Northwest Territories and British Columbia."[34]

Bruce Brown employed a familiarised and proprietary manner regarding the endangered Olympic

Peninsula wild salmon, following in the patrician-naturalist footsteps of Canadian Roderick Haig-Brown. There was a pedagogish, admonitory tone throughout, chiefly directed at encroaching, plebeian-human habitat. The only non-Natives permitted in these pristine areas, went the gist, should be wild-life officials, government scientists, and selected eco-sensitive naturalist/sportsmen of wealth, education, and status. Mountain in the Clouds was a culmination of local-colour fish stories Brown wrote for the Seattle Post-Intelligencer, and the completed work was well received in Kirkus Reviews, and by Never Cry Wolf Canadian author and eco-conscience Farley Mowat. Brown is an award-winning journalist and script-writer, with articles published in The New York Times, The Washington Post, Atlantic Monthly, Audubon magazine and the like. Brown also penned the comic novel, Dr. Whacko's Guide to Slow-Pitch Softball, and the PBS-TV series, The Miracle Planet. In October 1995, Brown was working on "a history of the corporation" for Scribner's [a corporation] and putting out the computer magazine, Bug Net.[35] It was at this time that the writer attended a presentation by Brown, 'Wild Salmon and You', given at Peninsula College, Port Angeles. The writer enjoyed Brown's lecture as well as his book, but found correlating Salmon People with salmonid fishes a Herculean task. But for Bruce Brown, an eco-sensitive man of our times, the task has been easily accomplished through cultural preferences and valued aesthetics. This writer, having read Mountain in the Clouds so long ago as 1987, was well prepared for the Bruce Brown of 1995.

Moreover, the benign and pleasant Brown is a touchy-feely "Mr. Rogers" in the growing constellation of 1990s fisheriographer-environmentalists. This writer says "well prepared", for by the 1990s a subculture of wild-fish metaphysics has matured after being spawned during the 1960s. A proportional new class of salmon metaphysicists has arisen, making a sumptious living collateral to salmon fishermen, processors and canners. A bona fide member of the new class, Tom Jay, visited Port Angeles in November 1994 to promote his co-authored book, Reaching Home: Pacific Salmon, Pacific People.[36] Local literature emporium Port Book and News, in the November Readings info. sheet described its guest-reader as ...."[a] poet, sculptor, and teacher, Tom Jay lives in Chimacum, Washington. He has chosen to link his personal and professional life to salmon. His latest work is 'Heroic Chum', an 8-foot tall bronze sculpture, and his largest art work is 'Salmon Woman and Raven,' over 16 feet tall. In addition to his art and writings, Jay is active in salmon restoration and is a founding member of the North Olympic Salmon Coalition and the Wild Olympic Salmon group...."

Two months later, January 1995, salmon metaphysicist Tom Jay was back again in Port Angeles, this time as guest-lecturer at Peninsula College. In 'Reaching Home -- The Salmon of the Heart', Jay recalled how he first became obsessed with Pacific salmon. Several years back, Jay had spent a summer fishing off Alaska to support his true vocation, sculpting. One day Jay's skipper called him over to help board a particularly large chinook. As the net encircled the big fish, it began to struggle against the net, at last breaking free and taking the net with it. Said Jay, on this salmonid epiphany:

"Watching the powerful swimming of the salmon broke open time for me.... The scene froze in my mind. Suddenly the salmon was much more than blood or money. I couldn't claim it or understand it, but I knew this was the way home.

"Everyone looks at the eternal mysteries of life. The salmon became the center for me.... I studied its folklore, its linguistics. It became the centering experience for my own little cosmos.

"If salmon leave, we will be lonely in a way we will always feel but never understand because we will have become the secret orphans of the land."[37]

Tom Jay co-authored Reaching Home with fisheries columnist Brad Matsen, but the origin of the book was developed by nature photographer Natalie Fobes ... after an initial $25,000 grant from the Alicia Patterson Foundation. Ms. Fobes has been the recipient of numerous awards, including the Scripps-Howard Meeman Award for environmental[ist] writing and a Pulitzer Prize nomination for her specific work on salmon. Ms. Fobes has had photographs and articles published in National Geographic, GEO, Newsweek, Audubon magazine and the like. She has also been contributing photographer on no less than three books. In her research for photo-ops, "Fobes dons a wetsuit to swim in icy salmon streams or spends weeks on fishing boats to achieve her powerful and unique images."[38] (Serendipitous work if one can find it, but it surely helps to get jump-started by big foundation money).

Co-author of Reaching Home with Tom Jay and Natalie Fobes was Brad Matsen, fisheriographer turned salmon metaphysicist. He is the previously-mentioned Pacific editor of National Fisherman and has produced several books, among them Northwest Coast: Essays from the Columbia River to the Cook Inlet; Ray Troll's Shocking Fish Tales; and Planet Ocean: A Story of Life, the Sea, and Dancing to the Fossil Record (also with Ray Troll). Matsen wrote the script for the PBS documentary film Alaska and the Pacific War, and articles for the periodicals Audubon, Whole Earth Review, Orion, Mother Jones, and Alaska.[39] The

November/December 1994 issue of <u>Seafood Leader</u> magazine contained a fuzz-ball critique of <u>Reaching Home:</u>

<u>Pacific Salmon, Pacific People</u>:

....."But it's the images that really capture the Pacific Rim's prized fish: Gillnetters swarming the line in Bristol Bay, hundreds of pinks captured in a Russian trap, an Ainu woman in Japan reverently carrying the symbolic first fish of the season, a pair of well-worked hands clutching a thick wad of crisp $100 bills. And while capturing those who live, work and die by salmon -- Natives, biologists, commercial fishermen from Canada to Kamchatka -- the book makes an eloquent pleas to stem the tide of disappearing runs and environmental degradation. <u>Reaching Home</u> won't help you sell more salmon, but it may help you appreciate them just a little bit more."[40]

WRONG! <u>Reaching Home</u> will sell <u>alot</u> of salmon ... metaphysical fish mongered by top salmon

salespersons Jay, Fobes, and Matsen. Having read Matsen's <u>National Fisherman</u> Pacific column for some time,

this writer purchased a copy of Matsen and Ray Troll's <u>Shocking Fish Tales</u> (1991). Matsen has been a

commercial fisherman, charter pilot, and merchant seaman.[41] He lives in greater Seattle and is at least of

partial Scandinavian descent. Thus <u>Shocking Fish Tales</u>, illustrated by graphic artist (and ex-New Yorker) Ray

Troll, seemed to promise all the ingredients for a personally satisfying fish story. But this writer finished

reading the book in anger and disappointment; the tenor of Matsen's text fueling both emotions. Matsen's

overall tone combined environmentally-correct sermonising with a hard-edged Evolutionism, with his language

carefully clothed in New Age eco-speak. But there was none of Bruce Brown's wishful projections or gentle

admonishments. Surely Brad Matsen's years spent at sea as a commercial fisherman have toughened him

beyond sharing the eco-whimsies of salmon metaphysicists; if so, he should remain a Pacific fisheries columnist

and nothing more. When Matsen and Troll's second co-authored book, <u>Planet Ocean</u>, appeared in 1995, this

writer read the back-cover review with interest:

"Planet Ocean is a wonderful visual and intellectual treat. Ray Troll's paintings and block prints are a vibrant tribute to Mother Ocean and all of our relations within Her. Brad Matsen's text integrates paleontology, geology, and biology into a holistic narrative about the origin of all life on Earth."[43]

Is it playing God, or seeking gold at the end of the New Age rainbow, which drives wild-fish

metaphysics? How else to explain Brad Matsen the mainstream Pacific fisheries columnist, or Brad Matsen

the New Age wild-fish metaphysicist? Maybe Matsen has been able to concoct a single, synoptic philosophy

out of eco-Evolutionary Secular Humanism. Anyway, together with Tom Jay and Natalie Fobes of <u>Reaching</u>

<u>Home: Pacific Salmon, Pacific People</u>, Matsen and co. are self-imagined mini-versions of Jacques Cousteau,

David Attenborough, and Jane Goodall ... potential sperm/ovary donors/donatrix at a future genetic superbank. The only immediate victim of this eco-play acting is the tired fisherman or processor, in his or her bunk, who reads with bewilderment of sacred salmonids and humanoid cetaceans. It's all a result of the New Age diffusion and immanence, although to the average Joe Six-Pack -- and this writer -- the salmon is but a fish and the orca is still a marine mammal. The victim to-be of fish metaphysics is the fishing and seafood industry, a problem the fish metaphysicists should ponder while scurrying down the money trail.[44]

The eco-sophistries of the Upper Echelons have yet to really affect the general mind-set of fishermen and processors, but the fish metaphysicists are doing their utmost to win industry hearts and minds. Meanwhile, to enable the Lower Echelons to better identify with their ascended masters, there are fishery columnists like Roger Fitzgerald, of <u>Alaska Fisherman's Journal</u> and <u>Seafood Leader</u>, to help tune them in. Fitzgerald's column, 'In Search of the Simple Life', would be better titled 'In Search of the Sybaritic Life.' Witty, urbane, and extremely knowledgeable about seafood, Fitzgerald ranges so far a-field as Thailand from Alaska to Chile on his assignments. This writer is an avid reader of 'In Search of the Simple Life', but objects to Fitzgerald's often referring to a wired life-style of drink and drugs along with his exotic fish-dishes. An avuncular and engaging "Dr. Gonzo,' Fitzgerald nonetheless manifests "greened", countercultural values in his style and content. Fitzgerald and the fish metaphysicists should be a tad cautious, however, in pushing too hard their countercultural and New Age values onto a socially conservative industry. The situational dynamics of intellectualoids vis-à-vis plain folks remind this writer of an incident in the life of the original Dr. Gonzo, Hunter S. Thompson[45]:

".... One thing that [Ken] Kesey, [Allen] Ginsberg, and all the hopeful radicals seemed to forget was that the Hell's Angels were anti-Communist. Although they weren't opposed to dropping acid with hippies and frolicking in the forest with their long-haired women, opposition to the [Viet-Nam] war was out of the question for most of them."[46]

The passage quoted above had to do with an occurence on 16 October 1965, when 15,000 demonstrators marched from the U.Cal. Berkeley campus toward the Oakland (U.S.) Army Terminal, where men and matériel were shipped to South-East Asia. Hunter Thompson, biker-reporter, had predicted that the assembled Hell's Angels would show their Americanism by attacking and turning the demonstration violent. A "sea of protestors" warily approached "hundreds of Oakland police" who were waiting and ready for trouble.

Thompson biographer Paul Perry described the following scene and its significance:

"As the marchers closed the gap, a small group of [Hell's] Angels pushed through the crowd and past the policemen. The renegades punched protesters, tore up signs, and broke a policeman's leg before they were finally subdued by the police.

"The leftists were shocked and tried to dismiss the well-planned attack as a mistake. But Hunter [Thompson] knew the Angels better than any outsider and, as far as he was concerned, it was the leftists, not the Angels, who just didn't get it."[47]

It might appear a long shot, but one could equate Brad Matsen and Roger Fitzgerald respectively with Ken Kesey and Allen Ginsberg; members of the seafood industry with the Hell's Angels. Reading, then comprehending, Matsen and Fitzgerald is akin to uncovering an anti-war admiral, or outing a gay archbishop. The reader may readily imagine young fishermen and processors tuning into Heavy Metal/Acid Rock music and taking recreational drugs ... but without subscribing to countercultural-New Age beliefs. This has been overwhelmingly the case in this writer's experience. If there is a moral to the Oakland Army terminal happening, or a "greened" connection of the mid-1960s to the mainstream culture of the mid-1990s, it is that the mental trappings of the Berkeley radicals and the physical accoutrements of the Hell's Angels -- and vice versa -- have become indistinguishably fused over time. Today's freaks and headmen, although sporting the pony-tails and earrings of yesteryear's hippies, are "armed and dangerous." True freaks and real headmen are extreme hard-cases, but they are slavishly imitated by millions of young people, including members of the seafood industry. Many of the tuned in and turned on like to refer to themselves as "Deadheads." Since his abrupt departure from Earth on 9 August 1995, Jerry Garcia of the Grateful Dead has been designated the cultural image of the last three tripped-out generations, transcending class, gender, and age.[48] On his untimely death (it was a miracle Garcia lived so long), "Captain [LSD] Trips" has been elevated to near-holy after-life standing by a laudatory press and adoring Deadhead élites.[49] Other inter-generational icons are Londoner Mick Jagger and the Rolling Stones, a post-mortem John Lennon and the Liverpudlian Beatles, but San Franciscan Jerry Garcia and the Grateful Dead have reigned supreme on the Ectopian Pacific Northwest Coast.[50]

Three generations of "Jerry's Kids" are now grown, and in the U.S. share their peer-compatriots' huge appetite for guns, drugs, and trucks. Indeed, Jerry's Kids and their offspring, like the biker-hippy fusion, are virtually indistinguishable from the formally-despised Good Ol' Boys. The names have changed from Leroy, Curtis, and Orville to Mitch, Butch, and Chuck. And those folksy, embroidery-stitched blue-jean pockets are as apt to contain live ammo as hard drugs. The strangely American predilection for firearms is typically illustrated by the bumper-sticker: "Insured by Smith and Wesson." A highly-visible, fully-loaded, rear-window rifle-rack is a mandatory feature of the equipage. If the truck in question has a trailer attached, there is often an ancillary sticker on the door warning: "Don't bother knockin' if this rig's a rockin." Yes, Jerry's Kids of three generations have come of New Age in a meaningless culture largely engendered by the Pepsi Generation of the 1960s. That "rising culture" (Capra, 1988), whatever the exaggerated claims of the current wisdom gurus, still plays Bud Bowl and "reads" Playboy. The hated police of not so long ago, the "sic 'em pigs" of Berkeley, now offer entertainment value. The boys -- and girls -- in blue have become violence-subjects and sex-objects in such network shows as Hill Street Blues, Cop Rock, Picket Fences, and NYPD Blue. (Even Columbo got pc and nasty into the' 90s.) Police radio-scanners are popular, and FOX TV's Cops heads the list of real-life police sub-culture programming guaranteed to gratify the vicarious violence-lust of the North American viewing public. (Canada has her own copy-cat series.) That thrilling lust has nothing to do with respect for law or love of order. Televised public executions are sure to be next on the (American) networks' high-ratings agendum.

Until the era of U.S. federal court-ordered public executions, TV corporations and video companies offer wild-animal sex and "snuff movies." The rationale given for watching these raw scenes is "a love for" and/or "an interest in" Nature. But those viewing Discovery's Fangs! are the very people watching Fox's Cops ... for the same reasons. One example of blood-prurience was a 4 October 1995 presentation on Wild Discovery (DSC) of Komodo monitor lizards. There were the obligatory cuts of Komodo dragons hunting and killing an injured deer. But on this particular programme the viewer was treated to televised feeding-time at a local Indonesian Komodo-dragon zoo. The camera recorded the actual slaughter of a young goat, the heaving of the carcass into the enclosed dragon-pit, and then capturing on film the mixed reactions of the on-looking tourists; who were themselves video-taping the gruesome event for home viewing.

A later PBS episode of Nature, aired 14 April 1996, was no less blood-salacious. 'In the Lion's Den', coldly narrated by Welsh actor ("the silence of the lambs") Anthony Hopkins, the African lion was constantly referred to as the top, superior predator. The eco-élitist tone was in keeping with the PBS self-image of top intellectuality. But there was nothing intellectual or animal-loving about the lingering, excruciating pictures of bestial ferocity. African lions have become models of Darwinist admiration rather than "Born Free" sentimentality -- the Jane Goodalls accomplished a similar mission several years ago for spotted hyaenas, "The Sisterhood of Death." One expects no less in a culture obsessed with sex, violence, and death. With life being held so cheaply, public-sector calls for legalised euthanasia and abortion on demand (plus the eventual televised executions), come as no surprise. The prevalent [Charles] Darwinian and [Margaret] Sangerite attitudes regarding life and death, poignantly reminds this writer of blurting out "Hey, everyone in this room is special!", in a Carlsborg tavern on a warm evening during August 1982.[51]

Back in 1982 the old "Live and Let Live" had been transformed to "Live and Let Die." The Republicans under Ronald ("Ray-Gun") Reagan had won the White House in 1980, and current wisdom (cw) informed us that the Decade of Greed had begun. With the liberal Democrats back in power under an MTV president, the 1990s have seen a much-hyped return to "Live and Let Live"; supposedly a socialistic, communal philosophy. But it's a simulacrum: The "I feel your pain" cosmetic-coating is so shallow, that only true-believing Clintonistas and the least-discerning fail to see through it. "Live and Let Live" in the 1990s is the only too surreal "Kill or Be Killed", a rising culture where life is nasty, brutish, and often shortened by terminal sexually-transmitted diseases, fatal drugs, or violent death. But "Jerry's [Garcia] Kids", now mostly middle-aged, refuse to admit any culpability in the three-decade, ongoing cultural demise. After a dozen years of Reagan-Bush-Quayle (1981-1993), Jerry's Kids, now fisherpersons and hippies with guns feign a hatred for Big Government; identifying themselves as libertarians rather than liberals. In a recent interview at Port Angeles, Washington, Arlo ("Alice's Restaurant") Guthrie even had the temerity to call himself a conservative: "Although Guthrie said he no longer uses drugs, he doesn't believe the government has any business telling people what they can or can't do in the privacy of their own homes...."[52] But a January 1995 Alaska Fisherman's Journal interview at Kake, Alaska, of a new fisherperson, indicated a hippies-with-guns truculence:

"Suzie Young is a fisherman. Not a fisher, not a fisherwoman, she says, but a fisherman. She came to Alaska 15 years ago to live the life of a fisherman, a life of independence.

".... Young says she likes men just fine; she just hasn't found one she can put up with. Young likes men that hunt.... 'No small-minded people are going to keep me from living the way I want,' she says.

".... Ten years ago, when she bought the 36 foot Eagle, it was rigged as a troller. She made the change-over to longlining herself.... [T]he Eagle has given Young the freedom to raise two of her children at sea -- her way.

"'You don't get credit for that', she says, scraping to the rhythm of 'Puff the Magic Dragon' playing in the wheelhouse.

...."I taught my boy to sew and my girl to hunt and managed to feed the family at the same time.... "'You can still be a lady and bust your balls', she says"....[53]

The State of Alaska tried to accomodate "Jerry's Kids" a decade or so ago, by legalising the limited possession and personal use of certain recreational drugs. Residents have told this writer that the since-aborted experiment badly backfired, with marijuana runs on the ferries and the 49th state becoming a haven for dealers and abusers. This writer could visualise cultivated "victory gardens", and designer-drug labs, being guarded by fierce breeds of killer-dogs, pit-bull (Staffordshire) terriers or German (Alsatian) shepherds, as they were in Hawaii. The drug culture of the Left Coast, coupled with armed, self-centred libertarianism, has infused a hardness of heart into our Pacific Northwest ethic. Even local mystery authors currently reflect a common mean-spiritedness. In the late 1980s, this writer read (and re-read) Richard Hoyt's Fish Story with delight; but by 1993 in Big Foot, Hoyt's resurrected protagonists had become cruel, vengeful, and murderous -- no different from the book's antagonists.[54] Big Foot's story-line dealt with a gumshoe-hero and his Native American sidekicks first uncovering, then battling, evil Euro-Paleface land-developers. Hoyt's virtual savagery visited on the whitebread corporate capitalists is excused by their intention to commit virtual eco-cide -- an unforgivable crime in the pc New Age. The only real (besides racial) difference between the good guys (natural men) and the bad guys (city slickers) was that the home-boys (outdoor insiders) won. It is an extension of PBS Nature's top, superior, leonine predator, or Jane Goodall's spotted hyaenas. There is a "Kill or Be Killed" mentality abroad in our land.

The wise men tell us that Nature abhors a vacuum. Perhaps as if to compensate for the new Alaska fisherperson interviewed earlier, there is the phenomenon of "AlaskaMen." When this writer last looked, the AlaskaMen magazine cover featured a pleasant-faced, bearded young "single dad" pictured alongside his pretty, smiling six-year old daughter. The issue in question, Spring 1995, was of a "New Purse Size" and had shed its initial pretty-boy beef-cake image.[55] A few years before, a trash-TV talk show had featured single Alaska men (rather than jock-strapped Chippendale dancers), who had found love via the dating data-bank of AlaskaMen. Seeing all those big Scandihoovian hunting-and-fishing guys, would have made Hjalmar Rutzebeck (Alaska Man's Luck) pleased and proud. Scandihoovian guys as hunks are rarely seen on North American television; Nordic-type adult males are usually relegated to the cast-off dust-bin as Skinheads, Neo-Nazis, "gay blades", crazed loner-snipers, or serial rapist-killers.[56] Despite AlaskaMen's turn to family values, the old image of Alaska men as sourdough coots, codgers, and curmudgeons is forever gone. An elderly Norwegian-American couple, of this writer's life-long acquaintance, report encountering bronzed Nordic god-like ski-coaches on Utah slopes. They turned out to be Alaska king-crabbers, instructing (less wealthy) vacationers during the off-season. In Port Angeles, one can nearly always spot the off-season Alaska fisherman: He's the fellow who has the Mexico or Maui sun-tan in mid-winter.[57]

So it's back to where we started, with Pacific Fishing magazine's ad of Gunnar and Pete lounging on the beach at Waikiki. In Brad Matsen's essay, 'Barging down the River', a photo by Natalie Fobes showed... "[a] fisherman hold[ing] $21,000.00 he made for nine days' work in 1988. Big bucks can be made -- and lost -- during a season in Bristol Bay, Alaska."[58] If AlaskaMen's new accent on marriage and the family mirrors a trend of any integrity, it can only be good for all members of the fishing and seafood industry. Those rich, young superior-predacious king-crabbers, doubling in the off-season as well-paid instructors on the Utah ski-slopes, are the élite of the industry and tomorrow's natural leaders. How they think and what they do with their youth, strength, talent, and wealth will have a profound effect on the future of the industry, culture, and society in Alaska and the Pacific Northwest. After all, it will take real Alaska men and women to raise real families, in a geographic entity not yet part of the New Age Global Village.

And now we return full circle from AlaskaMen to Alaska-menn.[59] This writer, when moving to Port Angeles, Wash. from Victoria, B.C. in 1987, had not been to Ballard for seven years. But Ballard follows Norwegian-Americans -- wherever they live -- through the pages of Western Viking, the locally-produced weekly. But, sometime toward the end of the 1980s, the editorship of Western Viking was assumed by one Dr. Alf Knudsen, a U.Washington musicologist with a pc agendum. Even the WV food page, Retter med Petter ("Recipes with Peter"), reflected a pc overlay. Caterer-columnist Petter Pettersen openly displayed his anti-clerical bias by constantly ridiculing the Christian roots of traditional holidays (i.e., "holy days"). The WV editorship, an unabashed booster of the present socialist-labourite government ruling Norway, once boasted of the parliament's (storting) mandatory quota of 40% female representation. Celebratory portraits drawn of these bossy, neo-feminist governesses established that an unhealthy percentage were thirty/forty somethings, unmarried, but living with co-vivants (samboere). The modern Scandinavian state exemplifies today's condom culture. Besides presenting flattering profiles of the vacuous royal family, with their vapid royal kid-clones, WV lovingly dogged the footsteps of Prime Minister Gro Harlem Brundtland throughout the 1990s: Statsminister Gro shouting and gestulating at the UN Rio Earth Summit; Statsminister Gro receiving a complimentary degree at Pacific Lutheran University. After a personally rewarding jubilaeum trip to Norway in 1994, this writer returned culturally fortified to the U.S.A.; confident enough to editorially challenge Western Viking, and to finally cancel an off-and-on eighteen year subscription.

The writer still claims Ballard as part of himself. Ballard continues to be the unofficial capital of Norwegian America. Fishermen's Terminal and the Hiram Chittenden Locks are important elements in the local marine-related industries, and such periodicals as The Fishermen's News, Pacific Fishing, Alaska Fisherman's Journal and (sister publication) Seafood Leader are all located in greater Ballard. The Ballard Sons of Norway lodge, Leif Erikson No. 1, is the flag-ship S/N lodge of the entire Pacific Northwest, although the Poulsbo (Lodge No. 44) is more beautiful and better-known. Like the "Evangelical" Lutheran Church, Sons of Norway is also undergoing the crucible of political-correctness.[60] The much-ballyhooed 1989 S/N "Norwegian of the Year", a privileged track-star athlete living in Colorado, was caught cheating on her U.S. alien status. Repeated letters to S/N International President Thorleif Bryn from this (naturalised U.S.) writer elicited no response. And during the early 1990s, a top S/N insurance salesman bilked a multitude of elderly lodge members of millions of hard-earned nest-egg dollars. The S/N International head-office at Minneapolis was slow to admit culpability; even slower to apologise with a mea culpa to the general lodge membership. Last and least, the S/N mountain cabin in the Cascades, "Trollhaugen", was grandly declared "smoke-free" circa 1990. This writer received a couple of free passes to "Trollhaugen" since then, but gave them away on principle. Although having smoked his last cigar in 1989, the writer had determined not to aid or abet nicotine-nazism in any way. Healthful-correctness is, after all, just another form of political-correctness.[61]

Besides having a pc government and one of the most punitive taxation systems on earth,[62] Norway (along with her Scandinavian neighbours) is also one of the least God-fearing. Gallup International took a sixty-nation survey during the mid-1970s of those professing a belief in God or "a universal spirit." The results were: 94% in U.S.A., 89% in Canada, 65% in Scandinavia. Of those believing in an afterlife, the results were: 69% in U.S.A., 54% in Canada, 35% in Scandinavia. Of those considering religion "very important", the results were: 56% in U.S.A., 36% in Canada, 17% in Scandinavia.[63] So the new-norske kids, so worldly-wise and precocious (verdensvante, veslevoksne) a whole generation later, are over-ripe candidates for the paradigm shift. For many Norwegians, the 1994 Winter Olympiade was the perfect vehicle to boldly show the world how far their country, on a cultural scale, had advanced into the New Age. The opening ceremony at Lillehammer evinced, too, the degree beyond which giant-and-troll (jette and jøtul) national mythology had graduated. Dr. Terje Leiren of the U.Washington Scandinavian Dept., and visiting guest columnist at Western Viking during 1994, waxed lyrical -- nay, near hysterical -- in describing the opening ceremony at Lillehammer. But this writer has chosen Norwegian-born columnist and thoughtful Christian, Berit Kjos, to bring the scene into sharper, more rational focus:

"The 'artistic portion' of the opening ceremony illustrates the 'new' spirituality sweeping through the Western World. A CBS reporter described the event: 'We introduce you to the mythical beliefs of the Norwegian people. Popping out of the ground are the Vettas, mythical characters rooted in ancient Nordic folk-tales...

"We know them as gnomes, pixies, trolls...' continued the reporter. 'The [V]ettas are an integral part of Norwegian beliefs... [t]hey are said to be knowledgeable and wise... And watch constantly over the activities of mankind....

"These Vettas make up the bulk of Norwegian fairy tales. All the children grow up learning all about them.'[64]

"....A massive egg was emerging from a glowing hole in the center of the arena. Gyrating to the beat of drums, the [V]ettas formed a dense circle around the rising egg. 'The message from the [V]ettas' intoned CBS, [is] 'that we should take better care of our environment! They're promoting world peace.'

"Chanting and raising their hands in worship, the [V]ettas bowed to the illumined egg which began to change into a globe. Bathed in blue light, the mystical representation of the earth opened releasing ... dove-shaped helium balloons in a dramatic expression...."[65]

As neither authoress Berit Kjos nor this writer, who both grew up in Norway, had ever heard of Vettas, the daemonic little earth sprites must have been revivified by neo-pagan persons in high (Norwegian) places. But this is not surprising in an Olympic setting: The "sacred flame", the oath to Zeus, the Olympic hymn all fit snugly in with the Olympic Religion of Baron Pierre de Coubertin, who revived the games in 1896. The Olympic Religion also conforms to the globalism of Taoist-inspired Avery Brundage, who influenced the Olympiades for decades.[66] But that such neo-pagan earth-based spirituality should be an official part of Norwegian public policy, is deeply disturbing to people of faith. Throughout the summers since the Lillehammer games, young arsonists in Norway (home-grown "Jerry's Kids") have been burning down historic stave-churches (stavkirker). Is this what the coming New Age portends for the United States and Canada? New Age beliefs and values, however, won't have to be shoved onto a resistant populace in either country. Elliot Miller, editor of the Christian Research Journal, has already told us why:

"A movement [i.e., the New Age] succeeds when its essential features have become so integrated and established in the larger community that it is no longer recognizable as a movement."[67]

NOTES

1.   Elliot Miller, ed. 'Is the New Age Old News?', <u>Christian Research Journal</u>, Vol.18, No.2, Fall 1995, p.4.

2.   Doug Le Blanc, 'Marketplace of the Gods', <u>Christian Research Journal</u>, Vol.18, No.1, Summer 1995, p.6; citation from Terry Mattingly of Milligan College, Johnson City, Tenn.

3.   "[T]he Republicans get feverish and clammy and speak in tongues and handle snakes.... The Republicans are going to be the Party That Canceled the Clean Air Act and Took Hot Lunches from Children, the Orphanage Party of Large White Men Who Feel Uneasy Around Gals."
              -<u>Time</u> commentary by Garrison Keillor, 13 March 1995; cited in <u>Human Events</u>, Vol.52, No.1, 12 January 1996, p.13. Keillor is the author of <u>The Book of Guys</u> (New York, N.Y.:Viking Penguin, 1993) and the Lake Wobegon follies.

4.   Tom Wolfe, <u>The Kandy-Kolored Tangerine-Flake Streamline Baby</u> (New York, N.Y.:Bantam Books, 1980 ed.), p.186. Originally published in 1963.

5.   <u>The Trumpet</u>, December 1995, p.3. HTLC newsletter.

6.   <u>The Trumpet</u>, November 1995, p.2 HTLC newsletter.

7.   Dave Hunt, 'Time & Eternity', <u>The Berean Call</u> (Bend, Ore.), January 1996, p.1.

8.   'Church in Society', <u>The Trumpet</u>, January 1996, p.4. HTLC newsletter.

9.   From the hymn "A Mighty Fortress is Our God" by Martin Luther. (Orig. German title: <u>Eine Feste Burg Ist Unser Gott</u>.)

10. The Sons of Norway International organisation is (still) headquartered at Minneapolis, Minnesota.

11. Robert J. Browning, <u>Fisheries of the North Pacific: History, Species, Gear and Processes</u> (Anchorage: Alaska Northwest Publishing, 1974 and 1980). Quite simply the best and most comprehensive book ever written on the subject.

12. William B. McCloskey, Jr., <u>Highliners: A Documentary Novel about the Fishermen of Alaska</u> (New York:McGraw-Hill Books, 1979 and 1981). An excellent, true-to-life fish-tale of contemporary Alaska.
         Author's note: In <u>Captains Courageous</u>, Rudyard Kipling's Harvey Cheyne undergoes the rite of passage from (low-minded) selfish brat to (high-minded) useful youth. William McCloskey's Hank Crawford matures from innocent aboard to callous (ed) young (Alaska) man.

13. Hjalmar Rutzebeck, <u>Alaska Man's Luck</u> (New York: Boni and Liveright, 1920), and <u>My Alaskan Idyll</u> (New York:Boni and Liveright, 1921). Both works reissued by Capra Press, Santa Barbara, Calif., 1988.
         Author's note: In this writer's opinion, the dialectician to most closely reflect the <u>Alaska-mann</u> political image was U.S.-born Thorstein Veblen, author of <u>The Theory of the Leisure Class</u> (1899). See Appendix G.

14. <u>Lutefisk</u> is a Norwegian wintertime dish of true cod treated in a lye solution as a preservative, and then carefully simmered. There has arisen a subculture of "lootefisk" among Norwegian-Americans,

neither fully understood nor really appreciated in Norway. <u>Lutefisk</u> itself to the uninitiated palate tastes like toxic waste. This writer loves well-prepared <u>lutefisk</u> and eagerly awaits the Sons of Norway lutefisk dinner served each November at Port Angeles, Washington.

15. Norman Mailer, <u>Of a Fire on the Moon</u> (New York:Grove Press, Inc., 1970), p.143. For New Age [old] religious views of God, see Appendix F.

16. Ernest Callenbach, <u>Ecotopia: The Notebooks and Reports of William Weston</u> (New York:Bantam Books, 1990 ed.), p.140. Orig. published in 1975.

17. William Irwin Thompson, <u>The American Replacement of Nature</u> (New York:Doubleday/Currency, 1991), p.45.

18. <u>Ibid.</u>, passim.

19. <u>Dolphin Log</u>, January 1995, p.3. The Cousteau Society, 870 Greenbrier Circle, Suite 402, Chesapeake, VA 23320.

20. P. J. O'Rourke, <u>Age and Guile Beat Youth, Innocence and a Bad Haircut</u> (New York:The Atlantic Monthly Press, 1995), p.331.

21. <u>The American Spectator</u>, Vol.28, No.8, August 1995, p.81.

22. David Andrew Price, 'Save the Whalers', <u>The American Spectator</u>, Vol. 28, No.2, February 1995, p.48.

23. <u>Ibid.</u>, p.48.

24. <u>Ibid.</u>, p.49.

25. <u>Ibid.</u>, p.49.

26. <u>Ibid.</u>, p.49.

27. <u>Ibid.</u>, p.49.

28. Op.cit., David Andrew Price, p.49.

29. The indigenous Asian Pacific salmon, <u>Oncorhynchus masou</u> (Japanese <u>masu</u>, cherry salmon) is a sixth species. Steelhead/rainbow trout, <u>Salmo gairdneri</u>, was promoted taxonomically during the early 1990s to Pacific salmon status, <u>O. mykiss</u>.

30. <u>Seafood Leader</u>, Vol.14, No.6, November/December 1994, p.48.

31. <u>Ibid.</u>, p.49.

32. For political and diplomatic essays on Pacific salmon, see this writer's <u>Fisheries of the Pacific Northwest Coast, Vol.1</u> (1991); for biological and aquacultural essays, see <u>Vol.2</u> (New York:Vantage Press, Inc., 1994).

33. New York:Touchstone Books, 1982.

NOTES (cont'd)

34.   Bruce Brown, 'Wild Salmon and You', <u>Studium Generale Program Notes</u>, Peninsula College (Port Angeles, Wash.), 12 October 1995, back page.

35.   <u>Ibid.</u>, back page. Bruce Brown lives in Sumas, Washington (1995). Roderick Haig-Brown (<u>Bright Waters, Bright Fish</u>, Timber Press, Portland, Ore., 1980).

36.   Seattle:Alaska Northwest Books, 1994. With essays by Brad Matsen, and 101 colour photographs by Natalie Fobes. Hard bound, $37.95. 144pp., 11 1/4" x 9 7/8". Promoted by spawning-salmon glossy postcards with caption reading ..."Now is truly the time of the salmon and its people."

37.   Tom Jay, 'Reaching Home -- the Salmon of the Heart', <u>Studium Generale Program Notes</u>, Peninsula College (Port Angeles, Wash.), 19 January 1995, front page.

38.   <u>November Readings</u>, Port Book and News (Port Angeles, Wash.), 12 November 1994, info. sheet.

39.   <u>Ibidem.</u>

40.   'Seafood Reader', p.152.

41.   Brad Matsen, 'Barging down the River: Salmon at the End of the 20th Century', <u>Pacific Northwest</u>, December 1994, p.51.

42.   Brad Matsen and Ray Troll, <u>Ray Troll's Shocking Fish Tales</u> (Bothell, Wash.: Alaska Northwest Books, 1991).

43.   Brad Matsen and Ray Troll, <u>Planet Ocean: A Story of Life, the Sea, and Dancing to the Fossil Record</u> (Berkeley, Calif.: Ten Speed Press, 1994). Back cover review by Leslie Marmon Silko, author of <u>Ceremony</u> and <u>Almanac of the Dead</u>.
      Author's note: For examples of Ketchikan-based artist Ray Troll's striking piscine creations, see 'A Portrait of the Artist as a Fish: Alaska Artist Ray Troll Turns Fish into Art, T-Shirts and Religion', <u>Seafood Leader</u>, Vol.15, No.1, January/February 1995, pp.68-72. This writer proudly wore a Ray Troll T-shirt when giving a fisheriography lecture at Peninsula College (Port Angeles, Wash.) in April 1992.

44.   The Associated Press reported that The Foundation for the Study of the Welfare of Whales at Wellington, N.Z., announced on 16 April 1996 its intention to analyse the level of pain whales suffer when beached (i.e., by Danish islanders) or harpooned at sea (i.e., by Japanese ships).... "All forms of commercial whaling are inhumane. So we are looking at euthanasia and also to prevent cruel commercial slaughter practices", said David Blackmore, an expert on the slaughter of domestic stock animals.
                                                         -<u>Peninsula Daily News</u>, 16 April 1996, p.A-8.

      NB. This writer concurs with Blackmore, but can the total UN-enforced ban on whaling world-wide be far behind?

45.   Gonzo journalist and wigged-out author of <u>The Great Shark Hunt</u> etc.

46.   Paul Perry, <u>Fear and Loathing: The Strange and Terrible Saga of Hunter S. Thompson</u> (New York: Thunder's Mouth Press, 1993), p.112.
      Author's note: Allen Ginsberg, Beat poet, of <u>HOWL</u> fame. Ken Kesey, of the Merry Band

of [LSD] Pranksters, author of <u>One Flew Over the Cuckoo's Nest</u> etc. This writer has chosen the late Jerry Garcia of the Grateful Dead -- who was much influenced by both Ginsberg and Kesey -- as cultural idol for '... Fisherpersons, and Hippies with Guns'. See Appendix H.

47.   Op.cit., Paul Perry, p.113.

48.   M.D. Carnegie, 'Jerry's Kids', <u>The American Spectator</u>, Vol.28, No.10, October 1995, p.56. See Appendix H for complete quotation.

49.   NB. Not all of the Fourth Estate felt Jerry Garcia and the Grateful Dead to be worthy "... generational icons ... [whose music] stitched together three generations" (editorial quoted from <u>The New York Times</u>). See Andrew Ferguson, 'The Gimlet Eye', <u>National Review</u>, Vol.XLVII, No.17, 11 September 1995, p.76.

50.   See Appendix H for further details.

51.   Author's note: The writer's drinking partner on that (and too many other a) night was James A. "Pinky" McEwen, then of Dungeness, Washington.
        Pinky died on 11 March 1996 in Petersburg, Alaska. This book is dedicated to his memory.

52.   Christina Kelly, 'Guthrie says he's old conservative, '<u>Peninsula Daily News</u>, 7 March 1996, p.A-3.

53.   Charlie Le Duff, 'Not by Any Other Name', <u>Alaska Fisherman's Journal</u>, Vol.18, No.1, January 1995, p.55.

54.   Richard Hoyt, <u>Big Foot</u> (New York:Forge Books, 1993). Compare Earl Emerson's "whodunits" involving the pc Seattle Fire Department.

55.   <u>AlaskaMen</u>, Issue 23, Spring 1995.

56.   Among other observations on ethnicity, Norwegian-descended U.S. economist Thorstein Veblen wrote:
        ".... These ethnic types differ in temperament in a way somewhat similar to the difference between the predatory and the ante-predatory variants of the types; the dolicho [cephalic]-blond [Nordic long-headed] type showing more of the characteristics of the predatory temperament -- or at least more of the violent disposition -- than the brachycephalic-brunet[te] [Alpine short-headed] type, and especially more than the Mediterranean...."
        Thorstein Veblen, <u>The Theory of the Leisure Class</u> (Mineola, N.Y.:Dover Publications, Inc., 1988), p.134. Orig. published in 1899. See Appendix G.

57.   Mac and Travis at the Port Angeles Boat Haven figured, over a 1 May 1996 telephone talk, that approx. 25% of all vessels -- including trollers, packers etc. -- which over-winter at P.A., are Alaska fishing boats.

58.   Brad Matsen, 'Barging down the River: Salmon at the End of the 20th Century', <u>Pacific Northwest</u>, December 1994, p.50.

59.   Author's note: Besides starting life in the Old Country, <u>Alaska-menn</u> (as defined in this context) were born during the Great Depression and World War II years, 1929-1945). "AlaskaMen" are mainly Boomers, Busters, and Gen. X'ers born in the U.S.A. and Canada.

60.   Sons of Norway, District 2 (Wash., Ore., Ida., Wyo., and Alaska), with Seattle as headquarters;

dovetails neatly with the Evangelical Lutheran Church in America, Region 1 (Wash., Ore., Ida., Mont., and Alaska), also with Seattle as headquarters.

61. Sons of Norway is supposed to be non-political, but this writer's local lodge leadership took it upon itself to make Olympic Lodge No. 37 a Peninsula 1992 Ross Perot HQ.

62. The Norwegian tax burden has even been noised abroad so far as Port Angeles, Washington. Jim Guthrie, 'Below Olympus', Peninsula Daily News, 19 April 1996, p.A-4: Local editor Guthrie quotes translated comments from Norwegian personal finance magazine, Dine Penger ("Your Money").

63. Source: Gallup Poll, The New York Times, 12 September 1976 and 31 December 1976. Cited in Maurice S. Rawlings, M.D., Beyond Death's Door (New York: Bantam Books, 1991 ed.), pp.125-126. Author's note: One would surmise that figures for U.S.A., Canada and Scandinavia would be appreciably lower in 1996 than in 1976.

64. Berit Kjos, 'Olympic Myths and Earthy Magic', Today, the Bible & You, April 1994, p.13.

65. Ibid., p.14.

66. Ibid., p.14.

67. Elliot Miller, 'Is the New Age Old News?', Christian Research Journal, Vol.18, No.2, Fall 1995, p.4.
    NB: At this writing, May 1996, Black and White churches throughout the American South, have been set a-blaze throughout the year....

Bibliography for Part I

1. Bodett, Tom. The End of the Road. Bantam Books, New York, 1990.

2. McCloskey, William B., Jr. Highliners. McGraw Hill Books, New York, 1981 ed.

3. McGiniss, Joe. Going to Extremes. Plume, New York, 1989.

4. McPhee, John. Coming into the Country. Bantam Books, New York, 1979. (Author of Encounters with the Archdruid.)

5. Rutzebeck, Hjalmar. Alaska Man's Luck. Boni and Liveright, New York, 1920.

6. _____ . My Alaskan Idyll. Boni and Liveright, New York, 1921.
   (Both reissued by Capra Press, Santa Barbara, Calif., 1988.)

7. Walker, Spike. Working on the Edge. St. Martin's Press, New York, 1991.

Main References

A. Alaska Fisherman's Journal Pilothouse Guide & Yellow Pages, Vol.18, No.5, May 1995.

B. Alaska Fisherman's Journal Pilothouse Guide & Yellow Pages, Vol.19, No.5, May 1996.

Part II: The Pacific Northwest Prepares for Cybercentury
(A Seattle, Washington Vision)

Section A: Cyberspace -- the New Noösphere

"Free speech in cyberspace: anonymity for creeps, curs"
- Mike Royko, The Seattle Times, 16 February 1996

"Mike [Royko] is one of the last newspapermen on earth who still hangs out in bars instead of computer stores or leg-waxing salons."
- P.J. O'Rourke in The American Spectator's Enemies List, 1996.

"Study predicts PC's won't be used in most homes by the year 2000."
- Associated Press, 24 March 1996

A Harris Poll taken in April 1994 revealed that only 34% of all U.S. adults had ever heard of the Information Superhighway. By late July 1994, that figure had increased to 48% after another Harris Poll; with most of us like those surveyed, not knowing much about key components of the Infobahn. These included On-Line services, E-mail, Digital Information, the Internet, and the Clipper Chip.[68]

On 9 February 1995, one Ron Gilster of the Communications Technology Center (CTC) journeyed to Peninsula College in Port Angeles, Washington, to present a humourous but enlightening look at the Information Superhighway and the Virtual Multiversity. This writer, one of the many compu-stupid attending the lecture, was not the only surprised audience member when Gilster predicated his opening remarks by declaring: "The Information Age is over! We are now in the Communications Age!"[69] This could only mean one thing to this writer: That Clifford Stoll, author of Silicon Snake Oil, was right. In his book, Stoll cited a certain David Thornburg's course materials for a fall 1994 Computer-Using Educators Conference:

"He [Thornburg said] that the information age is over, replaced by some sort of communications age. He want[ed] to reshape education because 'students are going to primary source materials to research their term papers without leaving their bedrooms. The days of running through the library stacks pulling reference materials are numbered.'
"Not much need for books and school libraries?...
"Slowly, the term computer-literacy is becoming passé, I'm told. In its place, educators speak of computer-aided education, networking, and technology seeding. If computer vendors seem filled with puffery, you haven't heard these people talk."[70]

Clifford Stoll, a brilliant computer expert himself, wrote Silicon Snake Oil as a compu-cautionary tale warning against excessive speeding down the Infobahn. This writer, a self-admitted cyber-idiot, bought the book with mixed feelings, not knowing what to expect. Imagine this writer's glee at reading early-on: "[Computers] isolate us from one another and cheapen the meaning of actual experience. They work against literacy and creativity. They will undercut our schools and libraries."[71]

This writer readily acknowledges that he has been cyberphobic ever since the Port Angeles Branch, of the North Olympic Library System, deep-sixed their card-catalogue system (mid-1990s). Without the index card-files, an old-fashioned fellow like this writer couldn't look up any information, could do no research on his own. The writer had even struggled to effectively use microfiche at U.Hawaii, so mandated computerisation was bad news. One was either compelled to get on-line, or (--worse--) pester the permanently surly P.A. librarians for access to information. The writer's sinking sensation at the time was explicated by misanthropic Southern satirist, Florence King: "Scriptophobia is winning. Computer jocks predict with relish 'the decline and fall of print' .... Joggers [the Thigh Culture] make calls from portable phones while listening to an audio book with the other ear, and I fight on...."[72]

In retrospect, this writer had been "digitally-hostile" ever since Pac-man had invaded the peace of his Hawaiian home in ca.1980. As Clifford Stoll observed fifteen years later: "Watch any kid play Nintendo to sense the shallowness of computer games."[73] There have been geometrical evolutionary changes throughout the '80s and '90s; some vaguely disturbing, some plainly irritating. There has been a pile-up of compu-garbage littering and obstructing the Information Highway. And it doesn't take a computer expert to notice a central, glaring irony of the Communications Age. As Andrew Ferguson, senior writer for The Washingtonian, has remarked:

"As our means of communications accelerate, there are fewer things of interest to talk about and fewer interesting people to talk about them with. Anyone who doubts this need only sign on to one of the 'chat rooms' offered by CompuServe or America Online. 'Megadeath rules!' one communicator will argue. 'Megadeath sucks!' another will counter, and thus the conversation will develop, for hours and hours. So little to say, so many ways to say it"....[74]

Perhaps one reason for the vapidity of "chat room" chit-chat is the seeming preponderance of thirtysomething yuppies jamming the Infobahn. In early 1996, the results of an Emerging Technologies Research Group survey found that the average Internet "surfer" is a 36 year-old (presumably white) male, has a collegiate education, and comes from a household with an overall income of $62,000 U.S.[75] The satirical magazine, Spy, has characterised the promise of the global village/network/information highway as fast-becoming a "text-only party line for lonely technophiles.... and [introducing] much-needed phenomena such as electronic stalking and interactive pornography to our culture."[76] Vapid chit-chat aside, CD-ROM technology is now able to compress the contents of an entire encyclopaedia onto a single compact disk, where in a matter of months the information is outdated.[77] So, except for the cyber-surfers and lonely technophiles, the new computer technology has advanced so swiftly that the average (North) American has been unable to adapt. Professor Terry Winograd, of computer science at Stanford University, has contended that the new information technology is now overwhelming rather than aiding Americans.[78] John Cunniff, business analyst for The Associated Press, has observed: "But unless the information generated by the new technology is made intelligible, technology may do much to complicate lives and very little to develop communication and understanding. It may, in the end, simply give us more of what we don't understand."[79]

Besides the endless, meaningless compu-chat and near-undecodable information overload, this writer most fears computerisation for the inherent loneliness it threatens. The Internet has promised us personal and political liberation; we may plan elaborate vacations, discover exotic new recipes, and make faceless new friends in cyberspace, identifiable only by code-numbers and aliases.[80] Some of these disembodied spirits become imaginary lovers for the lonely technophiles, and the mainstream press tells tales of "relationships" and marriages undermined by electronic pen-pals in cyberspace. As Thomas Fleming of Chronicles magazine has commented, "This is some nightmare out of Poltergeist [the movie], when the ghosts on the screen invade our living rooms."[81] Last, but not least, of this writer's immediate concerns about computerisation is the absolute alienation of cyberspace. The writer had to go no farther than the local Port Angeles newspaper to find thoughts on cyberspace fully commensurate with his own:

"There is very little, if any, difference between sitting glued to daytime or nighttime soap opera and being rooted to a computer screen, completely isolated from family and/or other human beings. I shudder when I hear proclamations about how convenient and lonely our lives will soon be.... You will never have to utter a human word, if you, personally, don't want to. This is kind of like solitary confinement, I imagine."[82]

Computerisation is big-time business in the writer's home state of Washington, the site of the Bill Gates-Microsoft phenomenon. A local television ad for Volvo in 1995 showed newlyweds driving off to Las Vegas on their honeymoon. They were the quintessential 1990s grown-up Grunge-Online Seattle fun-couple:

He, goateed and satanic like a younger Roberto Duran; she, a hard-faced Sharon Stone look-alike, hardly the blushing bride. When this writer first relocated to Port Angeles in 1987, the Oak Harbor-based Interwest Bank "misplaced" $16,000 U.S. home down-payment for an entire week. A wired bank manager, lolling in front of a computer modem, wearing a Maui Wowee T-shirt and lizard-skin cowboy boots, does not inspire this writer's financial confidence. But as a political small-government free-market conservative, this writer has to admit that the Information Revolution -- i.e., the wide-open and inexpensive circulation of ideas -- can definitely work for the greater good. Some of this writer's initially bad impressions of the Information Revolution were allayed by the rôle of desktop computer and fax machine in the 1980s breakup of the Soviet (Evil) Empire. The same free flow of ideas were facilitated by Johann Gutenberg's creation of movable type, which led to the Protestant Reformation during the sixteenth century. In the 1990s, the Internet may be bringing on another Information Revolution. An example of this was reported in 1995 by Time magazine, cited by the conservative periodical Human Events:

"...[S]ome Iranian scholars have gained access to the Internet, exposing them for the first time to the ideas of Shakespeare, Mill, and other Westerners. Iran's government may find it increasingly difficult to contain this information flow."[83]

Today, in 1996, the Internet is a "mega-network" of 50,000 computer systems in ninety nations. Thirty million individuals have world-wide access to the Internet via telephone-lines and personal computers (PCs), send electronic (e-)mail, "download" software, purchase computer-related products, and gather news and information. And the number increases 10% monthly.[84] More important than scope and numbers, however, are the uses to which the Internet is being put. Ordinary citizens now possess the means to circumvent -- indeed subvert -- existent bugbears imposed by perennial power-structures: Taxes, tariffs, Mickey-Mouse governmental regulations. The Internet also provides the private citizen with a public forum to disseminate information and ideas ... as well as a way to receive them.[85] (It has been said that the powerful Democrat Speaker of the House, Tom Foley of Washington State, was unceremoniously unseated in the Election of 1994 over the Internet.) Moreover, empowering citizens on the Internet has reduced the influence of the traditional media, long dominated in Norway, the United States, and Canada by the liberal-leftish élites. Throughout this writer's half-century lifetime, mostly government-run channels in Norway and Canada, and the Big Three networks in the United States, have dominated televised news -- placing their own "spin" on world and domestic affairs. They have been mostly aided and abetted by a few radio syndicates, and several large news services and newspapers. That all changed with the advent during the 1980s of cable television; there was CNN (recently dubbed the "Clinton News Network"), but also C-SPAN and many other stations catering to the many needs, tastes, and proclivities of the vast and varied North American viewing populace. Talk radio (Rush!) has also emerged as an aspect of the Information Revolution, where listeners and callers can later compare notes and express their views ... on the Internet.[86]

For purely fiscal conservatives and economic libertarians, the great spokespersons for cyberspace as political tool have been Alvin and Heidi Toffler (The Third Wave, 1980). In their 1995 book, Creating a New Civilization,[87] the Tofflers glowingly extolled the virtues of Third Wave "computer-based capitalism" as opposed to Second Wave "smokestack socialism."[88] As indicated earlier in this chapter, it was largely the Information Revolution -- powered by the computer and new communications media -- which brought down the Iron Curtain dividing Europe. Political freedom of thought transforms into ideas; political freedom of expression translates into action ... freedoms not always granted by tyrannical governments, but always guaranteed by the free flow of information. The Information Revolution promises the identical fate to befall the reactionary gerontocracy running China as that which ruled Russia. The Tofflers have correctly stated that Mikhail Gorbachëv was the first (and last) Soviet dictator to recognise the historic reality of the Information Revolution.[89] In The American political context, the Tofflers have averred that:

"....[T]he most important political development of our time is the emergence in our midst of two basic camps, one committed to Second Wave civilization, the other to Third. One is tenaciously dedicated to preserving the core institutions of industrial mass society -- the nuclear family, the mass education system, the giant corporation, the mass trade union, the centralized nation-state and the politics of pseudorepresentative government. The other recognizes that today's most urgent problems, from energy, war and poverty to ecological degradation and the breakdown of familial relationships, can no longer be solved within the framework of an industrial [i.e., Second W(ave] civilization."[90]

Thus spake the Tofflers of their frightening FutureWorld. The Toffler-envisioned Third Wave promises utilitarian benefits and individual rights for the commonweal, but this writer wonders (and worries) about Third Wave plans for the free nuclear family and independent nation-state. The Tofflers have even brought the dualistic Second Wave vs. Third Wave conflict to a fine point in American politics. A Toffler theory has phantasised that 1984 Democrat presidential candidate, Gary Hart[pence], won the New Hampshire primary for having called for "new thinking." The old Second Wave power structure (another Red China-type council of elders imbued with 19th century Marxist ideology) behind the Democrat Party united to stop Hart, and chose ... "solid, safe, Second Wave thinker Walter Mondale instead."[91] Another Toffler theory has credited the uneasy, strange-bedfellows anti-NAFTA alliance of Second Wave -[Ralph] Naderites with Second Wave [Pat] Buchananites. Indeed, according to the Tofflers, the whole Second Wave vs. Third Wave political-power war being waged in Washington, D.C., has so far been a no-contest. In 1991, for example, the U.S. Congress passed an infrastructure bill allocating $150 billion to bridges, highways, roads, and pot-holes; a provision of jobs and profits to Second Wave unions and companies. The Tofflers have reluctantly admitted that although physical infrastructure is important, Third Wave digital networks are getting short shrift by government -- far less any federal intent of subsidising the electronic Infobahn.[92]

Despite the Tofflers' personal association with House Speaker Newt Gingrich, they have pinned political cyber-hopes on the unlikely person of Vice President Al Gore. Furthermore, the Tofflers have surmised that much of the imbalance in the U.S. Capital is due to Gore's failure as yet to "reinvent government" along Third Wave lines. Certainly Gore has often used the phase, "the Information [Super] Highway"; it might even be the only original expression ever uttered by the wooden vice-president. But the present Democrat administration (1993-) is seen as still mired in Second Wave swamps of centralised, swollen, and inefficient bureaucracies which characterise federal agencies and civil service unions. The Tofflers have concluded:

"The Democrats' reflexive reliance on bureaucratic and centralist solutions to problems like the health insurance crisis is drawn straight from Second Wave theories of efficiency. Despite an occasional politician like Vice President Gore, who recognizes the importance of high technology and who once served as (Co[-]chair of the Congressional Clearinghouse on the Future, the Democrats remain so heavily indebted to their Second Wave backers in industry, the unions and the civil service, that as a party, they remain largely paralyzed in the face of the twenty-first century."[93]

Fellow futurist John Naisbitt (who co-authored Megatrends 2000 along with wife, Patricia Aburdene) doesn't believe in political parties at all, and has even proclaimed their death.[94] Naisbitt was specifically referring to the 1993 electoral débacles in France, Canada, and Japan, but also made mention of American Bill Gates as the leadership rôle-model of today: ..."Bill Gates and the millions of entrepreneurs we haven't heard of. The world is being run by the collective judgments and actions of individuals."[95] Naisbitt made the point that all computer developments affecting the whole earth have occurred quite recently. Since its inception at the Pentagon during the late 1970s, the Internet was broken down in 1986 and distributed to other agencies in the U.S.A. and internationally for purposes of research, education, and commerce. This happened just a decade ago! By 1990, the Internet had gone mostly commercial, and in 1995 linked several millions around the world through nearly a million "hosts."[96] The nature of leadership itself is changing as the political power-base is spreading out, diffusing itself from formerly localised area-nodes (the old districts, wards and neighbourhoods). The new Toffler-Naisbitt leadership will be pragmatical rather than ideological, as economical concerns will increase and political issues will decrease; with the voters having ... "better access to information against which to judge them."[97]

In the Third Wave FutureWorld of the Tofflers and the Naisbitts, economics is the be-all and end-all question. As global manufacturers, financial institutions, and merchandise retailers continue to do business in an increasingly single, world-wide market-place, more and more industries will follow the current trend. And as the world-wide market-place gets ever larger, the small units connecting it will get yet smaller. Certainly the main mantra throughout John Naisbitt's Global Paradox, for both government and industry, has been: "The almost perfect metaphor for the movement from bureaucracies of every kind to small, autonomous units is the shift from the mainframe to PC's, with PC's networked together."[98]

That smaller is better is a theme oft-returned to by Naisbitt, with a virtually-audible Amen! emanating from the Tofflers in the (virtual cyberspace) background. It is the Information Revolution of telecommunications that simultaneously drives the global economy and concurrently creates smaller but stronger connecting parts. It is the new technology which permits unwieldy bureaucracies to deconstruct -- to decentralise from fat Second Wave corporations to lean Third Wave companies -- "to push power and decision making down to the lowest possible point."[99] John Naisbitt has cited Bill Gates, "Microsoft Corp.'s pioneering president, "as having described what is occurring as the creation of a "'new digital world order.'"[100] If such a statement alarms technophobes or conservatives, there remains the mollifying knowledge that telecommunications, in the hands of the Western news media, helped end the wars in Afghanistan, Angola, and Nicaragua; challenged the gerontocracy ruling China; and, as noted, in Europe brought the Berlin Wall and Iron Curtain crashing down.[101]

Reassuring or not regarding the rôle of telecommunications in the collapse of the Communist "Evil Empire", FutureWorld prophets such as John Naisbitt and Alvin Toffler have assumed the inevitable demise of the nation-state. Acerbic paleo-conservative columnist, Samuel Francis of Chronicles, has likened the predictions of Karl Marx and Friedrich Engels regarding the fate of nationalism to those of Alvin Toffler in The Third Wave (1980).[102] Francis cited Toffler at length in his Chronicles column:

"It is questionable how effectively national borders can be sealed off -- or for how long. For the shift toward a Third Wave industrial base requires the development of highly ramified, sensitive, wide open "neural network" or information system, and attempts by individual nations to dam up data flows may interfere with, rather than accelerate, their own economic development.... All such developments -- the new economic problems, the new environmental problems, and the new communications technologies -- are converging to undermine the position of the nation-state in the global scheme of things."[103]

Samuel Francis reminded the reader that exactly the opposite came true during the (ensuing) 1980s and 1990s. Just as Marx's working-class proletarians enthusiastically supported their particular patriotic cause during the Great War of 1914-1918, so have the collapse of Communism and the end of the Cold War given re-birth to nascent nationalisms all over the globe. Francis also indicated that FutureWorld prophesies have been based solely on economic calculations, overlooking deeper gut issues of nationalism, culture, and religion. As the Clintonistas tirelessly informed the American body politic, over and over again in 1992, "It's the economy, Stupid!" But as Francis commented:

"....[T]he coronation of Economic Man as the absolute monarch of modern political thought not only ignores and distorts human reality but also serves to destroy and erase human social and cultural realities the monarch does not much care for anyway. Relying on "the market" as the universal answer to every question of public discussion, the adherents of Economic Man merely accelerate the institutional destruction out of which the power of the mass state emerges as an alternative answer to the questions Economic Men skip over..."[104]

A main text used by this writer in preparing for Part II (on cyberspace), was Creating a New Civilization by Alvin and Heidi Toffler; with foreword by Newt Gingrich (R--Ga.). Ever since "Mr. Newt" took up the gavel as Speaker of the House of (the 104th) Congress in January 1995, the Pennsylvania-bred Georgia Republican has been under a withering fire from the pens of the Fourth Estate. And Gingrich's high-profile acquaintanceship with the New Age guru-like Tofflers has been a favourite grist for the news-media mill. Not all criticism directed at Gingrich, vis-à-vis the Tofflers, has been from the liberal mainstream press.... No, indeed! Richard Brookhiser of National Review has uncharitably written:

"Everything the Tofflers say is trivialized by their theory of history. Humanity has gone through three waves: agriculture, industrialism, and the wave that's happening now, the information age. I first heard the big theory in my interview with Gingrich ten years ago, and that was the best way to be exposed to it. It's the kind of thought you come up with at a dinner party when you've had a few drinks and you're on a roll. It's sweeping, plausible, partly true; in that context, the holes don't matter. But the Tofflers have built an entire world view on it."[105]

According to the perspicacious Brookhiser, the Toffler weltanschauung looks like history but is more a clever trendology in the (old) game of threes: "Posit two eras, and predict a third. If you win, you not only foresee the future, you own it."[106] In the Toffler trendology, influences from previous eras persisting in to succeeding eras are conveniently left out (or forgotten). And although the Tofflers accentuate the turmoil caused by one Wave clashing with the next, they don't acknowledge that the turbulence might last for centuries. An example of this persistence is humanity's contemporary ideals of masculinity and notions of warfare -- still with us after millennia, from the pre-First Wave dreamtime of hunting and gathering."[107] Positive proof of continuing public high-regard for warriors is reflected in the 1996 (an American election year) political phenomenon of U.S. General Colin Powell. Generals Dayan, de Gaulle, MacArthur, and Eisenhower are further exemplars which come to this writer's mind. Brookhiser continued: "Dying and reviving gods, the myths of agriculture, haunt Christmas trees and The Waste Land. This is a criticism of trendology on its own terms."[108] Modern customs and mores -- derived from time immemorial -- are additional evidence that the Tofflers are skewed in their thinking. Brookhiser's ultimate criticism is that the language of trendology ignores the question of truth, ... "whether framed by philosophers, prophets, or poets. Plato, St. Paul, and Shakespeare would all be baffled by the Tofflers...."[109] But, then again, the Tofflers would most probably be baffled by the truth as framed by Plato, St. Paul, and Shakespeare.

Palaeo-conservative commentator Samuel Francis of Chronicles has referred to the thought of the late Eric Voegelin to explicate the Toffler-Gingrich Third Wave trendology. Francis believes that the Toffler world-view, with Gingrich's enthusiastic political promotion of that view, are "almost literal manifestations of what Voegelin called 'gnosticism.'"[110] Gnosticism and neo-Gnosticism have been discussed earlier in this work; let it suffice to say that Voegelin saw Gnosticism -- neo or not -- as the spiritual and intellectual prototype of modern totalitarianism. Voegelin, Francis has informed us, identified four "symbols" that

characterise Gnostic movements: (1) A conception of history as unfolding in Three Ages ("Waves"); the last

stage (the "Third Realm") in which man, society, and the earth are perfected through <u>gnosis</u> (Gr."knowledge").

Former symbols of Gnostic movements are Marxist Communism, with its "[T]hird [A]ge" of proletarian rule,

and National Socialism (Nazism) with its ill-starred Third Reich. Voegelin's second symbol (2) was that of

the Leader; the third symbol (3) that of the Prophet. Voegelin's fourth and final symbol (4) was that of a

"brotherhood of autonomous persons."   To Eric Voegelin, the "[B]rotherhood" (in modern Gnostic

movements) consisted of the party, the race, the workers, or other aggregated groups fingered by fate as the

"historic agents" of paradigm shift; the mystical-but-secular salvation of the New Age.[111]

Gleaning from the apocalyptic interpretations of Eric Voegelin, Samuel Francis has likened the Third

Wave itself to the Third Realm, with Alvin Toffler as the Prophet, and with Newt Gingrich as the Leader of

the Realm. The Brotherhood has been envisioned by Francis as emerging in time when "those who adhere

to the paradigm and to Mr. Gingrich's unquestioned leadership of it crystallize."[112] The whole point of this

exercise by the doubting Francis was to prove that (1) the new technology (of computerisation) has more

potential to enslave private citizens than decentralise public power, and (2) the new technology, itself, is the

<u>gnosis</u> of the Third Wave [i.e., New Age] Gnostic movement. Francis concluded with a pessimistic clincher:

...."The dehumanized vision of the future that he [Prophet Toffler] and Leader Gingrich share may
yield a certain amount of decentralization and 'opportunity' in the short run, but as the machines of the Third
Wave replace social institutions and moral disciplines, make no mistake about how much freedom from the
first and second waves will remain on the beach."[113]

This writer has always feared the cold impersonality of computers. Ever since the moonshot of 1969,

the coming universal digital_isation has filled the writer with dread. On computers, Norman Mailer wrote in

<u>Of a Fire on the Moon</u> (1970): ...."The computer became the new frontier, a frontier of air-conditioned

windowless rooms with fluorescent panels in the ceiling and electronic shirrings and gurglings. The men who

rode the limits of this range were computer programmers who wore horn-rimmed glasses and shirts of

synthetic fabric...."[114] But there was more, much more, to it than Mailer's comic-strip picture of technocrats

in the late 1960s: Computerisation was an entire new dimension -- cyberspace -- with new rules and its own ecology. The computer to Mailer was "... an electronic mode of calculating which might yet change the nature of thought itself."[115] Mailer credited the digital computer with the power of running man's mind through an accelerator, which could catapult the mortal mind out into the universe, or explode its remains on earth. Perhaps for this reason, Mailer "... could never pass through a room containing a bank of computers without a moment of woe, as if he had just walked through an amphitheater where some species of higher tapeworm was quietly ingesting the vitals of God"....[116]

Like Alvin Toffler in 1980 and John Naisbitt in 1990, Norman Mailer on the eve of the 1970s foresaw that the computer would become smaller, faster, more accurate, and with a greater ability to store information.[117] But, unlike the futurists following him, Mailer regarded the new brainpower as being plastic: "[I]t would push to fill vacuums, press on to simulate what had hitherto been out of range of simulation, occupy problems whose outer margins would be lost as the center was sucked into the binary system..."[118] And although hardly a futurologist, novelist Mailer was notably prescient in 1969 for his sense of the imminent Information Age:

..."Because the computer was the essence of narcissism (the computer could not conceive of its inability to correct its own mistakes) a view of the Seventies suggested a technological narcissism so great that freak newspeak was its only cure -- only the threat of a murderous society without could keep computer society from withering within. How those societies would mingle! Acid and pot had opened the way."[119]

Those societies would mingle allright, but not in exactly the way Mailer imagined. The hippies and the bikers, sworn enemies during the 1960s, became indistinguishably fused over a generation; so too the ovine Mailer compu-nerds meshed with the 1960s counterculture. The mutated results of the technological and psychospiritual mixture are the vulpine cyber-dweebs of the 1990s, with roots deep in the New Age. In the spring of 1995 Time magazine put out a cyberspace Special Issue. A feature article, 'We owe it all to the hippies', was subtitled, "Forget antiwar protests, Woodstock, even long hair. The real legacy of the sixties generation is the computer revolution."[120] Two of the high-lighted computer revolutionists were one Bill Gates and a Mitch Kapor. (Bill Gates of Microsoft will be dealt with at length in Section B.)

Mitch Kapor, co-founder of Lotus software, is a prime example of New Age computer revolutionist. According to Psychology Today, Kapor became a full-time Transcendental Meditation (TM) initiator after leaving Yale. He then turned to psychology and computers, becoming "too successful."[121] Since then, Kapor has co-founded the Electronic Frontier Foundation, a non-profit organisation developed to "foster democracy and protect civil liberties on the electronic superhighway."[122] Mitch Kapor believes that cyberspace itself is a new spiritual frontier,[123] and that computer technology offers an advanced method of personal liberation. Achieving true freedom from the prison of one's own mind is possible in both traditional Buddhist practice and the new computer technology, he told Psychology Today. Kapor visualises himself as an engaged Buddhistic healer, "relieving suffering wherever it is possible."[124]

Jaron Lanier is another hot-shot whiz-kid rising fast in cyberspace. Stewart (Whole Earth Catalog) Brand has portrayed him as naming, largely inspiring, and partially equipping the cyber-phenomenon known as Virtual Reality; that weird, computerised sensory-immersion. Brand has informed the Time Special Issue readers that Lanier "grew up under a geodesic dome in New Mexico, once played clarinet in the New York City subway and still sports dreadlocks halfway down his back."[125] Another Time Special Issue contributing writer was more cyber-dramatic:

"With shoulder-length red dreadlocks and an intense gaze, Jaron Lanier is a striking presence, even in the strange universe of performance art. But then he does nothing so routine as, say, recite sonnets while cartwheeling nude across a stage. Lanier is a virtual-reality performance artist. In his piece, The Sound of One Hand, which has played to packed theaters in Chicago, Toronto and Linz, Austria, he appears onstage framed by the image of a virtual world he enters when he dons special goggles and a DataGlove. His audience sees what he sees -- and what he does, which is bend and stretch like some contorted stork. His movements elicit eerie, tinkling notes from the computer-generated virtual instruments he is playing: a Cybersax, a CyberXylo and a Rhythm Gimbal."[126]

From the tenor of the articles contained in the Spring 1995 Time Special Issue, the casual reader might have expected the Second Coming. In particular, Stewart Brand praised the lords of cyberspace. Disingenuously twisting the old Sixties saying, "Do your own thing," into "Start your own business,"[127] Brand brought new standards to depths of doublespeak unplumbed by even the present political pilot-fish at the Clinton White House. In other words, by following Timothy Leary's notorious mantra -- "Turn on, tune in, drop out" -- Brand's 1960s college kids also "dropped academia's traditional disdain for business.... Reviled by the broader social establishment, hippies found ready acceptance in the world of small business."[128] Brand's grandiloquent assessment of his Sixties generation's accomplishments in cyberspace was final imprimatur that "where self-reliance leads, resilience follows, and where generousity leads, prosperity follows. If that dynamic continues, ... then the [I]nformation [A]ge will bear the distinctive mark of the countercultural 60's well into the millennium."[129]

Stewart Brand (age 56 in 1995) has been right about the Sixties generation's influencing the Information [New] Age, but attributing that to "self-reliance" and "generosity" is an absurd conceit. This writer attended Boston University from 1963-1965, returned to college (U.Miami) after two years in the Army, 1967-1969, and well remembers the hippies. They were mostly the rebellious sons and wayward daughters of the White upper-middle classes' best and brightest citizens. Hippies seemed to predominate on the college campuses of the U.S. Northeast, Northcentral, and West ("Left") Coast. In New England and South Florida, they were often the educated offspring of indulgent well-to-do WASP and Jewish families; the very foundations of the Eastern Establishment. When these drug-using tie-dyed college kids "dropped out", they usually went "underground", seeking employment at leftist journals, beat coffee-houses, or at "alternative" teaching. This writer does not recall hippies generally finding "ready acceptance in the world of small business" -- quite the contrary: Hippies sought out their own kind in the countercultural underground economy, mainly peripheral to the very institution out of which they had dropped. During the mid-1960s at Boston University, hippies (still in school) were overwhelming at Humanities, Communications, and Liberal Arts; underwhelming at Science, Technology, and Business Administration. Pete Seeger, and Peter, Paul, and Mary sang of a world in a language alien to M.I.T. slide-rule techno-grubs. When the countercultural underground surfaced and became assimilated into -- but not absorbed by -- the 1970s popular mainstream, science, technology, and business followed suit in the roiling cauldron of psychospiritual brew. As Norman Mailer observed in 1969, "How those societies would mingle! Acid and pot had opened the way."[130] Alvin Toffler pointed out in 1991 that knowledge (i.e., information), wealth, and violence equal power,[131] and sometime during the 1970s the hippies at Communications and the compu-nerds at Technology discovered this equation and ... presto! A generation later, the fanged cyber-dweeb rules the air!

This writer has called Stewart Brand's crediting the Information Revolution to hippiedom's "self-reliance" and "generosity" an absurd conceit. 1960s hippies, still at university during the 1970s, had relied on the financial largesse of their upper-middle class parents or State sponsors; hippies dropping out had relied on like-minded members of the Velvet Underground. As for generosity, hippies had been open-handed in drug distribution only after a big score. They (then) got "high with the help of their friends," (and) they got "by with the help of their friends." But Stewart Brand and other Sixties apologists in today's Establishment press only praise those cool hippies who have ultimately achieved wealth, fame, and power. Those Dr. Jeckyll/Mr. Hyde hippies at Communications and compu-nerds of Technology who stayed in school during the 1970s, outwardly conformed to the former Establishment's rules and regulations. On weekdays they wore Hush Puppies desert boots; on weekends and at night they wore the tire-tread Cong sandals. These were the computer hackers accurately assessed by Stewart Brand as spearheading the Information Revolution.[132] Despite this writer's overdrawn metaphor of "fanged cyber-dweebs", it accurately describes the empowerment of the 1990s libertarian lords of cyberspace. The current crop owes its very existence -- certainly their wealth, fame, and power -- to the free-wheeling, pony-tailed computer hackers of the 1960s who liberated cyberspace. Today's dweeb-lords of the air are enjoying the fruits of hard-earned labour by that first generation.

In 1978, countercultural author William Irwin Thompson predicted that in computer science, "traditional Ahrimanic technologists" would eventually compete with "New Age Luciferian technologists."[133] In 1996, they have been joined in battle for a decade and more, and the New Age Luciferian technologists are winning the cyber-war. Are, then, the MTV whiz-kids -- the hackers-cum-technicians -- the new lords of cyberspace, the new noösphere? It would seem so. it is instructive that William Irwin Thompson characterised the New (noetic) Men as New Age Luciferians. Thompson's contemporary and colleague, New Age leader David Spangler of the Findhorn Community, in 1977 made an extraordinary statement he termed the Luciferic Initiation:

> "Lucifer works within each of us to bring us to wholeness, and as we move into a [N]ew [A]ge, which is the age of man's wholeness, each of us in some way is brought to that point which I term the Luciferic Initiation; the particular doorway through which the individual must pass if he is to come fully into the presence of his light and his wholeness.
>
> "Lucifer comes to give us the final gift of wholeness. If we accept it, then he is free and we are free. That is the Luciferic [I]nitiation. It is one that many people now, and in the days ahead, will be facing, for it is an initiation into the New Age."[134]

On a lighter note, humourist Ian Shoales of Duck's Breath newsletter told readers of one Dan Farmer, co-creator of a software programme designed to find weak security points in any computer system linking the Internet. Farmer and co. eventually came up with Security Administrator Tool for Analyzing Networks, a-k-a

SATAN.[135] Shoales related that SATAN entered the digital domain on the Internet at 7 a.m., 5 April 1995, "a day that will live in infamy."[136] The unfortunate Dan Farmer was subsequently sacked for his part in releasing SATAN into cyberspace. Shoales, with tongue in cheek, exhorted his public to "... exorcize the Father of Lies [Lucifer/Satan] from our operating systems before it's too late. We need digital priests! Virtual garlic!"[137]

But there is undoubtedly a New Age "Luciferian" cast to contemporary cyberspace. A New Age journal advertises "Life without The New Times is like an astrologer without a computer"[138] -- the assumption being that it is a given for Aquarian astrologers to be on-line. The Learning Channel (TLC) has likened interactive Virtual Reality to the weird, surreal dimensions of Alice Through the Looking Glass. In Virtual America,[139] evangelical writer George Barna observed that American cultural beliefs and values will be decreasingly transmitted via the written word, but ..."will instead become part of the new communications strategy"....[140] As reading for knowledge and pleasure gives way increasingly to use of alternative media, the American public derives its political and cultural (current) wisdom from pre-"digested and interpreted information conveyed in bite-size pieces (e.g., sound-bite journalism). Some analysts refer to ours as the 'post-literate age.'"[141] The oral tradition has declined along with functional literacy, and schools, government, and business rely more and more on interactive and video media (T.V., video-cassettes, laser discs) to "...convey the crux of our culture to young people. Expect much to get lost in the translation," Barna warned.[142] As to how to help budding 1990s MTV whiz-kids prepare for the Luciferic Initiation, Christian periodical Today's Front Page has advised, "Give them New Age computer and video games that introduce them to the world of spells, powers ... make them so exciting that they retreat into a fantasy world that opens the door to the occult."[143]

And to think that all this flower-power (action) and weeding (reaction) was seeded (insemination) during the 1960s counterculture! Personifying the strands linking the counterculture to 1990s cyberspace, has been Dr. Timothy ("Turn on, Tune in, Drop out") Leary. The Harvard professor and LSD guru died 31 May 1996, at age 75 years, of cancer.[144] But what is significant -- for our purpose here -- is that Timothy Leary, enamoured of high-tech, expired at his web-site. Indeed, Leary had seriously considered committing suicide in cyberspace. Furthermore, the drug-doctor's groupies and fans had been able to follow their hero's deteriorating health through his site on the World Wide Web. Leary's home-page announced his death, a modest "Timothy has passed," and that the Leary last words were "Why not?" and "Yeah!."[145] Before he died, Leary (the inner-space traveler) had decided that Celestis, Inc. of Houston, Texas, would pack seven grams of his ashes into a small aluminium capsule and blast them into orbit.[146] Celestis, Inc. is a two years-old space funeral company which, for $4,800.00, will launch into the firmament the burnt offerings of at least 15 rich-and-famous persons this autumn (1996). This flight, the Founders' Flight, will include some of the charred remnants of celestial hitchhiker Gene Roddenberry, creator of Star Trek, whose partial remains have been resting in a burial urn since 1991; the year Roddenberrry "assumed room temperature."

But why would Timothy leary, countercultural guru and sage, wish his ashes sent into space, the outer limits, rather than to be scattered in the sea or spread over a mountain-top? Leary confidante and friend of 25 years, a Ms. Carol Rosin, has answered, "He always wanted to travel in space and had some experiences doing it -- mentally, consciously -- and now he will have the chance to really do it."[147] (Oh, wow.) A truly closing Strawberry Statement -- an odic paean -- to the wigged-out life and web-site death of Timothy Leary was issued as epitaph in Newsweek magazine, a mainstream [counter]cultural vehicle of the current wisdom (cw):

.... "After his release [from prison] in 1976, the ever-resilient Leary spent the rest of his life being famous for being famous. He kept the pot boiling as a 'stand-up philosopher' and a software designer, touting the PC for the same reasons he had touted LSD: as an opener of the doors of perception and a whoopee cushion under the seats of power. At least in public, he remained the dauntless, wisecracking psychonaut to the end. He was 'thrilled' to be dying, couldn't wait for those mysterious minutes between the last heartbeat and fade-out of the brain. His last words were 'Why not?' It was the one-liner he'd been fine-tuning all his life."[148]

Theodore Roszak, in 1969 a member of the history department at Cal.State Hayward, wrote The Making of a Counter Culture which was put out that same year. The book was subtitled: Reflections on the technocratic society and its youthful opposition,[149] and still stands as a truly significant work. Like Charles Reich's The Greening of America, The Making of a Counter Culture exemplifies the 1960s era. Unlike Reich, however, Roszak was neither so easily taken in by weekend plastique hippies of the time, nor as quick to genuflect at the hastily-erected altars to proliferating Zen stud-muffins published in Playboy. Concerning ("Terrible") Timothy Leary, Roszak -- to his credit -- had already smelled an Alpha fox so far back as 1967.

Quoting from a <u>New York Post</u> interview, Roszak commented in his book:

....."Leary ha[d] begun to assimilate the psychedelics to a bizarre form of psychic Darwinism which admit[ted] the tripper to a 'new race' still in the process of evolution. LSD, he claim[ed], [was] 'the sacrament that will put you in touch with the ancient two million year old wisdom inside you', it free[d] one 'to go on to the next stage, which is the evolutionary timelessness, the ancient reincarnation thing that we always carry inside.'"[150]

Timothy Leary, countercultural icon, passed out and on at his web-site ... how ironic! Surely though, as evangelists Dave Hunt and T.A. McMahon have reminded us, the counterculture began as a largely political movement questioning the Viet-Nam War and which decried the "evils of a materialistic society."[151] Technological science had offered no answers to ultimate questions and had, instead, brought mankind to the edge of nuclear winter and environmental collapse.[152] The counterculture became a spiritual [New Age] movement that sought solace through mind-expanding drugs and solutions in mystical Eastern religions. The ultimate answers [went the current wisdom] lay in the realm of spirituality.[153] But Theodore Roszak, a chronicler of the counterculture, remarked that after Flower Power, Peace and Love, had set in ..."[a]t the level of our youth, we begin to resemble nothing so much as the cultic hothouse of the Hellenistic period, where every manner of mystery and fakery, ritual and rite, intermingled with marvelous indiscrimination."[154] Roszak wrote the preceding during the 1960s, but he could just as well been comparing the Hellenistic period to today's New Age.[155] The Encyclopaedia Brittanica tells us that:

....."In the Hellenistic age there was a growing distrust of traditional Greek rationalism and a breaking down of the distinction between science and religion. Hermes-Thoth was but one of the gods and prophets (chiefly Oriental) to whom men turned for a divinely revealed wisdom."[156]

Change "Greek rationalism" to "Western Civilisation" and "Hermes-Thoth" to "Shamballa forces,"[157] and one has the "cultic hothouse of the Hellenistic period" fully evolved in the 1990s New Age. As this writer has expressed before, the demon seeds sown in the cultic hothouse of the 1960s have bloomed into the flowers of evil ("<u>les fleurs du mal</u>") today. Theodore Roszak's <u>The Making of a Counter Culture</u> was (also) a seminal planting of the 1960s. Roszak had -- during that turbulent era -- had articles published in such leftist organs as <u>The Nation</u>, <u>Liberation</u>, <u>New Politics</u>, and <u>The New American Review</u>. He introduced <u>The Making of a Counter Culture</u> with a quote from fiery British poet, William Blake: "Rouse up, O Young Men of the New Age!" As a liberal author, Roszak nonetheless pleasantly surprised this writer with his canny observations and

222

(oh, horrors!) right-on labels (e.g., "psychic Darwinism" of Timothy Leary) stuck to countercultural idols and others.[158] But there has been another aspect of Roszak's book almost forgotten in the contemporary maelstrom of cybermania, and the subtitle tells it all: Reflections on the technocratic society and its youthful opposition. That is why the good Doctor Leary's expiration at his PC web-site was so ironic -- whatever happened to countercultural technophobia?

Rebels against the Future by Kirkpatrick Sale originally came out during May 1995.[159] And, according to Sale, since the book's appearance ... "the issue of technology and its discontents has burst on the public consciousness as seldom before and a broad array of neo-Luddites of all kinds -- doubters, dropouts, naysayers, victims, recoverers, and out-and-out technophobes -- has surfaced to give it voice.... At least a dozen books were published denouncing the promises of cyberspace and demonstrating ways to find the exit ramps from the information highway...."[160] And, as Sale has noted, it was in the midst of all this cyberphobia that the Unabom[b]er forced The Washington Post and The New York Times to publish his manifesto, 'Industrial Society and Its Future' in September 1995. Within the pages of the polemic, the Unabom[b]er accused computer-age machines of having "'destabilized society, have made life unfulfilling, have subjected human beings to indignities, have led to widespread psychological suffering ... and have inflicted severe damage on the natural world.'"[161] Sale has concluded that although there was no public approval of the Unabom[b]er's actions, a "widespread and vociferous response' was elicited by his hatred and rejection of modern technology.[162]

Since then, of course, we know that the Unabom[b]er suspect is one Theodore John Kaczynski, sometime U.Cal. Berkeley mathematics professor, arrested by U.S. federal agents on 3 April 1996 in Lincoln, Montana.[163] The Unabom[b]er manifesto and the apprehension of Ted Kaczynski have reignited the neo-Luddite debate amongst academicians and literati, and continues unabated. Kirkpatrick Sale's study on Luddism, Rebels against the Future, was almost presciently coincidental. The eponymous Luddites (1811-1812) took their name from the mythical Ned Ludd of Lincolnshire (Robin Hood country) and northern England; they were mostly weavers, combers, and dressers of wool. Workers and artisans in home-cottage industries, the potential Luddites felt threatened by the encroaching Industrial Revolution. New-fangled, complicated and massive machinery would intrude on their ancient and settled trades, along with huge multi-storied buildings invading the Lincoln-green hills and valleys. Yet worse, Sale has passionately indicated, the soon-to-be Luddites ...

"...[S]aw their ordered society of craft and custom and community begin to give way to ... industrial society and its new technologies and systems, new principles of merchandise and markets, new configurations of countryside and city, beyond their ken or control. And when they rose up against this for fifteen tempestuous months [1811-1812]... they did so with more ferocity and intensity than anything Robin Hood ever mustered, and were put down with far more force that King John ever commanded."[164]

The original principles of Luddism, Sale has asserted, are presently reflected in neo-Luddite opposition to progress, mechanisation, growth, competition, exploitation, consumption.[165] The neo Industrial Revolution is cyberspace, with neo-Luddites engaging technomaniacs on the currently automated battlefield. Who exactly are the neo-Luddites? Kirkpatrick Sale has painted [himself and] them a decidedly vivid Green:

...."They are to be found on the radical and direct-action side of environmentalism ... they are on the dissenting edges of academic economics and ecology departments ... they are everywhere in Indian Country throughout the Americas, representing a traditional biocentrism against the anthropocentric norm; they are activists fighting against nuclear power, irradiated food, clear-cutting, animal experiments, toxic wastes, and the killing of whales, among the many aspects of the high-tech onslaught."[166]

The neo-Luddites are also those whose trust in technology has been shattered by the proofs and evidence of industrial error and terror -- from Bhopal to Chernobyl and Love Canal; from PCBs to the Exxon Valdez oil spill and [reports/rumours of man-made] ozone holes. Finally, to cap it off, Sale has lamented (along with a plaintive note of pc victimology) that dormant neo-Luddites are all those who have been "confused or demeaned, or frustrated" by inoperable high-tech at home or the workplace.[167] Although the digital computer is non-polluting and energy-efficient, Sale has declared the instrument inherently evil: It is designed to calculate in a linear, fact-based logic which is the scientific method. Kirkpatrick Sale, a "neo-Luddite neo-leader" (Joe Klein, Newsweek, April 1996) has seen the digital computer as fulfilling the scientific desire ...

"[F]or ordering nature, ultimately reducing all its 'secrets' to reductive analysis and manipulation ... they [computers] are designed to give humans not merely analytical but physical control over nature, putting all its elements to human use whenever possible, altering its systems and even its species for human enhancement, ultimately changing its atoms to create new compounds and life forms for human aggrandizement."[168]

Sale continued throughout his work to belabour the point of how industrial technology has ravished Mother

Nature, giving humankind the dubious gifts of "atomic bombs and death camps, toxic wastes, traffic jams, strip mining, organized crime, psychosurgery, advertising, unemployment, or genocide."[169] Certainly the preceding is an absurd succession from the tortuous mind of Kirkpatrick Sale. Although this writer is assuredly a cyberphobe, such skewed arguments against technology prompt him to seriously reconsider the sensible words of P.J. O'Rourke:

....."The Industrial Revolution allowed millions of ordinary folks an opportunity to obtain decent houses, food, and clothes (albeit with some unfortunate side effects, such as environmental damage and Al Gore)."[170]

Kirkpatrick Sale, like Charles A. Reich before him, hates the logic and linear thinking responsible for scientific reductionism, hence its feared offspring, technology, and therefore its grandchild, technocracy. Sale names a stranger-than[science] fiction pantheon of supposed neo-Luddite All-Stars, of varying achievement or celebrity, some of whom will be familiar to readers: Fritjof Capra (Taoist Quantum physicist), Rachel Carson (Buddhistic environmentalist), Paul Goodman (Gestalt-therapy Anarchist), Herbert Marcuse (Freudian Marxist), Arne Naess (Deep Ecologist), Jeremy Rifkin (New Age Geosophist); and authors Farley Mowatt (Never Cry Wolf), Theodore Roszak, and Kurt Vonnegut (Galapagos).[171] If Sale's "A" List of neo-Luddite candidates look like 1960s-1990s Countercultural-Establishment figureheads, it is no coincidence. As neo-Luddite neo-leader, Sale revels in praising such Green terrorist groups as Earth First! and Sea Shepherd Conservation Society for their horrendous acts of "ecotage."[172] Regarding the condemnation of technocracy, the only commonalities of the low-key Roszak and the high-whine Sale have been two sources -- Jacques Ellul[173] and Lewis Mumford.[174] But whereas Jacques Ellul wrote: "The artificial world is radically different from the natural world, [with] different imperatives, different directives, and different laws... [such that] it destroys, eliminates, or subordinates the natural world."....;[175] Kirkpatrick Sale would whine: "Whatever material benefits industrialism may introduce, the familiar evils - incoherent metropolises, spreading slums, crime and prostitution, inflation, corruption, pollution, cancer and heart-disease, stress, anomie, alcoholism -- almost always follow."[176]

Traditional, non-industrial societies in America admired by Sale are the Amish and the Iroquois (i.e., the

"Irokwa").[177] Perhaps their popularity is due to their numerical paucity and political powerlessness. No matter, the Noble Savage appears nobler from a (safe) distance, and the Amish version of God seems somehow less threatening than the (nearby) Judaeo-Christian One. But this is the sort of imagery and life-style that appeals so strongly to Christian "Fundi" Greens of Western Europe, Deep Ecologists of North America, and Unabom[b] suspect Ted Kaczynski, formerly of Lincoln, Montana. In the closing chapter of Powershift, Alvin Toffler warned darkly of "...self-described 'fundamentalists', who wish to plunge society into pre-technological medievalism and asceticism. They are 'eco-theologues', and some of their views dovetail with the thinking of religious extremists.... They wish to restore a religion-drenched world that has not existed in the West since the Middle Ages. The environmental movement provides a convenient vehicle."[178] The difference, though, between these reactionary "eco-theologues" and Deep Greens, is that the former worship God the Father (and Creator) and the latter Mother Earth (the creation). The Fundamentalist (Christian "Fundi") Greens of Western Europe, and to a lesser extent in North America (where Gaia rules the Greens), perceive the earth in a Biblical context: An Edenic paradise now marred and sullied by a diabolic technology. The Christian Greens yearn to re-impose the non-polluting, environment-friendly Mediaeval Village on the earth, thus reëstablishing the perfect paradise of harmony and sustainability., Toffler has noted the... "congruence between the views of the eco-theologues and the fundamentalist revival, with its deep hostility to secular democracy."[179]

Not satisfied with merely calling eco-theologues [i.e., Christian Greens] undemocratic, Toffler summoned the buzz-names of the Ayatollah Khomeini and ... Adolf Hittler. Since 1939, if all other vilifications aren't enough, evoke the dread name of Adolf Hitler and attach it to the accused. Since 1979, all religious fundamentalists -- whether Jewish, Christian, or Muslim -- have been demonised as would-be Ayatollahs [Khomeini]. Toffler quoted French sociologist Alain Touraine as having written, "If we reject reason in the name of salvation from ozone depletion, we will court a Green fundamentalism, an eco-theocracy of the Ayatollahs Khomeini variety.'"[180] Toffler reminded readers that it is in Germany (1991) where the European Green movement is most militant. The Wandervogel youth of the 1920s were ..."the hippie-Greens of the Weimar Republic, roaming the countryside with their rucksacks, carrying guitars, wearing flowers, holding Woodstock-like festivals, high on spirituality and preaching a return to nature."[181]

But which spirituality? Adolf Hitler who ruled Germany by the early 1930s, also exalted pre-Industrial

Revolution times, praised the organic, extolled physical fitness, and utilised biological analogies and

comparisons to justify racial purification ("ethnic cleansing"), along with Sangerite eugenics and abortion for

the unfit. A sad irony is that Adolf Hitler and his inner circle of Nazi cronies were deeply steeped in the

occult [Theosophist Thule Society], which was anything but Christian. Yet Toffler and others have implied

that fundamentalist Christianity is responsible for eco-extremism; these are the very people who have linked

Martin Luther to the German-Jewish Holocaust. This writer contends that "hippie-Greens" of today share far

more of a common spirituality with the Wandervogel movement and Nazi utopians than with Christian "Fundi

Greens." In closing, Alvin Toffler both asked and answered questions:

> "Can one really imagine a Neo-Green Party, with armbands, Sam Browne belts, and jackboots, setting out to enforce its own view of nature on the rest of society? Of course not, not under normal conditions. But what if conditions are not 'normal'?[182]

> ...."But it is a mistake to view them [eco-theologues] as an isolated or trivial phenomenon. The religious revival and the Green movements alike breed ultras who would be happy to jettison democracy. At their extremes, these two movements may be converging to impose new restrictions on personal and political behavior in the name of both God and Greenness. Together they are pushing for a power shift toward the past."[183]

But a Christian FundiGreen takeover (of anything) is not of immediate concern in North America,

where Green spirituality, if any of the Wandervogel variety, has been coöpted by the New Age. In the United

States, surely, the environmentalist movement per se has devolved into a palace civil war of opposing liberal

élites: TechnoGreens versus neo-Luddites; cyber-punks against technophobic freaks. All jesting aside,

however, those who control cyberspace have at their command so mighty a weapon as telecommunications or

nuclear energy. But even here, in this crucial sphere, we observers are afforded a last laugh. In his excuse

for neo-Luddites employing high-tech to spread anti-tech propaganda, neo-leader Kirkpatrick Sale has

rationalised:

> "That is also why so many of them [neo-Luddite neo-leaders] are willing to use, at least in the near future, the technologies at the heart of the system they oppose, including telephones, faxes, jet planes, and photocopiers; as John Davis says, though he is one of the neo-Luddites and editor of Wild Earth quarterly, he 'inclines toward the view that technology is inherently evil' but 'disseminates this view via E-mail, computer, and laser printer.' It is a contradiction and a compromise, however, that sits easily with no one and is justified only in the name of the urgency of the cause and the need to spread its message as wide [sic] as possible."[184]

Thus it all essentially boils down to use and control of cyberspace. Clifford Stoll, computer expert and critical author of Silicon Snake Oil, is confident that the Internet will survive and thrive.[185] What has prompted Stoll's thoughtful book -- and to some degree this chapter on cyber-worship -- is the old Marshall McLuhan (1911-1980) saw that the medium (itself) is the message. To McLuhan, the essence of communication lay not in the truth or falsehood, wisdom or folly, of the message passed between persons, but in the technological nature of the transmitting medium.[186] Furthermore, McLuhan divided the intervening media into "hot" and "cool." Low-participatory media such as radio and movies were "hot"; high-participatory media such as television and the telephone were "cool." On the McLuhan scale, the Internet, especially the Usenet, would definitely be considered "cool."[187] But the Internet is merely a medium -- cool McLuhan message or not. Cyber-watcher Stoll has told us to

"... Read the computing literature to feel the aridity of the culture of computing. Or follow Usenet net news to see dolts posting utter drivel or flame wars reminiscent of the Ostrogoths and Visigoths...."[188]

But what does Clifford Stoll expect? An entire generation has been brought up under the aegis of the counterculture. MTV videos and occultic computer games for adolescents serve as natural gradations from Saturday morning cartoon shows, an American-made television tradition, featuring inferred sexuality, virtual violence, and subtle spiritist messages. Compu-nerds and cyber-dweebs (i.e., the Ahrimanic and Luciferian technologists of William Irwin Thompson) arose from this countercultural swamp; the latter whiz-kids -- as described in this work -- imbued with New Age thinking, along with a sense of vast personal empowerment. In his book Saturday Morning Mind Control, evangelical writer Phil Phillips has observed:

"Today's cartoons are filled with religious propaganda. That may not bother you, if you are a follower of Eastern thought, Hinduism, new-age philosophy, Zen, or a participant in occult practices.... If you are a Christian or an orthodox Jew, take heed. Your child is being taught something that is the opposite of what you believe!

"Much of religion has to do with the issue of power -- what it is, who has it, how one gets it, and how it works. Your child's perception of power is tangible. 'Mine', says a child. 'Yours', he may have to ultimately admit. The perception of power on today's cartoons is quite different. The power has a spiritual source: a supreme power, a force, an entity beyond the person who or which causes that person to have power or not.... The power is absolute. It possesses. it controls."[189]

Author Phillips named She-Ra, Princess of Power; He-Man, Master of the Universe; Teenage Mutant Ninja Turtles; and Black Star as some of the worst offenders. But even The Smurfs and Care Bears have a

New Agey feel to them.[190] Sometime in the mid-1980s this writer took his (then) pre-teen daughter to Jim (the Muppets) Henson's animated film "The Dark Crystal," and was shocked at the occultic symbolism throughout. In the background of cartoons and kiddie shows plays the everpresent heavy-metal rock music, with groups like KISS -- with face-paint, S&M leather outfits, and darting tongues -- appearing in televised ads. All this aired fluff and garbage prepares pre-adolescents for the culture of cyberspace. And cyberspace does have a culture, as surely as architecture, animal husbandry, or the United States Army each has a culture. As for cybersmarts being good for kids, opinions vary. In a USA Weekend article, 14-16 June 1996, Douglas Rushkoff queried 'Are "screenagers" wiser than adults?' Rushkoff maintained that technology had "positive effects" on children. A Denver, Colorado, teacher named Liz Goodwin would later disagree, writing that the only benefit to young people of cyberspace was increased hand-to-eye coördination.[190] Otherwise, Ms. Goodwin asserted that: (1) Young people are unaware of how technology affects them as they have never known anything else; (2) they are used to "scanning" rather than hearing or seeing, with a resulting reduced attention-span; (3) they will have less resistance to media hypnosis ("Ever heard of 'Nike'?"); and they will have trouble distinguishing fact from fiction.[191]

With impaired ability to separate reality from virtual reality, many children, who don't (or can't) become cyber whiz-kids, will end as home-page flies in the World-Wide Web. Awaiting both the compu-stupid and compu-smart are cyberporn and drive-by shootings on the Infobahn. All this lies down the Information Superhighway, despite the visions and promises of a Yellow Brick Road by the cyber-lords of the air. It could all terminate in a terrible techno-scenario, as in the 1983 Canadian movie "Videodrome" (starring James Woods), or the frightening FutureWorld of Alvin Toffler and John Naisbitt. It all depends on power, and who or what will control the cultural ecology of cyberspace. Right now, in 1996, the New Age Luciferian technologists command the airwaves.

Section B: Wired for the Web-site: Microsoft Corp. and Cyber-city, U.S.A.

"In many ways, Seattle is the quintessential American city of the '90's.... It's New York with clean streets. Paris with better manners. London with better coffee. Los Angeles with a professional football team."

          - John F. Kennedy, Jr., in a luncheon speech to the Seattle Advertising Federation.[193]

"A Stones association with Microsoft [Windows '95] is a strategic alliance: Bill Gates, the multibillion-dollar Jesus of nerd-dom is now as hip as Mick Jagger.... Redmond, Wash., is the New Magic Kingdom."

          - Steven Levy, Newsweek, 4 September 1995
          (Author of Hackers: Heroes of the Computer Revolution, 1984)

"... [Bill] Gates's shambling, awkward public persona helped for years to disguise his acquisitiveness."
          - Jerry Adler and Rob French, Newsweek, 20 May 1996

In the 11 November 1996 issue of Fortune magazine, Seattle led the list of best 15 U.S. cities to combine work-place with family-life. Seattle previously topped the same list in Fortune for 1992, but this time out the magazine went beyond evaluating cities solely from a business perspective. In 1996 life-style quality, incidence of crime, educational value, urban accessibility to commuters, and availability of cultural pursuits and artistic interests were all ingredients making up the list. Quoth contributing editor Geoffrey Precourt at a Seattle news conference, flattering his audience, "[You have] known all along [that] ... this is the best place to live and work."[194] Precourt continued with "the factor of livability" becoming ever more significant as businesses weigh places best suited for moving and expansion. And "Seattle went off the chart" when life-style was considered as important -- or more -- than business. "Seattle went higher-up", in Precourt's words, when good schooling was ranked above short commuting as a life quality. "We even factored in the weather," concluded Precourt in Seattle; the buzz-phrase being "pure-air days" in an urban setting.[195]

All preceding smarminess aside, Seattle has come a long way in the eighteen years (1978-1996) since this writer dwelt in Ballard. Seattle is now the self-designated Emerald City, but still insists on playing the rôle of newly-urbanised, clueless naïf. On the 20 May 1996 cover of Newsweek magazine were emblazoned the headlines: "Swimming to Seattle ... Everybody Else Is Moving There. Should You?" This is the sort of rhetorical question that infuriates dog-in-the-manger no-growth groups like Lesser Seattle, of which the Emerald City is rife. On visiting Seattle for the very first time in May 1971, this writer was often and abruptly enjoined to "Have a nice stay but don't move here!" As touchy ex-New Yorker the writer would fire back: "Oh, not to fear! I would far prefer to live in Vancouver, B.C. ... Now there's a city!"

Also appearing on the Newsweek cover was Michael Kinsley, former New Republic editor and liberal CNN Crossfire irritant; now Microsoft cyber-editor of Slate. But Kinsley was photographed wearing rain-slicker and Sou'wester fortifying the nautical image which Seattle adamantly portrays: "We're, like, a more laid-back, looser Boston without the snow, ice, or Eastern pollution" etc. But Seattle is also Grunge City, U.S.A., and is perversely proud of its dubious status: "Yah, we're environmentally-correct, squeaky-clean and all, but we can also relate to Gen-X alienation." This is the city of late, self-destructed rocker Kurt Cobain of Nirvana; of his grieving widow Courtney Love, and her band, Hole. (This 52 year-old writer wouldn't dare to attempt describing the grunge scene. It is enough said that heroin has become the come-back drug of choice.[196])

As a concession to Seattle's status as West Coast fishing fleet headquarters, Newsweek's cover depicted an open-mawed Pacific salmon heading for Kinsley's sharp nose. But there was nothing reported on the industry in that issue despite the salmon. There was, however, mention of Melissa Rossi, the Seattleite working on a biography of grunge rocker Courtney Love.[197] There were also (gratefully) brief portraits of isolated artiste Anne Grgich, architect-for-Microsoft Wendell Lovett, Seattle mayor Norm Rice, former city councilwoman Ruby Chow, Super Sonic Shawn Kemp, and, naturally, Microsoft cybernauts Bill Gates and Paul Allen.[198] There came the expected ode to Seattle's admittedly beautiful natural surroundings, the Emerald City set by sparkling Puget Sound in between the rugged Olympics to the west and the towering Cascades to the east. This is Spandex-attired yuppy hiking and biking country, with an élitist back-to-nature spin. As the Newsweek editors observed:

...."Seattle is a city gone mad with connoiseurship. The humblest Safeway sells fresh lemongrass by the stalk. Bars are chockablock with rows of single-malt whiskies; the products of some of the nation's most esoteric bicrobreweries gush from the taps; wine lists are heavy with Washington state Chardonnays....

"The provenance of each ingredient is specified down to the method of capture for seafood; diners at one downtown restaurant are assured that their fish was caught by long line rather than in a net, sparing their lunch a lot of needless suffering."[199]

The last is a bit disingenuous of the restaurant, as any fisherman worth his salt will tell you that a quickly caught, butchered, and iced fish has firmer, better-tasting flesh anyway. But Seattle is an Emerald City full of blather and blarney to match its megabuck wheeler-dealers, Bill Gates of Microsoft or Starbuck's CEO Howard Schultz. Gates, of course, "owes less to [his] programming genius than his foresight in locking up the rights to the operating system used in IBM's first personal computers."[200] Former New Yorker Schultz, who bought the local 11-branch Starbuck's [coffee] chain in 1987, has since opened more than 800 outlets world-wide ... but still has emphasised Starbuck's Seattle origins; a city of "quality, integrity, authenticity, honesty, friendliness and fresh air and water."[201] (CEO Schultz sells as syrupy a Seattle as Starbuck's espresso, but not all Seattleites are sold; preferring Starbuck's when it was small and local.)

Besides being the yuppy-epicentre of relentless Microsoft and aggressive Starbuck's, Seattle is culturally a downer blend of home-grown White trash, working-class grunge, and (denied) imported California-style New Age affectation. Grunge, according to the Newsweek editors, is the "musical expression of the alienation of blue-collar youth, in the depressed logging towns of Seattle's hinterlands. Its accoutrements -- flannel shirts, workboots and knit caps -- [are] what people wear when they have to stay warm when they can't afford North Face down parkas."[202]

Yet gloomier still, commensurate with the Emerald City's lowering skies, are the reasons why (1) Seattleites drink so much coffee, and 2) New Age thinking is so popular. Cartoonist Lynda Barry, in a Newsweek Lifestyle comic-strip, 'Seattle's Siren Song', has explained why. The answer to comic-question (1) was shown as a harried, middle-aged woman ordering "Two pounds of your Javanese dark suicide inhibitor roast, please." The merchant asks, "For here or to go?" The shopper replies, "For here." The answer to comic-question (2) was shown as a bespectacled, balding man announcing to a younger woman: "I tried the healing mind rainbow and the magnetic bed but I am still very depressed"; to which she responds, "Well, you need a personal power geode! It's on sale which is a reality you created."[203]

That same semi-hip, semi-predatory New Age grunge is disseminated throughout the University of Washington and environs (the "U" district), along with a militantly pervasive pc since the 1970s. When this writer's daughter came of college age and decided to study at U.W. ("Uddub"), the father tried his best to convince her to attend his old alma mater, Seattle Pacific University, instead ... at least for undergraduate work. After an initial year at the U. Oregon at Eugene, the daughter transferred to U.W. for her sophomore year. So "Grunge Academy" it was. At this writing, October 1996, she is still there majoring in psychology. But she has been forewarned and forearmed concerning pc newthink and newspeak, while pursuing her courses with her father's financial and moral support. The U.W. School of Fisheries had earned this writer's profound respect, so U.W. couldn't be too pc, surely? An Associated Press article published last summer, however, reconfirmed the writer's suspicions:

"Such a deal. When the University of Washington hired Chavonda Jacobs, it made her an acting assistant professor; gave her an office, a nine-month salary of $60,000, no teaching responsibilities for her first year, and a travel allowance for two trips to North Carolina; and lined up a summer job for her with the Weyerhaeuser Co.

All this, and Jacobs is still more than a year away from her doctorate, and didn't even apply to the U.W. But such sweet offers are part of the territory in the ivory tower push to diversify college faculties. In Jacobs' case, she is the only black woman in the country earning a doctorate in wood and paper science, a highly specialized field dominated by white men."[204]

At the very end of Newsweek's mini-portraits of Seattle 'Movers, Shakers and Coffee Makers', were sketches of Microsoft multibillionaire cybernauts, Bill Gates and Paul Allen. Their bio-paragraphs rated no more ink than, say, Eddie Vedder of Pearl Jam or Seattle Mariner Ken Griffey, Jr., but we all know that Bill Gates and Paul Allen are the new Wonderful Wizards of Oz in the Emerald City. Thus Newsweek described Bill Gates as "[t]he boy billionaire ... looking beyond his virtual stranglehold on PC operating systems as he gears up to take on Netscape in a battle of the Web-browsers. At stake: the ability to shape the Internet's future."[205] Paul Allen's brief bio-let told us that he was ..."the other Microsoft billionaire. Allen is [ploughing] money into interactive entertainment ventures, backing start-ups like Starwave and sinking $500 million into DreamWorks SKG. His pet project: a $60 million museum devoted to late Seattle rocker Jimi Hendrix."[206]

Lesser Seattleites, Northwest NIMBYs (Not In My Backyard), and their allies in the local media were quick to repudiate Newsweek's "Swimming to Seattle" edition. A home-town version of The New York Times was especially miffed over the Newsweek Paul Allen profile. In it, the Microsoft co-billionaire had put up $20 million in "seed money" to persuade Seattle voters to approve a plan demolishing a portion of the city for a park, the ill-conceived "Seattle Commons', which ... sound[ed] both elitist and socialist to many residents --

notably the thousands whose homes or businesses would have been displaced."[207] Came the tight-lipped rejoinder: "[The] Actual count was 130 businesses and 600 housing units."[208] Moreover, the same New York Times [News Service] rebuttal eagerly cited a contemporaneous Rolling stone story (30 May 1996) which bleakly portrayed Seattle as a "junkie's haven."[209] Indeed, The New York Times seemed to take the position that the grim drug anecdotes served as "an antidote"; presumably to the good press praising the Emerald City, as a viable safe-place for New American migrants fleeing (other) urban hells of El Dollarado. But Seattle, as Grunge-Heroin City, is itself an urban hell despite all posturing to the contrary. Rolling Stone tersely reported that "'In Seattle if you know your way around, heroin is like takeout food. You can have your dope delivered ... or you can resort to a downtown drive-through.'"[210] (That should keep potential immigrants away!) For a lighter conclusion, Newsweek quoted a bartender/adman/would-be fisherman:

"Seattle is a place you go when you're on your way somewhere else. Everybody's a damn poet, or else they're a drummer. I'm sick of synchronized-hair bands that pound out their four chords and shake their hair back and forth in unison. I want somebody to honk their horn and give me the finger when I cut them off, so I'm moving back East. Next year."[211]

Of the two co-wizards of the Emerald City, Bill Gates is the far better known. Throughout 1995, there did not seem a day that he was not mentioned by the media. Gatesmania culminated in a four-hour televised PBS special -- Triumph of the Nerds: The Rise of Accidental Empires in Silicon Valley -- broadcast by KCTS-Seattle, on 21 August 1996. Featured were interviews with Microsoft's Bill Gates and Paul Allen, and Apple Computer founder Steve ("Big") Jobs.[212] Not being compu-smart at all, this writer didn't pay attention to the social or corporate antics of William H. Gates III before 1995, despite a flood of information on Mr. Microsoft. And not all his press was good; on a scale of 1 to 10, Spy magazine awarded Bill Gates a "5" for "inherent loathsomeness."[213] In the same satirical Spy sketch, a paragraph cited from Business Week referred to Microsoft's monopolistic misdeeds. So the next time this writer visited Port (Angeles) Book and News, he regarded a Home Microsoft CD-ROM with some interest. The one on display was Microsoft 'Dangerous Creatures'; pictured were a bear, panther, and serpent. The sub-title offered: "Explore the Endangered World of Wildlife." Not pictured was perhaps the most dangerous Microsoft creature of all -- Wm. H. Gates III, though hardly endangered. The Associated Press anticipated NBC TV's 1995 puff-piece ("Tycoon") on Bill

Gates with a mini-portrayal of their own:

"William Henry Gates is not an enigma, even though most of the skinny, bespectacled, mop-haired computer geek that he once was long since has vanished inside the sleek, well-fed tycoon in a $2,000 suit....

"Gates, hailed as 'the Thomas Edison of software', is no Edison and doesn't pretend to be. He is, rather, an intensely focused, intensely competitive entrepreneur who's made a fortune by marketing other people's ideas."[215]

By mid-1996, a 17 June issue of Time magazine (a leading reposit of cw) ranked Bill Gates right after Bill Clinton in order of ten "most powerful" people in America.[216] Mr. Microsoft, at Number Two, beat out political and media heavyweights such as Alan Greenspan, Rupert Murdoch, Michael Eisner, and Newt Gingrich.[217] And there was that well-known spring 1995 news-photo of Bill Gates "riding shotgun" with Bill Clinton in the presidential golf-cart, as game partner.[218] As the Associated Press quipped: "The dude is THAT important."[219] By early autumn 1995, Bill Gates had topped Forbes magazine's list of 400 richest Americans ... for the second year in a row.[220] Gates' personal wealth had increased from $9.35 billion in 1994 to $14.8 billion in 1995. Microsoft co-founder -- and Portland Trail Blazers basketball team owner -- Paul G. Allen was in 16th place in 1994; in one year his software shares had put him in the fourth spot of richest Americans with a fortune of a cool $6.1 billion.[221] By summer 1996, Bill Gates and Paul Allen had both made the Forbes top-ten list of the world's wealthiest billionaires.[222] But by this time No. 1 Gates was the clear favourite and the man to beat. In 1996, Gates' personal worth had expanded to $18.0 billion, with No. 8 Allen's increased to $7.5 billion.[223] By autumn 1996, the Forbes annual ranking of 400 richest Americans was a foregone conclusion, with Microsoft's Gates and Allen at first and fourth place[s] respectively. Bill Gates had swollen his net worth to $18.5 billion -- a gain of circa $500 million in less than 100 days![224] "The rich [do] just keep getting richer."

Bill Gates and Paul Allen are the two wealthiest persons in Washington State; two of the richest and most powerful men of America and the world. Despite media mutterings of monopolistic manipulations by Bill Gates, Microsoft Corp. is a hugh Pacific Northwest success story of which we are justifiably proud. But this writer smelled a rat-stink issuing through Windows 95; not from misgivings of Gatesian royalties, but from a feral rock-concert countercultural stench of cannabis and ketchup; of blood and urine, sweat and sperm. The suspect malodour emanated from the August advent of the Microsoft Windows 95 advertising campaign.

The designated theme song was "Start Me Up" by the Rolling Stones, that one British tabloid guesstimated

cost Microsoft so much as $12 million for the rights to use.[225] Said Jim Ward of Wieden & Kennedy, the

Portland (Ore.) ad agency which handled the Microsoft account, "We approached the Stones, and there was

a lot of instant synergy between them and Microsoft."[226] Indeed. Steven Levy, the author of Hackers:

Heroes of the Computer Revolution (1984), commented at length (and veritably) on the computer-rock

connection:

> "Certainly we are at a moment when what was once down is now very much up. Thirty years ago,
> around the time a Seattle private-school student named Bill Gates was twiddling his first bits, the Rolling
> Stones emerged as the dark side of the British pop invasion -- scruffy-looking, London rats[227] whose songs
> were too hot for Ed Sullivan to handle uncensored. One album title said it all: they were exiles on Main
> Street. Clear across the spectrum was the world of computers. Anyone who mastered them was considered
> an egghead or a twit -- not the type of person you'd have a beer with, let alone feature in a beer commercial.
> Who would have thought that in 1995, both deviant forces -- computers and rock -- would meet smack in the
> middle of the mainstream?"[228]

Well, to be appropriately modest, this writer has seen the computer-counterculture connection

becoming an amalgamated synergy for decades -- the primary purpose for including this part of Chapter 3.

And none proves the point more than co-wizard Paul Allen's obsession with rock-and-roll in general and Jimi

Hendrix in particular; Seattle's late, great musical icon.[229] At about the time of the "Start Me Up" Windows

95 campaign, the Seattle Post-Intelligencer newspaper featured a 12-page article, 'Experiencing Jimi Hendrix'

(30 August 1995). The Voodoo Child is still a serious business in the Emerald City. In early 1995, what had

been first envisioned as a small gallery of specifically Jimi memorabilia (black felt hat, Fender Stratocaster

guitars, 6,000 personal artifacts etc.), had evolved into a grandiose $50-60 million project glorifying and

enshrining Pacific Northwest pop music and culture. The former Jimi Hendrix Museum became the

Experience Music Project, to be located at the Seattle Center, site of the 1962 World's Fair. When plans were

originally announced during 1992, the Jimi Hendrix Museum was to occupy 15,000 square feet, at a cost of

$400,000. The Experience Music Project, when construction commences in 1997, will lease 35,000 square feet

of prime downtown land at the intersection of Broad Street and Denny Way, between the Space Needle and

the Pacific Science Center. Although still heavily Hendrix-accented, the brainchild of Paul Allen promises a

500-seat theatre, a multimedia library, and interactive music-making technology.[231]

Paul G. Allen saw his musical icon twice, during 1968 and 1969. Gushed the billionaire in a March

1996 <u>USA Today</u> ("McPaper") interview: "…. Once it was raining, and there was a tarp over [H]im. Suddenly, [H]e stepped into the rain and kept playing, almost defying electrocution…. Jimi was so great. Like a bolt out of the blue."[232] One can well imagine the instant idol worship of a 14-15 year-old boy; it is harder to understand the lasting fascination of a 42 year-old man. But sometimes even the (very) filthy rich don't always get everything they wish. As mentioned above, Paul Allen in 1992 decided he wanted to build a museum-as-memorial to local legend Jimi Hendrix. Allen also handed over a cheque for a $5 million interest-free loan to Al Hendrix, Jimi's father, and Janie Hendrix-Wright, Jimi's half-sister, for a legal battle over the deceased rock-star's estate. Last year (1995), the Hendrix family won their suit for the rights to Jimi's music. But by then the mercurial Paul Allen's personal ambition had even outpaced his Jimi Hendrix fixation. The Microsoft co-magnate now wanted his project transformed from the relatively modest Jimi Hendrix Museum into the mega-bucks Experience Music Project … "to embrace rock music as a whole."[233] Meanwhile, Janie Hendrix-Wright had stayed busy, fiercely protecting Jimi's music legacy, as CEO of Experience Hendrix. This put a damper on Paul Allen's Experience euphoria, with Janie Hendrix-Wright shortly commenting, "We just agreed to disagree."[234]

As also stated earlier, there will be ample Jimi memorabilia and paraphernalia at the Experience Music Project to satisfy hard-core, true-blue Hendrix believers. As for Paul Allen himself, when he isn't overseeing Web-site Starwave and the NBA's Portland Trail Blazers, or meddling with the Seattle Commons, he's (according to <u>USA Today</u>) practising plinking "Purple Haze." Recalled the Microsoft co-founder, "In High School I had two passions: computer programming and [rock] music. Who knows? If things had been different…."[235] But Jimi Hendrix is dead, and Paul Allen remains a super-wealthy, frustrated wanna-be rock-star. One month before Jimi would have turned 54 years -- half a lifetime again from age 27 -- a news-photo was printed of the Experience Music Project's architectural model. Wayward, waving cables shown on the mini-building's roof represented broken guitar-strings; a wired Hendrix trademark.[236] Also for true believers, is the <u>Roomful of Mirrors</u> (from the song title) Web-site of the Jimi Hendrix Foundation. <u>Newsweek</u> has described it as "[p]art shrine, part fan-zine, the site mixes high-culture and low-culture perspectives on Hendrix -- such as a deconstruction of his concerts and a Q&A with Hendrix 'from the astral plane.'"[237]

The big software news-story of March 1995 was the proposed collaborative effort between Bill Gates and Hollywood's show-biz "Dream Team"; DreamWorks SKG triumvirate movie director Steven Spielberg, movie producer Jeffrey Katzenberg, and music producer David Geffen.[238] In a Hollywood run by hipsters, hucksters, and hustlers, these three are the master manipulators of analogue emotions and nutra-sweet dreams. This writer once watched a 1989 TV episode of <u>Columbo</u>, 'Murder, Smoke and Mirrors,' in which the L.A. police lieutenant (played by raspy-voiced Peter Falk) hunts down a murderous hot-shot, boy-wonder film director. The cinematic weasel, convincingly portrayed by actor Fisher Stevens, was an uncanny type-composite of Steven Spielberg ... and Bill Gates. Anyway, Microsoft Corp. was to join forces with entertainment studio-conglomerate DreamWorks SKG, each to invest $15 million into a new software venture, to be tentatively called DreamWorks Interactive. Microsoft Corp. would also become a minority investor in DreamWorks SKG, but no concrete terms were disclosed. Talks between the two parties had been going on for some six months, it was reported.[239] Microsoft's Bill Gates was poised on a course of folly and frivolities regarding Hollywood, as Microsoft's Paul Allen had of vanity and vagaries vis-à-vis Jimi Hendrix. <u>Seattle Post-Intelligencer</u> reporter Vanessa Ho vividly described the 23 March 1995 software summit at Redmond:

"First, Jeffrey Katzenberg strolled in, sipping his usual can of Diet Coke. Steven Spielberg, David Geffen and Bill Gates followed, and before anyone could say, 'Let's do lunch,' a star-struck hush permeated the room as the men who gave us 'The Lion King', 'Jurassic Park' and Nirvana sat down with the richest man in America....

"[Gates] looked especially unhip next to Spielberg, who sported his trademark bomber jacket, casually skuffed loafers and a baseball cap, with the bespectacled smiley-face logo of Microsoft's 'Bob'....[240]

"In revealing how the joint venture emerged, the men told of their mutual admiration. Spielberg called himself 'a game junkie' and said he played Microsoft's Flight Simulator with [wigged-out comedian] Robin Williams; Gates said, 'Just as Steven admits he plays games, I watch movies.'"[241]

The Redmond summit of software couldn't have preceded by much time a spring gala fund-raising dinner given for the Democrat Party by ... Spielberg-Katzenberg-Geffen. According to <u>National Review</u>, S-K-G raised about $1 billion for themselves and, at $50 thousand per plate, S-K-G were "...prepared to do what it takes to beat the [Republican] [P]arty of the Rich in '96."[242] Over a year later, long-time liberal-cause contributrix Barbra ("Funny Girl") Streisand would join a gaggle of Gollywood celebrities at a $2,500-a-plate fund-raiser for Bill Clinton, on 12 September 1996, at a supermarket tycoon's Bel-Air estate. (And Streisand would be performing "live" for the first time since 1994.) Among the nibs and nobs of filmdom attending would be ... Spielberg-Katzenberg-Geffen.[243] Steve ("Big") Jobs of Apple Computer, who announced for Clinton's re-election in August 1996, might have donated his $100,000 to the Democrat Party at that very dinner.[244] The lords of cyberspace appear to have political agenda[s] noticeably similar to those of the entertainment élites.

But what about the compulsive alliance of Hollywood and Silicon Valley? Cyber-writer Steven Levy has characterised the enforced union as a "... resemblance to an arranged match between two wealthy dynasties, where each legacy coldly evaluates its potential gains and suffers through the wedding night."[245] This marriage-made-in-hell has resulted from a brief, cool courtship by La-La Land of Nerdville. According to the savvy Levy, Hollywood evinced an interest on hearing ... "scary buzzwords like Information Superhighway and Digital Convergence descending on Tinseltown like a cloud of locusts...."[246] The current wisdom (cw) amongst Hollywood big-wigs is that while interactive video game content can be addictive (to participants), nobody as yet has figured out how to mesh virtual reality with (non-participatory) celluloid phantasy, for a greater cleaning out of the lowest cultural denomimated (lcd) motherlode. All Hollywood needs, then, is a "digital messiah" to do for interactive what Sergei Eisenstein, the Russian film director (1898-1948), did for the movies.[247] So who could that wunderkind be? Steven Levy has surmised that the word "genius" in Hollywood can only mean one person ... Steven Spielberg:

...."Guess who showed last week at the Electronic Entertainment Expo? Spielberg. It turns out that His Stevenhood has invested in a game company and has already begun shooting footage for his first made-for-computer production. Whether or not the program breaks new ground, it does represent a wake-up call from Hollywood to Silicon Valley. 'He's heee-re.'"[248]

The reader/observer should spare any misplaced empathy for Bill Gates as nerdy mouse being thrown to Hollywood weasels. For this "mouse" is a rat in MouseTards, and pity for him is synonymous with sympathy for the devil. Bill Gates reminds this writer of Frank L. Boyden, the late and lauded headmaster of Deerfield Academy in Massachusetts. This writer attended Deerfield for (all) four years (miserable years of 1959-1963), and well remembers Dr. Boyden. The Headmaster for all his helpless, shuffling ways -- which endeared him so to generations of Deerfield parents, students, and alumni alike -- was cold, calculating, and horribly intelligent.[249] Of Bill Gates, Newsweek's Jerry Adler and Rob French have characterised how his ..."shambling, awkward public persona helped for years to disguise his acquisitiveness."[250] That could have described Frank

Boyden to a "T".

Bill Gates started to really show his micro-sharp teeth so early as July 1994, when the U.S. Justice Department agreed to settle the four-year anti-trust investigation of Microsoft Corp.[251] By October 1994, Microsoft was already emboldened enough to announce its intent on buying Menlo Park (Calif.)-based Intuit, maker of personal finance software programme Quicken. Microsoft Corp. would purchase Intuit Inc. in a swap of 1,336 Microsoft shares for each Intuit share.[252] By February 1995, a reflective Federal Judge Stanley Sporkin deeply believed that the Justice Department had been far too lenient with Bill Gates and co. in its July 1994 anti-trust non-action. Therefore Judge Sporkin ruled against the U.S. federal settlement with Microsoft Corp.[253] Judge Sporkin, a former chief of enforcement at SEC (Securities and Exchange Commission), also deeply believed that Bill Gates and co. had been competing unfairly all along, and, if Microsoft remained unchecked, would continue to do so. Wise compu-scribe Steven Levy has explained the process in railway terms:

"....Bill Gates not only owns the tracks, he sells the trains. Every computer requires an operating system as the platform for the applications (spreadsheets, word processors, etc.) that run on the machines, and the Microsoft MS-DOS/Windows combination -- the tracks -- constitutes the world's platform of choice, running on about 70 percent of all desktops. Microsoft also is the market leader in applications -- the trains...."[254]

Thus Microsoft competitors, like Lotus and Novell, are compelled to coöperate with Gates and co. on operating-systems issues; their "trains" run on Microsoft "tracks." Another advantage for Microsoft running the tracks, is that Gates and co. know all future plans of Lotus, Novell et al. Furthermore, if Microsoft alters its operating-system -- i.e., switches the gauge of its tracks -- Gates and co. are able to accomplish their goals in concert with their applications division.[255] The end result, of Judge Sporkins's misgivings toward Microsoft's monopolistic power, was the Justice Department's (after some waffling) new anti-trust complaint, blocking the Microsoft-Intuit merger. The suit was filed Thursday, 27 April 1995, at U.S. District Court in San Francisco. Microsoft's appeal of the ruling was pending.[256]

Also swirling about Bill Gates and co. during spring 1995, were stories of Microsoft purchasing electronic rights to works of art, with intentions to become premier purveyor of electronic art.[257] Cyber-expert and critic Clifford Stoll wryly commented, "I'm not worried about Bill Gates taking over the art world.... Aside from technical inaccuracies of reproducing art on a computer, I find it disconcerting to view a work of art in the same place that I read nasty arguments on the Usenet. Going to a museum is an escape from daily tasks and a trip into another world."[258] Far less charitable on cybermania and Bill Gates was Time magazine art critic, Robert Hughes: "....In the not too distant future, when Bill Gates realizes he has succeeded in spending $30.8 million on the only Leonardo manuscript that doesn't have a single drawing of real aesthetic significance in it, he will be able to off-load it for $60 million onto David Geffen or Michael Ovitz. Thus civilization progresses."[259]

In a 2 October 1995 Forbes magazine interview, to celebrate Microsoft's 20th anniversary, Bill Gates seemed almost chastened by Judge Sporkin's temporary legal de-railment earlier that year. And Microsoft had been criticised for its tardiness in developing software which would work in concert with the Internet.[260] The Internet, of course, is a global data network that has approx. 20 million users. Although it has been in existence since ca. 1980, the Internet only became fashionably "in" with yuppiedom during 1995 ... and mainly due to the World Wide Web. The Web and cojoining software, like Netscape, makes the Internet ..."easy to use" and, as USA Today technology editor Kevin Maney has opined, "The Web is the place to be."[261] In the Forbes interview, Gates likened Microsoft's eventual fate to that of IBM (International Business Machine[s]) and DEC (Digital Equipment Corp.). [The quantum change was from mainframe to mini-computers to PCs (personal computers). Today's electronic communications, as represented by the Internet and other networks, could change the way software is utilised. Compu-geeks, nerds, and hackers would then be less dependent on PC programmes, hence rely more on those "downloaded" from a network.[262]] Microsoft's slowness in adapting to Internet-friendly software could pose a danger to the Magic Kingdom in Redmond, as in the manner the PCs displaced the mighty IBM mainframe. A resigned but brave Gates summed up:

"The Internet is the seed corn of a lot of things that are going to happen, and there are so many parallels to when Paul [Allen] and I were involved in the beginnings of the PC....
"We said back then, 'Don't DEC and IBM know they're in deep trouble?' Here we are, staring at the same kind of situation....
"The odds are against us, and that's what makes it so much fun and so challenging."[263]

But Bill Gates, Paul Allen, and Microsoft were hardly headed for the corporate dumpster in 1995. An NBC special programme, "Tycoon", aired on the evening of Friday, 26 May, narrated by fruity-voiced News anchor Tom Brokaw.[264] Despite "Tycoon's" factual errors, the programme effectively projected Microsoft's vision of our electronic-digital future. Alluded to in the special (but not too gratuitously), was NBC's coming joint venture with Microsoft to develop an on-line service.[265] This writer says "not too gratuitously "as the introduction of the Microsoft Windows 95 software package engendered a veritable media furore, both print and visual. Among those leading the loudest cheers, remarked Philip Jenkins of Chronicles, was Gannett's USA Today ... (coincidentally) available on the "Microsoft Network", along with NBC.[266] And the Washington Post speculated that the intense interest in Windows 95 shown by CNN and cable-mates, might have been directly related to a Turner Broadcasting System[s] union proposed with Microsoft Corp. Finally, in the U.K., Bill Gates bought up a day's issue of the formerly-eminent [The] Times [of London] and distributed it gratis; complete with Windows 95 advertising materials.[267] This act was additional proof that the sun has forever set on mini-England, and William H. Gates III is indeed one of the most powerful men on the planet.

To clinch a special deal or press a particular agendum, Bill Gates and co. have used the truculent Business Software Alliance trade group, and the Washington, D.C., office of the Seattle law firm of Preston, Gates, Ellis & Rouvelas Meeds ... where Bill Gates, père ("Dad"), is a partner.[268] (The BSA -- with allies IBM, Novell, and Sybase -- is considered a Microsoft mouthpiece by competitors.) During the summer of 1995, Microsoft (Bill Gates, fils) hired Washington, D.C., attorney, Jack Krumholtz, as its first capital city, bona fide lobbyist.[269] By mid-May 1996, Gates and co. were knocking on the White House door to curb international software piracy, and help quash congressional attempts to limit immigration of high-tech ("gimme software") workers.[270] Microsoft, D.C., also lobbied to ensure that digital-TV standards, backed by U.S. regulators, would be compatible with [Microsoft, Corp.] computers. Explained [now Microsoft] D.C. lawyer-lobbyist Jack Krumholtz: "With the convergence of telecom and computers, the policy debate in Washington becomes a lot more relevant.'"[271] As for the summer 1996 "branding"/merger of the Microsoft Network with NBC, Newsweek's Rick Marin has observed:

".... MSNBC is a meeting of brand names, a merger of convenience. The deal gives NBC a 24-hour news network paid for in large part by someone else. And from its $500 million investment, Microsoft gets another product -- news -- for its metastasizing software empire. Incredibly slick (the set is like a really cool Starbucks), there are times when the channel looks like a giant ad for Microsoft."[272]

The fanged cyber-dweeb is truly lord of the air!

But what now of Paul Allen, the other Microsoft founder? While Bill Gates has been thinking globally, Paul Allen has been acting locally back in Seattle, the Emerald City. He has been staying busy with Web-site Starwave, the Experience Music Project, and the NBA's Portland Trailblazers. As if all that weren't enough, Allan has had designs on buying the NFL Seattle Seahawks from hated Californian, Ken Behring, and for renovating the Kingdome or building a "natural grass" whole new stadium.[273] Allen has already spent up to $20 million to buy an option to purchase the Seahawks, and must decide either way by July 1997.[274] During late August 1996, representatives of Paul Allen and King County did some hard-ball negotiating concerning the Kingdome obligations. Allen's people contended that King County Executive Gary Locke (Washington State governor-elect after Election '96) promised unconditionally to reduce the 10-year lease if Allen bought the Seahawks. King County representatives responded that no such pledge had been made. The upshot was that Allen's Football Northwest, Inc., requested a written guarantee from Gary Locke, wherein King County would renegotiate the 10-year lease down to 3 years.[275] Allen and co. would (ostensibly) use the shorter lease to obtain a "better place to play" for the Seahawks, whether a renovated Kingdome, a remodeled Husky Stadium, or an entirely new "natural grass" venue. Locke and co. would (ostensibly) protect King County's interests by having a "local buyer" purchase the Seahawks before Allen could possibly move the NFL team.[276] As of this writing, 30 November 1996, involved negotiations were still going on, with Allen's Football Northwest, Inc., awaiting a recommendation, due 5 December, from King County's Seahawks/Kingdome Renovation Task Force.[277] Whichever way things go, Paul Allen is used to always getting pretty much what he wants ... and he probably will this time too.

1995 was the Year of the Information Mega-mergers. There occurred the [in]famous corporate couplings of CBS and Westinghouse, NBC and Microsoft (Bill Gates), Capital Cities/ABC and Disney (Michael Eisner), CNN (Ted Turner) and Time[-Life] Warner, and MCA [Universal] and Seagram (the Bronfmans).[278] As the reader may notice, Microsoft was right there up front, along with spiritual soul-mate Disney, in its search for synergy. In the 4 December 1995 issue of Newsweek was a full-page ad for The Road Ahead by Bill Gates (Viking Penguin, New York, 1995), with companion Interactive CD-Rom included.[279] Also, in the same issue, appeared a centre two-page spread for Disney Interactive, which announced in capital letters:

"ONCE AGAIN, THE MAGIC OF DISNEY BEGINS WITH A MOUSE."[280] (Advertised right next to Disney Interactive was The Wisdom of Jerry Garcia, Wolf Valley Books.) And, finally, a Newsweek ad for cyber-accessories was aptly titled 'Turn On, Tune In, Shop Out', as it was openly aimed at former rebel compu-hackers; now well-paid pc cyberdweebs: "Turned from anarchy to technology? Earth Care's hemp briefcase is perfect for porting that laptop [computer] around Redmond, Wash."[281]

To this writer, there is more than meets the eye to the Microsoft/Disney connection. Besides the Microsoft-DreamWorks SKG software summit of March 1995, in which ex-Disney whiz-kid Jeffrey Katzenberg ..."strolled in, sipping his usual can of Diet Coke",[282] Microsoft and Disney have much in common. One might readily imagine Boomer/Buster, Microsoft/Disney nerds and dweebs sending out for NutraSweet sodas and cardboard pizzas, while thus laid back, deciding the eventual destination of hundreds of millions of cyber-dollars. It reminds this writer of the arrogant squirts and pilot-fish unconcernedly wonking values-free policy at the Clinton White House. These policies, like the Microsoft/Disney infotainment overload, have a huge impact on the hearts and minds of gullible America and beyond. Disneyism, in fact, has long been a form of American civic religion. Pilgrimages are made to Disneyland, California, and Disney World, Florida, where sojourners stay in Disney hotels and eat Disney food. At home, the Disney disciples purchase Disney products at Disney shops, read dumbed-down versions of European fairy tales in Disney books, listen to Disney songs on Disney records, and watch Disney movies at theatres and on video-cassettes.[283] The Disney popular culture has been pervasive in America ever since World War II. Although always sub-adult and often silly, Disney popular culture didn't evolve into an American civic religion until after Walt Disney's death in 1966. During the 1980s and 1990s, the Disney organisation fell under the rule of evil men, becoming a New Age countercultural vehicle attacking traditional values. Disney has been boycotted by Southern Baptists and condemned by Roman Catholics alike. Quite recently, Disney did the pc thing by extending benefits for live-in gay employees. In her book, The American Amusement Park Industry, historian Judith Adams has propounded that Disney World has grown into a spiritual shrine comparable to Canterbury, Lourdes, and Mecca: "'The perfect world of Disney has replaced the biblical Garden of Eden as the American vision of paradise.'"[284]

Microsoft has only existed since 1975, but today, in the words of Steven Levy, "Redmond, Wash. is the New Magic Kingdom."[285] Moreover, the Microsoft Redmond campus already has 25 buildings on 260 acres, with corporate plans to build an additional 1.5 million square feet at Redmond throughout 1996 and on.[286] Microsoft (in mid-1996) provided more than 11% of Redmond's total property tax revenue, and a full 21% of Redmond's daytime workers were employed at Microsoft.[287] For good corporate relations, Microsoft has promised to match individual charitable contributions up to $12,000 per annum, and for ec approval, Microsoft recycles 46% of on-campus waste.[288] Like Disney, Microsoft has come to dominate many of our daily consumer functions. Cyber-commentator Steven Levy has written:

".... You can bank with Microsoft, you can book travel with Microsoft, you can buy music from Microsoft, you can read book reviews from Microsoft. Watch cable TV on the Microsoft (and NBC) channel.... People may find themselves brushing against Microsoft often, as they work, shop and entertain themselves. And at the end of the day, a Windows-based home-control system may even shut off the bedroom light."[289]

Levy reported that some Microsoft executives believe that the software giant could actually double in size and market evaluation with the next five years (2001 A.D.).[289] Microsoft has even figured out a way to ride the Internet on the trail to new prospects. There had been a cyber-flap during summer 1996, when competing Netscape Communications had complained to the U.S. federal government that Microsoft used its operating-systems advantage to force PC-makers to pre-install its (own) Internet programmes on their machines, instead of competitors' products.[290] According to Levy, the Internet has "turbocharged" Microsoft's progress rather than hindering it. This writer doesn't understand the details (either), but Microsoft has been in Steven Levy's words, "[r]evitalized by its cyberspace initiative, [and] ...is ready to gobble up the limitless opportunities that will come from the Net's restructuring of commerce itself."[291]

In 1990, Seattle economist Dick Conway conducted a study of Boeing, to find out how heavily dependent the State of Washington was on the aircraft manufacturer. Boeing is still Washington's largest private employer, with 85,000 workers of 20% of the state's total.[292] Dick Conway did a similar study on Microsoft in 1995, and found that Microsoft employed 9,940 workers then, and now employs ca. 11,000 in the state and more than 18,000 throughout the world.[293] Indeed, Microsoft was the single largest contributor to the economic expansion of Washington State throughout the early 1990s. Furthermore, economist Conway found that Microsoft pumped so much money into state coffers during the preceding five years -- via salaries, stock options, construction spending, and support-industry jobs -- that the software corporation actually rescued King County from the brink of recession.[294] And there's more. The average Microsoft employee earns $58,860 a year, but Microsoft employees as a whole cashed in on $793.3 million in stock options during 1995, and this doesn't count the stock sold by Chairman Gates himself, who owns approx. 25% of Microsoft Corp. Thus, according to Seattleite Conway, with exercised stock options the average Microsoft worker made $138,270 in 1995![295] Concluded the enthused Conway: "The economic impact [of Microsoft] is interesting. Relative to the size of the company, it's as large as you're going to find.... [Microsoft] is no Boeing, [but] it has provided a lot of clout in single years."[296]

Compu-reporter Steven Levy has written that the general public -- most assuredly the proud denizens of the Evergreen State -- are "charmed in part by Gates' tousled high-tech Horatio Alger role," and accept Microsoft as cyberspace future... "to be viewed as a mix of scary inevitability and 'Jetsons'-style frisson."[296] At the closing of the Piscean Era (1996), with the dawning of the Age of Aquarius (1997) on Seattle-Redmond, is it over a synchro-cybercity or a Virtual Rocktropolis? Is William H. Gates III an Ahrimanic lord of the air or a Luciferian fanged cyber-dweeb? Only the next (Microsoft?) millennium will tell. Whichever, the pure power of electronic cyberspace, on a par with thermonuclear energy, is an awesome force to be in the white hands of a boyish man barely forty years of age. Scribes are fascinated by Bill Gates, and are still trying to figure him out. On the cover of U.S. News & World Report, 25 November 1996, Bill Gates is depicted as the martyred San Sebastián, his naked torso pierced by arrows. Inside are back-to-back stories on the Wizard of Redmond: 'Heaven's Gates' by Randall Stoss (pro), and 'The Struggle for Bill Gates' Soul' by Eric Schmidt (con). And little wonder! As Steven Levy has warned, "If you think the world's biggest software company is powerful now, you haven't seen anything yet. Bill Gates and his overachievers are headed for your house, your car and your wallet.[297]

They are also headed for your mind and how you think.

Section C: Cyberfishers on the InterNet, Compuprocessors OnLine

    .... "Clearly the Internet is the way of the very near future.... It's almost going to be essential for people like us, who are supposed to be helping people, to put it [seafood information] on the Internet."

- Gunnar Knapp, Salmon Marketing Information Service

    "Strangely, CB [citizens band radio] fulfills many of the goals of the emerging National Information Infrastructure. It supports cheap universal access with neither censorship nor restraint of communications. It supports both commercial and private applications. Heavily used, too.

    "Yet what a barren landscape. Conversations are strangely vacant of substance. Over the citizens band [see the Internet], I hear long rambling monologues interspersed with short, vicious attacks. Requests from lost drivers [see skippers] are sometimes met with wrong directions...."

- Clifford Stoll, Silicon Snake Oil

    Today's North Pacific fisheries will have to deal with cyberspace the way the U.S. Armed Forces handle thermonuclear energy; with caution, care, and wise use. In 1996, the Internet and the World Wide Web are no longer the private domain of computer nerds and hackers, but are accessible to anyone with on-line capabilities. The Internet was started as a way for U.S. government computers to inter-communicate for scientific and military purposes.[298] The Internet was originally set up to accomodate the many types and sizes of computers and software used by the many branches of the U.S. federal government. The Advanced Research Projects Agency NETwork (ARPANET) was the eventual name given the collection of connected computers in the late 1960s.[299] During the 1970s, the U.S. federal government funded through its own creation, DARPA (Defense Advanced Research Projects Agency), a cheaper implementation of the TCP/IP communications system, which became available to colleges and universities. TCP/IP (Transmission Control Protocol/Internet Protocol) was a set of protocols explaining how computers would inter-communicate.[300] By the early 1980s, colleges and universities had begun utilising the TCP/IP to connect their computers together, and by 1989 the World Wide Web was a fact of cyber-life. The Net and the Web -- the arrangement of accessible Internet sources from computer systems world-wide -- are the most powerful tools currently available for research and development ("R&D"), as well as communication.[301]

    The crucial significance of cyberspace for the fishing and seafood industry has been well stated by one Alwin McGartlin, CEO of Mandeville, Louisiana-based Market Select Network, a global seafood buying and selling service: "Companies that do not use computer technology as a management, marketing and sourcing tool in the future will soon find themselves out of business.'"[302] What McGartlin meant, as a fish broker, was the use of e-[electronic] mail, Internet discussion groups and bulletin board, and access (via computer) to information stored in databases. An example of the latter has been clarified by Dr. Michael Morrissey, director of the Oregon State University Seafood Laboratory at Astoria, Oregon: "Say we're interested in whiting [Pacific hake, Merluccius productus], we'd tell the computer and it would give us a list of abstracts from the last 10 years dealing with whiting."[303]

Besides on-line research and inter-communications, there is bureaucratic information related to seafood -- fishing closures, processing regulations, nutrition labeling and the like -- available electronically. Another example is the Import Support and Information System (ISIS), a joint FDA/US Customs programme allowing importers and brokers to give U.S. officials shipment particulars by computer. In return, the importers or brokers receive an immediate electronic response, revealing whether the shipment will be released or held for further review.[304] For those industry members still not ready (or willing) to cyber-surf the (do-it-yourself) Aqua-net, there are commercial in addition to non-commercial services at hand, and their numbers are growing exponentially. Some non-commercial services featured in Seafood Leader's December 1994 issue were: (1) Fisheries Ecology -- "An international forum for fisheries scientists interested in research and species identification"; (2) Fishfolk -- "Mailing list for fishery management issues, including the social and economic issues resulting from the declining catches in the U.S. and Canada"; and (3) Fishnet -- "This forum contains items including files of abstracts, a business directory and a fish drug index."[305]

Editor Bruce Buls, of The Alaska Fisherman's Journal, has written that "links" to other (Web-)sites is a major attraction of the Web.[306] For instance, if a marine supply store closes a deal with a major supplier, the store can set up a link which allows the user to click onto that supplier's Web-site. Besides linking to commercial Web-sites, users may be helped finding links to non-commercial sites, like those mentioned earlier, providing important information. For example, the home-page for Seattle Marine (supply house) offers links to NMFS (National Marine Fisheries Service), ADF&G (Alaska Department of Fish and Game), the [Pacific] halibut commission, weather services and other governmental agencies. Seamar.com, according to editor Buls, also offers links to various Web-sites for marine sciences, fisheries organisations, safety programmes, "relevant periodicals' and the like.[307] Web-sites in the industry will proliferate for many reasons: Fishery Web-masters like the speed at which material can be added, subtracted, changed, or deleted; the lack of paper saves money and permits instantaneous change or updating. And if a mistake is made on a Web-site catalogue, it may be fixed almost as fast. Netscape CEO James Barksdale has been quoted by Time magazine as saying, "The Internet is the printing press of the technology era."[308] And as Seafood Leader's editor-in-chief, Peter Redmayne, has posited:

> ..."[T]he Internet unlocks some powerful tools for business. Forget international faxes ... now you can E-mail your shrimp supplier in Bangkok with a local phone call. And instead of printing and sending a brochure halfway around the world, you can post it on your [Web-]site, saving time and money.
> "The Web will change the way business does business, including the seafood business. It won't happen overnight, but it will happen."[309]

Peter Redmayne of Seafood Leader wrote the preceding editorial for the November/December 1995 issue. A year later, Seafood Leader featured an article by Daniel Shaw titled: 'Computing the Future: From Software to Cyberspace, Seafood definitely Computes.'[310] By late 1996, computerisation within the industry was booming on two fronts, seafood-specific software and Internet services -- indeed, computers have become "indispensable business tools."[311] Just the sheer bulk of seafood-related information on the Internet is overwhelming ... and expanding. According to Daniel Shaw, "dozens" of seafood companies have posted their own home-page(s) on the World Wide Web for advertising purposes, with a corollary growth of Internet clearing-houses for seafood information and seafood itself. Although these Internet clearing-houses all have their own angle, they agree on the computer-medium's effectiveness as advertising, marketing, and sales business tool.[312] In late 1996, leading seafood services on the Net are provided by outfits like Seafood On-Line of Los Angeles, the Seafood Exchange of Redondo Beach, Calif., and FIS International Co., Ltd., of Tokyo. Seafood companies pay these Net clearing-houses to post their latest product prices, inventories and information so that fish brokers -- world-wide -- may see what's available at the "click of a mouse."[313]

Back here in the Pacific Northwest, a Seattle corporation, Innovative Internet Marketing Systems Inc. (IIMS), lets clients like Alaska Smoked Salmon International sell on-line by credit card at a retail level. IIMS also has links to (the) NMFS, NOAA, Sea Grant, and other fishing/seafood-related information agencies.[314] The president of IIMS is none other than Bob Maillet (he of the Ocean Pacer, son of Norman Maillet) of

Anchorage, Alaska, a self-confessed "computer junkie" and fifth generation New Bedford (Mass.) scalloper.[315] The former scalloper/ex-crabber, who has even ventured into sea-snail (tsubu) fishing, got hooked on computers after purchasing a small IBM modem to do the books for his container-leasing business. Maillet's old skipper, crabber Jan Jastad, owner/operator of the Western Viking, was out "pot codding" in 1995 and got hooked while reading about the Internet during slack time. Jastad became interested in the Net's future, and Maillet soon had his old skipper intrigued with the commercial potential of buying and selling fish on-line, with instant world-wide access for the cost of a local 'phone call. Jan Jastad decided in favour of financially backing his -- and Bob Maillet's -- dream. Jastad is now secretary-treasurer of IIMS, while Maillet is president.[316] IIMS' space in cyberspace, "fishmart.com", is the Web-site whence seafood producers, wholesalers, traders, and brokers are able to publicise their available products, thereby be contacted by retailers. Moreover, fishmart.com (which has an office at the south end of the Ballard Bridge in Seattle) is tied into the United Nations Trade Point Development Centre, with links to 75,000 computers world-wide in five minutes.[317] Furthermore, fishmart.com is developing (February 1996) a kind of industry Yellow Pages -- i.e., the Maritime Pages -- as an extra service for fishermen, with listings of gear suppliers, electronics dealers, electrical contractors, employment services, boat-yards, safety equipment suppliers etc. Sometime in early 1997, seafood giant UniSea will be climbing on board to give fishmart.com a try.[318] This is not bad business for a Ballard company started by a couple of ex-crabbers in 1995!

But the North Pacific industry is not just about the fish business and making money; it is also about fish management. And fish managers may soon be able to get vital [updated] statistics with a mere keystroke, when FIMS, a new integrated computer network, comes on-line. The pilot version of the Fishery Information Management System (FIMS), designed by LGL Alaska Research Associates, was to be demonstrated at industry meetings and trade shows throughout 1995. FIMS promises to organise data into sets within what is called a "relational data-base.[319] Information will be presented in the form of maps; in this case a map of Alaska, from which users may concentrate on the region of their choice, then continue to zoom in to the point where individual fishing vessels can be identified and thereby pertinent information derived. This programme of FIMS is known as a Geographical Information System (GIS), and is a well-suited system for handling the needs of fisheries managers. Fishery and climatic data can be linked together; economic information factored

in, a fisherman's boat or name verified, mode of fishing -- e.g., trap or trawl -- identified, exact

latitudinal/longitudinal location ascertained. [320] LGL Alaska Research Associates representative, one Steve

Davis, is director of the LGL Fishery Management Program and an outspoken advocate of GIS. He has

projected that the GIS would be maintained by data from a number of accessible sources -- including the

Alaska Fisheries Science Center in Seattle, the Alaska Department of Fish and Game (ADF&G), and the

Commercial Fisheries Entry Commission. As FIMS broadens in scope, Steve Davis has been sanguine that

FIMS could also include oceanographic data from U.Alaska and the National Oceanic and Atmospheric

Administration (NOAA).[321] Davis has expostulated:

"With a GIS type of system, we could put a map up on a screen during a [North Pacific] Council meeting and you could ask questions like, 'We're interested in reducing by catch of halibut, herring, crab and salmon' .... You ask the computer to sort through its data and try to solve the problem by finding an area where bycatch can be minimized and catches of pollock and cod can be maximized.... The Council could do in one meeting what it took five years to do prior to having the system in place.... Having a map showing them (NMFS) where those hot spots [for bycatch] are will help them make those [fishery] decisions.... Fishermen might be able to enter their own data from a log book, and compare it with NMFS survey information and garner some insight into areas that might provide some productive fishing."[322]

Improved fishing, reduction of [trawl] by-catch, gains in stock assessment, fishery-marine mammal

interactions, and better enforcement of the North Pacific Council's decisions -- what more could cyber-

technology do for fish, fishermen, and fisheries management? Surely the enthusiastic Steve Davis, former

deputy director of the North Pacific Council and current (1995) director of the LGL Fishery Management

Program, is right on all counts!

The North Pacific industry is neither occupied solely by business and profits nor even wise fisheries

management, but also concerned with the fisherman's standard of living -- and political organisation to ensure

a decent one. Political organising in today's complex cyber-world means taking advantage of new

communications technology, in additional to traditional means such as joining a labour union. In response

to the new challenge, the Pacific Coast Federation of Fishermen's Associations (PCFFA), under the regional

directorship of Glen Spain, went on-line in early 1996. Indeed, the regional director in a February (1996)

feature in The Fishermen's News, called for all West Coast fishermen to get on the Net and organise in

cyberspace.[323] Besides giving basic tips on how to operate a computer and surf the Web, Glen Spain enumerated the advantages of Net services to fishermen. One of PCFFA's co-ventures during 1996 has been with the Institute for Fisheries Resources (IFR), the Association's habitat conservation affiliate, to organise both fishermen and fishing information on the Net. The joint Net project is named "FISHLINK", described by Glen Spain as an ..."electronic network linking West Coast fisheries organizations and associations (both commercial and recreational, U.S. and Canadian), as well as folks working on fisheries protection issues from conservation organizations, agencies and tribes. It is also intended to be a rapid alert network for fisheries-halibut-protection issues which all of these groups face."[324]

Although all sectors of the North Pacific industry seem to be quickly going on-line in the mid-1990s, for some prognosticators it's not fast enough. An example of cyber-reluctance is that computerised fish-tickets, according to Pacific Fishing's Joel Gay, "are receiving a cool welcome."[325] Homer (Alaska) fisherman and tender operator, Bill Wiebe, has spent much time and trouble during the last several winters developing a small computer; a computer that he believes will help tender operators, processors, and the Alaska Department of Fish and Game move into cyber-Century 21. Wiebe believes that his little computer, "Ticketally", will replace the present industry's paper and pencils with computers and modems -- and the quicker the better. "Ticketally" means that, instead of filling out a fish-ticket by hand, the tender operator or dock worker will type in the vessel's name, the skipper's name, and the brailer weights into a tiny lap-top computer. After the delivery, the receiver will push a button and ... presto! A printer will then kick out a mathematically-correct, computerised, fish ticket.[326] But one ADF&G statistician, Herman Savikko, who orders some $40,000 worth of fish-tickets per annum, said that his cyber-reluctance stemmed from a state funding problem, rather than a distrust of Bill Wiebe's computer. Fishermen and processors in Alaska have relied on paper fish-tickets ever since the 1930's, said Herman Savikko, and going cyber would engender major discussion involving all sectors of the industry.[327]

Although the home of Seattle, Emerald Cybercity of Century 21, Washington has not taken the plunge into cyberspace regarding state fisheries. Lee Hoines, of Washington's Department of Fish and Wildlife (WDFW), has said that local processors aren't clamouring for a cyber-system, and that he was too busy with the old paper/pencil system to develop something brand-new: "Until we get some impetus [i.e., state money], it's a low priority.'" And as to security concerns of accuracy in digital data, Hoines has asked, "How do we verify what they're sending us? Personally, I think it would be easier to cheat on a computer than to cheat on paper."[328] But on a factory trawler equipped with satellite telephone service, the omni-presence of computers and modems is hardly surprising, so sending information over the Net will become increasingly common. Cyber-technology -- "Ticketally" etc. -- has yet to make its way onto most smaller fishing vessels. Gunnar Knapp, of the Salmon Marketing Information Service, has said that he, and other seafood information providers, have to make technological decisions based on budgets; both their own and those of their customers. Knapp has concluded that, "'Clearly, the Internet is the way of the very near future.... It's almost going to be essential for people like us, who are supposed to be helping people, to put it on the Internet.'"[329]

As the world's technological capabilities are increasing, the cost of owning electronic gear is decreasing, so sonars and other sophisticated fish-finding equipment aren't the only fancy gadgets and gizmos found in highliner wheelhouses. On more and more vessels, separate electronic units are being replaced by centralised computer systems; computers with programmes which send and retrieve satellite information in detailed graphics. In the very near future, industry movers and shakers confidently predict, sophisticated software in on-board computers will integrate harvest information with management regimes and market dynamics.[330] On-line skippers will click through "menus" for the latest by-catch up-dates, past catch records, species abundance and distribution, plus meteorological and oceanographic information. These compu-smart skippers will run the programmes alongside the more traditional business applications which monitor fuel, expenses, crew-shares, and administrative tasks.[331]

One industry cyber-outfit, Fisherman's Associate, has been parallelling the most recent Wall Street compu-finance technology, known as "neural networking", which selects from the existent stockpile of data to analyse trends in market trading, then makes a cyber-educated forecast, and finally integrates information from how stocks and commodities have fared. The point is that the computer teaches itself to predict market trends with increasing accuracy. This idea transferred to the fishing industry will, in the words of Pacific Fishing writer Charlie Ess, "incorporate data from what is actually caught with what the satellites say and what the fish-finding side of the instrument purports to have seen, with the hope that, eventually the computer will offer a holistic approach to fishing success. Critics of neural networking, however, contend that computer databases will forever be plagued with insufficient data."[332] Data will only proliferate, asserts Charlie Ess, when the private and public sectors combine their efforts. NASA (National Aeronautics and Space Administration) recently contributed funding to furnish East Coast fishermen with satellite data to help find fish. The ultimate hope of West Coast cyber-fishers is that a totally integrated computer system will soon be in place where they can click on a species, such as albacore, and instantaneously have their digital disposal temperature, bathymetric and weather   cyber-information relative to Thunnus alalunga ... and then steer their boats in the tuna direction. When fisheries become more IFQ-oriented, concludes Ess, fishermen will be custodians of their own data.[333]

The dawning of 1997, the first year of the Age of Aquarius, finds this writer at his desk in Port Angeles, Washington. Snow is piled high and deep all around the house, and Christmastide 1996 witnessed the worst winter storms in the Pacific Northwest for many decades. But there were no electric power outages in this writer's home, or in many other dwellings on the Olympic Peninsula and Vancouver Island. It has been, therefore, highly conceivable that, had this writer still been in the local fish business, he could have taken a seafood spin on the World Wide Web -- even when snowed in. The digitally-competent browser doesn't have far to look for the location of seafood Web-sites. Three of the first listings in Seafood Leader Sourcebook 1996 serve as prime examples:

1.   Alaska Seafood Marketing Institute
     (http://www.state.ak.us/local/akpages/COMMERCE/asmihp.htm)
     "ASMI's home page includes access to their bi-monthly newsletter, recipes, sales aids, educational informational and industry-related materials on Alaska seafood, and the 1995 Directory of Alaska Seafood Suppliers. Links to ADF&G, the University of Alaska's Institute of Marine Science, and NMFS."[334]

2.   AquaNet H.P.
     (http://www.brainiac.com.aquanet/aq)
     "AquaNet is an information service for the aquatic world.   Subjects include aquaculture, conservation, eduction, fisheries, marine science, and oceanography, maritime heritage, ocean engineering and seafood.   Other features include a calendar of events, business news and employment listings."[335]

3.   BIOWEB
     (http://bioweb.org.)
     "BIOWEB is a virtual Canadian company made up of Canadian Biotech News and the Resudox Online Service, Inc. that has created a site for learning more about biotechnical research and community development in Canada.   Areas covered include, healthcare, Ag-biotech, environmental applications,

aquaculture, forestry and industrial sup[p]liers. Information is available on the history of Canadian aquaculture, the industry's growth potential and a list of Canadian companies involved in aquacultural biotechnology."[336]

What a wealth of information at the North Pacific industry member's fingertips! As the Seafood Leader Sourcebook editor, John Pappenheimer, has inquired of his readers: "...[W]hen you find yourself surfing to a computer in Tasmania, and from there to Canada and back to the USA all in a matter of minutes for the price of a local [Seattle] call, how can you not be awestruck by the promise of this technology?"[337]

But ... the promise of cyber-technology is accompanied by the real threat to individual privacy, communication between people on a personal level, and literacy in the classical sense. Books -- and CD-ROMs(!) -- have already proliferated warning of the dangers of going digital to traditional emphasis on reading, writing, and [a]rithmetic.[338] This writer has endeavoured to articulately describe and accurately document a hitherto (for him) unknown subject. Despite a personal animus against cyber-yuppies with their voice-mail and vanity plates, the writer has tried (even harder) to remain objective throughout this report. There remains no doubt regarding the benefits of cyber-technology for the North Pacific fisheries in the United States and Canada. The benefits are as good for fish management, conservation, and recruitment as they are for fish harvesting, processing, and distribution. But those in the industry -- an essentially conservative calling -- should be wary of cyber-culture itself. Like thermonuclear power, cyberspace is a powerful tool for both good and evil. It could be especially devastating if falling into the hands of a few bad men (or women); sort of like Hollywood movies or Network TV news. But cyberspace is coming to the fisheries as surely as Christmas Future.

Clifford Stoll, author of Silicon Snake Oil: Second Thoughts on the Information Highway, pointed out in 1995 the cultural perils of computerisation.[339] A cyber-expert himself, Stoll pooh-poohed the technocratic phantasy that computers and networking will somehow create a better society ... that access to information, better communications, and electronic programmes can cure societal problems.[340] Stoll wrote that he doesn't believe the technocrats, and this writer concurs, that there are no simple technological solutions to societal problems: "There's plenty of distrust and animosity between people who communicate perfectly well. Access to a universe of information cannot solve our problems: we will forever struggle to understand one another. The most important interactions in life happen between people, not between computers."[341]

The power-potential of cyberspace was chillingly manifested on the pre-Christmas _Time_ magazine cover, 16 December 1996: 'Jesus Online: How the Internet Is Shaping Our Views of Faith and Religion.'[342]

Post-Net: An Internet Interpolation
From: olympians @ olympus net
Date: 1/15/1996 11 39
Subject: Downsizing Government (hmmmm)
Address: To olympians @ olympus net

------- Forwarded message -------
Date: Mon. 15 Jan 1996 00:26:21-0500
Subject: Downsizing Government

"SECRETARY OF THE INTERIOR BABBIT ANNOUNCES HISTORIC COOPERATIVE AGREEMENT BETWEEN NASA AND THE U.S. FISH & WILDLIFE SERVICE.

"WASHINGTON, D.C. October 5, 1995. Secretary of the Interior Bruce Babbit called a press conference today to announce the implementation of a new cooperative agreement between the U.S. Fish and Wildlife Service and the National Aeronautics and Space Administration. Secretary Babbit called the agreement an historic step towards successful implementation of Reinventing Government, Stage II, that has been developed by the Clinton Administration.

"Under the terms of the new agreement, packs of wolves, imported from Canada, will be introduced into several NASA centers .... 'Wolves are an endangered species that need special protection to allow their populations to increase,' said Babbit. 'Private landowners have objected to releasing wolves in National Parks, fearing that they will wander onto private lands and attack livestock. This agreement presents an innovative compromise that will allow the wolves to prosper in areas where the public will have no objection to their pres ence'....

"An information brochure, entitled 'Adapt or Die', will be distributed to all NASA employees. The brochure explains the ecological basis for this new management policy. It also points out that there are severe penalties for harming endangered wolves, even in self-defense. It says, 'Keep in mind that humans are not an endangered species and, therefore, lack protection under the law.'"[343]

NOTES

68. 'The Road to the Future,' with Ron Gilster. <u>Studium Generale Program Notes</u>, 9 February 1995, Peninsula College, Port Angeles, Wash.

69. Op.cit., Ron Gilster, <u>ibidem</u>.

70. Clifford Stoll, <u>Silicon Snake Oil: Second Thoughts on the Information Highway</u> (New York:Doubleday, 1995), p.132.

71. <u>Ibid.</u>, p.3.

72. Florence King, 'Scriptophobia', <u>National Review</u> Vol.XLVII, No.8, 1 May 1995, p.92.

73. Op.cit., Clifford Stoll, p.12.

74. Andrew Ferguson, 'Very Unimportant Person,' <u>National Review</u>, Vol.XLVII, No.7, 17 April 1995, p.76.

75. 'Profile of a "surfer": thirtysomething male', <u>Peninsula Daily News</u>, 17 Janaury 1996, p.C-3. The ETRG survey was sponsored by 30 corporations with interests in the Internet; interviewed 1,000 people by telephone, only persons age 18 and over, during November-December 1995; and had a margin error of ±3%.

76. 'Technocrap', <u>Spy</u>, Vol.9, No.9, January/February 1995, p.56.

77. <u>Ibid.</u>, p.56.

78. John Cunniff, 'Talk cheap in Information Age', <u>Peninsula Daily News</u>, 23 April 1995, p.D-2.

79. <u>Ibid.</u>, p.D-2.

80. Thomas Fleming, 'Talking to Strangers', <u>Chronicles</u>, Vol.20, No.2, February 1996, p.11.

81. <u>Ibid.</u>, p.11.

82. Rayna Abrahams, 'The isolation of computer age', <u>Peninsula Daily News</u>, 2 May 1996, p.A-4. Rayna Abrahams is a free-lance writer living in Forks, Washington.

83. Matthew R. Estabrook, 'Internet Revolution Can Empower People', <u>Human Events</u>, Vol.52, No.6, 16 February 1996, p.18.

84. <u>Ibid.</u>, p.18.

85. <u>Ibid.</u>, p.18.

86. <u>Ibid.</u>, p.18.

87. :<u>The Politics of the Third Wave</u> (Atlanta:Turner Publishing, Inc., 1995).
Foreword by Newt Gingrich.

NOTES (cont'd)

88.   <u>Ibid.</u>, pp.62-63.

89.   <u>Ibid.</u>, p.63.

90.   <u>Ibid.</u>, p.73.

91.   <u>Ibid.</u>, p.74. This writer recalls that Gary Hart was mostly undone by Donna Rice aboard the <u>Monkey Business</u>.

92.   <u>Ibid.</u>, p.74.

93.   <u>Ibid.</u>, p.75.

94.   John Naisbitt, <u>Global Paradox</u> (New York:Avon Books, 1994), p.50.

95.   <u>Ibid.</u>, p.50.

96.   <u>Ibid.</u>, p.51.

97.   <u>Ibid.</u>, p.55.

98.   <u>Ibid.</u>, p.18.

99.   <u>Ibid.</u>, p.357.

100. <u>Ibid.</u>, p.112.

101. <u>Ibid.</u>, p.125.

102. Bantam Books, New York, 1981.

103. Samuel Francis, 'Voices in the Air', <u>Chronicles</u>, Vol.19, No.5, May 1995, p.11.

104. <u>Ibid.</u>, p.11.

105. Richard Brookhiser, 'Tout Newt', <u>National Review</u>, 20 March 1995, p.68.

106. <u>Ibid.</u>, p.68.

107. <u>Ibid.</u>, p.68.

108. <u>Ibid.</u>, p.68.

109. <u>Ibid.</u>, P.68. NB: Would "Mr. Newt" be baffled by these ancient truths? The U.S. electorate hopes not!

110. Samuel Francis, 'Gnostic Newt', <u>Chronicles</u>, Vol.19, No.4, April 1995, p.9.

NOTES (cont'd)

111. Ibid., p.9. The Leader,Prophet, and Brotherhood, sound variously like the Anti-Christ, False Prophet, and Archons of The New Testament. Eric H.W. Voegelin (1901-1985), German-born American political scientist and philosopher of history.

112. Ibid., p.9.

112. Ibid., p.9.

114. Norman Mailer, Of a Fire on the Moon (New York:Grove Press, Inc., 1970), p.354.

115. Ibid., p.352.

116. Ibid., p.352.

117. Ibid., p.355.

118. Ibid., p.355.

119. Ibid., p.142.

120. Stewart Brand, 'We Owe it All to the Hippies', Time Special Issue: Welcome to Cyberspace', Vol.145, No.12, Spring 1995, pp.54-56. Stewart Brand created the Whole Earth Catalog.

121. Eugene Taylor, Ph.D., 'Desperately Seeking Spirituality', Psychology Today, Vol.27, No.6, November/December 1994, p.62.

122. Ibid., p.62. Co-founded with a lyricist for the Grateful Dead. See Stewart Brand, Time Special Issue, p.56.

123. Eugene Taylor, Ph.D., Psychology Today, p.56.

124. Ibid., p.62.

125. Stewart Brand, Time Special Issue, p.56.

126. Ginia Bellafante, 'Strange Sounds and Sights' ("Musicians and artists are redefining their work by embracing the computer -- and shaking up the world of culture"), Time Special Issue, p.14.

127. Stewart Brand, Time Special Issue, p.55.

128. Ibid., p.55.

129. Ibid., p.56.

130. Op.cit., Norman Mailer, p.142.

131. Alvin Toffler, Powershift: Knowledge, Wealth, and Violence at the Edge of the 21st Century (New York:Bantam Books, 1991).

NOTES (cont'd)

132. Stewart Brand, <u>Time Special Issue</u>, p.55. Brand has cited Steven Levy's 1984 work, <u>Hackers: Heroes of the Computer Revolution</u>.

133. William Irwin Thompson, <u>Darkness and Scattered Light</u> (Garden City, N.Y.:Anchor Press/Doubleday, 1978), p.117, ff.

134. David Spangler, <u>Reflections on the Christ</u> (Moray, Scotland:Findhorn Publications, 1981 ed.), p.45.

135. Ian Shoales, 'Exorcize cyberdemons now!', <u>Northwest Comic News</u> (Eugene/Springfield, Ore.), Spring 1995, No.146, p.6.

136. <u>Ibid.</u>, p.6.

137. <u>Ibid.</u>, p.6.

138. Ad in <u>The New Times</u> (Seattle, Wash.) Vol 10, No.9, February 1995, p.2.

139. Subtitled <u>What Every Church Leader Needs to Know About Ministering in an Age of Spiritual and Technological Revolution</u> (Ventura, Calif.:Regal Books, 1994).

140. Op.cit., George Barna, p.139.

141. <u>Ibid.</u>, p.36.

142. <u>Ibid.</u>, p.139-140.

143. <u>Today's Front Page</u>, April 1995, p.10. With <u>The Screwtape Letters</u> of C.S. Lewis in mind, the monthly ran a hypothetical ad: "To my Dear Slimeball: Secret letters from a Senior Demon to His Slippery Sidekick."

144. "60s drug guru dies of cancer', <u>Peninsula Daily News</u>, 31 May 1996, p.A-2.

145. <u>Ibid.</u>, p.A-2.

146. 'Ashes to go boldly into space', <u>Peninsula Daily News</u>, 7 June 1996, p.A-10.

147. <u>Ibid.</u>, p.A-10.

148. David Gates, 'Odyssey of a Psychonaut: Timothy Leary's well-advertised trip: 1920-1996', <u>Newsweek</u>, 10 June 1996, p.92.

149. Anchor Books, Doubleday & Company, Inc., Garden City, N.Y., 1969.

150. <u>Ibid.</u>, p.167. Roszak quoted Leary from interview with the <u>New York Post</u> magazine, 14 September 1967, p.45.

151. Dave Hunt and T.A. McMahon, <u>The Seduction of Christianity</u> (Eugene, Ore.:Harvest House Publishers, 1985), pp.47-48.

NOTES (cont'd)

152. <u>Ibid.</u>, pp.47-48.

153. <u>Ibid.</u>, pp.47-48.

154. Op.cit., Theodore Roszak, p.141.

155. The post-Alexandrian Mediterranean world, from the late 3rd century through the 1st century B.C., in Greece and Greek-speaking territories.

156. 'Micropaedia' (Chicago, Ill.:Encyclopaedia Brittanica, Inc., 1990), p.875.

157. With the feminisation of Western culture and society, more personalised deities of the 1990s are identified as "Gaia", "Sophia." The "Shamballa Force" was coined by Theosophist Alice A. Bailey (1939).

158. Please see Appendix M.

159. <u>: The Luddites and their War on the Industrial Revolution</u> (Reading, Mass.:Addison-Wesley Publishing Company, 1996 ed.) Author's note: Is Kirkpatrick Sale the son of Roger Sale, author of <u>Seattle Past and Present</u> (U.W., 1976)?

160. Op.cit., Kirkpatrick Sale, Preface, p.IX.

161. <u>Ibid.</u>, p.X.

162. <u>Ibid.</u>, p.X.

163. For a profile of Ted Kaczynski, refer to Appendix J.

164. Op.cit., Kirkpatrick Sale, p.3.

165. <u>Ibid.</u>, p.16.

166. <u>Ibid.</u>, p.20.

167. <u>Ibid.</u>, p.21.

168. <u>Ibid.</u>, pp.231,232.

169. <u>Ibid.</u>, p.275.

170. P.J. O'Rourke, <u>The American Spectator's Enemies List</u> (New York:The Atlantic Monthly Press, 1996), pp.147-148.

171. Kirkpatrick Sale, pp.240,255. For a comparative list of political labels, see Appendix M.

172. <u>Ibid.</u>, pp.248-249.

NOTES (cont'd)

173.   The Technological Society (New York:Alfred A. Knopf, 1964). Translated from the French by John Wilkinson.

174.   The Myth of the Machine (New York:Harcourt, Brace & World, 1967).

175.   Kirkpatrick Sale, p.266.

176.   Ibid., p.265. NB: Let the reader be the judge of which pronouncement makes more sense.

177.   Ibid., pp.271-276.

178.   Op.cit., Alvin Toffler, Powershift, 'CODA: Yearnings for a New Dark Age', pp.369-370.

179.   Ibid., p.371. Toffler mentioned in passing that Ivan Illich, social critic and ecological theorist was opposed to "'managerial fascism'" or "simple-minded Ludditism." Yet ... Kirkpatrick Sale has listed Ivan Illich as a neo-Luddite, Rebels against the Future, p.240.

180.   Ibid., p.372. Toffler cited Alain Touraine, 'Neo-Modern Ecology,' New Perspectives Quarterly, Spring 1989, n.p.

181.   Ibid., p. 372. Toffler cited John de Graff, 'The Dangers of Counter-Culture,' Undercurrents, April/May 1977; esp. Chapter 11.

182.   Ibid., p.372.

183.   Ibid., p.373.

184.   Op.cit., Kirkpatrick Sale, p.256.

185.   Op.cit., Clifford Stoll, p.12.

186.   Op.cit., Theodore Roszak, p.217.

187.   Op.cit., Clifford Stoll, p.46.

188.   Ibid., p.12.

189.   Phil Phillips, Saturday Morning Mind Control (Nashville, Tenn.:Thomas Nelson, Inc., 1991), p.109. Quoted by Jeffrey A. Baker, Cheque Mate: The Game of Princes (Springdale, Penna.:Whitaker House, 1993), p.147.

190.   Op.cit., Jeffrey A. Baker, pp.148-149.

191.   'News and Views', USA Weekend, 26-28 July 1996, p.7.

192.   Ibid., p.7. Liz Goodwin, letter to ed., "Cybersmart or cyberstupid?"

NOTES (cont'd.)

193. <u>Peninsula Daily News</u>, 20 October 1996, p.C-4.

194. 'Seattle tops for family, work', <u>Peninsula Daily News</u>, 22 October 1996, p.A-7.

195. <u>Ibid.</u>, p.A-7.

196. The eds, 'Harvest O'Heroin,' <u>Spy</u>, Vol.10, No.6, November/December 1996, p.72. Deaths of rock-stars from heroin since 1988 include: Hillel Slovak (Red Hot Chili Peppers), Shannon Hoon (Blind Melon), and Jonathan Melvoin (Smashing Pumpkins).

197. Jerry Adler with Rob French, 'Seattle Reigns', <u>Newsweek</u>, 20 May 1996, p.51.

198. <u>Ibid.</u>, p.51, ff.

199. <u>Ibid.</u>, p.53.

200. Op.cit., Jerry Adler and Rob French, p.53.

201. <u>Ibid.</u>, p.54.

202. Op.cit., Jerry Adler and Rob French, p.54.

203. Lynda Barry, 'Seattle's Siren Song', <u>ibid.</u>, p.55.

204. 'U.W. struggles to diversify,' <u>Peninsula Daily News</u>, 4 July 1996, p.A-5.

205. <u>Newsweek</u>, 20 May 1996, p.58.

206. <u>Ibid.</u>, pp.58-59. There will be more on Microsoft's involvement with Dream Works SKG and the (unrelated) Experience Music Project. See Appendix I for a discography of Jimi Hendrix.

207. <u>Ibid.</u>, p.57.

208. 'Magazine plugs into Puget Sound -- again,' <u>Peninsula Daily News</u>, 14 May 1996, p.A-5.

209. <u>Ibid.</u>, p.A-5.

210. <u>Ibid.</u>, p.A-5. From <u>Rolling Stone</u>, 30 May 1996.

211. <u>Newsweek</u>, 20 May 1996, p.57.

212. Steve Jobs announced his political/financial support for the Clintons at that time. Shortly afterwards, Jobs donated $100,000 to the Democrat Party. See 'Meanwhile, Clinton Loves Rich Dinners', <u>Time</u>, Vol.148, No.15, 23 September 1996, p.35.

213. <u>Spy</u>, Vol.9, No.9, January/February 1995, p.61.

214. <u>Ibid.</u>, p.61.

NOTES (cont'd.)

215. 'Bill Gates -- Microsoft's "Tycoon"', <u>Peninsula Daily News</u>, 26 May 1995, p.B-9.

216. 'Power? Gates has lots of it,' <u>Peninsula Daily News</u>, 10 June 1996, p.A-8.

217. <u>Ibid.</u>, p.A-8. If <u>Time</u> were to be believed, grunge widow Courtney Love of Hole -- "female-rocker-as-open-wound" -- was listed in top 25 of "most influential" [Americans]. Courtney Love lives in Grunge City and is America Online at alt.fan.courtney-love. <u>Yahoo! Internet Life</u>, Vol.2, No.5, October 1996, p.31.

218. 'The Other Bill Goes to Washington,' <u>Business Week</u>, 13 May 1996, p.57.

219. 'Bill Gates -- Microsoft's "Tycoon"', <u>Peninsula Daily News</u>, 26 May 1995, p.B-9.

220. 'Gates again tops list of America's richest', <u>Peninsula Daily News</u>, 2 October 1995, p.A-5.

221. <u>Ibid.</u>, p.A-5. All three of Washington State's richest individuals in 1995 were from Microsoft Corp.

222. 'Microsoft chief still richest, but Asian tycoons gaining', <u>Peninsula Daily News</u>, 1 July 1996, p.A-6.

223. <u>Ibid.</u>, p.A-6.

224. 'Microsoft exec tops list of Forbes' richest,' <u>Peninsula Daily News</u>, 30 September 1996, p.A-5.

225. 'Microsoft rolls out Stones', <u>Peninsula Daily News</u>, 18 August 1995, p.A-6.

226. <u>Ibid.</u>, p.A-6.

227. Source of the countercultural stench!

228. Steven Levy, 'Gimme Software', <u>Newsweek</u>, 4 September 1995, p.54.

229. See Appendix I for more on Seattle's home-town hero.

230. 'Purple haze seen in Seattle', <u>Peninsula Daily News</u>, 7 February 1995, p.A-7.

231. <u>Ibid.</u>, p.A-7.

232. Marco R. della Cava, 'Billionaire's dream blends art, technology', <u>USA TODAY</u>, 15 March 1996, p.1-D.

233. 'Hendrix's sister, museum founder "agreed to disagree"', <u>ibid.</u>, p.2-D.

234. <u>Ibid.</u>, p.2-D. See Appendix I.

235. <u>Ibid.</u>, p.2-D. The Experience Music Project's Web-site is at :http://www.experience.org.

236. 'Seattle rock museum's design takes shape,' <u>Peninsula Daily News</u>, 27 October 1996, p.C-3.

NOTES (cont'd.)

237. N'gai Croal and Toriano Boynton, 'A Few Good Web Sites,' <u>Newsweek</u>, 7 August 1995, p.10. <u>The Roomful of Mirrors</u> Web-site is at: http://www.wavenet.com/jhendrix.

238. 'High tech goes Hollywood,' <u>Peninsula Daily News</u>, 23 March 1995, p.A-6.

239. <u>Ibid.</u>, p.A-6.

240. Vanessa Ho, 'Three cool dudes and a rumpled rich guy', <u>Seattle Post-Intelligencer</u>, 23 March 1995, p.A-1.

241. <u>Ibid.</u>, p.A-8.

242. <u>National Review</u>, Vol. XLVII, No.10, 29 May 1995, p.56.

243. <u>Peninsula Daily News</u>, 25 August 1996, p.C-8.

244. 'Meanwhile, Clinton Loves Rich Dinners', <u>Time</u>, No.148, No.15, 23 September 1996, p.35. See note 212.

245. Steven Levy, 'Waiting for Spielberg', <u>Newsweek</u>, 29 May 1995, p.56.

246. <u>Ibid.</u>, p.56.

247. <u>Ibid</u>, p.56.

248. <u>Ibid.</u>, p.56.

249. See John McPhee, <u>The Headmaster</u> (New York:The Noonday Press, 1992 ed.), <u>passim.</u> Originally publ. in 1966.

250. 'Seattle Reigns', <u>Newsweek</u>, 20 May 1996, p.54.

251. James Kim and Becky Beyers, 'Federal lawsuit imperils Microsoft purchase plan', <u>USA TODAY</u>, 28 April 1995, p.2-B.

252. James Kim and Becky Beyers, <u>ibid.</u>, p.2-B. Cf. John Flinn and Tom Abate, 'U.S. sues to halt big Microsoft deal', <u>San Francisco Examiner</u>, 27 April 1995, p.A-1.

253. 'Stanley Sporkin, Trustbuster,' <u>Newsweek</u>, 27 February 1995, p.45.

254. Steven Levy, 'Antitrust and Common Sense', <u>Newsweek</u>, 6 March 1995, p.78.

255. <u>Ibid.</u>, p.78.

256. Tom Flinn and Tom Abate, 'U.S. sues to block big Microsoft deal', <u>San Francisco Examiner</u>, 27 April 1995, p.A-14.

257. Clifford Stoll, <u>Silicon Snake Oil</u> (New York:Doubleday, 1995), p.85.

NOTES (cont'd.)

258.   Ibid., p.85.

259.   Robert Hughes, 'Take This Revolution...', Time Special Issue, Vol.145, No.12, Spring 1995, p.77.

260.   'Internet may spell doom for Microsoft', Peninsula Daily News, 17 September 1995, p.D-1.

261.   Kevin Maney, 'Fear, loathing mark rush to Internet', USA TODAY, 28 April 1995, p.2-B.

262.   'Internet may spell doom...', ibid., p.D-1.

263.   Ibid., p.D-1.

264.   'Bill Gates -- Microsoft's "Tycoon"', Peninsula Daily News, 26 May 1995, p.B-9.

265.   Ibid., p.B-9. NB: Although fronted by NBC's Brokaw, "Tycoon" was produced outside the network.

266.   Philip Jenkins, 'The Matter of Money', Chronicles, Vol.20, No.2, February 1996, p.14.

267.   Ibid., p.14.

268.   Catherine Yang, 'The Other Bill Goes to Washington', Business Week, 13 May 1996, p.57.

269.   Ibid., p.57.

270.   Ibid., p.57.

271.   Ibid., p.57.

272.   Rick Marin, 'Rebooting the News', Newsweek, 29 July 1996, p.77.

273.   'Allen favors fresh start, new stadium for Hawks', Peninsula Daily News, 24 April 1996, p.B-1.

274.   'County, Allen at odds on stadium', Peninsula Daily News, 25 August 1996, p.B-3.

275.   Ibid., p.B-3.

276.   Ibid., p.B-3.

277.   'Allen plans to ask state for help with stadium', Peninsula Daily News, 5 November 1996, p.B-1.

278.   'Mine Is Bigger Than Yours', Newsweek, 25 December 1995-1 January 1996, p.14.

279.   Newsweek, 4 December 1995, p.86.

280.   Ibid., pp.50-51. NB: A computer "mouse."

281.   Ibid., p.8. Redmond, of course, is corporate headquarters for Microsoft. Accent on "hemp" is this writer's.

NOTES (cont'd.)

282.   Vanessa Ho, 'Three cool dudes and a rumpled rich guy', <u>Seattle Post-Intelligencer</u>, 23 March 1995, p.A-1.

283.   Mitchell Landsberg, 'Disney doesn't pussy foot', <u>Peninsula Daily News</u>, 7 August 1995, p.A-6.

284.   <u>Ibid.</u>, p.A-6.

285.   Steven Levy, 'Gimme Software', <u>Newsweek</u>, 4 September 1995, p.54.

286.   'Microsoft amazing firm', <u>Peninsula Daily News</u>, 17 May 1996, p.A-8.

287.   <u>Ibid.</u>, p.A-8.

288.   <u>Ibid.</u>, p.A-8.

289.   Steven Levy, 'The Microsoft Century', <u>Newsweek</u>, 2 December 1996, p.57.

290.   'David and Goliath battle over Internet', <u>Peninsula Daily News</u>, 20 September 1996, p.A-6.

291.   Op.cit., Steven Levy, 'The Microsoft Century', p.57.

292.   'Microsoft did most for state economy, study says', <u>Peninsula Daily News</u>, 5 December 1996, p.A-6.

293.   <u>Ibid.</u>, p.A-6.

294.   <u>Ibid.</u>, p.A-6.

295.   <u>Ibid.</u>, A-6. NB: Emphasis on "average" is this writer's.

296.   Op.cit., Steven Levy, 'The Microsoft Century', p.59.

297.   <u>Ibid.</u>, p.57.

NOTES (cont'd.)

298.   'Introduction to the World Wide Web', with Stan Compton. <u>Studium Generale Notes</u>, 7 November 1996, Peninsula College, Port Angeles, Wash., p.1.

229.   <u>Ibid.</u>, p.1. NB: As early as the late 1960s, according to Stan Compton. As reported in John Naisbitt's <u>Global Paradox</u> (New York:Avon books, 1995, p.51), the Internet itself was initially created by the Pentagon during the late 1970s.

330.   <u>Ibid.</u>, p.1.

301.   <u>Ibid.</u>, p.1.

302.   Karen McGeorge Sanders and D.T. Sanders, 'Seafood in Cyberspace', <u>Seafood Leader Aquaculture & Seafood Processing Yellow Pages</u>, Vol.14, No.7, Dec. 1994, p.10.

303.   <u>Ibid.</u>, p.11.

304.   <u>Ibid.</u>, p.11.

305.   'Surfing the Aquanet', <u>ibid.</u>, p.13.

306.   Bruce Buls, 'Surfing the Fish Net', <u>Alaska Fisherman's Journal</u>, Vol.19, No.11, Nov. 1996, p.20.

307.   <u>Ibid.</u>, p.20.

308.   <u>Ibid.</u>, p.20. Bruce Buls has cited <u>Time</u> magazine.

309.   Peter Redmayne, 'Seafood Surfer', <u>Seafood Leader</u>, Vol.15, No.6, Nov./Dec. 1995, p.5.

310.   Vol.16, No.6, Nov./Dec. 1996, pp.58-61.

311.   <u>Ibid.</u>, p.58.

312.   <u>Ibid.</u>, p.58-59.

313.   <u>Ibid.</u>, p.59.

314.   <u>Ibid.</u>, p.59.

315.   Bill Rudolph, 'Fishing with the World Wide Web', <u>Alaska Fisherman's Journal</u>, Vol.19, No.2, February 1996, p.13. NB: For a short story of the Maillets (formerly of Bedford, Mass.), and New England-style scalloping in Alaska waters, see C.D. Bay-Hansen, <u>Fisheries of the Pacific Northwest Coast, Vol. II</u> (New York:Vantage Press, Inc., 1994), pp.70-76.

316.   <u>Ibid.</u>, p.13. Ie., February 1996.

317.   <u>Ibid</u>, p.13.

318.   <u>Ibid.</u>, p.13, 18.

319.   Mark Gillespie, 'Fish On-Line', <u>Alaska Fisherman's Journal</u>, Vol.18, No.2, February 1995, p.26.

320.   <u>Ibid.</u>, p.26.

NOTES (cont'd.)

321. Ibid., p.26.

322. Ibid., p.26-27.

323. Glen Spain, 'Organizing on the Internet', The Fishermen's News, Vol.52, No.2, February 1996, p.18.

324. Ibid., p.18.

325. Joel Gay, 'Getting Wired: Fisheries Inch into Cyberspace,' Pacific Fishing, Vol.XVII, No.6, June 1996, p.37.

326. Ibid., p.38.

327. Ibid., pp.38-39.

328. Ibid., p.40.

329. Ibid., p.41.

330. Charlie Ess, 'Electronic Ears & Eyes', Pacific Fishing, Vol.XVII, No.11, November 1996, pp.32, 33.

331. Ibid., p.32.

332. Ibid., p.37.

333. Ibid., p.37.

334. 'Take a Seafood Spin on the World Wide Web', Seafood Leader Aquaculture & Seafood Processing Sourcebook 1996, Vol.15, No.7, December 1995, p.19.

335. Ibid., p.19.

336. Ibid., p.19.

337. Ibid., p.3.

338. The latest offering has been Sven Birkerts, The Gutenberg Elegies: The Fate of Reading in the Electronic Age (New York:Fawcett-Columbine, 1996).

339. New York, Doubleday, 1995.

340. Clifford Stoll, p.50.

341. Op.cit., p.50.

342. Newsweek, America's other current wisdom (cw) magazine, voted Scott Adams, creator of "Dilbert", as their cartoonist of 1996 -- which was most assuredly the virtual year of the Alpha Geek.

343. Via Internet from Port Townsend, Wash., Olympus Net. Many thanks -- mange takk! -- to Sons of Norway member Paul Enga of Port Angeles, Wash.

Bibliography for Part II

8. Atelsek, Jean. <u>All about Computers</u>. Ziff-Davis Press, Emeryville, Calif., 1993.

9. Barna, George. <u>Virtual America</u>. Regal Books, Ventura, Calif., 1994.

10. Lalonde, Peter and Paul. <u>Racing Toward ...the Mark of the Beast</u>. Harvest House Publishers, Eugene, Ore., 1994.

11. Sale, Roger. <u>Seattle Past and Present</u>. U.Washington, Seattle and London, 1976.

12. Stoll, Clifford. <u>Silicon Snake Oil</u>. Doubleday, New York, 1995.

13. Toffler, Alvin and Heidi. <u>Creating a New Civilization</u>. TurnerPublishing Inc., Atlanta, Ga., 1995.

Main References

C. Seafood Leader <u>Aquaculture & Seafood Processing Yellow Pages 1995</u>, Vol.14, No.7, December 1994.

D. _____ . <u>Aquaculture & Seafood Processing, Sourcebook 1996</u>, Vol.15, No.7, December 1995.

Part III: The Fish of Science and the Pisces of Magic
(Scientific vs. Magickal Perspectives)

NB: Part III (of Chapter 3) was originally titled 'Technomarine and Weird Science.' After dealing extensively in Part I with neo-Darwinian fisheriography and New Age salmon metaphysics, this writer decided in Part III to compare Natural Scientism with New Age new physics; followed by a contrast of both with a Judaeo-Christian apologia. As stated in 'Interword' (before Ch. 3), "How persons [i.e., scientists] of power and influence view matter, life, energy, and the cosmos deeply affects the Church, the Academy, and the Culture at large...." Such institutions of power and influence deeply affect attitudes and ideologies in business and government, and through them the harvesting of fish and the processing of seafood.

Extrospection 1996

The worst old flavour of 1996 was Safeway's Lucerne Rocky Road ice-cream, a gummy chocolate ["chock-lit"] mish-mash interspersed with unidentifiable nuts and mini-marshmallows -- Yeeeech! The worst year-end toy was the Tickle-Me-Elmo doll. The worst new TV show of 1997 (so far) has been Politically Incorrect, hosted by sheep-faced wag Bill Maher. The unlikely-named offering has been anything but, with the host early (and predictably) revealing himself as just another pc member of the show-biz Left. But if Bill Maher (pronounced "Marr") wishes to regard himself as a free spirit and original thinker, who's to gainsay him? The comedian's smirking visage has already [dis]graced the cover of the 20 January 1997 issue of the (new) U.S. News & World Report.

And right on time for the ("Dr.") Martin Luther King, Jr. Holiday was Touched by an Angel's sell-out to ethnic diversity and multiculturalism. Good Lord! Besides ratings, what could Martha Williamson, producer of the CBS programme, have been thinking? This writer had been watching Touched by an Angel since its inception in 1994, and had seen the very lovely Monica (Roma Downey), and the extremely lovable Tess (Della Reese), solve human problems in wondrous angelic manner. Christian columnist Cal Thomas once requested viewers to write CBS in support of the faith and family-values show, and this writer was one of many fans who did. Indeed, the usually acerbic Brent Bozell III, of the Media Research Center, named producer Martha Williamson Person of the Year (1996).[344] But the 19 January 1997 episode of Touched by an Angel was packed with every reverse-racial stereotype and corporate-greed cliché imaginable: Big Tobacco, [ugly] White executives, a [handsome] young Black lawyer (Kadeem Hardison) employed by Big Tobacco, the former's [brave] mother (Ja'net DuBois) dying of lung cancer, his [venerable] father an oppressed corporate chauffeur "wukkin' fo' de Man." Like the 1972 movie "Sounder", in which every Black was Beautiful, every White man in the 19 January episode of <u>Touched by an Angel</u> was bad; except for Andrew the Angel of Death (John Dye). The message seemed to say that tobacco was grown and cultivated by [Southern] Whites to specifically addict then afflict Blacks; sort of like the scurrilous rumour of CIA-distributed crack-cocaine in L.A. to rid South Central of Blacks. Della Reese, though still playing Tess the angel, filled in as a [not so lovable] Oprahesque lawyer-lady. Where-oh-where was God supposed to be in all this, basically a health issue? The terrible spectre of political correctness has reared its ugly head in a feel-good programme [surely] intended for all.

But there were lessons to be learned from the storm of 1996. A neighbour of this writer's shoveled snow out in front of the adjacent driveway, so that his own motorised brats could get out. Otherwise it was mostly the wives who did the shoveling, while their husbands revved up their Broncos or Blazers in noisy, but futile, power displays. Otherwise, folks were friendly -- far friendlier than they usually were. Neighbourhood women, pausing from shoveling snow, smiled and waved, as did those few men who managed to drive around. The one driver, that this writer recognised who did <u>not</u> smile or wave, was the assistant (sub-) pastor of Holy Trinity Lutheran Church. The Age of Aquarius was already off to an inauspicious start.

Section A: Space and the Cosmos

"[L]ong hair and funky unwashed caverns were the zone of demarcation in the physics of smell, stink was the Siegfried [L]ine between magic and technology."
- Norman Mailer, <u>Of a Fire on the Moon</u>

"Like religion, science looks for the sources of everything, the ultimate things, for a total explanation of the universe. So physics is also, ultimately, a kind of metaphysics."
- Gerhard Staguhn, <u>God's Laughter</u>

The Age of Pisces did not bow out without its casualties. On Friday, 20 December 1996, Dr. Carl Sagan died at the Fred Hutchinson Cancer Research Center in Seattle. Sagan succumbed at age 62 to pneumonia, after a two-year losing battle with bone-marrow disease, a form of anemia known as myelodisplasia (or pre-leukemia syndrome).[345] What could this writer say of Carl Sagan that hasn't already been said? The Associated Press eulogised Carl Sagan as having "...helped transport an ivory tower realm [science] into the living rooms of ordinary people, enthralling millions ["and billions"] with his vivid writing and flamboyant television soliloquies."[346] Sagan won the Pulitzer Prize for Literature in 1978 for <u>The Dragons of Eden:</u> <u>Speculations on the Evolution of Human Intelligence</u>. Just two years later (1980), Sagan's 13-part PBS series, <u>Cosmos</u>, became the most watched limited series in the history of American public TV, a record only since surpassed by pixieish Ken Burns' <u>The Civil War</u>. Carl Sagan was "the science popularizer", a label the good doctor claimed he wore proudly.[347]

And Carl Sagan had substance besides style. He was David Duncan Professor of Astronomy and Space Sciences; director of the Laboratory for Planet[ary] Studies at Cornell U. (Ithaca, N.Y.); Distinguished Visiting Scientist at Cal. Institute of Technology's Jet Propulsion Laboratory; and co-founder and president of the Planetary Society.[348] Moreover, Carl Sagan -- handsome, articulate, affable -- transcended the above sum of all his parts; he has been the only scientist since Albert Einstein to enjoy public adulation in America and the world.[349] This writer has characterised Sagan as a believer in "Romantic [Natural] Scientism" (see Appendix M), although the brilliant astrophysicist has defied facile pigeon-holing. But surely Carl Sagan agreed with Karl Marx, when the latter stated that natural science alone was "'empirically establishable'"; all else was 'shadowy forms in the brain of men.'"[350] This is Scientism pure and simple, and Sagan lovingly debunked New Age theories of UFOs, space aliens, and ancient astronauts throughout his long and illustrious career. In <u>Broca's Brain</u>, Sagan expanded briefly on this theme:

"The interest in UFOs and ancient astronauts seems at least partly the result of unfulfilled religious needs. The extraterrestrials are often described as wise, powerful, benign, human in appearance, and sometimes they are attired in long white robes. They are very much like gods and angels, coming from other planets rather than from heaven, using spaceships rather than wings. There is a little pseudoscientific overlay, but the theological antecedents are clear: in many cases the supposed ancient astronauts and UFO occupants are deities, feebly disguised and modernized, but easily recognizable. Indeed, a recent British survey suggests that more people believe in extraterrestrial visitations than in God."[351]

Carl Sagan didn't believe in UFOs, space aliens, or ancient astronauts; neither did he believe in Mesmerism, dowsing, channeling nor orgone energy.[352] In fact, Carl Sagan disbelieved in all things supernatural whatsoever, was contemptuous of Creation Science, and seemed to harbour an especial grudge against evangelical Christianity.[353] No surprise there -- the devout Jew, Christian, or Muslim would expect such disbelief from the leading apostle of spiritless Scientism. Carl Sagan, however, was associated with "weird science" more than his naturalistic legacy might intimate. For example, in 1966 Sagan and Soviet astrophysicist I.S. Shklovskii discussed the possibility of extraterrestrial contact (i.e., UFOs, space aliens, or ancient astronauts) in their book, Intelligent Life in the Universe.[354] This joint venture by Sagan and Shklovskii was inspirational for -- and often cited by -- such paradoxical science [fiction] writers as the Briton, W. Raymond Drake, and the Swiss, Erich von Däniken; perpetrators of a borderline science always disparaged by Sagan. But ... Sagan himself thought and wrote about eventual alien first contact, and was a leading exponent of listening for possible radio signals from other civilisations. Nay, Sagan was obsessed with that possibility throughout his professional life. In 1984, Sagan persuaded none other than [His Steveness] Steven Spielberg, past creator of "E.T." and present cyber-weasel, to sponsor and fund the SETI (Search for Extraterrestrial Intelligence) project at Harvard, to the amount of $100,000. Since then, NASA supported the SETI programme with $100 million, until its ultimate demise in 1995.[355]

The first serious attempt to listen for possible extraterrestrial radio signals was tried at the National Radio Astronomy Observatory at Greenbank, West Virginia, in 1959 and 1960. The whole was organised by one Frank Drake (no relation of W. Raymond), later of Cornell U., and it was named Project Ozma after the princess in the Land of Oz -- an exotic, distant, and difficult-to-reach place. Frank Drake examined two relatively-nearby stars, Epsilon Eridani and Tau Ceti, for several weeks with negative results....[356] Since Project Ozma, there have been a half-dozen or more such projects -- at varying levels -- in the United States, Canada, and (former) Soviet Union. All the results were negative, but since the 1980s efforts have been made for inter-galactic radio contact by the Harvard University/Planetary Society META (Megachannel Extraterrestrial Assay) programme; the Ohio State U. search; the SERENDIP Project of the U.Cal. Berkeley;[357] and recently BETA. BETA (the Billion Channel Extraterrestrial Assay) is an 84-foot radio-telescope with all channels tuned to finding intelligent life elsewhere in the cosmos. A large aggregate of physicists, astronomers, and star-gazers gathered from Harvard and beyond to attend the 30 October 1995 turning-on of one of Earth's largest receivers. BETA, according to an Associated Press report, is a "300 fold upgrade" of the telescope activated nine years previously on the same Massachusetts hilltop.[358] Since the earlier META (Harvard U./Planetary Society) programme, first switched on in 1987, research scientists had isolated seemingly promising signals several times, but none had ever been duplicated. The new, improved BETA radio-telescope simultaneously beams three powerful antennae (Eastward, Westward, Earthward), and is backed by a sophisticated room-sized computer-system which breaks down the frequencies, trying to separate -- from a wall of static -- one, pure (alien) tone from Out There.[359] That single, flute-like note is fervently awaited by the 100,000 contributing members of The Planetary Society, plus a number of private corporations and foundations which pay $40,000 per annum to keep BETA functioning. It takes an average of six months for the radio-telescope to scan the entire firmament.[360]

Searching the dark skies for signs of extraterrestrial life is scientific; as is announcing that no proofs for UFOs or ETIs exist. Yet Carl Sagan, for all his Scientism, definitely hoped (and believed) that We Are Not Alone (Contact, Simon & Schuster, 1985). And although dismissing religious and spiritual practices as mere superstition, Sagan himself extolled the weird science of LSD psychedelic therapist Stanislav Grof.[361] Grof, moreover, was a major contributor to Taoist quantum physicist Fritjof Capra's milestone New Age work, The Turning Point (Bantam Books, 1988 ed.). In The Demon-Haunted World, Sagan decried "UFOs, channeling and other examples of Western pseudoscience ... along with such ancient Chinese practices as ancestor worship, astrology and fortune telling -- especially that version that involves throwing yarrow sticks and working through the hoary hexagrams of the I Ching."[362] But "that version" is exactly what quantum physicist Fritjof Capra practices as a bona fide Taoist. Notwithstanding the two above inconsistencies, Sagan's Scientism remains safe, solid, secure. There has been a trend in New Age science circles to refute reductionism; here Sagan's apologetics were at their best. In The Demon-Haunted World, the astrophysicist mounted a furious and effective counter-attack.[363]

The lasting impression, left from Sagan's final book, is of a science populariser of the old cw (current wisdom); of a passé scientific correctness. At the end of The Demon-Haunted World, Sagan paid his political dues to chemist Linus Pauling (1901-1994), a scientific good-guy, and Edward (H-Bomb) Teller, a scientific bad-guy.[364] Throughout his writings, Sagan revered the person, physics, and political activism of Albert Einstein (1879-1955).[365] Like Fritjof Capra, Sagan genuflected to feminist women and racial minorities, but looked to has-been cultural icons such as Isaac Asimov, Henry Steele Commager, and Theodore Roszak for inspiration.[366] Long before his death in December 1996, Carl Sagan had already been eclipsed by New Age

physicists in the popular science imagination. In a September 1996 Chronicles book review of The Demon-

Haunted World, John Caiazza wrote:

> "...Sagan himself has demons that escape his scrutiny, including his left-wing political convictions (evident throughout the book), the belief in extraterrestrial intelligence, and the notorious nuclear winter scare of a few years back. Sagan also includes religion -- especially Christianity -- which he smears rather than attacks by a clever method of guilt by association. His discussion of religion is immediately linked to the witch-hunting craze of the 16th century, on which he spends a significant part of his book.... Sagan's attacks on religion ... are pervaded by the musty odor of   18th- and 19th- century atheism.
>
> "....Sagan skates on the surface of significant issues, glibly reducing the anxieties of the human heart to hormonal imbalances, mankind's search for transcendence to a remembrance of childhood fears, and the conflict between faith and reason to a sort of intellectual wrestling match between 'science' and 'anti-science.'"[367]

In The American Spectator's Enemies List, compiler P.J. O'Rourke contributed that "...Annoyance

factor seemed to outweigh public danger in readers' minds. Carl Sagan, Whoopi Goldberg and C. Everett

Koop ... each collected a larger number of blackballs than did the ACLU...."[368] And a donation, by one

Timothy A. Curry of Seattle, characterised as primary pests "'...Carl Sagan and Jonathan Schell, purveyors of

nuclear winter, the most important scientific theory since phlogiston, phrenology, and the Piltdown Man.'"[369]

If the 1960s and 1970s were the decades of Carl Sagan and Scientism, the 1980s and 1990s have been

the decades of Fritjof Capra, mysticism and the new [meta]physics. Capra's 1975 seminal study, The Tao of

Physics: An Exploration of the Parallels Between Modern Physics and Eastern Mysticism,[370] spawned a second-

string of copy-cat books penned by wanna-be Zen stud-muffins. For the purposes of our study, this writer has

selected three works by new physics commentators to compare with those of Fritjof Capra: Heinz R. Pagels'

The Cosmic Code,[371] Gerhard Staguhn's God's Laughter,[372] and Michael Talbot's Mysticism and the New

Physics.[373]

> "Five years ago, I had a beautiful experience which set me on a road that has led to the writing of this book. I was sitting by the ocean one late summer afternoon, watching the waves rolling in and feeling the rhythm of my being, when I suddenly became aware of my whole environment as being engaged in a gigantic cosmic dance.... As I sat on that beach my former experiences came to life; I 'saw' cascades of energy coming down from outer space, in which particles were created and destroyed in rhythmic pulses; I 'saw' the atoms of the elements and those of my body participating in this cosmic dance of energy; I felt its rhythm and I 'heard' its sound, and at that moment I knew that this was the Dance of Shiva, the Lord of Dancers worshiped by the Hindus."[374]

A great LSD trip? No ... thus began Fritjof Capra's Preface to The Tao of Physics, shortly after the dedication to Carlos Castaneda, Werner Heisenberg, Krishnamurti, Alan Watts et al.[375] When Capra referred to "Eastern Mysticism" in his subtitle, he meant the religious philosophies of Hinduism, Buddhism, and Taoism.[376] From these Eastern philosophies a New Age religious cosmogony/cosmology has arisen, the "cosmic religion" of science; wherein Eastern mysticism and the new physics converge. ("Cosmic religion" was a designation of Albert Einstein's whose imprimatur, as Darwin's, is still essential to contemporary scientists - - weird or not.)[377] For Capra, the Eastern [i.e., Taoist] world-view is "organic, better expressing the New Age inter-connectedness of all things, than the mechanistic [i.e., Newtonian] Western view. And the further science penetrates the submicroscopic world, the more the Western physicist -- like the Eastern mystic -- has come to regard Man and the macro-Cosmos as a sealed-in system of ever-moving, interacting, and inseparable parts. According to Fritjof Capra, there is an essential harmony between the wisdom of Western science and the spirit of Eastern mysticism: It takes the enlightenment of quantum [meta]physics to show us -- beyond all absolutist technology -- the Tao, the path.[378]

The new physics is different from classical physics in many ways. The discoveries of modern physics, of quantum theory and relativity theory during the early part of the twentieth century, forever changed concepts of time, space, matter, object, cause and effect. The classic, mechanistic world-view of Isaac Newton (1642-1727), had held scientific sway for almost three hundred years. Quantum theory and relativity theory [therefore] seem, to New Age physicists, to vindicate Eastern mysticism; [thereby] justifying a more subtle, holistic, and "organic" world-view.[379] But both theories originated in the extraordinary mind of Albert Einstein (1879-1955), and resulted from applying the Western scientific method. On publishing the two articles on his theories in 1905, Albert Einstein revolutionised the realm of scientific thought. In the Special Theory of Relativity, space was neither three-dimensional nor was time a separate entity. Both, rather, were so closely connected as to form an entirely new four-dimensional continuum, "space-time." Space and time, like matter and energy, had become interchangeable. As a consequence, the Newtonian universal flow of time was refuted; absolute space negated. Augmenting Einstein's Special Theory of Relativity of 1905 was his General Theory of Relativity of 1915, in which he proposed that the force of gravity had the effect of actually "curving" space and time. Thus, Einstein invalidated millennia-old Euclidean geometry. The quantum theory would be completed by a team of physicists during the 1920s.[380]

The close connection between space and time, and their interchangeability as space-time, has encouraged New Age scientists to believe that Eastern mysticism and the new physics might also be interchangeable. Fritjof Capra tells us that both world-views are essentially dynamic, containing time and change as intrinsic elements. The dynamic character of the universe and its indivisible oneness, are the two basic elements of the Eastern world-view. It is at the dynamic unity of the universe where Eastern mysticism and the new [age] physics converge.[381] Scientific knowledge of the sub-atomic world gained during the twentieth century, has revealed the dynamic nature of matter. The sub-atomic particles which constitute atoms making up matter, do not exist as separated particles but as interacting entities within an integrated network. These integrated, interacting particles involve a constant flow of energy, where particles -- in exchange -- are endlessly created and endlessly destroyed in continuous variations of energy patterns. The inter-penetrating flow of particles is the stable stuff composing the building-blocks of the macro-world; building-blocks which do not remain static, but rhythmically oscillate in infinite motion. This is the Cosmic Dance of Fritjof Capra, the dance of the Hindu god Śiva [the Destroyer], the cosmic dance of universal energy. For the new physicist it is the dance of sub-atomic matter, a continuous dance of creation and destruction involving the entire cosmos, the very basis of existence itself.[382] For the New Age physicist it is religion as well as science.

For laypersons like this writer, unfamiliar with the language of new physics or the New Age, the quantum world is one which Heinz Pagels has dubbed "quantum weirdness."[383] The properties of the quantum world with its lack of objectivity, indeterminancy, and weird-scientific theory of observer-created reality, have prompted Pagels to remark that "Quantum weirdness does not exist for the macroworld."[384] Michael Talbot, author of Mysticism and the New Physics, has quoted E.J. Zimmerman on the same paradox: "'.... When a vast number of ... microscopic systems ... interact, the simplest and most fundamental result is the creation of a space-time framework which gives validity to the classical notions of space and time, but on the macroscopic level only.'"[385] After ingesting all the quantum physics with a New Age spin, this writer was vastly relieved to learn that quantum weirdness doesn't exist for the macro-world. So despite continuous particle movement in the micro-world, a chair is still a chair after all, and a beautiful work of art will retain its shape, colour, and form after many millennia. And hadn't the great Albert Einstein resisted quantum weirdness, with its especially crazy notion of an observer-created reality? On Einstein, Pagels commented, "The fact that an observer was directly involved with the outcome of measurements clashed with his [Einstein's] deterministic world view that nature was indifferent to human choices."[386]

Weird science indeed! Although Heinz Pagels may be considered an atheistic/scientific naturalist,[387] in the Scientism mould of a Carl Sagan, he believes somewhat in "quantum weirdness" himself.[388] The theory of subjective reality is a favourite of New Age [meta]physics and its apologists. Michael Talbot, in his Introduction to Mysticism and the New Age Physics, has matter-of-factly declared: ".... [A]ccording to the new physics, there is no physical world 'out there.' Consciousness creates all."[389] In Chapter 1, titled 'Observer and Participant', Talbot quoted physicist Jack Sarfatti as having stated, "An idea of the utmost significance for the development of psycho-energetic systems ... is that the structure of matter may not be independent of consciousness!'"[390] The New Age even has its own Newspeak -- in the words of Michael Talbot, a "reality-structurer" is that "[p]ortion of the human consciousness which affects matter-space-time."[391] Ah, the [a]cute arcane language of the new physics! It reminds this writer of nonsensical new words such as "waitperson", "speciesism", "religionist", "other-abled" and the like. But the real heavyweight of the new quantum weirdness is none other than Dr. Tao himself, Fritjof Capra. Never at a loss for producing near-insurmountable verbiage, Capra has made his own pronouncements on creation-by-consciousness:

".... The fact that all the properties of particles are determined by principles closely related to the methods of observation would mean that the basic structures of the material world are determined, ultimately, by the way we look at this world; that the observed patterns of matter are reflections of patterns of mind.[392]

".... That this is so is one of the fundamental tenets of Eastern philosophy. The Eastern mystics tell us again and again that all things and events we perceive are creations of the mind, arising from a particular state of consciousness and dissolving again if this state is transcended...."[393]

Fritjof Capra must be accorded the last word again. In November 1994, a trendy new art-film, "Mindwalk", was making the grand tour of the Chardonnay and Camembert circuit. The film's theme is of two men who visit a mediaeval abbey in France, where a professor of the new physics lectures them for hours on the ultimate meaning of life.[394] "Mindwalk" is based on the written work of Fritjof Capra, and is a celluloid exposition of Dr. Tao's belief that quantum physics prove the truths found in Eastern mysticism. Christian commentator Charles Colson, in a review of "Mindwalk", brought quantum weirdness down to brass tacks: As quantum mechanics has discovered, parts of atoms -- such as electrons -- sometimes behave as particles (confined to micro-places) and sometimes as waves (spread out in macro-space). New Age scientists have resolved this apparent contradiction by hypothesising that electrons merely appear as particles or waves; depending on the nature of the experiment. But if scientific experimentation is to determine the properties of an electron, hitherto passive observers actively create the properties of that electron ... or so say the new [meta]physicists. The Eastern mystical connection is that the entire cosmos is a creation of our minds; "'consciousness creates all.'"[395] Weird science indeed!

The new physics perceives the universe as a three [four]-dimensional hologram, a dynamic web of inter-related events in which each segment of the web determines the complete structure of the whole.[396] Not surprisingly, the new physics views consciousness itself as a holographic paradigm, the closest -- perhaps, according to Michael Talbot -- the new physics can approach Eastern mysticism, without either one losing its identity. It is the holographic model of consciousness presented by Jack Sarfatti's "cosmic consciousness", Sir James Jeans' "giant thought", D. Bohm and B. Hiley's "unbroken wholeness"; a hologram of the universe described by Eastern mystics for centuries.[397] Cosmic consciousness and reality that the self creates? We are right back to the spacy New Age of Teilhard de Chardin and Shirley Maclaine.

Checking out any indicative philosophical background of Heinz Pagels (The Cosmic Code) and Michael Talbot (Mysticism and the New Physics), this writer found some revealing facts. During the early 1980s when The Cosmic Code was first published, The Village Voice praised it as "[f]ascinating stuff ... much less patronizing than, say, Carl Sagan, and I think more truthful about where and what science is." There were other glowing critiques from Saturday Review, The New Republic, Kirkus, and Chicago Sun-Times.[398] Except for Phillip E. Johnson's description of Pagels as "an atheist" and "scientific naturalist" (see note 387), this writer could only glean facts from a 1984 paperback edition of a Bantam New Age Book: "Heinz R. Pagels is the Executive Director of The New York Academy of Sciences and adjunct professor at Rockefeller University. Dr. Pagels lives in Manhattan with his wife, the historian Elaine Pagels, and their son, Mark."[399]

Bingo! Somewhere during the mid-1980s, this writer had seen Elaine Pagels' The Gnostic Gospels displayed on collegiate book-shop shelves. More recently, The Origin of Satan (Vintage, New York, 1996) by Elaine Pagels, had appeared on those same academic book-store shelves. Was this guilt-by-association, or just married-mind-set? At least it had been a lead (see Appendix A).

Finding pertinent information on Michael Talbot was far easier. Unlike Heinz Pagels who offered a bibliography but no end-notes and few foot-notes, Michael Talbot's Mysticism and the New Physics contained both. On the strength of his bibliography and end-notes, Talbot had solid New Age credentials. Some of his references included (in alphabetic order): Śri Aurobindo, Annie Besant, Fritjof Capra, Arthur C. Clarke, Aldous Huxley, Carl G. Jung, Marshall McLuhan, Swami Panchadasi, Carl Sagan, and William Irwin Thompson.[400] Their writings speak in volumes for themselves.

Where does all this confusing and conflicting new knowledge leave the average Joe? This writer's personal quantum physics puzzlement has been best expressed by regular-guy writer, Norman Mailer:

"[T]he hard peasant facts upon which Aquarius' [Mailer's] education had been built, the consciousness that numbers were real units, hard as hours of work and miles one walked, now had to be discarded into some waste-nexus of the mind, some stink of the unusable like the [New] Jersey flats. The real fact was that distance [or space and time] was now an abstract concept..."[401]

In 1915, Albert Einstein presented his General theory of Relativity, in which he stated that space is not three-dimensional and time is not a separate entity from space. According to Einstein, space and time are different aspects of the same something. Space-time comprises a four-dimensional mutually inter-penetrated continuum, in which there is no Newtonian flow of time.[402] As mentioned previously, Einstein's space was not that of classical Greek geometry, but a "curved" space-time revealing itself in (especially) gravitation.[403] As Heinz Pagels readily admitted, "the curvature of three-dimensional space (four dimensions if we include time) is hard for our minds to grasp...."[404] A fourth dimension, with space and time comprising different aspects of the same something, boggles this layman's mind and disturbs his imagination. But, somewhat reassuring for this writer, even though time appears in the new physics equation as a spatial distance, it is not merely a fourth dimension of space. German physicist Gerhard Staguhn has posited that the mathematical linking of the three dimensions of space with one of time, necessitates a minus sign in the equation: A plus sign would make time simply a fourth dimension of space.[405] The minus sign is crucially significant because:

"It determines that signals emitted by events cannot travel backward in four-dimensional space-time. The minus sign strictly separates past and future; it ensures that an event can impart itself only in the future. In other words, one can only observe cosmic events that lie in the past...[406]

"The structure of space-time -- that is, three dimensions of space and one dimension of time - guarantees the existence of the universe as the scene of events whose causes lie always in the past and whose effects lie always in the future.[407]

Surely modern physics is on the horns of a philosophical dilemma, personified by the (romantic) Scientism of Carl Sagan versus the (quantum) Taoism of Fritjof Capra; true science against weird science, although hardly a case of torah opposed to tantra. Already discussed has been the rejection by the new physics of Scientism as rigid reductionism, and Sagan's strong defense thereof.[408] Predictably, Capra has toed the countercultural line by deprecating "rational thought" and "scientific knowledge" as the solely acceptable kind of knowledge. "Intuitive knowledge" or "awareness" is just as valid or reliable.[409] Except for their respective attitudes on science and religion, however, Sagan and Capra have much in common on political philosophy. Both share[d] open scientific contempt for the personal beliefs of René des Cartes, the mathematical theories of Isaac Newton, and the scientific methodologies of Francis Bacon. As creatures of the philosophical-political Left, Sagan and Capra eschew Roman Catholic and evangelical Protestant Christianity; reject Western and Eastern patriarchal tradition in favour of gender feminism; prefer global government over the nation state; hold similar views on tobacco, alcohol, and health care (i.e., ClintonCare) as a means of population control; and agree on the enforced redistribution of the world's industrial wealth.[410]

Both physicists also share a strange, bio-energetic fascination for psychoanalyst Wilhelm Reich (1897-1957), although drawing vastly different conclusions;[411] plus an almost morbid enthusiasm for psychedelic psychotherapist Stanislav (and helpmeet, Christina) Grof.[412] Grof's name was the very first, at the top of a long roster, of those whom Capra acknowledged for aid and advice in his Author's Note (The Turning Point). Like Sagan's list of Leftist has-beens, Capra's constellation of faded stars are right out of the 1960s, but were far more politically active. Included are: John Lennon and Bob Dylan, Daniel Cohn-Bendit ("Danny the Red") and Angela Davis, Herbert Marcuse and the [entire] Esalen community et al.[413] In The Turning Point's final chapter, 'The Passage to the Solar Age', Capra selected anti-nuke nuisance Helen Caldicott, along with

Gaia (the Goddess) and (again) John ["Imagine"] Lennon for special mention.[414]

Why all this slavering adulation of and slavish association -- by both scientists -- with these [counter]cultural élites? The answer is simply that Carl Sagan was -- and Fritjof Capra is -- a charter member of the post-1960s cultural élite himself. Heinz Pagels has probably best expressed one reason for the omniscient hauteur and swollen egomania of the new physicists: "No great science was discovered in the spirit of humility."[415] An intellectual aggression, Pagels has asserted, that is necessary for uncovering the mysteries of the cosmos; an ... "intellectual intolerance [which] is crucial to the conduct of inquiry."[416] Pagels has even appealed to the Kabbala, that body of mystical writings so dear to Jewish secularists and New Agers alike, to emphasise his point. The yetser hara (in Hebrew) is the "evil impulse" of desiring completeness -- a sin as (Pagels should know) only God can (or may) achieve completeness. Yet the desire of modern physicists is to imitate God and achieve completeness by ultimately possessing a unified theory of all physics.[417] In other words, are new physicists playing God in their endeavour to seek answers to questions only the Almighty ought to know? Those answers -- and questions -- have as much spiritual value for us as scientific significance. In the meantime, though, we laymen can concur with regular-Joe writer, Norman Mailer, that we didn't understand space....

".... Nor did we comprehend time. There were numerous theories of time, but time remained as fundamentally mysterious as the notion that space was infinite, or matter consisted of individual atoms whose makeup was as complex as solar systems, and then proved more complex. Each year the number of subatomic particles discovered was greater. To laymen who had grown up on electrons, protons, neutrons and positrons, there were now mesons and photons and mumesons, still more names and concepts no layman could follow, and science had less certainty today about the periodic table of the elements and the structure of the atom than at the turn of the century...."[418]

Author's note: Heinz Pagels was killed in a freak hiking accident in 1988, and Mark Pagels died at age 6 1/2 years. Elaine Pagels, a professor of religion at Princeton, dedicated her book, Adam, Eve, and the Serpent, to Mark. Special thanks to Ms. Holly Knowles Fisher of Port Angeles, Washington.

Section B: Earth and the Planets

"[E]ach generation of scientists rewrites its textbooks in such a way as to select from the past what is still considered valid and to suppress the multitude of errors and false starts that are also a part of the history of science."

-- Theodore Roszak, The Making of a Counter Culture, alluding to a quote by Thomas Kuhn, historian of science

This writer has never been a science fiction buff, and only knew who Arthur C. Clarke was from watching Arthur C. Clarke's World of Strange Powers on cable TV. This programme had been featured on the Discovery channel (DSC) during the early 1990s. Then in the mid-1990s, also on cable TV, came re-runs of "2001: A Space Odyssey" (1968, directed by Stanley Kubrick), followed by a Turner Super Station sweeps-week clincher, "2010" (1984, starring Roy Scheider). Of course, this writer had heard of "2001: A Space Odyssey"--ad infinitum--ever since the film had been released in 1968.[419] At that time, the writer had been a U.S. Army sports specialist stationed at USAREUR HQ in Heidelberg, West Germany, and had turned down impassioned appeals from fellow GIs to see the movie showing on post. Not inclined to sit through a long sci-fi offering, the writer (a Spec. 5 in 1968 who far preferred "spaghetti westerns" with Lee Van Cleef) chose instead to down some German lagers at the enlisted men's club. But a quarter century later, times--and the man--had changed. Although still not interested in science fiction, the writer had since become very interested in science fact ... and Arthur C. Clarke. So this time around he watched both "2001: A Space Odyssey" and "2010."[420]

"2001: A Space Odyssey" seems to have been seen by every sentient being on planet Earth, and there is no point in re-reviewing the film. It appears that the real legacy of "2001: A Space Odyssey" is HAL, the mellow-voiced computer that ultimately went haywire and took control of the space mission. Scheduled for publication on 12 January 1997 was a book titled HAL's Legacy: 2001's Computer as Dream and Reality.[421] The authors include Marvin Minsky, an MIT professor of computer science; and one David Stork (who conceived the book's central idea), a scientist who was inspired by HAL to attempt developing lip-reading computers.[422] The 12th of January 1997 is the significant sci-fi "date" on which HAL became operational.[423] The writer remained nonplussed throughout the viewing of both films. The suspenseful relief from boredom in "2001: A Space Odyssey" came when HAL refuses an astronaut entrance through the [landing] pod bay doors. ("'Open the ... doors, Hal', the commander says. 'I'm sorry, Dave, I'm afraid I can't do that,' HAL replies.")[424] Comedic relief from ennui in "2010" arrived when alpha tough-guy actor, Roy Scheider, pretends to play tender father to cinematic son. And "2010" ends with the climactic appearance--rather than the apparent creation--of a second sun named...Lucifer!

On 6 September 1996 PBS-TV aired a programme, "The Colours of Infinity", introduced by Arthur C. Clarke. The show gloriously displayed the "fractal geometry" of the Mandelbrot Set. This writer understood little of "The Colours of Infinity", but noticed that ageing countercultural rockers, Pink Floyd, provided the background music. The documentary also made honourable mention of New Age guru Śri Aurobindo. All of the above, plus the tenor of his two series on cable TV,[425] leave no doubt that venerable and distinguished astronomer, Arthur C. Clarke, is just another old atheist after all; complete with the now-familiar anti-Judaeo-Christian bias. One would expect less psychic bile from the inventor of the communications satellite and past chairman of the British Interplanetary Society. But Arthur C. Clarke has become an "Old Scratch"-type rôle model for younger New Age metaphysicists like Michael Talbot, author of Mysticism and the New Physics.[426] In his Fritjof Capraesque copy-cat work, Talbot dwelt briefly on Clarke's 1953 sci-fi book, Childhood's End.[427] In the sci-fi novel, Clarke envisioned Earth's first contact with ETIs. A star-fleet of huge space-ships hover over Earth for many years without descending. The aliens--they call themselves the Overlords--are in constant radio contact with Earth, but for those many years have avoided revealing themselves. After several generations, the Overlords finally come down to Earth from their immense star-ships. Michael Talbot has explained why it took so long:

"....The reason for their [the Overlords'] seclusion becomes obvious: the Overlords are beings from our [Earthly] mythology, exact likenesses of the devil. When asked if they have visited the [E]arth before and if the legends of the devil are some sort of memory of this visit, they [the Overlords] reply, 'It was not precisely a memory'. You already had proof that time is more complex than your science ever imagined. For that memory was not of the past, but of the future--."[428]

Today, Arthur C. Clarke is a prunish, superannuated spiritual soul-brother of the late Carl E. Sagan. For although gleefully debunking both religious "superstition" and borderline/paradoxical science, Clarke and Sagan seriously inquir[ed]: "Is anyone out there?" In his The Exploration of Space first published in 1951,[429] Clarke concluded a UFO-skeptical chapter with some thoughts on possible prehistorical visits of Earth by ETIs:

"Countless times in geological history strange ships may have drifted down through the skies of Earth, and left again with records of steaming seas, the first clumsy amphibians creeping upon the beaches and much later still, the giant reptiles. A few of those ships may have come from other planets of the Sun, but most must have been strangers to our Solar System, traveling from star to star [the ETis in their UFOs] in their search for knowledge. And some day, they may return."[430]

Before ending The Exploration of Space, Clarke gave us an eerie premonition to what would be a globalist-inspired work published thirty-five years later, in 1986--July 20, 2019: Life in the 21st Century.[431] For in 1951 Clarke prophesied: "We are slowly...evolving from that [local-yokel] mentality towards a world outlook. Few things will do more to accelerate...evolution than the conquest of space. It is not easy to see how the more extreme forms of nationalism can long survive when men have seen the Earth in its true perspective as a single small globe against the stars."[432] By "extreme forms of nationalism", Clarke probably equated patriotism of any kind (excepting British, of course) with Italian fascism, German nazism, or Russian communism. (This writer wonders how Clarke regards the Singhalese-Tamil civil war in his adopted Sri Lanka?) In 1986, Clarke ventured "[W]hen we have the Global Family ['The United States of Earth'], we will no longer need the United Nations. But until then...."[433] This is the form of unitary UnoMundo which New Agers pine for. And Carl Sagan, like Clarke so questioning of motives in religion, would--with Clarke-- be in automatic political accord. Arthur C. Clarke closed The Exploration of Space with a statement straight from the weird-science textbook:

"The world in which we live is drenched with invisible radiations, from the radio waves which we have just discovered coming from Sun and stars, to the cosmic rays whose origin is still one of the prime mysteries of modern physics. These things we have discovered within the last generation [1951], and we cannot guess what still lies beneath the threshold of the senses--through recent studies in paranormal psychology hint that the search may be only beginning."[434]

What Arthur C. Clarke is to New Age astronomy, Jeremy Rifkin is to New Age geosophy. They are both men of power and influence; Clarke in the planetary realm and Rifkin the terrestrial. But here all similarity ends. For unlike the up-front Arthur C. Clarke, Jeremy Rifkin is a Protean man of many masques, any one of which he may assume at any given moment. Looking somewhat like "Mean Gene" Okerlund of World Championship Wrestling (WCW), Jeremy Rifkin's face has appeared on U.S. television discussion/documentary shows, ranging from cable and public TV to faux-Christian programming. Jeremy Rifkin is virtually indefinable, being all things to many people. He is, ostensibly, concerned with The Earth.

Similar to the most annoying C. Everett Koop, Jeremy Rifkin is a nittering, nattering nutrition and nicotine

nazi. He is also an eco-meddler who has ridden the cresting wave of environmentalism to its absolute limit.[435]

Jeremy Rifkin's name appears everywhere. He has even made The American Spectator's Enemies List, being

nominated--along with PBS commentator Bill Moyers and Rep. Barney Frank (D-Mass.)--by contributor Peter

Cuikas of Leominster, Mass.[436] Jeremy Rifkin's name may be found in New Age [meta]physicist Fritjof

Capra's The Turning Point bibliography, right under that of Wilhelm ("Dr. Orgone") Reich.[437] As Wilhelm

Reich and the contemporary William Irwin Thompson, Jeremy Rifkin has eschewed modern technology

without seeming to comprehend that it has long since interpenetrated New Age consciousness (and vice versa).

Jeremy Rifkin's name finally--for the purposes of this study--showed up on Kirkpatrick Sale's holier-than-thou

list of neo-Luddites in Rebels against the Future, to wit:

> "Jeremy Rifkin is the president of the Foundation on Economic Trends, a Washington citizens' lobby
> fighting the spread of biotechnologies and the threat of global warming, and the author of a number of books
> attacking the foundations of industrial society."[438]

Although Rifkin did his undergraduate studies at U. Pennsylvania's Wharton School of Finance, his

statist models have been Mahatma Gandhi's India and Chairman Mao's China. The roiling, toiling masses of

the globe's two most overpopulated nations might help explain Rifkin's doom-and-gloom, mercilessly

Malthusian outlook. On the back cover of Rifkin's Entropy: A New World View, is a review by the

Minneapolis Tribune that tersely praised it as being "...an appropriate successor to...Silent Spring, The Closing

Circle, The Limits to Growth, and Small is Beautiful [alarmist books all]."[439] As Entropy: A New World

View is to serve as a main secondary source for this part of the study, the afore-mentioned titles have been

fair warning. Before Entropy: A New World View was first published in 1980, Rifkin had also written

Common Sense II, Own Your Own Job, Who Should Play God? and The Emerging Order (both with Ted

Howard), and The North Will Rise Again (with Randy Barber). Since 1980, Rifkin has come out with

Declaration of a Heretic and, more notably, Time Wars: The Primary Conflict in Human History (New York:

Touchstone Books, 1989). More recently, Rifkin has produced The End of Work: The Decline of the Global

Labor Force and the Dawn of the Post-Market Era (Putnam Books, 1995).

In Entropy: A New World View, Rifkin so early on as the Author's Note, divided his readers [a generous portion of humanity] into three categories: Those who [after reading Rifkin] regard the immutable Law of Entropy as (1) not convincing enough to restrain human action against the planet; (2) confining humankind inside an escape-proof cosmic prison; and (3) a Great Truth [pointed out by Rifkin] which sets humankind free. According to Rifkin, "The first group [the eco-criminals] will continue to uphold the existing world paradigm. The second group [the eco-clueless] will be without a world view. The third group [the Rifkin eco-enlightened] will be the harbingers of the [N]ew [A]ge,"[440]

The Entropy Law, the second law of thermodynamics, simply states that in the universe as a whole, disorder increases as time goes on (Sagan: 1995). The first law of thermodynamics declares that all matter/energy in the universe is constant, that matter/energy cannot be created or destroyed. Matter/energy's form may change but never its essence. The second law, the Entropy Law, says that matter/energy can be changed in one direction only; from usable to unusable, from available to unavailable, from ordered to disordered. In other words, whenever a semblance of order is created anywhere on earth or in the universe, a greater disorder is cause in the surrounding environment.[441] For doomsdayers such as Rifkin, this immutable law became perfect grist for his Malthusian mill. To Rifkin, the Entropy Law destroys the whole notion of (or hope for) progress, that man's science and technology are able to manage a more ordered world. But New Ager Rifkin quickly qualified the iron-clad Entropy Law vis-à-vis the spiritual plane:

"The spirit is a nonmaterial dimension where there are no boundaries and no fixed limits to attend to. The relationship of the physical to the spiritual world is the relationship of a small part to the larger unbound whole within which it unfolds. While the Entropy Law governs the world of time, space, and matter, it is, in turn, governed by the primordial spiritual force that conceived it."[442]

Before the end of his introductory 'World Views' chapter, Rifkin concluded by invoking the Ourobouric Concept of the classical Hellenes: "History is seen not as a cumulative progression toward perfection but as an ever repeating cycle moving from order to chaos."[443]

In this analysis of scientific versus magickal views of the world and the cosmos, we find differing interpretations of the laws of thermodynamics, the "science of complexity'" (Capra: 1988). But as Fritjof Capra has indicated in The Turning Point, the second law of thermodynamics--the Entropy Law-- is regularly violated in microscopic systems, which consist of few molecules. Macroscopic systems contain vast numbers of molecules; for instance a cubic centimetre of air holds ca. ten billion billion (10^{19}) molecules.[444] This is the obverse, in effect, of Heinz Pagels' observation that "Quantum weirdness [i.e., in the microworld] does not exist for the macroworld" (Pagels: 1984). But it is the interpretations of the physicists, both naturalistic and New Age, which affect us. In the metaphysical mind of Fritjof Capra, the Entropy Law is a "grim picture", involving as it does the isolated cosmic system having reached maximum entropy, or "'heat death'". All activity in that state has ceased, and all materials have evenly diffused throughout the void at like temperature. The Entropy Law, a product of [despised] Newtonian mechanics, has been effectively challenged (if not displaced) by nineteenth century Maxwellian electrodynamics and Darwinian evolutionism. The latter theories clearly went away beyond the imaginings of Newton and Descartes, with Darwinism seeing the biosphere evolving from disorder to order with increasing complexity.[445] Capra has postulated that

the first three decades of the twentieth century have all but dismissed the Law of Entropy (that "grim picture" applied to the cosmos rather than to biological evolution):

"Two developments in physics, culminating in relativity theory and in quantum theory, shattered all the principal concepts of the [hated] Cartesian world view and [despised] Newtonian mechanics. The notion of absolute space and time, the elementary solid particles, the fundamental material substance, the strictly causal nature of physical phenomena, and the objective description of nature--none of these concepts could be extended to the new domains into which physics was now penetrating."[446]

Entropy is, simply put, a measure of the amount of energy which can no longer be converted into work; or a quantity which measures the degree of evolution in a physical system. The term "entropy" is a combination of "energy" and Greek tropos, the word for evolution or transformation. Although "entropy" was first coined by German physicist, Rudolf Clausius, in 1868, the second law of thermodynamics was first formulated forty-one years earlier by French army officer, Sadi Carnot, in terms of thermal (steam) engine technology. The significance was the introduction into physics the idea of irreversible processes, of an "arrow of time".[447] Carl Sagan queried: "[I]f we live in a Universe in which the present Big Bang expansion will slow, stop, and be replaced by a contraction, might the Second Law be reversed? Can effects precede causes?"[448] Gerhard Staguhn has described an eerie future universe of maximum entropy--a universe without natural processes with a uniform temperature; an absolute stagnant universe in eternal balance, a cosmos terminated by heat: "In the state of maximum entropy there will be no time either. Time is, so to speak, just a function of the increasing entropy in the universe, reflecting the gradual transition of energy from order to disorder."[449]

What is truly significant about the Entropy Law for this study, is its effect on the cosmology of commentators like Jeremy Rifkin. For the latter believes that energy, per se, is not only the basis of human culture but life itself. With this in mind, Rifkin has expostulated that power within a society is wielded by whomever controls the "exosomatic instruments", which are used to transform, exchange, and discard energy. Ergo, those controlling the energy flow-line decide how work in society is designated, how economic rewards will be allocated among constituencies. Thus, according to Rifkin, class divisions--entailing privilege, exploitation, and poverty--are ultimately determined by the controllers of the energy flow-line.[450] The Protean Rifkin has designated the second law of thermodynamics as "the emerging entropy paradigm", although it was scientifically formulated during the last century. Furthermore, Rifkin has posited, "The ancient Greeks and the medieval Christian scholars...had intuited it [the Entropy Law] and integrated its central truth into their cultures and their world views."[451]

Jeremy Rifkin predicated an entire book, an environmental neo-Ludditic "strawberry statement", on the second law of thermodynamics. A Malthusian mind-set (similar to that of Paul Ehrlich or Norman Myers) became apparent about a third of the way into Entropy: A New World View, along with the invariably failed prophesies which, in another less grave context, would actually amuse the reader. Notably egregious examples of energy entropy were:

1. A study conducted during the late 1970's under the auspices of MIT, involving experts from industry, government, and academia concluded that the worldwide supply of oil would "'fail to meet increasing demands before the year 2000"'. The MIT report predicted that even if oil prices rose 50% above current 1970s levels, the world would likely experience an oil crisis between 1985 and 1995.[452]
2. A concurrent report [1978] undertaken by [none less] than the Trilateral Commission varied but slightly in its forecast: The Commission concluded that global demands for oil would exceed supply by the mid-1990s.[453]
3. In the Bulletin of Atomic Scientists, Emile Benoit of Columbia [U.] wrote that if world oil consumption continued at the 1978 rate, existing reserves would be exhausted within twenty-five years [i.e., 2003 A.D.]. Even if new discoveries of oil were to equal four times the present [1978] reserves, new finds would only buy an additional twenty-five years [i.e., 2028 A.D.] before total depletion of all global oil reserves.[454]
4. In his book The Twenty-ninth Day, ecologist Lester Brown [later president of Worldwatch Institute] estimated that there were enough oil reserves to supply every American with about 500 barrels. When refined, computed Brown, a barrel of oil yields ca. forty-two gallons of gasoline. Therefore, conjectured Brown, if the average American drove 10,000 miles per year, in a big car getting around ten miles per gallon, the driver would use up his entire remaining share of the world's oil reserve in less than twelve years.[455]

And regarding nuclear energy, Rifkin referenced none other than the nuclear-mad Helen Caldicott:

5. The Union of Concerned Scientists conjectured [1978] that by the year 2000 A.D., close to 15,000 Americans will have perished as a direct result of nuclear reactor leaks and accidents. Should there occur a full "China Syndrome" melt-down, the UCS prognosticated that 100,000 humans might die, with thousands of square miles of land contaminated for years to come.[456]

This writer has often wondered if Carl Sagan and Jonathan Schell, purveyors of nuclear winter, were ever publickly challenged? Or, when nuclear winter failed to materialise, were not-so-gently reminded: "We thought not!?" Surely those of the pre - 1998 unfulfilled prophesies, confidently enumerated as fact by the card-stacking Jeremy Rifkin, are to be considered ludicrous in 1997? The writer seriously doubts that the other dire predictions will prove accurate, either. Meanwhile, in 1997, Jeremy Rifkin sits in his (surely) sumptious office at his Washington, D.C.-based Foundation on Economic Trends; ferrety fingers drumming on his desk-top [modem], figuring out further ways to flim-flam the already over-flummoxed American people. Rifkin and his ilk are the same fussy meddlers who forced child-killing auto air-bags -- pro bono publico -- onto the American driver. But this is what "citizens' lobbyists" do to insure their (surely) sumptious life-style. Jeremy Rifkin will continue to dispense his alarmist propnostications to a gullible public for a goodly price, flowing with the current wisdom under the guise of doing good, until a lonely reader sometime in 2020 A.D. sits up in his bunk and says, "Hey! None of this came to pass!" All that nay-saying and fear-mongering by such as Jeremy Rifkin was just so much stuff and nonsense after all. This writer envisions Jeremy Rifkin -- somewhat like the Clintons on arising every morning -- speculating, "How are we going to fool them today?"

In what manner, then, does Jeremy Rifkin disagree or, if not, rationalise his entropic views (of the cosmos) with that of the new metaphysics? A come-along, get-along type regarding popular opinion, Rifkin would have to effect more twists and turns than the Ourobouric serpent in proving that Entropy: A New World View really was a New World View; that it was in absolute accord with the new[age] metaphysics, as espoused by contemporary Zen stud muffins of quantum mechanics. Slowly but surely, Rifkin brought forth his enviro-economic thesis throughout Entropy: A New World View in small but subtle doses; in a sort of punctuated equilibria. Behind every economic policy statement, Rifkin informed us, "looms [sic] the shadows of [Isaac] Newton, [René] Descartes, [Francis] Bacon, [John] Locke, and [Adam] Smith."[457] Today, as when Scottish economist Adam Smith wrote The Wealth of Nations more than two centuries ago, all economic systems are based on classical mechanical doctrine. Indeed, the entire Enlightenment weltanschauung is founded on the principles of Newtonian mechanics, Cartesian mathematics, and Baconian scientific

methodology.[458] It logically follows that both capitalist (free market) and communist (socialist command)

economic assumptions are grounded in these Western concepts. It was there that Rifkin neatly dove-tailed

his entropic world-view with that of the new [age] [meta]physics. So slime-eel smooth, in fact, was Rifkin's

transitional metamorphosis that it left this reader gaping:

> "The old Newtonian view that treats all phenomena as isolated components of matter, or fixed stocks, has given way to the idea that everything is part of a dynamic flow. Classical physics, which recognized only two kinds of classifications, things that exist and things that don't exist, has been challenged and overthrown. Things don't just 'exist' as some kind of isolated fixed stock. This static view of the world has been replaced by the view that everything in the world is always in the process of becoming. Even nonliving phenomena are continually changing. This process of becoming is really nothing more than the entropy law at work...."[459]

Was the above passage penned by Jeremy Rifkin ... or Fritjof Capra? Or was it written, perhaps, by

Heinz Pagels ... or Gerhard Staguhn ... or even Michael Talbot? No matter; the continuum of energy

transformation was more than sufficient to justify Rifkin's "It's a Small World After All" entropic agendum.

Neater still was how Rifkin correlated and paralleled an energy environment based on [fixed] "stocks" (fossil

fuels), to one of [dynamic] "flows" (solar power and renewable resources).[460] But Jeremy Rifkin, that man of

a thousand faces, had yet another trick up his sleeve -- a solution calling for a (gasp!) Christian stewardship

of planet Earth![461] This "Christian" stewardship was not to be of the FundiGreen (i.e., fundamentalist) variety

so disparaged by Alvin Toffler in Powershift (1991), absolutely not! New Ager Rifkin's Christian stewardship

doctrine was of a decidedly leftist hue, of unresistant acceptability to liberal "mainstream" theologians. Rifkin

enumerated, and excoriated, the conditions and mind-sets in opposition to the new Christian eco-stewardship:

> .... [P]rivate ownership of resources, increased centralization of power, elimination of diversity, greater reliance on science and technology, the refusal to set limits on production and consumption, the fragmentation of human labor into separate and autonomous spheres of operation, the reductionist approach to understanding life and the interrelationships between phenomena, and the concept of progress as a process of continually transforming the natural world into a more valuable and more ordered human-made environment have long been considered as valid pursuits and goals in the modern world. Every single one of these items and scores of others that make up the operating assumptions of the age of growth are inimical to the principles of ecology, a low-entropy economic framework, and, most importantly, the newly defined stewardship doctrine".[462]

Rifkin foresaw danger if the remnants of Christendom failed to embrace his proposed new stewardship

doctrine. The emerging (early 1980s) evangelical fervour could be harnessed and "ruthlessly exploited by right-

wing and corporate interests."[463] Furthermore, Rifkin warned of dark consequences if the religious revival provided the "cultural backdrop" for a potential fascist take-over of the U. S. A., during a weakened "period of long-range economic decline."[464] This possible period of economic decline would result, of course, from not heeding the economic/ecological advisements of Jeremy Rifkin.

The final pronouncements in Jeremy Rifkin's <u>Entropy: A New World View</u> contained no surprises at all; certainly not a new world view. The [small] world view of Jeremy Rifkin has been prevalent ever since the late 1960s, and has been spun, expanded, polished and presented in other [dis]guises since then throughout the 1970s, 1980s, and 1990s. Rifkin was original in that he approached energy- ecologism from the oblique angle of the second law of thermodynamics, the Entropy Law, and <u>that</u> was assuredly a new tack in promulgating politicised pseudo - science. Rifkin was -- and is -- merely one more New Age geosophist marching in lock-step with his fraudulent fellow-environmentalist Cassandras; only smarter hence richer.

Section C: The Ocean and Seas

"In the last analysis magic, religion and science are nothing but theories of thought; and as science has supplanted its predecessors, so it may be hereafter be itself superceded by some more perfect hypothesis, perhaps by some totally different way of looking at the phenomena -- of registering the shadows on the screen -- of which we in this generation can form no idea".

- Sir James G. Frazer (1854-1941), author of The Golden Bough

It is late May 1997, and the writer is sitting at his desk with his final issue of Currents before him. Currents is the informational newsletter put out by Friends of the Arthur D. Feiro Marine Lab in Port Angeles, Washington. The writer had been a "Friend of the Lab" for several years, but the membership cost of Currents had gone up and ... fish metaphysics had insinuated itself into the editorship. An example of this new ec (environmental/evolutionary correctness) was reflected in a Currents article: A new (live) Pacific octopus (O.dofleini) was on exhibit at the laboratory, and we, the people, were welcome to come and view the cephalopod; the public [i.e., plebeians] might even be "privileged to touch her" ... if the captive mollusc so desired. This eco-treat, naturally, was never denied the docents or permanent parties [those-in-the-know] at the marine lab.

Similarly, the Port Angeles Branch of the North Olympic Library System had gone pc and (PC) some years ago. As a "Friend of the Library", this writer had noticed the profusion of New Age titles which proliferated alongside computerisation. The P. A Branch was scheduled to move to august new quarters (1998), presently being erected next to an extensively-expanding Holy Trinity Lutheran Church. Thus the library and the church would be high-price, ex-urban neighbours and New Age soul-sisters.[465] Not to be outdone, the powers-that-be at the Arthur D. Feiro Marine Lab [i.e., Peninsula College] had themselves long contemplated expensive renovation on P. A. City Pier. In a hard-scrabble, cash-strapped town like Port Angeles (whose I. T. T. Rayonier pulp-paper mill closed its gates 1 March 1997), it seemed solely the agencies of state and federal government that thrived ... and sometimes the big-tent, feel-good churches.

A large poster is featured in a window of the Arthur D. Feiro Marine Lab. The wall-sized print is from the National Museum of Natural History, Department of Pal[a]eobiology, and depicts "The Arch[a]ean Age .... Three Billion, Five Hundred Million Years Ago .... "Pastel blues, off-whites, and fleecy swirls describe a primordial world of Aztlán cones and Aztec volcanoes, a graffito-type mural worthy of a fashionably-enraged East L.A. barrio artiste. But does the flippant Dept. of Paleobiology have any inkling of how many aeons comprise 3,500,000 years? Or is it just more "millions and billions", arbitrarity thrown out by "science-popularizers" as science junk-food to a credulously omnivorous populace? Was the Archean Age the oldest part of the Precambrian era, the Archaeozic Period? Or was it just more scholastic cuteness to impress the uneducated waiting outside the marine lab? For the writer these questions were moot as he hadn't entered the premises for years. With renovation and expansion, the Arthur D. Feiro Marine Lab will concomitantly grow yet more eco- and evo-correct. Surely this monolithic outlook was not what Art Feiro (1930-1982) had in mind![466]

Salmonid metaphysics and the cetacean religion were extensively covered in Part I of this chapter. In the section below, this writer examines the pantheistic philosophy which sees the sea it [her]self as part of the Goddess. And no one marine biologist elevated the sea to sacrosanct status earlier than Rachel L. Carson, authoress of The Silent Spring (1962). Silent Spring was the environmentalist book of the early 1960s, and set the grim tone of eco-imprimatur for all the alarmist scribblings to come. Rachel Louise Carson (1907-1964) studied biology at Pennsylvania College for Women, received her MA from the Johns Hopkins University in 1932, and then did graduate work at the Marine Biological Laboratory at Woods Hole, Massachusetts. Next, Carson taught at the U. of Maryland and at Johns Hopkins. After that, Carson had a distinguished career at the U.S. Bureau of Fisheries (the later U.S. Fish and Wildlife Service), where she was marine biologist and editrix-in-chief. By 1941 she had written Under the Sea-Wind, The Sea Around Us in 1951 (which won the National Book Award for that year), The Edge of the Sea (1955), and the falsely prophetic Silent Spring in 1962. For the purposes of this report, the writer has chosen The Edge of the Sea as pre-1962 Carson exemplar.[467] Silent Spring set a pseudo-science precedent: Rachel Carson predicted the biological end of the world by 1982 (twenty years later); in 1967, Paul Ehrlich came out with The Population Bomb, soothsaying starvation and overpopulation by 1980.[468] Needless to relate, there was neither population bomb nor global starvation in 1980, and the planet was still viable in 1982. But, perhaps to be charitable, The Silent Spring served as a needed wake-up call to an over-consuming, over-polluting American society of what might happen if the life-style continued as it had.

The Edge of the Sea was a volume in the Signet Science Library, books by leading scientists and educators to -- ostensibly -- present non-technical [i.e., proto-metaphysical] explanations of the latest discoveries, developments, and knowledge in science. A grant of a Guggenheim Fellowship helped finance Rachel Carson's first year of study, and some of her field-work along the Maine-to-Florida tide-lines.[469] Carson was not to disappoint her neo-Darwinian mentors. In the Preface she wrote: "For us as living creatures it [the sea shore] has special meaning as an area in or near which some entity that could be distinguished as life first drifted in shallow waters -- reproducing, evolving, yielding that endlessly varied stream of living things that has surged through time and space to occupy the earth."[470] Although the scientific/metaphysical battle is immediately joined, Carson became bolder in showing her colours as The Edge of the Sea unfolded:

"There is a common thread that links ... the spectacle of life in all its varied manifestations as it appeared, evolved, and sometimes died out. Underlying the beauty of the spectacle there is meaning and significance. It is the elusiveness of that meaning that haunts us, that sends us again and again into the natural world where the key to the riddle is hidden. It sends us back to the edge of the sea, where ... the forces of evolution are at work today, as they have been since the appearance of what we know as life; and where the spectacle of living creatures faced by the cosmic realities of their world is crystal clear."[471]

What meaning and what significance? Which key to which riddle? Is it the key of random evolutionism, to the riddle of natural scientism, that will unlock the elusive answer; thereby providing meaning and significance to [L]ife? Rachel Carson clearly thought so. In some umbral future envisioned by Carson, the ocean surf will grind the rocks -- at the edge of the sea -- to sand, returning the coast (the U.S. Eastern littoral) to its original state. Then -- in Carson's mind's eye -- those coastal forms will blend and merge in a shifting, kaleidoscopic pattern..."in which there is no finality, no ultimate and fixed reality -- earth becoming fluid as the sea itself."[472] Rachel Carson concluded The Edge of the Sea, confessing to an uneasiness that some universal truth lay just beyond her grasp; the elusive answer to the mystery of life itself.[473] This writer seriously doubts if the [neo-]Darwinist religion (the Buddha cum Evolutionism) provided Rachel Carson with either an answer to the mystery of life, or meaning to her own, before she died in 1964.

The writer begs the reader's indulgence for the brief telling of a neo-Darwinian parable. Surely the sorriest sermon (pathetic, really) on the (rarely challenged) Darwinist religion was delivered (ca. 1995) by the

PBS-TV programme The New Explorers, produced by wanna-be evolution-evangelist Bill Kurtis. In the particular episode presented, an elderly (presumably) British faux-colonial couple (perhaps from Adelaide, Australia, or Christchurch, N.Z.) investigated the thirteen sub-species of "Darwin's finches" on the Galápagos Islands. Dressed in safari dust-jackets and khaki shorts (showing dessicated shanks), the creaky couple self-importantly pointed out differences in seed sizes and finch-bill variations. (These micro-evolutionary changes had come about as a result of a severe island drought during 1977.) Accordingly, the prissy and pernickety buff-clad couple behaved as if the greater availability of past-drought seed (hence the predominance of larger-beaked finches) indicated a proof-positive theophany of their great god, Charles Darwin. The irony of the entire exercise, staged by a gloating Bill Kurtis, was that natural selection (in a micro-evolutionary sense) had been proven once again ... but little else. (And all could conceivably be reversed again under antonymic condition.)[474] But the fussily fastidious, faux-colonial pair on camera acted blissfully unaware of the anti-climatical nature of their shared exposition. The New Explorers ended with a parting shot of their weathered, tan-wearing bodies; with a final close-up of their wrinkled, withered visages which expressed the combined all-accepting, smugly-certain look of the true [Darwinist] Believer.

An unoriginal but early, equally-eco-anxious Cassandra to succeed Rachel Carson was Wesley Marx, author of The Fragile Ocean. Indeed, Rachel Carson had only lain in her grave for six years before Wesley Marx's book was published in 1970. That year marked the very first Earth Day (22 April), and also the high-tide of environmentalist panic. A quick perusal by the reader of The Fragile Ocean's back cover proves the point. Among the advertised better-known works were: S/S/T and Sonic Boom Handbook by William A. Shurcliff; Perils of the Peaceful Atom: The Myth of Safe Nuclear Power Plants by Richard Curtis and Elizabeth Hogan; and The Environmental Handbook: Prepared for the First National Environmental Teach-In, edited by Garrett De Bell. The titles themselves amply reflect the authors' mind-set.

Of Wesley Marx's "deep concern" with the frail ocean, a Ballantine Books editor made his pitch: "Impassioned in his indictment of Man's ruthless exploitation of the seas, Wesley Marx also writes with lyric joy, reminiscent of Rachel Carson's, of the ocean's splendor, communicating his sense of wonder at its enormous power and fertility, as well as his growing fear for its future."[475] In his acknowledgements, Wesley

Marx flatteringly deferred to his inspirational muse: "Any author who purports to discuss the ocean is indebted to a woman who contributed so gracefully to its public appreciation -- Miss Rachel Carson."[476] Also in the frontispiece, and to appear later in the book, is the Wesley Marx theme (Wesleyan? Marxist?), a single sentence which sets the tone throughout The Frail Ocean:

"Are we perhaps fated to mark the ocean with ruin, to plunder, pollute, and contend until we have a ghost ocean bereft of all but the voice of its waves?"[477]

What was once The Cruel Sea -- a World War II story written by Nicholas Montsarrat (1910-1979) --had become The Frail Ocean by 1970. It is all very "old hat" today, but Sierra Club-type ecologism was still fairly unfamiliar to the vast majority of North Americans in 1970. Readers and TV viewers could still become indignant and concerned about the environment, both terrestrial and marine, for the very first time. And Wesley Marx covered it all -- starting with the kelp forests and riverine/estaurine nurseries for anadromous fish from the Aroostook River, Maine, to the St. Johns River, Florida. Marx enumerated these "upward-running" fish ranging from alewives, Atlantic salmon, sturgeon, shad, to striped bass.... The whole topped off with the obligatory Gray Whales Homily as clincher. Among the many Marxian threats listed were: Red tides, beach erosion, dam-building, oil spills, land reclamations, sanitary fills, sewage outfalls, dredging projects, private marina construction, the dumping of refuse and industrial wastes off the U.S. mainland, residual atomic wastes in Micronesia; ending at Minamata mercury poisoning in 1960s Japan.[478]

It was all there, all to be rehashed and re-digested, discussed forever on the air-waves and scribbled in literally thousands of like books, ever since 1962. But to his credit, imitative as he might have been of Rachel Carson, Wesley Marx did write his opus magnum during the mid-late sixties, and undertook a thorough study utilising primary sources. Marx produced both instructive and interesting chapters (though hardly of "lyric joy") on Hugo Grotius and Law of the Sea, "flag-flying fish" (i.e., yellow-fin tuna in the tropical East Pacific), the U.S. "Naval Ocean", and the problem of the Soviet [Russian] fishing fleets. In this writer's opinion, Marx's weakness lay in his underlying sub-thesis, in which he implied that the freedom of the seas could only be guaranteed by global governance (i.e., the UN's Intergovernmental Oceanic Commission [IOC]). Only then, went the Marxian inference, could the Goddess be truly safeguarded from Man.[479] (In pc language, "man" is the perpetrator, humankind--the victim.)

In 1997, twenty-seven years later, this writer sincerely hopes that Wesley Marx is alive and well enough to have witnessed the world-wide collapse and discrediting of Socialism, and to have noticed the vast improvement in the marine environment since 1970. If so, Wesley Marx ought to immediately admit how over-wrought he was then, how much he had exaggerated the extent of "plunder and pollution" of the [frail] ocean, and get about writing a revisionist follow-up work: State of the Oceans, 2000 A.D. The latter should include--to the very last detail -- each and every clean-up and improvement in North American marine ecosystems since 1970. (Marx must make honourable mention of the man-made revivification of Chicago's Lake Michigan waterfront to the Windy City.) It is now June 1997, so Wesley Marx has two and a half years until the year 2000 to complete the proposed study. Naturally, the book -- if written -- would never sell. But at least such a revisionist book would have been written! (For instance, rumours of a global population plunge would ruin such Malthusian fear-mongers as Paul Ehrlich and Norman Myers....) Nonetheless, this obscure writer believes his proposal to be just and fair, addressed to an individual ostensibly dedicated to the truth and having expressed passionate concern for the marine environment.

If Wesley Marx is unable or unavailable to word-process State of the Oceans, 2000 A.D., perhaps the task could be assumed by the 86-year-old reigning eco-Pontifex Maximus of oceanography, Jacques-Yves Cousteau. Captain Jacques was one of this writer's childhood idols, but has since devolved from the personable and knowledgeable master of the Calypso (with those glasses of red wine and Heinz ketchup bottles on the table in the mess) into the élitiste species-ist of today (i.e., cetaceans are of a higher order than humans). Even the Cousteau Society's publication, Dolphin Log, serves as an agency enhancing Captain Jacques worship.[480] But there is no denying Jacques-Yves Cousteau's great accomplishments in the field of oceanography. For almost a half century, Cousteau and crew on the Calypso have criss-crossed and circum-navigated the world's seas and oceans. In 1950 (seven years after co-inventing the aqualung) Cousteau purchased Calypso, a converted minesweeper, and sailed to the Red Sea. The trip led to the discovery of a multitude of previously unknown marine plants and animals, and to the publication of The Silent World.[481] Five years later, Cousteau and crew embarked on a 13,800-mile voyage around the world that resulted in replenishing international aquariums with rare marine plants and exotic fishes. Cousteau and co. also produced and directed a 90-minute movie version of "The Silent World." The film won the prestigious Palme d'Or award at the 1956 Cannes International Film Festival, and an Academy Award (Hollywood) a year later.[482]

By 1960, Jacques-Yves Cousteau had arrived. In that year, Cousteau appeared on the cover of Time magazine, and in 1961 received the National Geographic Society's Gold Medal in a ceremony attended by President John F. Kennedy.[483] It was at this time that the writer lost touch for over a decade with Jacques-Yves Cousteau. School, college, marriage, children, and the U.S. Army beckoned; this writer didn't really re-connect with Cousteau until the PBS series The Cousteau Odyssey premiered in 1977.[484] But the writer was doomed to disappointment -- The Cousteau Odyssey contained an academic arrogance that seems to taint anything aired on "public" television". And this time around Captain Jacques was telling us how to treat the oceans and seas (dictating the do's and don't's of marine environmentalism), rather than teaching us about the world's waterways. Sometime during the 1970s, Captain Jacques formed the Cousteau Society in Norfolk, Va., a marine environmental organisation with the avowed goal of educating the public about problems such as industrial pollution, over-fishing, the decline of coral reefs etc. etc.[485] In 1979, Cousteau's elder son and heir-apparent, Philippe, perished tragically in a sea-plane crash. But except for strong empathy felt for the bereaved father, this writer's interest by that time had vanished in all things Cousteauan.

During the 1990s, Jacques-Yves Cousteau has not slowed down. In 1997, Captain Jacques was hard at work building Calypso II, the renowned original having sunk off Singapore last year (1996). In 1998, Cousteau plans to study the diseased (deceased?) Ganges River of India, the great waterway sacred to Hindus (and assuredly a valuable New Age connection). Cousteau's message has always been: "Take care of water, for it is the earth's lifeblood."[486] Today, Cousteau's message is to divers and children: "I would like to turn the divers into [blue-helmeted?] soldiers of the water. Second, I would like to have the [Al Goresque] children of the world better educated.... We have to teach the children water is vital to survive and they have to take care of it.'"[487] As a living legend and senior statesman of the earth's oceans and seas, Jacques-Yves Cousteau could also impart hope and increased motivation in those same children by leaving one final legacy: A State of the Oceans, 2000 A.D.-type book (accompanied by CD-ROM or VHS video) showing and telling all the vast man-made improvements in the world's marine ecosystems since Earth Day, 1970. Considering the 45-plus-years on-going adulation accorded to Jacques-Yves Cousteau, his version of a State of the Oceans, 2000 A.D. could, and should, sell to a still-adoring public.

The oceans and seas are the source of much of the life on our planet, and are still subject to scientific inquiry along with eco-politics. True scientists are constantly discovering hard facts of real significance in the oceans and seas. Just last summer, mid-August 1996, a study published by the journal Science revealed that researchers had decoded the 1,700 genes of a microbe called Methanococcus jannaschii. This microbe was found to be a member of a life class known as Archaea.[488] J. Craig Venter of the Institute for Genomic Research was quoted by the Associated Press as saying, "This is a very different life form from what we know.... Two thirds of the genes in this organism are new to science and biology."[489] In other words, M. jannaschii is one of a class of hitherto unrecognised class of life-forms; it, and others like it, make up what is essentially a third branch of the tree of life.[490] J. Craig Venter, senior author of the study, explained that the microbe is extremely different from the other two basic class-branches of life, bacteria and eukaryotes, which include plants, animals, and human beings. The main difference between the latter life-forms is cellular structure. The cells of eukaryotes have nuclear structure but bacteria do not. The Archaea microbes share characteristics with the organisms in the two other "domains" (i.e., classes), but are fundamentally different in the way they live and function. That Archaea (named for their ancient heritage) appear related to both bacteria and eukaryotes..." 'gives us hints that they may be precursors to all life forms on the planet,'" Venter has (predictably) postulated.[491] (Archaea's position on the tree of evolution is still uncertain etc. etc.)

According to the Associated Press, the existence of Archaea was first thought of so long ago as 1977 by Carl Woese and Ralph S. Wolfe of U. Illinois Urbana. Only recently has their proposal gained acceptance as the new life-form has been found in the least likely places; to wit:

"The Methanococcus jannaschii was discovered living on the edge of a volcanic vent on the floor of the Pacific Ocean in 8,606 feet of water. It required temperatures of 185 degrees Fahrenheit, just 27 degrees from boiling, and must be in pressures of about 3,700 pounds per square inch.... M. jannaschii lives without the ... effects of sunlight and without organic carbon as a food source. The [Archaea] microbe lives on carbon dioxide, nitrogen and hydrogen expelled by the volcanic vent and gives off methane... as a waste."[492]

Oh, wow! Or as Newsweek magazine breathlessly put it, Imagine an organism which thrives in near-boiling water a mile and a half down on the bottom of the Pacific, under pressures "that would easily squash all but the most specialized submarines."[493]

The deep ocean seabed, and sub-seabed, have always been of interest to hard-rock marine scientists. For instance, in October 1996, an extraordinary article appeared in The Atlantic Monthly magazine under 'The Environment' heading:

"In 1976 a giant coring device mounted to a ship plunged repeatedly into the bottom of the Pacific Ocean, three miles below the surface, bringing up 100-foot-long tubes of mud and clay with the consistency of peanut butter. The primeval muck told a tale of geologic serenity. Sediment records from the cores indicate that the region -- roughly 600 miles north of Hawaii and spanning an area four times the size of Texas -- has been tranquil for 65 million years, unperturbed by volcanic activity or by shifting of the earth's tectonic plates...."[494]

One Charles Hollister, geologist and senior scientist at the Woods Hole Oceanographic Institution, sees more than mere marine substratum when he regards the thick, dark ooze; he perceives what might provide the perfect place on the planet to sequester high-level nuclear waste, the most potently radioactive by-products of public (military, naval) or private (civilian) activity. Indeed, Charles Hollister initially suggested the idea of sub-seabed disposal so long ago as 1973; after he had had a conversation in Washington, D.C., with a chemist from the Sandia National Laboratories of New Mexico. The chemist, a William Bishop, had mentioned the many problems associated with a proposed nuclear-waste repository in Lyons, Kansas. Recalls the ever-enthusiastic Hollister, "I immediately thought of the clays in the deep-sea floor, which I knew, from previous studies, clung tenaciously to the radioactive particles that had settled there as a result of atmospheric nuclear testing."[495]

But Charles Hollister's common-sensical concept has been deep-sixed, at every twist and turn, from the early 1970s by (i.e., U.S.) eco-politicians et al. It has been a long, hard, up-hill slog, but from 1974 onward the idea of deep-seabed disposal had grown into a global effort, involving ten nations and 200 scientists under the auspice of the Paris-based Organisation for Economic Coöperation and Development. The international team of scientists conducted experiments from 1974 until 1986, the results of which supported Hollister's hypothesis: If waste canisters were deposited just ten metres below the ocean floor, any leakage of toxic substances would be bound up by the sticky clays for millions of years. Deeper interment would provide an even greater margin of safety. Says a still-optimistic Hollister: "The stuff sticks to the mud and sits there like heavy lead.... Nothing's going to bring it into the biosphere, unless we figure out how to reverse gravity."[496]

Even the invariably ec Atlantic Monthly allowed that sub-seabed disposal is a promising solution to the problem of radioactive waste, but [still] "faces stiff opposition from the [U.S.] federal government, the nuclear industry, and environmental interests."[497] As The Atlantic Monthly has readily admitted, the mud and clays of the deep-seabeds may provide the safest burial grounds for nuclear/toxic wastes.[498] Environmental writer Steven Nadis directly posed the question, "Why won't the United States make a modest investment to find out if sub-seabed burial would work?"[499] And Charles Hollister, who originally hit on the notion twenty-four years ago, has plaintively concluded: "I have no problem with a ban on sub-seabed disposal.... I think it should be banned until we do more experiments. What troubles me is people who are trying to ban research on the subject."[500]

Sub-seabed disposal is definitely a sad case of Charles Hollister, geologist and senior scientist at the Woods Hole Oceanographic Institution, being caught between a rock (the U.S. federal government, the nuclear industry, environmental interests) and a hard [science] place.

A third deep-seabed story during the latter part of 1996 attracted this writer's attention. Gas-loaded rocks have been found off the Oregon coast which have the potential to supply a goodly portion of the world's energy needs.[501] The gas in the white rocks is methane hydrate, and oceanographers from Oregon State U., Canada and Germany, aboard a German research ship, recently discovered the snow-white methane hydrate on a 2,000-foot-deep sea-ridge, located approximately 50 miles west of Newport, Ore.[502] Said Robert W. Collier, an associate professor of marine geochemistry, "The sea floor there is paved with hydrates.... We've known that hydrates were out there, but the real surprise is that they're at the surface of the sediment.... They reach a zone where the methane hydrate solidifies.... Now there's the potential for being able to take samples that we can study without a great deal of difficulty."[503]

Methane hydrates are abundant in offshore sediments and in arctic regions, and quantities have been estimated to be at twice the globe's known coal, oil, and natural gas deposits combined. As the major deposits of the methane hydrate are at abyssal depths, technology must be developed to extract and collect the rocks.

(So inflammable is the methane hydrate, that place a lighted match near such a rock and it will ignite.) Necessity being the mother of invention, the required technology should follow shortly. The scientists on the German research vessel off the Oregon coast made close observations, using video surveys of the Newport sea-ridge. The international team detected a nine-square-mile plume of methane above the submarine summit, and found the plume was fed by methane bubbles issuing from deep-seabed fluid vents.[504] It was from bubbles rising from deep-seabed volcanic vents that the Archaea-class microbe (M. jannaschii) was learned of, and then announced by the journal Science in mid-August 1996.

The ocean and seas are entities in themselves, with the fish that interest us being mere temporary denizens. The oceanographer is not an ichthyologist although both are marine scientists (of a kind). The New Age oceanographer may define the sea herself as goddess, in a manner similar to the wild-fish metaphysicist anthropomorphing cetaceans and salmonids (as we have seen throughout this chapter). But where could a "cultural anthropologist" fit into this equation? The cultural anthropologist this writer has in mind is Thor Heyerdahl of Kon-Tiki Expedition fame, now celebrating his jubilaeum of the 1947 4,300-mile sailing from South America across the Pacific to Polynesia.[505] Thor Heyerdahl was possibly more of a childhood ikon of this writer's than even Jacques Cousteau. Heyerdahl, after all, was Norwegian too, and the images of those bearded Scandihoovians a-drift on a balsa-wood raft, braving the high seas ... were stirring indeed to a young soul. There is an entire museum-wing outside Oslo, Norway, dedicated to the Kon-Tiki Expedition (Kon-Tiki Museet) and surely every Norwegian, and visiting North American of Norwegian descent, has been to this virtual shrine. Thor Heyerdahl was one Norwegian of the modern era we were all proud of.

Heyerdahl's accomplishments have equalled, and even surpassed, those of Cousteau. During 1940-1941, Heyerdahl completed the Northwest America Expedition (and once lived and worked in British Columbia); the Galápagos Islands in 1952; Easter Island (Rapa Nui) from 1955 to 1956; the Ra Expeditions of 1969 and 1970, in which Heyerdahl sailed in a reed boat from Morocco to Barbados; the Tigris Expedition in 1977, that ranged from the Persian Gulf to Pakistan back to Arabia and the Red Sea; and the Maldives Expedition off the southwest coast of India, 1982-1984.[506]

As a Pacific history graduate student at the U. Hawai'i at Manoa (1979-1981), this writer was to hear that all Thor Heyerdahl's much-heralded theories about Pacific Basin migrations were ... theories, and bass-ackward ones at that. But these scholastic doubts have never detracted from Thor Heyerdahl's achievements, in the writer's estimation. As a young man, Heyerdahl enrolled at the University of Oslo and studied biology and anthropology, earning degrees in both disciplines. Heyerdahl embarked on his first expedition in 1937, the day after he had married his sweetheart, Liv Torp; they spent their honeymoon on the French Polynesian island of Fatu Hiva in the Marquesas. The couple started their connubial life together in a hut made of leaves and straw, eating nothing but fish and fruit during their year-long sojourn (Dude!) And it was on Fatu Hiva that Thor Heyerdahl started chasing his ignis fatuus ... but bravely, with style.[507]

Today, Thor Heyerdahl is 83 years old, almost as long-in-the-tooth as his celebrated contemporary, Jacques Cousteau. Heyerdahl has lately been touring the United Sates to promote his most recent book, Green Was the Earth on the Seventh Day: Memories and Journeys of a Lifetime (1996). Heyerdahl's books have been translated into 65 languages and have sold more than 60 million copies around the world. This is not bad for a Norwegian kid born in the small town of Larvik! Among Heyerdahl's books have been: Kon-Tiki, Aku-Aku, Easter Island: The Mystery Solved, The Ra Expeditions and his latest, Green Was the Earth on the Seventh Day, already being re-printed in 1997.[508] During recent years, Heyerdahl has been excavating pyramids near Tucume, Peru, and on Tenerife, the (Spanish) Canary Islands; he and the present Mrs. Heyerdahl (the former Miss France) make their home in both Pacific and Atlantic locations.[509]

Thor Heyerdahl, the latter-day Viking, is this writer's leading candidate to write the State of the Oceans, 2000 A.D. for the posterity of the coming century. Although designated a "cultural anthropologist", Heyerdahl is enough of an Oceanic Man to speak with the authority of impressive maritime credentials; Oceanic Man enough to write the hypothetical but deterministic State of the Oceans, 2000 A.D. Heyerdahl has, ironically, confessed to having to overcome an early fear of water. In an October 1996 interview with Sons of Norway member Alice Cristofoli of Castlegar, B.C., Heyerdahl said:

"I think my greatest achievement was to conquer my own fear of the water -- because when I was 5 years old, I fell into a lake and, at 12, into the sea -- and I decided that I was never going to learn to swim or even to try....And I overcame that. So I think that I first taught myself -- and later, I've tried the best I could to tell the rest of the world -- that the ocean isn't such a terrible abyss as we think."[510]

But in 1997 Thor Heyerdahl might not be so modest as he acts; he, like his renowned peer Jacques

Cousteau, is coming into his dotage but, for now, is still a lionised Lion in Winter. Since winning an Oscar for best documentary -- Kon-Tiki -- in 1951, Thor Heyerdahl has received a multitude of medals, awards, and honours for his writings, teachings, and films. Just last October (1996) at Minot, North Dakota's Høstfest, Heyerdahl was presented with the International Scandinavian Cultural Award.[511] He has "been there, done that" and basked in celebrity status for decades. Would all the fame gained, riches accrued, and the "pride of life" prevent Heyerdahl from publickly approving the present state of the oceans? Have the health and welfare of the globe's oceans and seas been vastly improved since the Ra Expeditions (1969, 1970)? Or, have Thor Heyerdahl's later years proven too comfortable for him to mount the effort in behalf of our young people? (They need hope. For thirty plus years our children have been told that the world's waters are dead or dying.)

This writer fears that the answers to all three questions above are Yes. And were Thor Heyerdahl convinced that the ocean and seas had become cleaner and better than in 1970, that worthy would be certain to call for direct supervision -- over all the world's waters -- by his beloved United Nations Organization. Thus do the mighty idols fall! And what of Heyerdahl and Cousteau's scientific/spiritual successors? As we have already observed from the scientific/spiritual transition of physics (Albert Einstein) to metaphysics (Fritjof Capra), New Age oceanography and cultural anthropology will be far removed from a Jacques Cousteau or a Thor Heyerdahl. And how will New Age Oceanic Man perceive himself and his future place in marine science? One might specify that transition as "Back to the Future":

"The powers described by the mystics through the ages are now being described by scientists, proof that underlying the material world is a vast nonsubstantial world. The priests [i.e., witch doctors, medicine men] of old were also the scientists. Today, the priest [i.e., shaman, curandero] and the scientist are coming back together again."[512]

And that signifies the real "End of Science" (true, objective, empirical) and the second advent of [weird] science/magick.

Author's note: "Magick" is used in this chapter to connote the practice of the occult; "magic" denotes the art of conjuring. "Magick" was coined by British Satanist Aleister Crowley (1875-1947).

Jacques-Yves Cousteau (1910-1997) died 25 June 1997 in Paris, France, He succumbed to heart problems and a respiratory infection. Cousteau is survived, among others, by his younger son, Jean-Michel.

NOTES

344.   Brent Bozell III, 'Hollywood's Winners and Losers in 1996', <u>Human Events</u>, Vol.53, No.3, 24 January 1997, p.14.

345.   'Science popularizer dies', <u>Peninsula Daily News</u>, 20 December 1996, p.A-11. See Appendix N.

346.   <u>Ibid.</u>, p.A-11. Quotes and brackets are this writer's.

347.   <u>Ibid.</u>, p.A-11.

348.   Carl Sagan, <u>The Demon-Haunted World: Science as a Candle in the Dark</u> (New York:Random House, 1995), frontispiece and back cover.

349.   For a scientific and religious profile of Albert Einstein, see Appendix K.

350.   H.B. Acton, <u>What Marx Really Said</u> (New York:Schocken Books, 1967), pp.77-80. Cited in Theodore Roszak, <u>The Making of a Counter Culture</u> (Garden City, N.Y.:Anchor Books, 1969) pp.91-92.

351.   Carl Sagan, <u>Broca's Brain</u> (New York:Ballantine Books, Inc., 1980), p.67. See also Appendix L.

352.   Carl Sagan, <u>The Demon-Haunted World</u>, pp.68-69, 74, 204-205 ff. See the "Orgone Energy" of Wilhelm Reich (1897-1957) in Appendix F. Reich founded the sexual politics of Orgonomy, and wrote <u>The Function of Orgasm</u> (1927). He invented the Orgone box, and died in a U.S. prison.

353.   <u>Ibid.</u>, pp.128-129, 334-335 ff.

354.   Carl Sagan, <u>Broca's Brain</u>, p.79.

355.   <u>Newsweek</u>, 12 October 1992. Cited by Maurice S. Rawlings, MD., <u>To Hell and Back</u> (Nashville, Tenn.:Thomas Nelson Publishers, 1993), p.208.

356.   Carl Sagan, <u>Broca's Brain</u>, p.316.

357.   Carl Sagan, <u>The Demon-Haunted World</u>, p.179. NB: The SETI programme was briefly resurrected via private financing in 1995, under an appropriate name: Project Phoenix. <u>Ibid.</u>, p.396.

358.   'Hello, out there: Anybody listening?', <u>Peninsula Daily News</u>, 1 November 1995, p.C-2.

359.   <u>Ibid.</u>, p.C-2.

360.   <u>Ibid.</u>, p.C-2.

361.   Carl Sagan, <u>Broca's Brain</u>, pp.357, 365. See Appendix A for the "Spiritual Emergence" of Stanislav Grof and wife, Christina.

362.   Carl Sagan, <u>The Demon-Haunted World</u>, p.17.

363.   <u>Ibid.</u>, pp.270-271, 274.

364.   <u>Ibid.</u>, pp.417, 419.

NOTES (cont'd.)

365.   See Broca's Brain, passim. Cf. Appendix K; Albert Einstein as "Scientific Ideal."

366.   The Demon-Haunted World, p.436.

367.   John Caiazza, 'Science on Parade', Chronicles, Vol.20, No. 9, pp.26-27.

368.   P.J. O'Rourke. The Atlantic Monthly Press, 1996, p.12.

369.   Ibid., p.44. Letter from Timothy A. Curry, Seattle.

370.   Bantam Books, Inc., New York, 1977 ed. Orig. published by Shambhala Publications, Inc., 1976.

371.   :Quantum Physics as the Language of Nature (New York:Bantam Books, 1984 ed.).

372.   :Man and His Cosmos. Translated from the German by Steve Lake and Caroline Mähl. HarperCollins Publishers, Inc., New York, 1992.

373.   Bantam Books, New York, 1981 ed. I.e., Bantam New Age Books: "Looking for Meaning, Growth and Change."

374.   Fritjof Capra, The Tao of Physics, p.xv. Emphasis Capra's.

375.   Ibid., frontispiece. The In-Crowd pronounces it "Daoism."

376.   Ibid., p.5.

377.   Heinz Pagels, p.8; Gerhard Staguhn, pp.94, 96; Michael Talbot, pp.5, 161.

378.   Fritjof Capra, The Tao of Physics, pp.10-12.

379.   Ibid., pp.42, 43. Cf. Heinz Pagels, p.136; Michael Talbot, p.89.

380.   Ibid., pp.50-51. Cf. Appendix K.

381.   Ibid., pp.159, 117.

382.   Ibid., pp.211, 233.

383.   Heinz Pagels, The Cosmic Code, p.48.

384.   Ibid., pp.131, 83.

385.   E.J. Zimmerman, 'The Macroscopic Nature of Space-Time', American Journal of Physics, Vol.30, No.2 (1962). In Michael Talbot, p.87.

386.   Op.cit., Heinz Pagels, p.48.

387.   Phillip E. Johnson, Darwin on Trial (Downer's Grove, Ill.:InterVarsity Press, 1993 ed.), p.119. Cf. pp.118, 202. Also in Heinz Pagels, p.68.

NOTES (cont'd.)

388.   Cf. Pagels, p.76. NB: <u>The Cosmic Code</u> -- published by Bantam <u>New Age</u> Books!

389.   Op.cit., Michael Talbot, p.15.

390.   Jack Sarfatti, 'Implications of Meta-Physics for Psychoenergetic Systems', <u>Psychoenergetic Systems</u>, Vol.1, Gordon and Breach, London (U.K.), 1974. Cited in Talbot, p.36.

391.   Op.cit., Talbot, p.189.

392.   Fritjof Capra, <u>The Turning Point: Science, Society, and the Rising Culture</u> (New York:Bantam [New Age] Books, 1988 ed.), p.93.

393.   Op. cit., Capra, <u>The Tao of Physics</u>, p.266.

394.   Charles Colson, 'Quantum mysteries: The New Age comes to science', <u>The Citizen's News</u> (Sequim, Wash.), Vol.3, Issue 10, 17 May 1996, p.7.

395.   <u>Ibid.</u>, p.7. Quote is from Michael Talbot, p.15. NB: Chuck Colson, former Watergate felon, has been involved with Prison Fellowship Ministries for many years.

396.   Michael Talbot, p.59. Cf. Capra, <u>The Tao of Physics</u>, p.276.

397.   <u>Ibid.</u>, pp.59, 86.

398.   Heinz Pagels, <u>The Cosmic Code</u>, front page.

399.   <u>Ibid.</u>, back page.

400.   <u>Mysticism and the New Physics</u>, pp.191-204. NB: In a note about the author at book's end, the Bantam bio-let said that Michael Talbot, in addition to studying physics on his own at Michigan State U.... "has had a lifetime involvement with the paranormal."

401.   Norman Mailer, <u>Of a Fire on the Moon</u> (New York:Grove Press, Inc., 1970), p.106.

402.   Michael Talbot, p.75. (Emphasis Talbot's.)

403.   <u>Ibid.</u>, p.76.

404.   Op.cit., Heinz Pagels, p.28.

405.   Gerhard Staguhn, <u>God's Laughter</u>, p.67.

406.   <u>Ibid.</u>, p.67.

407.   <u>Ibid.</u>, p.68. NB: Why hasn't so-called "hard science" forever stilled all idiotic talk of time-travel?

408.   Carl Sagan, <u>The Demon-Haunted World</u>, pp.270-271, 274. See note 363 in this chapter.

409.   Op.cit., Fritjof Capra, <u>The Turning Point</u>, p.39. See Appendix C and Charles A. Reich, <u>The Greening of America</u>, <u>passim</u>.

NOTES (cont'd.)

410. Sagan and Capra, passim. New Ager Capra waxes eloquent on the wonders of "alternative" and holistic medicine.

411. The Demon-Haunted World, pp.69,74; The Turning Point, pp.186, 343-345. Wilhelm ("Dr. Orgone") Reich, who died in prison, combined Left-wing politics with sexual liberation. See note 352 in this chapter and Appendix F.

412. Capra, The Turning Point, pp.371-372, 386; Sagan, Broca's Brain, pp.357, 365. See note 361 in this chapter and Appendix A.
    NB: Stanislav Grof's clinical research in consciousness psychotherapy employed LSD and other psychedelic substances for seventeen years -- with only legal restrictions eventually halting the practice.

413. The Turning Point, pp.9, 12.

414. Ibid., pp.415-417.

415. Op.cit., Heinz Pagels, p.303.

416. Ibid., p.303.

417. Ibid., p.297.

418. Op.cit., Norman Mailer, p.165.

NOTES (cont'd)

419. Based on Arthur C. Clarke, <u>2001: A Space Odyssey</u> (New York, N.Y.: New American Library, 1991 ed.).

420. From Arthur C. Clarke, <u>2001, Odyssey Two</u> (New York: Harper Collins, 1994 ed.).

421. 'Machines advance, but lack common sense;' <u>Peninsula Daily News</u>, 19 November 1996, p.A-7.

422. <u>Ibid.</u>, p.A-7.

423. <u>Ibid.</u>, p.A-7.

424. <u>Ibid.</u>, p.A-7.

425. Both <u>Arthur C. Clarke's World of Strange Powers</u>, and <u>The Mysterious Universe of Arthur C. Clarke</u>, could be watched on the Discovery channel (DSC) during the early/mid - 1990s.

426. New York: Bantam Books, 1981.

427. New York: Ballantine Books, 1953.

428. Op.cit, Michael Talbot, pp.105-106.

429. New York: Pocket Books, 1979 ed.

430. Op.cit, Arthur C. Clarke, <u>The Exploration of Space</u> (1951), p.217.

See also Appendix O.

431. New York: MacMillan, 1986.

432. Op.cit., Arthur C. Clarke (1951), p.224.

433. See Chapter 2, Part II, note no. 136.

434. Op.cit., Arthur C. Clarke (1951), p.230. Emphasis this writer's.

435. Jeremy Rifkin, ed. <u>The Green Lifestyle Handbook: 1001 Ways You Can Heal The Earth</u> (New York: Henry Holt & Co., 1990). Copyright the Greenhouse Crisis Foundation.

436. New York: The Atlantic Monthly Press, 1996, p.30. Compiled by P. J. O'Rourke.

437. New York: Bantam Books, 1988 ed., p.438.

438. Reading, Mass.: Addison-Wesley Publishing Company, 1996 ed., p.254. See Appendix J for the nature of neo - Luddism. NB: This writer, who has written this and two other books entirely by hand, wagers that Jeremy Rifkin has the latest in data-processing techno- gadgetry.

439. New York: Bantam Books, 1981 ed. Co-written with Ted Howard. Some editions of <u>Entropy: A New World View</u> appear to be a-k-a <u>Into the Greenhouse World</u> (New York: Bantam Books, 1980 and 1989).

NOTES (con't)

440. Ibid., Author's Note, first page. NB: All brackets and contents this writer's.

441. Ibid., p.6.

442. Ibid., p.8

443. Ibid., p.12. NB: From Ourobouros, the great mythological self-devouring serpent. This sounds as comfortably Hinduistic as Hellenistic.

444. New York: Bantam Books, 1988 ed., p.73.

445, Ibid., p.74.

446. Ibid., p.74. Brackets and contents are those of this writer. Cf. Pagels (1984), pp.100-102; Sagan (1995), p.332; Staguhn (1992), pp.185-187.

447. Rifkin (1981), p.35; Capra (1988), pp.73,72.

448. Sagan (1995), p.332.

449. Staguhn (1992), p.187.

450. Rifkin (1981), p.58.

451. Ibid., p.59.

452. Lee Schipper, 'Energy: Global Prospects 1985-2000', Bulletin of the Atomic Scientists, March 1978, p.58. Rifkin, P.101.

453. Hobart Rowen, 'Oil Supply, Adequate, Possibly to 1990s, Trilateral Commission Study Concludes', Washington Post, 14 June 1978, p.D-9, Rifkin, p.101.

454. Emile Benoit, 'The Coming Age of Shortages, Part I', Bulletin of the Atomic Scientists, March 1978, p.9. Rifkin, p.101.

455. Lester R. Brown, The Twenty - ninth Day (New York: Norton, 1978), pp.99-100. Rifkin, P.101.

456. Helen Caldicott, Nuclear Madness (Brookline, Mass.: Autumn Press 1978), p.51. Rifkin, p.108.

457. Jeremy Rifkin, p.128.

458. Ibid., p.135.

459. Op.cit., p.223

460 Ibid., p.224.

461. Ibid., p.234. For Tofflerian fear of, and loathing for, FundiGreens, see 'CODA: Yearnings for a New Dark Age' in Powershift, p.371 (note 179 in this chapter).

NOTES (con't)

462.   Op.cit., p.235. NB: This writer suspects that Rifkin, who decried "increased centralization of power", is all for global governance.

463.   Ibid., p.235.

464.   Ibid., p.235. NB: New Agers and secularists alike share a marked aversion to Orthodox Jewry, evangelical Christianity, and fundamentalist Islam.

NOTES

465. Author's note: On the prototypes of five-foot-high glass panels, the Friends of the [P.A.] Library had hired two Seattle artists to create "contemporary" muses. Rather than the nine classical muses of Greek mythology, the artists depicted on the proposed panels ... "a Buddha of healing; Siva as Nataraja, the Hindu god of the arts; Aphrodite of Melos; Kuyu Shonin, the Wandering Monk, a Chinese folk dancer, a Dogon ritual dancer from Africa and Barong, mythological figure of Bali, Indonesia [sic]." Brad Lincoln, 'Library's art fuels debate,' Peninsula Daily News, 30 May 1997, p.A-2.

466. A plaque is inscribed on the P.A. Marine Lab building: "Marine Laboratory dedicated to the memory of Arthur D. Feiro (1930-1982). A prominent marine biologist, educator, and community leader; whose dreams, efforts, and labors brought this project to reality. He lived the Rotary motto 'Service Above Self'. (Presented by the Rotary Club of Port Angeles, 1984)."

467. Signet Science Library, New York, 1955.

468. The American Spectator's Enemies List (New York: The Atlantic Monthly Press, 1996). See letter from Adrian H. Krieg of Acworth, N.Y., p.88.

469. Rachel Carson, The Edge of the Sea, pre-Preface.

470. Ibid., Preface.

471. Op.cit., Rachel Carson, p.15.

472. Ibid., p.215.

473. Ibid., p.216. For a meaning of Darwinism, see Appendix O.

474. Phillip E. Johnson, Darwin on Trial (Downers Grove, Ill.: InterVarsity Press, 1993 ed.), pp.19,25. See especially footnote no. 3, p.25. NB: Darwinism purports to tell us who and what we are and where we came from.

475. Wesley Marx, The Frail Ocean (New York: Ballantine Books, 1970), frontispiece.

476. Ibid., p.VI. NB: "Miss Rachel Carson"! How cloyingly touching!. One is reminded of Oscar Night among the Hollywood glitterati, hearing the introduction of "Miss Elizabeth Taylor" or "Miss Carol Channing".

477. Ibid., frontispiece, cf.p.7.

478. Ibid., p.69. The writer plans a future chapter (or monograph) entirely on Micronesia.

479. Ibid., pp.171-245, passim; and 'Mare Liberum Revisited.'

480. For an example of this, see Dolphin Log, January 1995, p.3. Cf.note 19 in this chapter.

481. 'Call of sea still sounds loud, clear: Oceanographer gave water a voice with French accent,' Peninsula Daily News, 16 February 1997, pp.C-1,C-2.

482. Ibid., p.C-2.

NOTES (cont'd)

483. <u>Ibid.</u>, p.C-2.

484. <u>Ibid.</u>, p.C-2.

485. <u>Ibid.</u>, p.C-2. The Cousteau Society, 870 Greenbrier Circle, Suite 402, Chesapeake, VA 23320.

486. <u>Ibid.</u>, p.C-1.

487. <u>Ibid.</u>, p.C-2. Cousteau cited by the Associated Press; brackets and contents this writer's.

488. 'In a global family tree, scientists discover a brand new branch,' <u>Peninsula Daily News</u>, 25 August 1996, p.C-3. See ref. to Arch[a]en Age at beginning of Section C.

489. <u>Ibid.</u>, p.C-3.

490. 'More Than Just a Blob', <u>Newsweek</u>, 2 September 1996, p.54.

491. <u>Ibid.</u>, p.54.

492. Op.cit., AP, 'In a global family tree ...,' <u>Peninsula Daily News</u>, 25 August 1996, p.C-3.

493. 'More Than Just a Blob', <u>Newsweek</u>, 2 September 1996, p.54.

494. Steven Nadis, 'The Sub-Seabed Solution', <u>The Atlantic Monthly</u>, October 1996, p.28.

495. <u>Ibid.</u>, p.28.

496. <u>Ibid.</u>, p.30.

497. <u>Ibid.</u>, p.28.

498. <u>Ibid.</u>, p.30.

499. Op.cit., Steven Nadis, p.38.

500. <u>Ibid.</u>, p.39. Emphasis included in Hollister citation.

501. 'Ocean may hold future fuel', <u>Peninsula Daily News</u>, 21 November 1996, "Energy."

502. <u>Ibid.</u>, "Energy".

503. <u>Ibid.</u>, "Energy". Robert W. Collier of OSU quoted by the Associated Press.

504. <u>Ibid.</u>, "Energy".

505. 'Thor Heyerdahl Yesterday and Today', <u>The Sons of Norway Viking</u>, Vol.94, No.6, June 1997, cover.

506. <u>Ibid.</u>, p.7. Leslie Rodlie, 'Beyond the Kon-Tiki'.

507. <u>Ibid.</u>, p.7. Cf.'Micropaedia', Vol.5, <u>The New Encyclopaedia Britannica</u> (Chicago: Encyclopaedia

NOTES (cont'd)

Britannica, Inc., 1990 ed.), p.907.

508. Ibid., pp.29,6.

509. Ibid., pp.6,32.

510. Ibid., p.7. Op.cit., Thor Heyerdahl.

511. Ibid., pp.28-29.

512. Los Angeles Times, 28 July 1975, Part 1, p.125. The quote is from Bam Price, associate of former astronaut and present psychic researcher Edgar Mitchell. Cited in The Berean Call (Bend, Ore.), May 1997, p.3.

Bibliography for Part III

14.   Capra, Fritjof. <u>The Tao of Physics</u>. Bantam Books, New York, 1977.

15.   Carson, Rachel. <u>The Edge of the Sea</u>. Signet Books, New York, 1955.

16.   Clarke, Arthur C. <u>The Exploration of Space</u>. Pocket Books, New York, 1979. (Originally published in 1951.)

17.   Marx, Wesley. <u>The Frail Ocean</u>. Ballantine Books, Inc., New York, N.Y., 1970.

18.   Pagels, Heinz R. <u>The Cosmic Code</u>. Bantam Books, New York, 1984.

19.   Rifkin, Jeremy with Ted Howard. <u>Entropy: A New World View</u>. Bantam Books, New York, 1981.

20.   Sagan, Carl. <u>Broca's Brain</u>. Ballantine Books, Inc., New York, N.Y., 1980.

21.   Staguhn, Gerhard. <u>God's Laughter</u>. Harper Collins Publishers, Inc., New York, 1992. (Orig. publ. as <u>Das Lachen Gottes</u> in 1990 by Carl Hanser Verlag, Germany.)

22.   Talbot, Michael. <u>Mysticism and the New Physics</u>. Bantam Books, New York, 1981.

Acknowledgements

My special thanks go to Paul Enga of Port Angeles, Washington, for the hilarious 'Downsizing Government' which he found while surfing the Net. "Yo Paulie!"

———————————

I am indebted to MCA Records Inc., for a 1994 reissue of <u>Jimi Hendrix: blues</u>. These recordings have created the near-perfect atmosphere of "noise, paranoia" (William Irwin Thompson, <u>Pacific Shift</u>, p.142) required as background "pollution" to writing on electronic communications ("Economy IV").

Part IV: ...And The Ichthys of Religion

<u>(Special Supplement in Judaeo - Christian Apologetics)</u>

"No watch without a watchmaker: -- Isaac Bashevis Singer

"Science without religion is lame, religion without science is blind" -- Albert Einstein

"For the believer an explanation is unnecessary, for the nonbeliever an explanation is impossible"
-- Franz Werfel, author of <u>The Song of Bernadette</u>

There is a <u>third</u> worldview beside those of Natural Scientism and New Age metaphysics, a view this writer will dub Judaeo - Christian determinism; a kind of Ancient Earth creationism. The writer strongly believes that the latter view most effectively combines the wisdom of Judaism and Christian revelation with the hard-rock empiricism of true science. It is also a real alternative to Darwinism and Disneyism, or a case of Tantra versus Torah. Judaeo-Christian determinism, then, offers a third way -- a wholly different view of the entire cosmos and life on earth. Norman Mailer expressed perfectly the dichotomy of science and religion:

"[O]ne recognized that to believe in progress and believe in God as well might make it necessary to conceive of our Lord as a vision of existence who conceivably was obliged to compete with other visions of existence in the universe, other conceptions of how life should be."[513]

Mailer wrote the above during the late 1960s, and today our Lord has to compete with spiritless scientism, along with multi-spirited metaphysics, for predominating conceptions of how life is or should be. In the weird-science world of the 1990s, it is considered as pointless for an Orthodox Jew to observe 613 laws of the Torah (365 proscriptions, 248 exhortations), as it is witless for the evangelical Christian to profess: "Now faith is the substance of things hoped for, the evidence of things not seen" (Hebrews 11:1). But, as Nancy Pearcey and Charles Thaxton have amply proven in <u>The Soul of Science</u> (1994), it was in the Judaeo-Christian West that empircal science emerged as a discipline and way to knowledge; not in the Hindu-Buddhist- Taoist East. Christians and Jews in the West had accepted the Biblical teaching that the cosmos was real, and therefore could be investigated by rational methods.[514] There are many persons of faith who believe that recognition of the divine is not obtained through scientific knowledge; <u>that</u> knowledge encompasses man, his existence and experience in <u>this</u> material would. They believe that "[c]omprehension of the divine is attained [solely] through our spiritual side."[515] However, this writer agrees with the late Rabbi

Mendel Schneerson who, on reconciling science and religion, wrote:

"One can ...say that secular or scientific wisdom deals with what the universe is, while spiritual wisdom deals with why it is and what it means to one's life. True science and true religion, therefore, are two sides of the same coin. The emphasis is on 'true' -- not a science that denies G__d or a religion that sees science as its enemy. Both of these attitudes stem from the same flaw: the belief that G__d, who created the natural universe and its laws, cannot co-exist with His creation! Any scientific theory that seems to contradict His laws will ultimately be scientifically proven to be unverifiable even by the most diligent scientific exploration."[516]

The last is admittedly a step farther than most people of faith dare to tread. With increasing attacks on Judaeo - Christian tenets, though, by both advocates of Natural Scientism and New Age metaphysics, people of faith ought to take that extra step. They cannot look to the [liberal] Church or the [secular] Academy for support -- these former bastions of Christendom and Western values have long been occupied by the enemies of God. As a result, a furious, frontal counter-attack must be mounted, rather than a sustained, half-hearted rear-guard defense. And conditions are ripe for re-taking the lost citadels of religion and education: Unfolding new discoveries in the sciences -- from archaeology to zoology -- are proving forever more the absolute truth in God's word; the Hebrew Scriptures and New Testament.

A good place to initiate the counter - attack is at the Entropy Law, the second law of thermodynamics. Jeremy Rifkin, of course, wrote an entire book on entropy as we have seen.[517] The second law of thermodynamics describes the probable behaviour of particles (molecules, atoms, electrons, etc.) of a physical system. The Entropy Law simply states that any physical system left to itself will decay with time, as matter tends to become increasingly disorganised (Barrett and Fisher: 1984).[518] The immediate implication of the Entropy Law is two-fold: (1) The whole material universe should have turned into "a cloud of dust"[519] aeons ago, and (2) there has to be a vast, organising force to counteract the vast, disorganising force within the nature of things to keep the material universe in order; this force has to be non-material ...or it too would become disordered. The only non - material force able to counteract the disorder of the material universe must be an omniscient and omnipotent God.[520] And in light of the Big Bang Theory, the Entropy Law, and the expanding universe -- all precepts subscribed to by "the scientific community" -- the cosmos by definition would have to have had an origin. A powerful First Cause, like the Great Watchmaker (the God of theism), would then logically answer the question of the universe's origin. That non-material force, which keeps the cosmos in check and perfect balance, is the One and same unknowable Designer who created the cosmos.[521]

Rabbi Daniel Lapin is the South African - born and Mercer Island - based founder and president of Toward Tradition, an organisation devoted to politically uniting American Jews and Christians. But the multi - talented ·rebbe· is also a former investment broker ... and physics teacher. He therefore speaks with scientific as well as religious authority:

"The monotheistic traditions, beginning with Judaism, teach that God's act of creation preceded and transcended, the physical laws that we know today. Without His intervention, the universe remains captive to the third [sic] law of thermodynamics: entropy is always increasing. In other words, defeating entropy is a God-like act. While only He can reverse entropy at the universal level, we humans can at least create small oases of physical and spiritual light ..."[522]

The scientific questions of anti-matter, the parallel universe, the fourth dimension, space - time and time - dilation pose a set of paradoxes for persons of religious faith. These questions appear different from one another but, this writer strongly believes, all are various sides of the identical paradox. Maurice S. Rawlings, medical doctor and Christian author of the best - selling Beyond Death's Door, wrote of a make - believe space - journey scenario in his follow-up book, To Hell and Back.[523] As the would-be trip encompasses several paradoxes simultaneously, a major part is well worth quoting:

"The following week the [astrophysics] professor had us imagine that we were on a space ship orbiting a black hole. The space ship would accelerate faster and faster as it approached the black star. With the increasing speed, time would become slower and slower until it was completely lost as it exceeded the speed of light. Never another tick of the clock. Impossible to grow old. The fountain of youth. Neither time nor the occupants would grow old. They would have entered eternity without death, and found a permanent glimpse of glory without dying.

"This world of infinity, the eternity proposed by science, is also the realm of spiritual existence. It could be the eternity proposed by all the bibles of all religions. The place of heaven and hell. Not merely a glimpse of glory or a glimpse of hell, but an eternal dwelling.

"Perhaps there are other bridges to eternity besides death, speed, and time. Since eternity and infinity have become bywords of science, Einstein's relativity has become more relative. More scientists are spirit-minded, but many seek information through the mysteries of spirit guides, rather than the traditions of religion. As a primary probe, the metaphysical is beginning to replace the telescope.

"Our astrophysics teacher mentioned the possibility of some sort of heaven existing in the time warp of space .... Of course, at this speed, no noticeable time would elapse during the two million year trip to Andromeda -- but how much further [sic] would it be to reach the proposed heaven...?"[524]

Let's start with the enigma of time - dilation. Nancy R Pearcey and Charles B. Thaxton, in The Soul of Science, made mention of the late Herbert Dingle, a distinguished physicist who found serious flaws in

Einstein's theory of relativity. Dingle had originally been a strong proponent of relativity. Among the theory's assumptions, Dingle had trouble accepting the idea of time-dilation. The concept of time-dilation requires, for example, that if two persons travel at different speeds, then time will slow down for the faster traveller and he therefore will age more slowly. But ... if all motion is relative, either person may be seen as travelling faster. However, reasoned Herbert Dingle, unless the idea of time-dilation specifies some distinguishing mark, the theory requires each traveller to age more slowly than the other (Pearcey and Thaxton: 1994).[525] Hence the idea of time - dilation still (in essence) remains a mystery.

The thorny paradox of time-dilation brings us back to the concept of space-time analysed earlier in Part III. Einstein stated in his General Theory of Relativity that space is not three-dimensional, and that time is not a separate entity from space. Indeed, Einstein's space and time are different aspects of the same something. And, we learned, space-time comprises a four-dimensional, mutually interpenetrated continuum, in which there is no Newtonian (i.e., tradional) flow of time (Talbot: 1981). In addition, Einstein's curvature of space-time -- revealing itself in gravitation -- was a difficult theory for the [average] human mind to grasp (Pagels: 1984). There was now a fourth dimension; three of space and one of time as a spatial distance. (Hold on, dear reader, a fifth dimension -- not the Soul group of the '60s -- will be coming our way later on!) Riding to this layman's mental-stress rescue was German physicist, Gerhard Staguhn; who reassuringly explained that fourth dimensional time (as a spatial distance) was not merely a fourth dimension of space. The mathematical linking of the three dimensions of space with one of time, necessitates a minus sign in the equation; a plus sign would make time just a fourth dimension of space.

That minus sign is crucially significant as it strictly separates past causes with future events (Staguhn: 1992 ed.). Yet the phantasy of past-time travel still persists. On 14 April 1996, the Discovery cable TV channel broadcast a Discover Magazine programme on the very topic. According to Discover Magazine, going back in time would land the time-traveller in a parallel universe, shaking hands with himself backwards. Surely this is Disneyism -- or theoretical weird-science -- at its most silly and irresponsible?

But there is alot more to be said about space-time, a concept which had been around long before Albert Einstein presented his General Theory of Relativity in 1915. In Judaism, tzimtzum can be translated from the Hebrew as "contraction". This is the parallel universe of eternity, of heaven and hell, where the Godhead (Elohim) may withdraw Himself to enable a finite cosmos to exist; to come into being via a process of emanation.[526] Since God is infinite and omnipresent, without tzimtzum there would be no vacant place into which the space-time structure of a separate creation could be engendered.[527] Tzimtzum, or space-time, also contains the ["other"] parallel universe, the theological fourth dimension. The parallel universe / fourth dimension, this writer strongly believes, is the eternity of Judaeo-Christianity, the infinity of Natural Scientism. Judaism's hellish sitra achra (Aramaic for "other side") is a by-product of tzimtzum in the way the parallel universe / fourth dimension is a by-product of space-time.[528] The sitra achra (a waste by-product) came into being as part of the process of emanation by a self-limiting Godhead, so that a finite universe could exist apart from the parallel [supernatural[universe. Jewish lore and legend tell us that the site of the sitra achra is on the "left hand side'; in the hole of the great abyss ruled by Samael ("poison of God"), the evil angel (a Jewish Satan), and Lilith, Adam's malignant first consort and mother of all daemons.[529] (Christianity has its own version of the infernal pit ...it is known as Hell!)

Since the cultural advent and popularisation of the New Age during the late 1960s, there are many versions of the parallel universe or the fourth dimension. Evangelist Dave Hunt of Bend, Oregon, has delved alot into New Age thinking, and in his (and T.A. McMahon's) best selling The Seduction of Christianity, flatly stated: "No one person has contributed more to the merger of science and religion than the French priest/palaeontologist Teilhard de Chardin."[530] Hunt has quoted sociologist/anthropologist H. James Birx in an L.A. Times interview saying: "A future fourth layer [dimension], the theosphere, is envisioned by Teilhard as the culmination ...when the converging ...human spirits transcend space and matter and mystically join god-omega at the omega point."[531] (Robert Muller, who served 36 years at the U N, is a product of "Teilhardian enlightenments", and Hillary Clinton guru Jean Houston -- among many other New Age leaders -- have been profoundly influenced by the thoughts, beliefs, and writings of Teilhard de Chardin.)[532]

The fourth dimension as New Age theosphere has become an intrusive, disturbing element in contemporary syncretic Christianity. A prime example of the blending of Eastern mysticism with charismatic Christianity has been the "fourth dimension" teachings of South Korean pastor, Paul Yonggi Cho. Stating that a line is one-dimensional, a plane two-dimensional (the two include the one), and a cube three-dimensional

(the three include the two), Yonggi Cho has then declared:

"Then God spoke to my heart, 'Son ... the spirit is the fourth dimension .... [as] the third dimension
includes and controls the second dimension, so the fourth dimension includes and controls the third
dimension, producing a creation of order and beauty ....'
"There are three spiritual forces in the earth. The Spirit of God, the spirit of man, and the spirit of
Satan.... All three spirits are in the realm of the fourth dimension, so naturally spirits can hover over the
material third dimension and exercise creative powers....."[533]

At first glance, Yonggi Cho's conception of the fourth dimension seems spiritually plausible, but there

is a glitch here somewhere ... Ah! of course: Yonggi Cho, in true New Age fashion, has placed the spirit of

man on a par with Satan's and, indeed, on a level with that of the transcendent God. In the garden of Eden

the serpent had said to the first woman, "[Ye] shall be as gods...." (Gen:3:5b). Aeons before, the pre-satanic

Lucifer had claimed, "I will make myself like the Most High" (Isa. 14:14). This attitude is known today as

the Human Potential Movement, ie., releasing the god within you. But this ultimate rebellion against God,

this insistence on personally divine status, is the moving spirit of the New Age. (And Christianity is not alone

in being syncretised with New Age teachings. According to glamour magazine In Style, Rabbi Philip S. Berg

preaches Kabbala to Hollywood heavyweights Sandra Bernhard, mother/daughter Diane Ladd/Laura Dern, Jeff

Goldblum and others. This writer wonders how many members of Rabbi Berg's blasé class would have showed

up to study basic Torah? For notes on Kabbala see Appendix K.) [534]

Last, but not least as an astrophysical problem for people of faith, is the matter of anti-matter. As

a lay Christian and (assuredly) a non-scientist, this writer can only guess and speculate as to the nature of anti-

matter and its significance to Judaeo-Christianity. On the scientific face of it, the question of anti-matter

appears simple. As the Disney magazine, Discovery, has put it:

"Any time a particle is created from nothing, the universe will simultaneously spew up its antiparticle,
which will have the same mass and other characteristics but will have the opposite charge and will head off
at an equal speed in the exact opposite direction. Thus protons are made with antiprotons; electrons with
antielectrons, known as positrons....."[535]

Images, both scientific and religious, literally swarm over one's mind, but the key phrase here is

"created from nothing", ex nihilo. (Only a transcendent God can create something from nothing.) In other

words, what we have here is a two-fold universe of direct opposites; characterised by yin and yang, by male and female, by light and dark, by good and evil, by Christ and anti-Christ. Is this, then, the parallel universe we've all heard so much of? And is it -- the infinite eternity -- made up of antiparticles composed of antiprotons and antielectrons?

Author and practitioner of paradoxical science, Erich von Däniken, has said that the earth is entering "the interstellar third millennium." Von Däniken, a Swiss, and W. Raymond Drake, a Briton, regaled the world public throughout the 1970s with tall stories of ancient spacemen populating Earth from afar. Celebrated late astronomer, Carl Sagan, and real-live NASA astronauts have laughed at the wild claims of borderline science. But does an arrogant Scientism have all the answers? Christian authors Dave Hunt and T. A. McMahon have made the point that Scientism, as a religion, requires a leap of faith -- unsupported by evidence -- for the true believer. Carl Sagan had unlimited faith in the cosmos to produce -- via macro-evolution of course -- ever higher life-forms.[536]

Astrophysicist Robert Jastrow is the founder and former director of NASA's Goddard Institute for Space Studies, which played a role in the Pioneer, Voyager, and Galileo space probes. He has written several books, including Red Giants and White Dwarfs and Journey to the Stars (Bantam Books, New York, 1970) Jastrow, a UFO/ETI enthusiast, has posited that life on some celestial bodies could have been macro-evolving for 10 billion years or more than on Earth. Jastrow has suggested that ETIs, from these distant places, could be so far evolved ahead of man as man is beyond the earthworm.[537] According to Dave Hunt, Jastrow has even ventured that ETIs might in fact have evolved beyond the need for bodies -- they are pure intelligence.[538] Jastrow has remarked for the record that extra-terrestrial life

"...may be far beyond the flesh-and-blood form that we would recognize. It may [have[...escaped its mortal flesh to become something that old-fashioned people would call spirit[s]. And how do we know it's there? Maybe it can materialize and then dematerialize. I'm sure it has magical powers by our standards.[539]...

But Robert Jastrow, astrophysicist, had a nasty shock in store for the 144th national conference of the Association for the Advancement of Science. For Jastrow rudely reminded some 800 of his fellow scientists that (1) the cosmos had a beginning; (2) that evidence indicates an intelligent design by a Creator.[540] Worse, the self-professed agnostic Jastrow has written candidly about his fellow scientists:

"Astronomers are curiously upset by ...proof that the universe had a beginning. Their reactions provide an interesting demonstration of the response of the scientific mind -- supposedly a very objective mind -- when evidence uncovered by science itself leads to a conflict with the articles of faith in their profession....

"There is a kind of religion in science; a faith that ... every event can be explained as the product of some previous event.... This conviction is violated by the discovery that the world had a beginning under conditions in which the known laws of physics are not valid ... the scientist has lost control.

"If he really examined the implications, he would be traumatized. As usual, when the mind is faced with trauma, it reacts by ignoring the implications...."[541]

But at today's New Age NASA, the thinking of former Apollo 14 Commander Edgar Mitchell, and like-minded others, have become predominant. Mitchell, the sixth astronaut to walk on the moon and holding a Doctor of Science degree from M.I.T., nevertheless founded the Institute of Noetic Sciences to channel the collected psychic efforts of ESP (extra-sensory perception) groups.[542] Noetic, as we have learned, is derived from the noösphere, that dream-area envisioned by Telhard de Chardin as accommodating the eventual cosmic union of all souls. Twenty years ago, satirist Tom Wolfe observed that "the Flying Saucer folk" were starting to reveal their space phantasies as essentially religious in nature. The Flying Saucer folk quite literally believed in an "other order" -- an order under the command of ETIs in UFOs.[543] Noetic evolution is deeply held, by such as Edgar Mitchell and the Flying Saucer folk, as the billion-plus-year psycho-spiritual synchronicity of mind and matter. Higher alien beings and ascended masters are the existential result.[544] Regular Joe author, Norman Mailer, has expressed his own spin on cosmic consciousness:

"'It came upon the senses that in the hour of death, consciousness might separate into other dimensions, dissipate into other orders of the immense and the miniscule, consciousness might at last be off on terminal voyages to microbes, molecules, or the stars."[545]

With the final dissipation of human consciousness into microbes, molecules, or the stars, there could well be a future recycling of the human body into compost-fertiliser or ground into edible, protein-rich "soylent green" (from "Soylent Green", the film released in 1973, starring Edward G. Robinson and Charlton Heston). Is this the end of evolution, both spiritual and physical?

There is alot of talk about evolutionism these days, mainly as a tenet of faith being increasingly -- and vocally -- challenged by members of "the scientific community" itself. The late Carl Sagan scathingly referred to several scientists of faith in his final book, The Demon - Haunted World:

"Astronomer George Smoot described his discovery of small irregularities in the radio radiation left over from The Big Bang as 'seeing God face-to-face'. Physics Nobel laureate Leon Lederman described the

Higgs boson, a hypothetical building block of matter, as 'the God particle'.... Physicist Frank Tipler proposes that computers in the remote future will prove the existence of God and work our bodily resurrection."[546]

It is ironic that Carl Sagan died a few months before the 1997 publication of Michael Drosnin's, The Bible Code (New York: Simon & Schuster), a work connecting computers to scriptural prophesy. (That "remote" future is already here, Dr. Sagan!) No matter; Sagan was devoutedly atheistic and would have pooh-poohed Drosnin's work anyway.[547] But there are scientists who not only believe in God, but are nay-saying Darwinism in the public forum. Human Events magazine announced, 5 July 1996, the recently published premiere issue of Origins & Design; an interdisciplinary, peer-reviewed quarterly committed to analysing theories of origin and beliefs on design, their philosophical foundations, and their influence on the culture at large. The quarterly editorial term boasts "outstanding credentials" in molecular biology, philosophy, the philosophy of science and interdisciplinary studies.[548] And the editorial advisory board of Origins & Design is "something else" -- it includes: Michael Behe, biochemistry (Lehigh University); Dean Kenyon, biology (SF State U); Charles Thaxton, chemistry (at Prague); Michael Denton (U. of Otago, N.Z.); Phillip Johnson, law (U. Cal. Berkeley); Robert Kaita, plasma physics (Princeton University); and Siegfried Scherer, taxonomy/molecular biology (at the Technical University of Munich).[549]

If all of the above was not enough, Sharon Begley of Newsweek magazine wrote an article, 'Heretics in the Laboratory' (with Peter Burkholder), published in mid-September 1996. The subtitle saucily asked: "Can a creationist be a good scientist? and vice versa?" Readers of the Newsweek article should've answered Yes, as Begley and Burkholder -- despite themselves -- name four creationists -- Kurt Wise, palaeontology/geology (William Jennings Bryan College); Russell Humphreys, power generation (Sandia National Laboratory); John Baumgardner, geophysics (Alamos National Laboratory); and Michael Behe (see above) -- who are good scientists! Indeed, Michael Behe in his recent book, Darwin's Black Box: The Biochemical Challenge to Evolution (New York: The Free Press, 1996) has postulated that biochemical systems of the level of vision, the immune system, and blood clotting are so complicated (cellular and molecular matters of which Charles Darwin had to have been in complete ignorance) that they could only have been designed by an intelligent Creator.[550]

Evolutionism -- contemporary neo-Darwinism -- is being increasingly doubted by responsible scientists, but nonetheless remains the official religion in academia. In the mainstream Protestant Church, liberal theologians are trying -- in vain -- to reconcile Darwinism; and there was that shockingly accommodating statement on macro-evolutionism which recently (1997) issued from the Pontifical Academy at Vatican City.[551] This writer has attempted to deride and discredit Darwinism via the fossil record, "punctuated equilibria", and Archaeopterix in the appendices.[552] Entire books are currently being written against Evolutionism, and so this writer will leave the fray (1) to the warrior-scientists, and (2) the readers with the story of "Lucy." Lucy, Australopithecus afarensis, was an almost complete humanoid female skeleton found in Ethiopia in 1974. (The skeleton was known to the cognoscenti as AL-288-I, but as Lucy to the rest of us.) Christian physicist Alan Hayward has had fun casting uncertainties on Lucy's humaness in a peculiarly British way:

"Much was made of Lucy by her finder, Don Johanson, and others. He assigned her a date of around three million years ago, and claimed that she represented the earliest known ancestors of the human race. Books and magazines began to publish imaginative drawings of Lucy and her family, looking almost as human as the nudists on Brighton Beach.
"Then in 1983 two American anthropologists, Stern and Susman, rather spoiled the artists' fun.[553] They published the results of a re-examination of Lucy's skeleton which had led them to very different conclusions. Many of her bones were more like chimpanzee bones than those of a human. She probably did not walk upright like a woman, but in a slouched position like an ape. And she probably spent much of her time climbing trees, since her skeleton was better suited to that than walking.
"So really what was Lucy? A forerunner of the human race, or just an extinct species of ape? The short answer is that there is no way of knowing." (Hayward: 1995 ed.).

The most effective critic of Darwinism to date, Phillip Johnson, in Reason in the Balance, has maintained that only creation by God can account for man's sense of morality. Nature- "red in tooth and claw" -- is amoral, therefore man's conscience disproves Evolutionism. Evangelist Dave Hunt has suggested that were Evolutionism true, we -- as a society -- ought to close all hospitals, cease all medications, and let the weak perish: Kindness and compassion have no place in an evolutionary world where only the fittest survive.[554]

At this juncture the reader might inquire, What possible connection could link neo - Darwinism to New Age thinking? As has been explicated throughout this chapter, science and magick are two opposing sides of the same triangle; the third side being religion. But "religion" in this study has meant monotheistic Judaeo-Christianity, and in that context New Age beliefs are magickal. And it is under the rubric of religion, then, where Natural Scientism (as neo - Darwinism) meets New (Age meta-) Physics and merge, melding into one. For the New Physics shares with the New Age -- along with Hinduism, Buddhism, Taoism -- an abiding faith in Evolutionism. The grand old man of "Young Earth" creationists, Henry M. Morris, has characterised New Age/New Physics as "accepting the space-time cosmos as the only ultimate and eternal reality and denying any real transcendent Creator of the cosmos."[555]

Finally, there is DNA (deoxyribonucleic acid). Living organisms are structured around the remarkable system known as the DNA molecule, wherein is encoded all the necessary information to direct the growth and form from the germ-cell to the completed organism (Morris: 1986 ed.). Nancy Pearcey and Charles Thaxton have quoted Aristotelian expert, Jeremy Campbell, who wrote that DNA represents "'a coded model of a biological goal.... It is the form of matter'" (Pearcey and Thaxton: 1994).[556] Although the "coded model" of the DNA molecule is immense in variation potential for both plants and animals, the DNA programme foresees, and vouchsafes, that any such variation remains within the fixed limits represented in the genetic systems of the parents (Morris: 1986 ed.). Theologian Henry M. Morris, that grand old man of creationism, has commented:

".... The tremendous amount of ordered information in even the simplest living organisms is so great that it is almost impossible to imagine that scientists could ever synthesize it from elemental chemicals, no matter how long they took, and even more inconceivable that it could ever happen by chance."[557]

(The DNA-type molecule -- composing just about all living flesh -- is itself made up of the basic earth elements of carbon, hydrogen, oxygen, nitrogen et al.).

The evolutionists still fervently hope that DNA can be replicated in the laboratory; it is their abiding faith in "abiogenesis". The latter hypothesis is the imagined, gradual development of complex molecules from the basic earth elements into self-duplicating molecules, which the evolutionists then assume to be living. The evolutionist neo-Darwinians retain their weird belief in spontaneous generation, despite its utter demolition by Louis Pasteur and others during the 19th century.[558]

Christian apologist J. P. Moreland has likened DNA to the human language. The DNA genetic code is transmitted as if by an intelligent communicator, in the same way one identifies a new language from a stone tablet or from outer space.[559] The information in DNA resembles human language -- whether translated or not -- in that it contains a meaningful sequence of symbols which transmits information.[560] Who, or what

328

intelligence, wrote the genetic code in DNA? Moreland has concluded that this information existed prior to -
- and outside of -- the genetic code, and that information was imposed by a Mind.[561] Pearcy and Thaxton have

concurred with Moreland and other Christian believers in accounting for the genetic code in DNA:

> "What is lacking is an agent -- an author who creates the DNA message, composing it according to
> the principles of grammar and recording it on a material medium. Creationists argue that the unique
> informational properties of DNA are best explained by an author, a creator of life.
> ...."If books and computer programs require an intelligent origin, so too does the message in the DNA
> molecule."[562]

AAs will recall Fulton Oursler as the brave editor of Liberty magazine, who, in autumn 1939, dared

to print the piece 'Alcoholics and God', thereby helping pave the way for Alcoholics Anonymous.[563] But the

same Fulton Oursler was the author of The Greatest Story Ever Told, a moving rendition of the Messianic

gospel. Oursler's book was later made into an inspiring movie of the same name, but long before cheap

imitations like "Jesus Christ Superstar' and "Godspell" came along.[564] During winter 1996, this writer spotted

The Greatest Story Ever Told in a local P.A. bookstore out-bin, advertised as costing less than a dollar. From

the printing on the pages-edge, the browser saw that the discarded paperback had at one time been the

property of River Ridge High School Library. Fulton Oursler's Christian classic had most probably been

dumped from the River Ridge H.S. Library to make way for the more popular [timely and cool] R. L. Stine's

truly frightful "Goosebump" series.[565] (Yeah, I know; but it gets the little clots to read.) This writer

immediately seized the battered paperback -- it was near Christmas and The Greatest Story Ever Told would

refreshen good memories of Yuletides past.

Oursler's book was warmly re-read, but also a forgotten lesson was re-learned concerning the genetic

code (found in DNA) and God-given individuality. Expanding on Yeshua of Nazareth having said that "the

very hairs of your head are all numbered," Oursler wrote:

> "Thus He emphasized the uniqueness of the individual and they [His listeners] loved it, though little
> comprehending the literal import of His words. But two thousand years later, in the laboratories of modern
> criminologists, the spectrograph and spectro-photometer show us that the hair on every mortal head is
> different from all others; and more, that each individual hair is 'numbered', is different from any other hairs
> on the same head! Not only are there no two thumbs or fingerprints alike in all humanity, but even the lines
> and whorls and loops and corrugations on the hoofs of cows and bulls and the feet of dogs and cats are all
> unparalleled. It is science today that shows individuality to be of persistent uniqueness in God's world, just
> as Jesus taught it."[566]

But, related through the faithful Oursler, Yeshua of Nazareth tackled magickal views of human individuality in addition to scientific views of human uniqueness. Oursler assumed that He (Yeshua) had heard the talk of Oriental travellers [proto-New Agers] passing through the marketplace; the chattering about Nirvana and the denial of human individuality. From the Eastern voyagers sojourning in Palestine, Yeshua had learned of the Vedic holy books of India, and the Sutras, and tales from their Sacred Mahabharata. The wise men from the East believed that the life of a man (unless he had already attained godhood) meant no more than a droplet of water falling into the vast ocean. All uniqueness, individual identity would be forever lost ...a mere man (or woman) signifying nothing. Yeshua Meshiach -- Jesus Christ -- would recall men to the truth that made them free. In the words of Fulton Oursler:

> "Man, individual [unique] man, with his infinite capacity to know the bliss of growth, the joy of action, the wonder of beauty, was the creature to whom He would address Himself; to man who had immortal individuality."[567]

Pre-Script

For 3,000 years a secret code has remained hidden in the Bible. Buried under the original Hebrew of the Torah (the Pentateuch, the Five Books of Moses), lies a complex network of words and phrases; indeed, a whole new revelation. As agnostic U.S. journalist Michael Drosnin has written, There's a Bible beneath the Bible: Under the Book there is a complete computer programme. The information encoded within the second Book could only have been released through the invention of the computer; thereby to be liberated into the dimension of cyberspace.[568] But Sir Isaac Newton among others, so far back as the 17th century, had believed that a blue-print of future history is encoded in the Bible -- and tried to find it. Their quest had been in vain for they lacked the one key to opening the hidden text -- a computer![569] The Bible Code author Michael Drosnin, and evangelists like Dave Hunt, have posited that no other scriptural text save the Masoretic Hebrew Text provides the amazing encoded messages, which also forms the basis for the 1611 King James Version of the Bible.[570] As more and more computerised information spills out from under the pages of the Torah, less and less new discoveries can be dismissed as sheer coincidence. These new discoveries involve computer-searching for central words at certain letter intervals which fit a consistent pattern. The original work was done by mathematical statiticians Doron Witzum, Eliyahu Rips, and Yoav Rosenberg at the Jerusalem College of Technology and the Hebrew University.[571] Continued research by Witzum, Rips and Rosenberg, in which they took the names of the 34 most prominent Jews from the ninth to the nineteenth centuries, revealed that all thirty-four -- along with approximate birth/death dates -- appeared in the Masoretic Text. The astounded researchers added the names of the 32 next most prominent Jewish leaders into Biblical cyberspace ...with the same accurate findings. The results were published in the <u>Statistical Science</u> journal, whose perplexed editor reported:

> "'Our referees were baffled: their prior beliefs made them think the Book of Genesis could not possibly contain meaningful references to modern day individuals, yet when the authors carried out additional analyses and checks the effect persisted. The paper is thus offered to <u>Statistical Science</u> as a challenging puzzle'"[572]

Evangelist Dave Hunt has wryly noted that the Bible Code is perhaps a puzzle to atheists. This writer now asks, Is cyberspace -- hitherto a New Age area -- the arena where in true science encounters the real [living] God?

NOTES

513.   Norman Mailer, <u>Of a Fire on The Moon</u> (New York: Grove Press, Inc., 1970), p.150. NB: Tough-guy Mailer has often addressed messianic themes. See Mailers <u>The Gospel According to The Son</u> (New York: Random House, 1997).

514.   Chuck Colson, 'Quantum Mysteries: The New Age comes to science', <u>The Citizens News</u> Sequim. (Wash.), Vol.3, Issue 10, 17 May 1996, p.7.

515.   See letter from Duśica Savić Benghiat of Pacific Palisades, Calif., to <u>Chronicles</u>, Vol.21, No.5, May 1997, p.5.

516.   Menachem Mendel Schneerson, <u>Toward a Meaningful Life: The Wisdom of The Rebbe</u> (New York: William Morrow and Company, Inc., 1995), pp.194-195. Italics in original.

517.   Jeremy Rifkin with Ted Howard, <u>Entropy a New World View</u> (New York: Bantam Books, 1981).

518.   See Boris P. Dotsenko, Chapter 1, 'Flight to Faith', pp.5-6.

519.   Op.cit., Boris P. Dotsenko, pp.5-6.

520.   <u>Ibid</u>., pp.5-6. Cf. Henry M. Morris (1986 ed.), pp.18-19.

521.   Paul Copan, 'The Presumptuousness of Atheism,' <u>Christian Research Journal</u>, Vol.18, No.4, Spring 1996, p.8. NB: The Big Bang Theory and expanding universe may sound contradictory to the Entropy Law, but they are not. Alan Hayward (1995 ed.) has cited an article published by the American Institute of Physics:

> "'[S]tandard big-bang cosmology recognizes that the Universe was at a low entropy at its outset and undergoes entropy increases globally through each step of its evolution. When a star condenses or when a galaxy forms, there is a local ordering and a great increase of heat. The second law is not violated because the decrease of entropy in one place is offset by a far greater increase somewhere else.'"

> See D. G., 'Mainstream scientists respond to creationists', <u>Physics Today</u>, February 1982, pp.53-55. Quoted in Alan Hayward, pp.153-154. Hayward has also reminded us that entropy only deals with <u>thermodynamic</u> processes; not with all natural processes (pp.183-184). Cf. Henry M. Morris, p.59.

522.   Rabbi Daniel Lapin, 'In Praise of Shame', <u>National Review</u>, Vol.XLVIII, No.17, 25 September 1995, p.87. Cf. J. P. Moreland, pp.33-35.

523.   Maurice S. Rawlings, M. D., <u>To Hell and Back</u> (Nashville: Thomas Nelson Publishers, 1993).

524.   Op.cit., Maurice S. Rawlings, pp.205-206. NB: Dr. Rawlings, a cardiologist, wrote both his definitive, [literally] hands-on studies about near-death (NDE) and out-of-body experience (OBE).

525.   Pearcey and Thaxton have cited Herbert Dingle, letter to the editor, <u>The Economist</u>, 5 March 1977. See also Herbert Dingle, <u>Science at The Crossroads</u> (London, U.K.: Brian and O'Keefe, 1972). In <u>The Soul of Science</u>, pp.181,272.

526.   Alan Unterman, <u>Dictionary of Jewish Lore and Legend</u> (London, U.K.: Thames and Hudson, Ltd., 1991), p.202. Cf. Henry M. Morris, p.21.

NOTES (cont'd.)

527. <u>Ibid</u>., p.202. Cf. Henry M. Morris, pp.22-24.

528. <u>Ibid</u>., p.188. Cf. <u>Holy Bible</u>, Matt. 25,ff.

529. <u>Ibid</u>., p.188. Cf. <u>Holy Bible</u>, Rev. 21, ff. NB: Some ancient sources and modern writers refer to Einstein's space-time as [solely] the fourth dimension. But quantum physicists speculate that there could be a <u>fifth</u> dimension, a state described by religious texts as "a depth of good and a depth of evil". See Michael Drosnin, <u>The Bible Code</u> (New York: Simon & Schuster, 1997), p.50.

530. Dave Hunt and T. A. McMahon, <u>The Seduction of Christianity</u> (Eugene, Ore.: Harvest House Publishers, 1985), p.77.

531. <u>Ibid</u>., p.77. <u>Los Angeles Times</u>, op.cit., pp.I-B,1 (n.d.). Brackets this writer's. See Appendix L for UFOlogy and Kenneth Ring's <u>Omega Project</u>.

532. <u>Ibid</u>., pp.77-78. Pierre Teilhard de Chardin (1881-1955), "godfather of the New Age".

533. <u>Ibid</u>., p.111. Cited is Paul Yonggi Cho, <u>The Fourth Dimension, Volume Two</u> (Bridge Publishing, 1983), pp.38-40. See also Dave Hunt's remarks, 'The New Age and The Church', <u>The John Ankerberg Show</u> (Chattanooga, Tenn: The John Ankerberg Evangelistic Association, 1988), p.9.

534. David Wallis, 'Scene + heard', <u>In Style</u>, Vol.3, No.12, Dec. 1996 (n.p.). NB: Also studying Kabbala in Tinseltown were Roseanne, Barry Diller, and Dolly Parton (go figure). <u>USA Today</u> 11/96. Cf. <u>The Berean Call</u>, January 1997, p.4.

535. Gary Taubes, 'The Anti-Matter Mission', <u>Discovery</u>, Vol.17, No.4, April 1996, p.74.

536. Cf. Dave Hunt and T. A. McMahon, p.92

537. Dave Hunt, 'What About ETIs?', <u>The Berean Call</u> (Bend, Ore.), April 1995, p.1. See Robert Jastrow, 'The Case for UFOs', <u>Science Digest</u>, Nov./Dec. 1980, pp.83-85.

538. Remarks by Dave Hunt, 'The New Age and The Church', <u>The John Ankerberg Show</u>, p.18.

539. <u>Geo</u>, Feb. 1982, 'Geo Conversation', an interview with Dr. Robert Jastrow, p.14. Quoted by Dave Hunt in <u>The Berean Call</u>, April 1995, p.2.

540. <u>Radix</u>, July/Aug. 1979, Paul Arveson and Walter Hearn, 'God and The Scientists: Reflections on The Big Bang', pp.9-14. In Dave Hunt and T. A. McMahon, p.96.

541. <u>The Los Angeles Times</u>, 25 June 1978, Part VI, pp.1,6. In Hunt and McMahon, pp.96-97.

542. Tom Wolfe, <u>Mauve Gloves & Madmen, Clutter & Vine</u> (Toronto: Bantam Books, 1997), p.131.

543. Op.Cit., Tom Wolfe, p.131.

544. Hunt and McMahon, pp.39-40. Cf. Pierre Le Compte de Noüy, <u>Human Destiny</u> (New York: The New American Library of World Literature, 1949), <u>passim</u>.

NOTES (cont'd)

545.   Norman Mailer, Of a Fire on The Moon, p.300

546.   Carl Sagan, The Demon - Haunted World (New York: Random House, 1995), p.335.

547.   NB: Journalist Michael Drosnin, despite all his own irrefutable evidence, remains a non-believer. CNN's Crossfire, 18 July 1997.

548.   'Announcing New Journal: Origins & Design', Human Events, 5 July 1996, p.21.

549.   Ibid., p.21. See Also Appendix P.

550.   Sharon Begley with Peter Burkholder, 'Heretics in The Laboratory', Newsweek, 16 September 1996, "Society" page. See also follow-up letters from Russell Humphreys and Michael Behe, Newsweek, 7 October 1996, pp.22,24. Cf. 'Q & A', The Berean Call, March 1997, p.3; J. P. Moreland, pp.213,221-222; Henry M. Morris, pp. 52-55; Alan Hayward, p.43.

551.   :'"We are convinced that masses of evidence render the application of the concept of Evolution to Man and other primates [to be] beyond serious dispute.'" The Vatican is gleefully quoted by Arthur C. Clarke in 'Foreword' (p.xiii to James Randi, An Encyclopaedia of Claims, Frauds, and Hoaxes of the Occult and Supernatural (New York: St. Martin's Griffin, 1995).

552.   See Appendix O. NB: The excellent Planet of Life televised series included an episode, 'Creatures of the Skies', dealing exclusively with Archaeopterix and evolution. It was evenly balanced, and broadcast on the Discovery channel, 20 May 1996 and 9 July 1997.

553.   Reported by J. Cherfas, 'Trees have made man upright', New Scientist, 20 January 1983, pp.172-178. Hayward has written that the irony was that the New Scientist is very pro-Evolutionism, very anti-Creationism, (in Hayward, pp.52-53).

554,   Dave Hunt, 'Evolution or God's Word?', The Berean Call, February 1997, p.2.

555.   Op.cit., Henry M. Morris, p.41. Science and The Bible was originally copyrighted in 1951. NB: This writer, with all due respect to Young Earth creationists, subscribes to the Ancient Earth creation theory because of the fossil record. Cf. Alan Hayward, passim.

556.   Jeremy Campbell, Grammatical Man: Information, Entropy, Language, and Life (New York: Simon & Schuster, 1982), p.270. In Pearcey and Thaxton, pp. 236-237.

557.   Op.cit., H. M. Morris, p.43.

558.   Ibid., p.42. See Appendix P.

559.   Op.cit., J. P. Moreland, p.68.

560.   Ibid., p.68. See Appendix P.

561.   Ibid., p.52. See Appendix P.

562.   Op.cit., Pearcey and Thaxton, pp.242-243

NOTES (concl'd.)

563.   The "Big Book" of <u>Alcoholics Anonymous</u> (New York: Third Edition, 1976), p.xviii.

564.   "The Greatest Story Ever Told" (1965), a George Stevens film starring Max von Sydow, received mixed reviews but this viewer loved it. "Godspell" (1973), was described by critic Bruce Williamson as "[a] patch of terra incognita somewhere between <u>Sesame Street</u> and the gospel according to <u>Laugh-In.</u>" "Jesus Christ Superstar" (1973), directed by Norman Jewison and starring Ted Neeley. Paul D. Zimmerman commented on this movie: "One of the true fiascos of modern cinema."

565.   Some of R. L. Stine's best-selling titles are: <u>Monster Blood</u>, <u>Go Eat Worms</u>, <u>Say Cheese and Die</u>, <u>Piano Lessons Can Be Murder</u>. From 'Children's stories raise goosebumps for school', <u>Peninsula Daily News</u>, 19 January 1997, p.C-8.

566.   Op.cit., Fulton Oursler, p.236.

567.   <u>Ibid.</u>, pp.108-109.

568.   Michael Drosnin, <u>The Bible Code</u> (New York: Simon & Schuster, 1997), p.25.

569.   <u>Ibid.</u>, p.21. NB: Economist John Maynard Keynes, Newton's biographer, found the physicist's papers packed since 1696 at Cambridge University, England.

570.   'Q & A', <u>The Berean Call</u>, September 1996, p.3.

571.   <u>Ibid.</u>, p.4; in Michael Drosnin 'Notes', p.217,ff.

572.   Quoted in <u>ibid.</u>, p.4; in Michael Drosnin, <u>passim</u>. NB: In addition to <u>The Bible Code</u>, other works on the same subject are: Grant R. Jeffrey, <u>The Signature of God</u> (Toronto: Frontier Research Publications, Inc., 1996); and Rabbi Yacov A. Rambsel, <u>Yeshua -- The Hebrew Factor</u> (San Antonio, Tex.: Messianic Ministries, Inc., 1996). And from the Israeli Hebrew codes scholars: Dr. Moshe Katz, <u>Computorah -- The Hidden Codes in The Torah</u>; and Professor Doron Witzum, <u>The Added Dimension (Maymad Ha Nosaf)</u>.

Bibliography for Part IV

23.   Barrett, Eric C. and David Fisher, eds. <u>Scientists Who Believe</u>. Moody Press, Chicago, 1984.

24.   Hayward, Alan. <u>Creation and Evolution</u>. Bethany House Publishers, Minneapolis, Minn., 1995 ed. (Originally publ. by SPCK, London, U. K., 1985)

25.   Moreland, J.P. <u>Scaling the Secular City</u>. Baker Book House, Grand Rapids, Mich., 1995 ed.

26.   Morris, Henry M. <u>Science and the Bible</u>. Moody Press, Chicago, 1986. (Orig. published in 1951.)

27   Pearcey, Nancy R. and Charles B. Thaxton. <u>The Soul of Science</u>. Crossway Books, Wheaton, Ill., 1994.

Acknowledgements

I am grateful to Holly Knowles Fisher of Port Angeles for supplying information on science and sharing her opinions on religion.

NB: The other 5th Dimension was arguably the very best pop-soul vocal group of the 1960s. They recorded the song "Aquarius/Let The Sunshine In", which became the New Age anthem of the 1970s, in addition to the haunting songs of Laura Nyro (tragically dead in early 1997). Cf. <u>The Greatest Hits on Earth</u> (1972), Arista Records, Inc.

P.O.V.: Evangelical Lutherans and the Electric Church

"This people honours Me with their lips,
But their heart is far from Me.
And in vain they worship Me,
Teaching as doctrines the commands
of men." -- Mark 7:6b-7 (NKJ Version)

"Let us never forget that there exists no other religious reality than the faith of the believer -- W.B. Kristensen, Religionshistorisk Studium (trans. by Eric J. Sharpe)

"Lutherans need to tell more about our identity than Garrison Keillor and the St. Olaf Choir" -- Robert J. Marshall

(NB: P.O.V. here means Point of View, not Port of Vallarta!)

The writer's daughter took her Easter school-break at Puerto Vallarta, Jalisco (Mex.), in March 1996.

A fortunate father, this writer soon received a lovely postcard, showing the beautiful Church of Our Lady of

Guadalupe (La Iglesia de Nuestra Señora de Guadalupe), overlooking the playa and the shimmering Bahía

de Banderas. The church building itself is topped by a magnificent cupola-like rendition of the crown

(corona) worn by the ill-fated three-year Empress of México, Carlotta (1864-1867). The ornate yet simple

corona atop the tall, stately Church of Our Lady of Guadalupe must dominate her prospect as few other man-

made objects on earth can.

In a similar way, Holy Trinity Lutheran Church of Port Angeles, Washington, wishes to dominate the

upper sky-line of her prospect. Holy Trinity Lutheran Church (HTLC) has a profound sense of self-

importance to the community at large. And HTLC has been expanding physically as well as spiritually. In

an HTLC campaign newsletter, Fling Wide the Doors, parishioners were informed of 'A Special Celebration':

....."The spirit of God dances among us, calls us to appreciate and enjoy life and invites us to participate in His divine song. The community of Holy Trinity invites you to join in a delightful celebration of our blessedness -- our FLING WIDE THE DOORS ALL-CHURCH BANQUET!"[573]

Although already a well-off and comfortable church, HTLC wanted more space and room to preach

the Gospel of Nice. Illustrative of this was the noëtic senior pastor's sermon on 14 July 1996: "The Best

News of All". (And what was that, pray?) "There is therefore now no condemnation for those who are in

Christ Jesus...."(Romans 8:1a). The ensuing interpretation, of course, was skillfully spun into the old lie of

After accepting the Lord, we may keep right on living as we always have. [Romans 8:1b reads: ..."[W]ho do not walk according to the flesh, but according to the Spirit."] This assured self-righteousness meshed perfectly with the HTLC membership's self-indulgent life-style. The expansive church parking lot was always filled with expensive Volvo Turbos, Crown Victorias, and "customized" big-tire Chevy trucks; giving mute but boastful testimony of a successful -- but <u>casual</u> -- church.

According to the HTLC newsletter, "God <u>dances</u> among us." This writer, in twenty plus years of studying Scripture and reading evangelical literature, has never come across one instance of God <u>dancing</u>. So the above was clearly a case of Tantra replacing Torah. The impersonal Tantric god <u>does</u> dance; it is an ecstatic expression of his/her/its deity. <u>Dancing</u> in itself is an exercise in cosmic consciousness and has often appeared in trendy New Age book titles, such as <u>Dancing in the Light</u> by Shirley Maclaine and <u>The Dancing Wu-Li Masters</u> by Gary Zukav. There is that LSD-type trip taken by Fritjof Capra in the cosmic dance of Śiva (<u>The Tao of Physics</u>). Even fisheriography hasn't escaped the cosmic dance -- Brad Matsen and Ray Troll's <u>Planet Ocean: A Story of Life, the Sea, and Dancing to the Fossil Record</u> (1994) is a recent example. Looking for the dancing deity, though, through real LSD (and other mind-bending drugs) has been around a long time. Theodore Rozsak, in his <u>The Making of a Counter Culture</u> (1969), cited a certain Ms. Jane Dunlap's dance with Mr. [LS]D in 1961:

"I saw the tiny grasses bend in <u>prayer</u>, the flowers <u>dance</u> in the breeze, and then lift their arms to <u>God</u>.
....'[To] one who accepts the God-pull of reversed gravity and maintains a geological time sense, the future seems
gloriously bright.'"[574]

A god who dances fits right in cosmically with the religiously, politically, and environmentally-correct God of Nice. On Earth Day Sunday, 20 April 1997, the printed HTLC service announcements contained A Psalm of the Earth [A Hymn to Al Gore]. After sinful man has raped the Earth, the "psalm" intoned, the implication was that nothing would remain save iron filings for warthogs and slag-heaps for hyaenas. For the Adult Education Hour, the HTLC announcements offered:

"<u>Keeping the Earth: Religious/Scientific Perspectives on the Environment</u>. Narrated by James Earl Jones, this inspirational video calls on all Americans to serve as good stewards of the natural world. Prominent scientists/religious leaders offer perspectives on the need to protect our environment and the diverse species that share it...."[575]

Since the inception of the New Song format during January 1995, church services at HTLC had become curiouser and curiouser. Always casually dressed anyway, the parishioners attending the 11 a.m. service had become downright silly, making their entrance bedight in the latest hiker/biker fashions. The ubiquitous Praise Team Leader, sporting a Rolling Stone (ca. 1964) hair-helmet throughout 1995 and 1996, by 1997 had scraped his long, thinning gray locks into a tight, obscene little Hausfrau bun. The Praise Team Leader, who pounded the keyboards up front, was sometimes accompanied by a wan young woman playing electric violin. Was she a budding Stephan[i]e Grappelli using HTLC services for music practice? This reluctant parishioner never dared ask.

The New Song format also served to further unleash HTLC's liberated clergypersons. The senior pastor -- our New [noëtic] Man -- was metamorphing into a veritable "Magician of Lublin" (1979, starring Alan Arkin), a double-talking (Yiddish: pilpul), theological wolf-in-sheep's clothing; shamelessly flummoxing his flock. The junior pastor, Boobus americanus, stared stupidly with the red-rimmed eyes of the serious ruminant, and delivered meandering sermonettes in the smarmy, familiar tones usually reserved for a Middle School sex-ed class. Doofus washingtonus, the junior flim-flam man, still mouthed Oprahesque platitudes about "relationships" ... but did he really believe his own psychobabble? This parishioner never could tell from observing the assistant pastor's heavy, expressionless mien or furious, porcine eyes belying the saccharine words. This was, after all, Pastor Guns "Я" Us.

Finally, there was Mr. New [cosmic] Christian, editor of the HTLC newsletter, The Trumpet. Not content with his usual feigned humility, Mr. New Christian had had himself listed after his pediatrician wife in the HTLC directory. In other words, Dr. Christian appeared as titular head of the family, with Mr. Christian listed under his given name along with those of his two young sons. He was certainly the super-sensitive type of '90s male, who reads Dear Abby's newspaper column, listens to Dr. Laura on the radio, and watches the Great Oprah on television. But Mr. Christian was also the wet type of weedy man who makes neighbourhood "pastoral" visits to church ladies -- not for reasons of dalliance -- while their husbands are off at honest work. At least Mr. Christian was intelligent enough to realise that he was eschewed as a creepy-crawly by the churchgoing men of the parish.

And so we go on to the New Song service itself. The format is on track with the "Praise & Worship"

(P&W) phenomenon, already notorious in evangelical circles. The P&W style, however, has become de rigeuer in the great mainstream corpus of American Protestant churches. The "praise song" is characterised by "four words, three notes, and two hours"[576], and a fitting new song was chanted over and over again on that last Sunday (13 July 1997) at HTLC:

> "Spirit of the living God, fall afresh on me,
> Spirit of the living God, fall afresh on me,
> Melt me, mold me, fill me, use me,
> Spirit of the living God, fall afresh on me."[577]

Is there a hidden S&M message here or just P&W nonsensical echolalia? These praise songs, along with brain-numbing mantra-like repetitions of isolated (hence meaningless) scriptural phrases, compose the bulk of the P&W service. Ecclesiastical commentator D.G. Hart has written with great insight of P&W in Chronicles magazine:

> "Gone are the hymnals which keep the faithful in touch with previous generations of saints. They have been abandoned... because they are filled with music and texts considered too boring, too doctrinal, and too restrained. What boomers and busters need instead, according to the liturgy of P&W, are a steady diet of religious ballads, most of which date from the 1970's, the decade of disco, leisure suits, and long hair. Gone too are the traditional elements of Protestant worship, the invocation, the confession of sins, the creed... the doxology, and the Gloria Patri. Again, these elements are not sufficiently celebrative or 'dynamic,' the favorite word used to described the new worship. And while P&W has retained the talking head in the sermon, probably the most boring element of Protestant worship, the substance of much preaching turns out to be more therapeutic than theological."[578]

The breakdown of any discipline or gravitas in the Church generally, and in the ELCA particularly, has direct consequences. In late 1996, when Playboy magazine required a representative (i.e., mainstream) student sampling for a sexual mores survey --" Pacific Lutheran University was a natural fit."[579] As part of a public/private school mix of various sizes nationally, the 3,600-student campus in Parkland (Wash.) -- "certainly nailed down our conservative and Northwest school categories'," said James Petersen, author of the report in the October 1996 issue.[580] If Playboy had truly believed PLU to be a conservative school, report author James Petersen would have scarcely bothered to survey the PLU student body. Moreover, PLU was perceived by Playboy as "a natural fit"... which indeed that pc institution is.

The Evangelical Lutheran Church (in both the U.S. and Canada) and Lutheran church schools (located mostly in the American North Central states) have not always been so laid back and permissive.

Traditionally, Lutheran church schools strictly adhered to Lutheran doctrine and Pauline christology. There had always been an ongoing attempt to appeal to the <u>synteresis</u> -- the "leftover spark of the divine" (Kittelson: 1986) present in everyone (i.e., conscience); especially Lutheran college students! The basic Lutheran view of "the world, the flesh, and the devil" ("<u>die Welt, das Fleisch, und der Teufel</u>") was jointly seen and believed by church and schools alike. Of course it was acknowledged that Martin Luther (1483-1546) had personal faults and flaws. Lutheran theological foes in protest were legion and included Martin Bucer, Wolfgang Capito, Anders Carlstadt, Desiderius Erasmus, Johannes Oecolampadius, Ulrich Zwingli. Were these, then, extra-evil men? Lutheran scholar James M. Kittelson has commented in his <u>Luther the Reformer</u> that, "When it came to matters of principle, he [Luther] never could acknowledge the other side's point of view."[581] But Martin Luther was also the humble Christian who could readily admit, "<u>Wir sind Alle Pettler</u>" ("We are all beggars").[582] And Martin Luther was unknowingly prophetic about his own future church, when remarking on the church of his day. In the Preface to <u>The Small Catechism</u> in May 1529, Luther exclaimed in revulsion:

> "Good God, what wretchedness I beheld! The common people...have no knowledge whatsoever of Christian teaching, and unfortunately many pastors are quite incompetent and unfitted for teaching. Although the people are supposed to be Christian...they live as if they were pigs and irrational beasts...."[583]

But <u>spirituality</u> is popular throughout the land, even if the Church herself is not. L. Dean Lagerquist, Associate professor of religion at St. Olaf College (Northfield, Minn.), has observed: "Spirituality is popular among some Americans when it promises a way to be religious without having to deal with the church, its long messy history or those often annoying folks who belong to it."[584] This writer wonders what L. Deane Lagerquist, an educated but seemingly down-to-earth Lutheran woman, thought of the participants at the Women of the ELCA Triennial Convention, held in Minneapolis during July 1996. For three days, almost 6,000 ELCA women "studied the Bible" and worshiped under the theme, "Proclaim God's Peace." There were "liturgical dancers", and the whole show was opened by close-cropped Bishopess April Ulring Larson.[585] After a self-pitying speech of gender victimisation by a Wilma Mankiller [sic.] of the Oklahoma Cherokee Nation, the ECLA womyn's convention was highlighted by the appearance of long-time Guatemalan irritant, Nobel Peace Prize winner Rigoberta Menchú Tum.[586] Look what they've done to our Church, Pa!

During that same month of July 1996, evangelist Dave Hunt wrote in his pastoral letter of one David W. Cloud, who had attended the installation of an ELCA bishop presided over by ELCA archbishop Herbert Chilstrom. Cloud told of Chilstrom speaking out on environmentalism and pacifism, but nowhere did the ELCA archbishop make mention of the cross, the blood, or the atonement of Jesus Christ.[587] David Cloud summed up:

"The entire experience was very sad and grievous to my spirit as I observed the pageantry, the solemnity, the appearance of piety which had been put on before the service just as a woman puts on her make-up...Not a hair was out of place, nor a voice off key in the two choirs, and the massive pipe organ gave off just the desired sounds... [but all] was contrary to the Word of God...."[588]

According to evangelist Hunt, a recent poll of Lutherans revealed that 3 out of 10 doubt the divinity of Jesus Christ, the same percentage reject His resurrection, 4 out of 10 are sceptical of God's very existence, and 7 out of 10 believe that All Roads Lead to [the] One.[589] Concerning Lutherans, possibly the unkindest cut of all has come from the Reverend James H. Fladland of Richmond, Virginia. He was included in P.J. O'Rourke's hilarious compilation of The American Spectator's Enemies List. The waggish O'Rourke introduced the Reverend Fladland as "a professional in the field of sin and knows an enemy of God and man when he sees one."[590] For the irreverent Reverend confessed:

"Much as it pains me to do so, I must nominate the denomination of which I am an ordained clergyman for this year's [1992] Enemies List. The Evangelical Lutheran Church in America has proved itself to be the most [pc] church body in the U.S., not just for the usual stuff (eg. Columbus-'bashing' and New Masses-sounding 'socioeconomic analyses') but by ensconcing in its very constitution the hideous principle of racial, sexual, and linguistic quotas."[591]

This sell-out of traditional doctrine and values hardly coincides with the historical portrayal of a courageous Martin Luther, boldly proclaiming at the Diet of Worms in front of Charles V, surrounded by imperial soldiers and representatives of Rome: "Here I stand. I can do no other. God help me! Amen."[592]

This writer attended two memorial services at Holy Trinity Lutheran Church last summer (1996). Both the deceased were elderly men who had been fellow Sons of Norway members. The first memorial service was held in late July, in behalf of a Dane born and raised in the state of Nebraska. He was a retired ELCA pastor, and age hadn't dimmed his radical views. The leftist pastor had lived in the Old Country for a while, and he attributed his "enlightened" religious and political views to that sojourn. Knowing of this writer's "fundamentalist" outlook, Pastor P. had once exclaimed with some asperity, "I guess you're one of those nut-cakes who's anti-abortion, aren't you?" The writer had replied with some equanimity, "Of course I'm for the life of the unborn, Pastor, aren't you?" Pastor P.'s memorial service had ended with a local Dixieland jazz combo playing "When The Saints Go Marching In". If nothing else, Pastor P. was certain of his eternal destination, so there would be no swan-songs by solemn Scandinavian hymnodists to usher him into the next world.[593] The writer fervently hoped that Pastor P. took with him..."the testimony of a good conscience."[594]

The second memorial service was held in early September, for a former South Dakotan of German ancestry. Willard S. had been a big man with a big heart, whom the writer knew from Alcoholics Anonymous in addition to Sons of Norway and HTLC. Indeed, Willard S. was accorded an AA-type memorial service, starring "God as you understand him [her/it]". Bill Wilson ("Bill W.") and Bob Smith ("Dr. Bob"), the founders of AA, had cunningly chosen "God as you understand him [her/it]" as their spiritual buzz-phrase, knowing that the Judaeo-Christian Him could not be forced down the throats of recovering alcoholics along with Depression-era coffee. But Holy Trinity Lutheran Church had no such excuse—"God as you understand him" conveniently nullified the potential threat of a personal, punishing Deity. But Willard S., although becoming a somewhat confused New Christian in later life, did not need HTLC or its double-talky pastors to get him to the Pearly Gates: He was already saved by grace through faith in Christ Jesus. The writer gently reminded Willard's widow of this crucial fact after the memorial service. Her warm embrace betokened that she understood.

And then there was the library-church imbroglio. As reported in the preceding Part (III), the Port Angeles Branch of the North Olympic Library System is scheduled to shift location sometime next year (1998). Commensurate with the move, the (pc-to-the-max) P.A. Friends of the Library decided to decorate the fancy new quarters with nine glass panels depicting "contemporary" muses. The Friends of the Library took it upon themselves to commission two Seattle artists specifically chosen to create the New Age panels. This writer labels them "New Age" as the prototype panels were not of the original classical muses of Greek mythology (the offspring of Zeus and Mnemosyne), but were instead of a Buddha of healing, Śiva as Nataraja (the Hindu god of the arts) and others.[595]

When some members of the P.A. community got wind of the type of deities etched into the glass panels…pandemonium ensued. But this time one Jew of faith and a few evangelical Christians turned the tables on both the New Agers and the secular humanists. Opponents maintained that the panels should not be placed in a public building (the library), because that would violate the principle of church and state. Proponents, disliking a dose of their own medicine, feebly retorted that the panels were mere secular objects: The "muses" mirrored the achievements of global multiculturalism. The debate in Port Angeles and environs raged throughout June 1997. Finally, by early July, the Friends of the Library board had had enough -- they voted unanimously to withdraw the nine glass panels.[596]

For this writer the new pc library was to be expected, especially as the Friends of the Library are local clerisy élites overseeing an arm of the public sector. One would anticipate as much from them. But the panels tumult brought in anti-"religious fundamentalism" proponents, a number of whom were from Holy Trinity Lutheran Church. On one occasion the writer had casually mentioned the panels controversy to the HTLC secretary, who jokingly responded that the church would gladly accept the offending panels were the library to back down. The time had definitely come for personal involvement in the fray, and, sure enough, the writer's letter to the local newspaper appeared on 16 July 1997. The second paragraph read:

"….I belong to a large, well-heeled, "mainstream" church which I will call the First Church of St. Timothy Leary. Alot of the granny-glasses/graybearded élites -- the movers and shakers of P.A. -- may be found here on Sunday mornings. My fellow parishioners always seem to end up on the [secular] side of a debate, rather than [on the Christian side]. Over the years, my fellow parishioners have been invariably pro-abortion on demand, special privileges for gays, for the right to burn the American flag. The most anti-P.A. High School Christian Club letter, a while ago, was written by a member of St. Timothy Leary's choir; a recent pro-Muses letter to the [Peninsula Daily News] was submitted by a St. Timothy Leary "Bible class" participant.

"I have finally accepted that I belong to the wrong church. But I can change my church; I'm stuck with the [l]ibrary."

Well, the die was cast…but the writer needn't have worried. Only the HTLC senior pastor telephoned to angrily complain about "going public"; the other telephone call was in enthusiastic support. There remained a twinge of conscience concerning the HTLC secretary -- a very likeable lady -- who had started this writer's train of thought leading to action. The HTLC secretary's baby-boomer husband served as an usher, and had passed the collection plate at the previous Sunday service. As the usher-husband swept by the pews, the writer had detected a tell-tale whiff of marijuana (religious peyote?) on that worthy's clothing. The heaviness of heart evaporated like pot smoke: This writer would be well quit the Electric Church. The sticky, intrusive fingers of the New Age counterculture has no place in a supposedly Spirit-filled church. And as for the ultimate meeting of science with religion, none less than Pope John Paul II has said:

"Science can purify religion from error and superstition; religion can purify science from idolatry and false absolutes."[597]

And if, or rather when, hard science meets and melds with true faith, there will be no place left for the metaphysical magick presently known as the New Age. For as British astrophysicist James H. Jeans (1877-1946) proclaimed, "God is a pure mathematician."[598] Perhaps that is why Thomas Jefferson wrote in 1801: "[T]he [Judaeo-]Christian religion...is a religion of all others most friendly to liberty, science, and the freest expression of the human mind."[599]

Thus, creationism has evolved into Creationism.

NOTES

573. HTLC, <u>Fling Wide the Doors</u>, campaign newsletter No. 3, 8 April 1996. Emphasis this writer's.

574. Jane Dunlap, <u>Exploring Inner-Space: Personal Experiences under LSD-25</u> (London, U.K.: Gallanz, 1961). Cited in Theodore Roszak, <u>The Making of a Counter Culture</u> (Garden City, N.Y.: Anchor Books, 1969), pp.175-176.

575. <u>Announcements</u>. Holy Trinity Lutheran Church insert to New Song brochure, 27 April 1997.

576. D.G. Hart, 'Evangelicals on the Durham Trail', <u>Chronicles</u>, Vol.20, No.4, p.40.

577. 1935. Renewed 1963 Birdwing Music [ASCAP]. Daniel Iverson, EMI Christian Music Publishing. CCU License No.906110.

578. Op.cit., D.G. Hart, p.40.

579. 'Magazine uncovers college opinion', <u>Peninsula Daily News</u>, 21 November 1996, p.A-5.

580. <u>Ibid.</u>, p.A-5. Emphasis this writer's.

581. (Minneapolis, Minn.: Augsburg Publishing House, 1986), p.296.

582. James M. Kittelson, p.297.

583. <u>Ibid.</u>, pp.216-217.

584. L. Deane Lagerquist, 'Arise to Live with God', <u>The Lutheran</u>, Vol.9, No.6, June 1996, p.15.

585. Carolyn J. Lewis, 'Peacemakers stir things up', <u>The Lutheran</u>, Vol.9, No.9, September 1996, p.38.

586. <u>Ibid.</u>, pp.38-39.

587. Dave Hunt, 'The Hope of the Gospel', <u>The Berean Call</u> (Bend, Ore.), July 1996, p.2.

588. Op.cit., David W. Cloud; quoted in <u>ibid.</u>, p.2.

589. Dave Hunt, 'Political/Social Activism?', <u>The Berean Call</u>, January 1997, p.2.

590. P.J. O'Rourke, ed., <u>The American Spectator's Enemies List</u> (New York: The Atlantic Monthly Press, 1996), p.111.

591. <u>Ibid.</u>, p.111. Letter by the Rev. James H. Fladland of Richmond, Va. Emphasis in letter. NB: The ELCA shamelessly retains "evangelical" in its name.

592. James M. Kittelson, p.161. From Karl Kaulfuss-Dietsch, ed. <u>Geschrieben von das Buch der Reformation</u>.

593. Eg., see Hymn No.314, "Who Is this Host Arrayed in White?" ("<u>Den Store Hvide Flok</u>"), by Hans A. Brorson (1694-1764). Based on a 17th century Norwegian folk tune. <u>Lutheran Book of Worship</u> (Minneapolis, Minn.: Augsburg Publishing House, 1978).

NOTES (Concl'd.)

594.   Ibid., p.208. 'Burial of the Dead'.

595.   See note 465 in this chapter.

596.   Brad Lincoln, 'A-musing twist for artwork', Peninsula Daily News, 3 July 1997, pp.A-1, A-2.

597.   Parade magazine, 1 March 1992. Cited in The Berean Call, July 1997, p.1.

598.   Paul Davies, Are We Alone? (New York: Basic Books, 1995), p.125. (Originally published in U.K.)

599.   Quoted in 'Conservative Forum', Human Events, Vol.53, No.38, 10 October 1997, p.21.

Bibliography

28. Bainton, Roland H. <u>Here I Stand: A Life of Martin Luther</u>. Abingdon Press, Nashville, Tenn., 1978 ed. (Orig. published in 1950.)

29. Kittelson, James M. <u>Luther the Reformer</u>. Augsburg Publishing House, Minneapolis, Minn., 1986.

30. Oursler, Fulton. <u>The Greatest Story Ever Told</u>. Pocket Books, New York, 1975 ed. (Orig. published in 1949.)

Special Supplemental Bibliography

1. Davies,Paul. <u>Are We Alone?</u> Basic Books, New York,1995.
    Orig. published in U.K. (SETI/cosmology)

2. Drosnin, Michael. <u>The Bible Code.</u> Simon & Schuster,
    New York,1997. (Cyberspace/prophesy)

3. Ferraiuolo, Perucci. <u>Disney and the Bible.</u> Horizon Books,
    Camp Hill, Penna.,1996. (Disneyism/Christianity).

4. Fletcher, Anne.M. <u>Eat Fish,Live Better.</u> Harper and Rowe,
    Publishers Inc., New York,1989. (Fish/nutrition)

5. Fukuyama, Francis. <u>The End of History and the Last Man.</u>
    The Free Press, New York,1992. (History/philosophy)

6. Gorsline, Jerry,ed. <u>Shadows of Our Ancestors.</u> Dalmo'ma/
    Empty Bowl, Port Townsend, Wash.,1992. (Pac.N.W. Natives)

7. Hersey, John. <u>Blues.</u> Random House, New York,1988 ed.
    (Fish conservation)

8. Hoyt, Richard. <u>Siskiyou.</u> Tor Books, New York,1984.
    (Ecotopia Indoors)

9. _____. <u>Fish Story.</u> Tor Books, New York,1987 ed.

    (Ecotopia Indoors)

10. Jamieson, G.S. and K.Francis,eds. <u>Invertebrate and Marine
    Plant Fishery Resources of British Columbia.</u> Canadian
    Special Publication of Fisheries and Aquatic Sciences 91,
    Department of Fisheries and Oceans, Ottawa,1986.
    (Pac.N.W. marine resources)

11. Jarvis, Norman R. <u>Curing of Fishery Products.</u> Teaparty
    Books, Kingston, Mass.,1987. Reprint of 1950 publication
    by Fish and Wildlife Service of the U.S.D.A. (Fish processing)

12. Jeffrey, Grant R. <u>The Handwriting of God.</u> Frontier Research
    Publications, Inc., Toronto, Ont.,1997. (Cyberspace/prophesy)

13. Keyes, Ken,Jr. <u>The Hundredth Monkey.</u> Vision Books, Coos
    Bay, Ore.,1982. (New World Order)

14. Kipling, Rudyard. "<u>Captains Courageous</u>". Lancer Books, Inc.,
    New York,N.Y.,1967 ed. Orig.published in 1897. (North Atlantic
    fishing)

Special Supplementary Bibliography (concl'd.)

15. Kurlansky, Mark. Cod: A Biography of the Fish
That Changed the World. Walker and Company, New
York, 1997. (North Atlantic fishing)

16. Noüy, Pierre Le Compte de. Human Destiny. The New
American Library of World Literature, New York,1949.
(Spiritual evolution)

17. Shute, Nevil. On the Beach. William Morrow and Company,
Inc., New York,1957. (Pax Americana)

18. Tappert, Theodore,ed. The Book of Concord. Augsburg
Fortress Publishing House, Minneapolis, Minn.,1987 ed.
(Lutheran doctrine)

19. Toffler, Alvin and Heidi. War and Anti-War: Survival
at the Dawn of the 21st Century. Little, Brown and
Company, Boston,Mass.,1993.(Third Wave futurism)

20. Vallée,Jacques. UFOs in Space: Anatomy of a Phenomenon.
Ballantine Books, New York,1987 ed. (SETI/cosmology)

Acknowledgements -- Cons and Pros

I received a rude shock when I tried to enlist the help of fellow fisheriographers within the Pacific Northwest industry. Brad M. of National Fisherman, Steve S. of Pacific Fishing, Wayne L. of Seafood Leader, Joe U. of Alaska Fisherman's Journal, and even local-yokel Harriet U. F. of Port Angeles, were all beseeched for help -- either directly or indirectly -- and chose to respond either marginally, evasively, or not at all. A literary pox on all their houses!

But my most sincere thanks go to Dr. Finnvald Hedin of Everett, Washington, for exemplary inspiration for all that is admirable in Norwegian - American Culture. And I must gratefully mention Mr. Francis E. Caldwell of Port Angeles, Washington (and Ketchikan, Alaska), for tacit reminders in keeping Future Fish on track as fisheriography. And, finally, without Ms. ("Miz") Ellie McCormick, owner/manager of Angeles Temporary Services, there would have been no FutureFish at all! Thanks to you all.

```
C.D.B-H.
Port Angeles, Wash.
July 1998
```

Appendix A

A Lexicon of New Age Nature Religions
(In Topical Order)

Component/Religion	As Defined by
1. "The Gaia Hypothesis" -- (the earth is a living, female organism)	James E. Lovelock, Lyn Margolis
2. Animism -- (souls are quasi-physical and can exist outside the body)	
3. "Extended animism" -- (akin to Taoist geomancy/feng-shui, basis of ecotheology)	William Irwin Thompson
4. Ecofeminism -- ("spiritual feminist circles" attracted to an earth goddess)	Fr. Robert A. Sirico
5. Ecotheology -- ("the universe is God") ("Neopantheism of academia")	Victor Ferkiss Dave Hunt, T.A. McMahon
6. Pantheism -- (God and the universe are identical, "god is in all things")	Berit Kjos
7. Scientism -- (belief in science alone) (accompanied by "nature spirits")	Carl Sagan William Irwin Thompson
8. Neo-Gnosticism -- (rôle and gender inversion of God the Creator with the Goddess)	Elaine Pagels Peter Jones
9. Monism -- (all reality is a single substance or principle, "one with all")	Berit Kjos
10. Shamanism -- ("the religion practised by a shaman .... priest or witchdoctor among some Ural-Altaic peoples .... A similar religion among North American Indians ...")	Webster's Dictionary Dave Hunt, T.A. McMahon

The "Spiritual Emergence" of Stanislav and Christina Grof:

1. Shamanic crisis
2. kundalini arousal
3. psychic opening/psychic healing
4. past-life experiences
5. "channeling"/direct spirit-contact
6. near-death experiences
7. UFO close encounters
8. possession states
9. astral travel
10. monistic consciousness

Appendix B

A Basic Primer of Comparative Philosophy

Tradition Thought/Persona	New Age Idea/Persona
1. Newtonian -- (Sir Isaac Newton) Mechanistic idea of universe: System that operates according to predictable, immutable law. World compartmentalised into distinct, constituent parts of larger mechanism. Personified by orthodoxy.	Einsteinian -- (Albert Einstein) Relativistic idea of universe: Humanity linked to all creation; interconnectedness of all things. Exponents: Buckminster Fuller, Gregory Bateson, Matthew Fox, Fri tjof Capra.
2. Left hemisphere of brain -- (analytical, verbal, logical, "common sensical")	Right hemisphere of brain -- (emotional, intuitive, silence, darkness, "cosmic delight") also, connection-making; orientation toward the maternal
3. Patrifocal (father-centred)	Matrifocal (mother-centred)
4. Dualism (good and evil, soul and body, angel and beast)	Monism (all is one)
5. St. Augustine	Matthew Fox
6. Archimedes (positivism, realism)	Pythagoras (Mystery/myth, cosmological)
7. Ahrimanic technologists (in computer science)	Luciferian New Agers (in computer science)
8. Judaeo-Christian theology	Pagan scientism -- (used during Enlightenment to free Judaeo-Christian theology). From Peter Gay, The Enlightenment:An Interpretation, from Vol. 1, 'The Rise of Modern Paganism' [New York:1966]; in Paglia, p.230.

The New Age Astrological Ages of Man

1.   Age of Taurus (the Bull) 4,000-2,000 B.C. ("Primitive, instinctual civilizations")

2.   Age of Aries (the Ram) 2,000 B.C. to A.D.1 (Judaism, conscience, and awareness of evil)

3.   Age of Pisces (the Fish) A.D.1-1997 (domination religiously by figure of Jesus Christ)

4.   Age of Aquarius (the Water-bearer) 1997? (Availability of choice in own way; restoration of the sensual and incarnate sense again -- i.e., New Age changes are "inevitable and irreversible").

Sources: Mitchell Pacwa, S.J., for main chart and major quotes.
See 'Catholicism for the New Age,' <u>Christian Research Journal</u>, Fall 1992, <u>passim</u>. For numbers 6 and 7, see William Irwin Thompson, <u>Darkness and Scattered Light</u>, p.117ff.; and for number 8, Camille Paglia, <u>Sexual Personae</u>, p.230. cf. Bibliography.

Appendix C

The Mind of Green: Consciousness I and II
(In the words of Charles A. Reich, 1970)

CONSCIOUSNESS I:

(Traditional conservatives--
"Just plain folks")

..."still thinks that the least government governs best. It votes for a candidate who seems to possess personal moral virtues and who promises a return to earlier conditions of life, law and order, rectitude and lower taxes. It believes that the present [1970] American crisis requires reducing government programmes and expenditure, greater reliance on private business, forcing people now on welfare to go to work, taking stern measures to put down subversion at home and threats from abroad, and, above all, a general moral awakening in the people." (p.28)

"Consciousness I ... takes pride in competence, ability and knowledge. But in the American innocent, from Billy Budd to Marshal Dillon, from 'just plain folks' to Andrew Carnegie, there always remained a dimension of reverence; many were genuinely religious, for one thing. The camping journals of Consciousness I people sound embarrassingly sentimental and florid, but the quality of wonder is still there." (p.76)

CONSCIOUSNESS II:

(Roosevelt liberals
--"Old-line leftists")

"[T]he consciousness largely appealed to by the Democratic Party [1970], the consciousness of 'reform.' Most political battles in America are still fought between Consciousness I and Consciousness II. Consciousness II believes that the present American crisis can be solved by greater commitment of individuals to the public interest, more social responsibility by private business and, above all, by more government action -- regulation, planning, more of a welfare state, better and more rational administration and management." (pp.61-62)

...."Much of the energy of Consciousness II has gone into battling the evils that resulted from Consciousness I -- prejudice, discrimination, irrationality, self-seeking, isolation, localism, outworn traditions and superstitions; Consciousness II has worn itself out fighting the know-nothingism of an earlier America"....
(p.64)

"If there is one characteristic that is shared by all ... Consciousness II -- aircraft [plant] employees, old leftists, young doctors, Kennedy men, suburban housewives -- it is the insistence of being competent and knowledgeable, on having 'already been there'".... (p.75)

Appendix C (conc'ld.)

CONSCIOUSNESS III: "Artists, beatniks, Holden Caulfields"
                               i.e.,   1960s political radicals
                                       1990s New Age Aquarians

                                       <u>Literature Cited/Bibliography</u>

1.   Buckley, William F., Jr. <u>God and Man at Yale</u>.
     Regnery Gateway, Washington, D.C., 1978
     (Reprint of the 1951 classic)

2.   Salinger, J.D. <u>The Catcher in the Rye</u>.
     Little, Brown and Company, Boston, Mass., 1951.
     ("Holden Caulfield")

The Ecological Goals of Deep Green
(As expressed by Christopher Manes, 1990)

1. Deindustrilisation of the West.

2. Reduction of human population.

3. Elimination of all use of fossil fuels, including automobiles, coal-fired plants, and manufacturing processes using petrochemicals.

4. End of all monoculture [exclusive cultivation of a single crop] and cattle production.

5. End of all commercial logging.

6. Restoration of wilderness on developed land.

7. Reintroduction of large predators, such as grizzly bears and wolves ....

Source: Christopher Manes, Green Rage (Boston:Little Brown & Co. 1990), p.34.
Quoted by Dixie Lee Ray and Lou Guzzo, Environmental Overkill (Washington, D.C.: Regnery Gateway, 1993), p.205.

Appendix E

A Glossary of Esoteric Ecospeak

1. Biocentrism   (from Greek bio = life) - "If everything is God, then everything is equal. And, if everything is equal, then everything has equal, intrinsic value. Hence, man must change from looking at the world from a 'man-centered' point of view (...anthropocentric) to looking at it from a 'life-centered' perspective."
   -Michael S. Coffman, p.89.

2. Biogenesis   (A Christian concept, like microevolution) ..."The development of life from preexisting life" (p.218). Recapitulation Theory: "...[T]he ontogeny of an individual is a recapitulation of the phylogeny of its group" (p.1893).
   - Webster's Third New International Dictionary (Springfield, Mass.:G.&C. Merriam Company Publishers, 1965).

3. Conservation biology   Ecological science that is biocentric militancy; "biocentic nihilism" (Michael S. Coffman, p.93).

4. "Cosmic ether"   New Age concept of "the web of life"--i.e., Any action by any human is interference.

5. Homo noeticus   New Age (noetic) man- "...a superbeing inextricably tied to and interconnected with his/her fellow-animals and the earth...."
   - Texe Marrs, Big Sister Is Watching You (Austin, Tex.: Living Truth Publishers, 1993), pp.110-111.

6. Mandala   (from Sanskrit=orb, from Hindu and other earth-centered religions) Geometric design "...drawn to protect from evil, invoke spirits, cast spells, contact the dead...."
   - Berit Kjos, Under the Spell of Mother Earth, p.184.

7. Metanoia   (from Greek) "... a fundamental shift in mind, as in a religious conversion."
   - Willis Harman in An Incomplete Guide to the Future (New York:Norton, 1976), p.33.

8.   Panentheism

"[T]he doctrine that God includes the world as a part though not the whole of [H]is being...."
- Webster's Third New International Dictionary, p.1630.
"All is in God" (Berit Kjos).

9.   Pantheism

[A] doctrine, that the universe conceived of a whole is God ... [the] doctrine that there is no God but the combined forces and laws that are manifested in the existing universe...."
- Webster's Third New International Dictionary, p.1632.

10.   Paradigm shift

"[A] sudden change in the global consciousness of the peoples ... of ... the world." -Dwight L. Kinman, p.39.
"World view, mental framework" [shift] -Thomas Kuhn, historian of science, in The Structure of Scientific Revolutions.
-   Quoted in Berit Kjos, 'New Promises Hide Old Agenda', Today's Front Page, March 1995, p.4.

11.   "Punctuated equilibria"

"Swift" ... "quantum leap" in spiritual evolution.   This can be effected by mass, raised consciousness as on World Healing Day, started in 31 December 1986 by John Randolph Price.

12.   Samadhi

(from Sanskrit, "cosmic consciousness") Enlightenment through death to the real things of the actual world.

Appendix F

A New Age Nomenclature for Lifeforce, "Healing Energy"

Prana	breath, energy (Hinduism)
Ch'i, Qi	Taoism, ancient Chinese medicine
Mana	Polynesian
Orenda	American Indian
Animal Magnetism	Franz Anton Mesmer
The Innate	D.D. Palmer, founder of chiropractics
Orgone Energy	Wilhelm Reich
Vital Energy	Samuel Hahnemann, founder of homeopathy
Odic Force	Baron Karl von Reichenbach
Bioplasma	Contemporary (1980s) Soviet parapsychologists
The Force	George Lucas, Star Wars trilogy

Source: Dr. Paul C. Reisser, M.D.; Teri K. Reisser; and John Weldon, The Holistic Healers (Intervarsity Press, 1983). Quoted by Caryl Matrisciana, Gods of the New Age (Eugene, Ore.:Harvest House Publishers, 1985), p.186.

Appendix G

Political Image: The Invidious Dynamics of Thorstein Veblen, American Economist

Veblen is most famous/notorious for his The Theory of the Leisure Class (1889), and coined the

phrases "conspicuous consumption", "pecuniary emulation", "predatory exploit", and "industrial exemption."

He also employed the saying "New [World] Order" (1918-19) to international post-World War I economics.

Thorstein Bunde Veblen was born 30 July 1857 in Manitowoc County, Wisconsin, to Norwegian-born

parents. He was the sixth of twelve children. Veblen was graduated from Carleton College, Northfield,

Minnesota, in 1880 after a stormy student-career:

"Always at odds with the faculty and unpopular on campus, Thorstein was an unorthodox student.
His speeches on suicide, alcoholism, cannibalism, and other distasteful subjects, plagued college officials, and
he quickly developed a reputation as a cynic."[1]

According to Carleton archivist Eric Hillemann, Veblen was disdained as a "free thinker" and

iconoclast during his years at the (then) conservative Christian college. Said Hillemann: "If Carleton had any

role in [Veblen's] accomplishments and formation, it was as something for him to react against."[2]

After graduation from Carleton College, Veblen taught at Monona Academy, Wisconsin, and then

attended Johns Hopkins for a semester. Veblen then went on to Yale where he earned a doctorate in 1884.

The United States was undergoing an economic depression at the time, so few academic positions were

available. Unable to secure a teaching position, Veblen returned to the family farm in Minnesota, where he

spent the next nearly seven years reading and studying in the attic.[3] In the words of Judge Sverre Roang, who

wrote a profile on Veblen, "'One may assume that it was in this period of enforced leisure during 1884 to 1891

that Veblen became a socialist but actually a Marxist in the dialectical sense.'"[4]

This writer hopes that Thorstein Veblen found time during his six-plus years of "enforced leisure" to

help his mother, Kari, around the house and his father, Thomas, in the fields, to thank them for their kindness

and forebearance for putting (up with) him up for almost seven years. Young Thorstein learned first-hand

of leisure!

For many reasons, no doubt including his cynicism and contempt for Christianity, Veblen was refused

a faculty position at St. Olaf College at Northfield, Minnesota. Now married, Veblen was kicked out of

U.Chicago (where he had secured a position in 1891) for marital infidelity, and in 1906 procured an assistant professorship at Leland Stanford. He was forced to resign three years later when his personal (love) affairs again became an issue. Veblen was a lecturer at U.Missouri from 1911-1918.[5] On Veblen's series of sexual affairs throughout his professional life, liberal economist John Kenneth Galbraith has commented that Veblen had "discovered that something -- mind, manners, dress, sardonic and challenging indifference to approval -- made him extremely attractive to women."[6]

Thorstein Veblen married twice. His first marriage failed when Veblen achieved fame, paying scant attention to his first wife. In 1920 Veblen's second wife died. He was teaching then at the radical-liberal New School for Social Research in New York City. Veblen-apologist and former student John Kenneth Galbraith has characterised his old teacher as "... not a socialist. He was a patron saint of Technocracy that minimized the problems of business management.... He was, of course, years ahead of his time."[7] But Veblen certainly sought to apply Darwinian evolutionism to the study of modern economic life, and he theorised, after World War I, that enduring peace would only be kept at the expense of "the rights of ownership."[8]

In 1926, Veblen returned to California; old, tired, resigned, and broke. Judge Sverre Roang described Veblen at this time as "wander[ing] off to his isolated cabin near Stanford, California; a deserted and lonely man -- feeble, pale, ill, wistful, demonic, proud."[9] On 3 August 1929 Thorstein Veblen died, a suicide, several weeks prior to the stock market crash; that seemed to ironically confirm his dire economic predictions. No labels have stayed stuck to Veblen, so he's not known to posterity as a Socialist, Communist, "Wobbly" etc. But Veblen had little use for labels anyway. At his own request neither tombstone, tablet, nor monument would be erected in his memory, anywhere or anytime. Veblen's ashes were scattered over the Pacific Ocean.[10] Judge Sverre Roang eulogised Thorstein Veblen as...

"a character of which legends are made: the prankster who pulled the leg of the stuffy administrator, secretly delighting his fellow students; the iconoclast who scandalized the proud professors by challenging their textbooks and pet theories; the ne'er-do-well who astounded everyone by becoming famous."[11]

None of the above qualities would endear Veblen to any teacher, Judge Roang's lauds notwithstanding! But this writer will leave Veblen's final obituary to Wesley C. Mitchell, U.S. economist, who had studied at U.Chicago under Veblen (and been influenced there by John Dewey). Mitchell called Veblen "a visitor from another world."[12]

Compare other notorious/famous Norwegians and Norwegian-descended North Americans: "Deep ecologist" Arne Naess with "Green Revolution" U.S. agronomist Norman Borlaug; shrill, eco-feminist Prime Minister Gro Harlem Brundtland with Nobel Prize-winning, Christian novelist Sigrid Undset; and strident, politically-correct actress Liv Ullmann with Canadian RCMP Sgt. Henry Larsen, Arctic explorer extraordinaire. (Larsen was born and bred in Hvaler, Norway, on the very island this writer's spouse grew up and still maintains a home.) Despite the obvious chauvinism of The Sons of Norway Viking (i.e., Columbus and Washington were essentially Norwegian!), there are as many black holes as shining stars in the Norwegian constellation. Thorstein Veblen, with his brilliance and striking good looks, is at present enjoying a Norwegian-American mini-renaissance. The revival is in part due to "current wisdom", declining church attendance, leftist economics, and academic yearning for existential anti-heroes. Thorstein Veblen fills that bill. To this writer Veblen had a rat's eye view of life, and for all his glowing rhetoric and biting ésprit, was a joyless satirist. Even the ghastly Karl Marx showed some humour ("Vive les saucissons!").

NOTES

1. Audrey Wendland, 'Outcast Genius', <u>The Sons of Norway Viking</u>, Vol.93, No.2, February 1996, p.18.

2. Joel Hoekstra, 'Veblen's Restored Farmstead, <u>The Sons of Norway Viking</u>, Vol.93, No.2, February 1996, p.17.

3. 'Micropaedia', <u>The New Encyclopaedia Britannica</u> (Chicago: Encyclopaedia Britannica, Inc., 1990 15th ed.), p.287.

4. Quoted by Audrey Wendland, p.18.

5. 'Micropaedia', p.287.

6. Quoted by Audrey Wendland, p.18.

7. <u>Ibid.</u>, p.18.

8. 'Micropaedia', p.287.

9. Quoted by Audrey Wendland, p.33.

10. Joel Hoekstra, p.16.

11. Quoted by Audrey Wendland, p.33.

12. 'Micropaedia', p.287.

<u>Bibliography</u>

Veblen, Thorstein. <u>The Theory of the Leisure Class</u>. Dover Publications, Inc., Mineola, N.Y., 1994. Originally published in 1899.

Appendix H

<u>Cultural Idol: Jerry Garcia of the Grateful Dead</u>

Garcia with his "long, frizzy hair and Uncle Sam top hat, became a symbol for American youth gone wild in drug-assisted, sparkle-eyed ecstasy.... The Dead drew two, maybe three generations into its swirling, tie-dyed tent, and its concerts usually seemed like family affairs in which traditions -- like sharing joints and bootleg tapes -- were passed on from old to young."
                                        -Mitchell Landsberg of the Associated Press[1]

Born 1 August 1942, died 9 August 1995 at Marin County's Serenity Knolls drug-rehab centre. Garcia grew up in San Francisco, Calif., nursed culturally on <u>Mad</u> magazine, Allen Ginsberg's <u>Howl</u>, Jack Kerouac's <u>On the Road</u>, and Lawrence Ferlinghetti's poetry. Ran away to the Army but was dishonourably discharged. Garcia's early musical group eventually evolved from a jug band into the Grateful Dead ... and a thirty-year acid test. The 'Dead grew infamous as the house band at LSD parties hosted by Ken Kesey and his Merry Pranksters during the 1960s. Loyal Garcia followers, "Deadheads," have always been associated with High Times. Garcia, later in life, would have to battle cocaine and heroin addiction; earlier drug use portrayed as daring, smart, hip. Garcia called heroin "the comfort drug." High-profile Deadheads include Peter Jennings, Bill Walton, Vermont Sen. Patrick Leahy, Massachusetts Gov. William Weld, "Batman Forever" director Joel Schumacher, U.S. Vice-Presidential power-couple Al and Tipper Gore.

Discography: "Their songs are more apt to be hard-luck stories [i.e., the <u>People's Band</u>] ... about desert rats, sharecroppers, footloose troubado[u]rs, gamblers and bums."
                                        -Malcolm Jones, <u>Newsweek</u> magazine[2]

7 November 1995: Deadhead Simon Radford at the Radio Astronomy Observatory in Tucson, Ariz., and Deadhead Ed Olszewski at U.Ariz.'s Steward Observatory, name an asteroid (100 miles across, orbiting between Mars and Jupiter) "Garcia" after their idol. "Garcia" name officially confirmed by the International Astronomical Union.

8 December 1995: The Grateful Dead ends thirty year tour.

Appendix H (cont'd.)

8 April 1996:   In a holy city [Rishikesh, India] where Hindu pilgrims seek salvation, Jerry Garcia's widow
                sprinkled the ashes of the Grateful Dead leader into the Ganges River following a lunar
                eclipse. .... "During the ceremony, [Bob] Weir -- Jerry Garcia's best friend --, prayed that he
                would 'travel to the stars'...."

                                                            -Associated Press[3]

A Deadhead Obituary

"....[T]he kids sure knew about Jerry, the mythic and mystic Jerry, a hyper-legend even among the hyper-
legends. Lots of rock bands have maniacal admirers, but the Grateful Dead were a bona fide world religion -
- with Garcia as its usually very high priest."

                                                -M.D. Carnegie, The American Spectator[4]

End Notes

1. Mitchell Landesberg, 'Generations mourn day the music died,' Peninsula Daily News, 11 August 1995,
   p.A-8.

2. Malcolm Jones, 'A Listener's Guide to the Dead,' Newsweek, 21 August 1995, p.49.

3. 'Singer's ashes go into Ganges', Peninsula Daily News, 8 April 1996, p.A-8.

4. M.D. Carnegie, 'Jerry's Kids', The American Spectator, Vol.28, No.10, October 1995, p.56.

Bibliography

1. Chute, Carolyn. The Beans of Egypt, Maine. Ticknor & Fields, New York, 1985.

2. Perry, Paul. Fear and Loathing: The Strange and Terrible Saga of Hunter S. Thompson. Thunder's Mouth
   Press, N.Y., 1993.

Appendix I

Musical Icon: Jimi Hendrix, Seattle's All-American Boy

Born 27 November 1942 in Seattle, Washington, to Lucille and Al Hendrix. At age 17, Jimi dropped out of Garfield High School and enlisted in the U.S. Army. After basic training in California, joined 101st Airborne Div. ("Screaming Eagles") paratroopers at Fort Campbell, Kentucky. After 13 months and 25 successful jumps, PFC Hendrix broke ankle on 26th jump; received honourable discharge from the Army. End of all-American phase of Jimi Hendrix's life.

"Not only was ... [Jimi Hendrix] free of slavish devotion to any previous or existing musical or social movement, [h]e himself seem[ed] synthesized, a true personification of Americana -- from the Boy Scouts and football to his stint as a paratrooper in the U.S. Army's 101 Airborne [D]ivision."[1]

After several months in New York City's Harlem, Hendrix went on to London, England, and eventually came under the managerial aegis of Bryan "Chas" Chandler (also The Animals bassist). By this time, Hendrix had developed his own eclectic music style and lyric compositions. Accompanied by two (white) British sidemen, Hendrix formed the Jimi Hendrix Experience. The band therefore had an intercontinental, interracial pedigree, and musically synthesised mainstream rock-n'-roll with black soul, jazz, and blues. But Hendrix, the original Voodoo Child, stamped Experience productions with his own Voodoo imprimatur and other erotic/exotic aspects of the African-American heritage -- all very evident and arguably essential aspects of the Hendrix sound appeal.

11 January 1967: Release of "51st Anniversary" by the Experience. The track expressed Hendrix's vocal opposition to traditional marriage. Hendrix marked performances by setting on fire, with lighter fluid, big Fender Stratocaster guitars during hot licks. Hendrix's behaviour becoming destructive with increased use of acid ("Owsley" LSD). Once in Los Angeles he hit a groupie in the face with a brick; she would require facial surgery. But Hendrix did find time, on a U.S. West Coast concert tour, to visit his father in Seattle. He also praised the U.S. Army as a good career opportunity for black Americans. Most rock stars in America during the late 1960s were, of course, in high-decibel opposition to the Vietnam War. However, in other ways, Jimi Hendrix was acting out his heavy-metal karma right on cue:

"[H]endrix['s] music had come to be associated with burgeoning drug use in America. To many, he [Hendrix] was the high priest of the counter-culture, a defiant symbol whose music and style set him apart from his contemporaries."[2]

Casual sex, wild partying, and trashing hotel rooms was hallmark behaviour of rock stars during the late 1960s. What set Hendrix apart from his peers was his extra edge ... a tri-racial identity as a "Voodoo Child of deep blues.... [T]he Hendrix family tree [had] roots in [Macon,] Georgia with Irish and Cherokee blood. And Irish lore is central to blues and Voodoo history."[3] Lucille, Hendrix's mother, had died in 1958, and Hendrix saw his "mothered boychild" self metaphysically reborn as a "Voodoo Chile bluesman."[4] For young Jimi, the last was a crucial rite of passage. Thus Hendrix envisioned himself as a multi-cultural phoenix, with a shamanic message cloaked in dream-séance metaphor. Christian researchers John Ankerberg and John Weldon have written:

"[J]imi Hendrix, whose basic philosophy was one of unbridled sex and drug use, commented, 'You can hypnotize people with music and when you get them at their weakest point, you can preach into their subconscious what we want to say."[5]

Just what did Hendrix want to say? And what prompted him to compose, sing, and play as he did? Fayne Pridgeon, a former Hendrix girl-friend recalled:

"He [Hendrix] was so tormented and just so torn apart, like he was obsessed with something really evil.... He used to always talk about some devil or somethin[g] that was in him, you know, and he didn't have [any] control over it.... [H]e didn't know what made him act the way he acted and what made him say the things he said, and songs ... just came out of him."[6]

21-22 October 1968: Jimi Hendrix and the Experience cut a "party" recording of "Calling All the Devil's Children." And the song, "Look over Yonder," was at first named "Mr. Lost Soul." A later album, Electric Church, the derisive title coined by Hendrix, was a 13 page collection of photos taken by Ron Rafaelli. One poster included a picture of Hendrix with two topless, admiring (white) female fans. Hendrix was very preoccupied during this period with science fiction and astrology.

Woodstock Festival, August 1969: Hendrix ..."still viewed drugs ... marijuana ... as a recreational exercise."[7] A close associate, Jim Marron, observed: "Hendrix was very scattered.... He was using marijuana, hashish, cocaine ... three to five times a week. Drugs were fast becoming a way of life.'"[8]

Earth Day, April 1970: Hendrix in a pre-Earth Day interview said, "There is a great need for harmony between man and earth and I think by dumping garbage in the sea and polluting the air, we are screwing up that harmony."[9] Also, in April 1970, Hendrix played bass accompaniment during a recording jam-session with acid guru, Timothy Leary, in "You Can Be Anyone This Time Around."[10]

17-18 September 1970, London: In the company of one Monika Danneman, Hendrix ingested an overdose of Vesparax sleeping tablets. He died by choking to death on his own vomit. But the fey Jimi Hendrix had already written his own prescient obituary:

"It's funny the way most people love the dead. Once you have died, you are made for life. You have to die before they think you are worth anything. And I tell you, when I die, I'm going to have a jam session. [I'll] have them playing everything I did musically, everything I enjoyed doing most."[11]

Post Script: July 1995

The music of Jimi Hendrix is coming home to Seattle. Hendrix's father, Al, will regain the rights to his late son's "prolific musical legacy" under a recent court settlement. The corporations controlling the rights since the 1970s will turn them over to Al Hendrix for "an undisclosed amount of money." The music itself, related rights, plus merchandising are worth $80-90 million; figured O. Yale Lewis, a lawyer for Al Hendrix. "'I'm so elated that it's all over with,' Hendrix, a 76-year-old retired gardener, told a news conference.... 'The money's OK too, but getting Jimi's music back, that's what was really important.'"[12]

END NOTES

1. John McDermott with Eddie Kramer, <u>Hendrix: Setting the Record Straight</u> (London, England:Warner Books, 1993), p. xvi.

2. <u>Ibid.</u>, p.210.

3. Michael J. Fairchild, 'Liner Notes', <u>Jimi Hendrix:blues</u>, MCA Records, Inc., 1994 re-issue, p.4.

4. <u>Ibid.</u>, p.3.

5. John Ankerberg & John Weldon, <u>The Facts on Rock Music</u> (Eugene, Ore.:Harvest House Publishers, 1992), p.23. Jimi Hendrix quotation cited from <u>Life</u>, 30 October 1969.

6. Ibid., p.42. Quote from Dave Hunt, <u>America: The Sorcerer's New Apprentice</u> (Eugene, Ore.:Harvest House Publishers, 1988), pp.239-240. Cf. Michael J. Fairchild, p.4.

7. John McDermott with Eddie Kramer, p.269.

8. Jim Marron cited in McDermott and Kramer, p.287.

9. Op.cit., Jimi Hendrix, p.311.

10. On the very day of this writing, Timothy Leary expired in Los Angeles. "'60s drug guru dies of cancer,' <u>Peninsula Daily News</u>, 31 May 1996, p.A-2.

11. Jimi Hendrix cited in McDermott and Kramer, p.412.

12. 'Family wins rights to rocker's music,' <u>Peninsula Daily News</u>, 16 July 1995, p.A-5.

Discography

McDermott, John with Eddie Kramer. <u>Hendrix: Setting the Record Straight</u>. Warner Books, London, England, 1993.

Appendix J

The Unabom[b]er: A Latter-day Luddite?

AND

On 3 April 1996, a man believed to be the notorious Unabom[b]er was found · seized in Lincoln,
                                                                            ^
Montana. After a seventeen-year man-hunt, U.S. federal agents had finally run to earth the individual

suspected of killing three persons and maiming 23 others. Law enforcement officials announced that the

federal agents had uncovered explosive chemicals and bomb-making materials at the remote, one-room cabin

of the suspect, one Theodore John Kaczynski. The New York Times described the arrested man:

> "The suspect is a 53-year-old former assistant professor of mathematics at the University of California
> at Berkeley. He graduated from Harvard College in 1962 and received a doctorate in mathematics from the
> University of Michigan several years later. His is just the sort of academic-oriented background that the
> authorities had attributed to the bomber, whose communications with the press had reflected an obsession with
> science and technology issues."[1]

That obsession with science and technology was manifested in a 35,000 word dissertation, 'Industrial

Society and Its Future,' published (under the threat of more bombings) during late September 1995 by The

New York Times and The Washington Post.[2] The Unabom[b]er manifesto severely censures the

dehumanisation of technologically-driven modern society. The tone throughout is rather that of a stern,

Christian Green earth-steward (Rifkin:1981, Toffler:1991) than of the infamous Unabom[b]er ... until the final

pages, wherein comes the call for assassinating enemies of the planet. Theodore John Kaczynski, the alleged

Unabom[b]er, is no hypocrite. He grew up in Evergreen Park outside Chicago, Illinois, in a suburban three-

bedroom working-class home surrounded by elm trees. Despite his scholarly brilliance and the promise of a

great academic career, Kaczynski "dropped out," and since the early 1970s lived in a tiny (10' x 12'), hand-

constructed shack fifty miles northwest of Helena, Mont. The cabin, without either electricity or running

water, was located at the edge of Lolo National Forest. (That Kaczynski chose the Treasure State of Montana

in which to hole-up is fitting in the mid-1990s. Montana has been dubbed "The Last Best Place" by western

writer William Kittredge, and has become the area of refuge for disparate folks ranging from the Montana

Freemen to Mr. and Ms. Jane Fonda-Turner.[3]) The Unabom[b]er has been so-called as some of his early

targets represented universities (science) or airlines (technology).[4] As to Kaczynski's motivations, New York

<u>Times</u> columnist Richard Pérez-Peña has commented:

"Mr. Kaczynski's sharp turn away from society occurred after he spent several years in the 1960's on two college campuses -- in Ann Arbor, Mich., and in Berkeley -- that were seedbeds of a counterculture that reacted profoundly against not only the war in Vietnam, but against materialism and many of society's standards as well. It is unclear whether Mr. Kaczynski was a part of that movement, but few who were surrounded by it came away unaffected."[5]

The Unabom[b]er manifesto has been characterised as a polemical essay of political philosophy, social science, and technology -- a mélange of ideas popular on college campuses during the 1960s when Kaczynski taught at U.Cal.Berkeley.[6] But the Unabom[b]er is <u>not</u> another leftist "environmental whacko"; indeed, a source told the <u>San Francisco Examiner</u> that Kaczynski was "disgusted with the widespread drug use and liberal politics'. Maybe so: the Unabomber manifesto is harshly critical of leftism."[7] Whichever politics Kaczinski subscribed to, he described himself as "'strictly anti-communist, anti-socialist, anti-leftist', but most of all, anti-science and [anti]-technology."[8] This stamps Ted Kaczynski as something other than a <u>left-wing</u> eco-nut, protestations to the contrary by (this writer's favourite) conservative commentators notwithstanding.[9]

Ray Archer, an editorial writer for the <u>Arizona Republic</u>, put the case for the right strongly but wrongly:

"Why, the Sierra Club and the left wing of the Democratic Party are no more responsible for the Unabomber than the National Rifle Association or the right-wing of the Republican Party and talk radio were for the cowardly and despicable acts of the madmen who blew up the federal building in Oklahoma City last year [19 April 1995], killing 168 people."[10]

Even Joe Klein of <u>Newsweek</u> conceded, "Still, the terrorist's left-wing orientation seems indisputable. In the Nation last year, Kirkpatrick Sale -- a neo-Luddite neo-leader -- embraced him [Kaczynski] (after suitable hand-wringing over the violence): 'Unless [the Unabomber's] message is somehow heeded ... we are truly a doomed society hurtling toward a catastrophic breakdown.'"[11] Although Joe Klein was in error as his conservative colleagues about the Unabom[b]er's politics, he has gotten much closer to the truth. For Klein mentioned "neo-Luddite neo-leader "Kirkpatrick Sale, who has claimed the Unabom[b]er as one of his own. Sale, author of <u>Rebels against the Future: The Luddites and Their War on the Industrial Revolution (Lessons for the Computer Age)</u>, considers himself a neo-Luddite. Is the Unabom[b]er, then, a neo-Luddite too?

Theodore John Kaczynski, the mathematics scholar of several prestigious multiversities, lived as a near-hermit for more than twenty years in a hand-built shack; without plumbing, electricity, and who grew his own vegetables, chopped his own wood for heat, and kept a cache of food in a root cellar. Kaczynski was regarded by the local people of Lincoln, Montana, as a polite but scruffy recluse, who bicycled to town and

was a frequent user of the public library. It was around Kaczynski's lonely dwelling, in the wild woods near

the Continental Divide, that the FBI watched and waited for their man. As Newsweek magazine reported:

> "[T]he FBI had assembled enough high-tech spying equipment to stage a James Bond movie. Special agents from the [B]ureau's elite Hostage Rescue Team peered down from the trees through night-vision goggles while highly sensitive listening devices eavesdropped on any words the suspect might have chanced to mumble. Thousands of miles overhead in space, satellites surveyed the desolate home the suspect rarely left in the raw of winter."[12]

The reader might think, "Hardly a fair contest!" But Ted Kaczynski is, after all, a man thought to have

murdered three persons and injured 23 others. He drew sustenance from enviro-nihilism, read anarchist and

radical eco-journals, and as recently as 1994 attended an Earth First! meeting in Missoula, Mont. According

to Jeff Jacoby of The New York Times, Kaczynski addressed an explosive to the Timber Association of

California's Sacramento headquarters, unaware that it had been replaced by the California Forestry

Association. A Gilbert Murray, the CFA's president and father of three, opened the package and died on the

spot. Kaczynski did the dastardly deed after reading a 1989 eco-terrorist tract titled 'Live Wild or Die.'

Number One on the eco-hit list had been the Timber Association of California.[13]

Is Ted Kaczynski, the Unabom[b]er suspect, a latter-day Luddite? This writer would reply an emphatic

Yes! The difference between Luddism and neo-Luddism may be paralleled with a comparison of Conservatism

to neo-Conservatism. If author Kirkpatrick Sale has identified himself as a neo-Luddite, Ted Kaczynski

qualifies as a true-blue Luddite who practised what he preached. A despised, smelly grade-grubbing grind at

Harvard, Kaczynski surely couldn't have fit in with the beat-hip, cool-cat, upper-class crowd of early 1960s Zen

rebels. Twenty years later, Kaczynski didn't cruise to environmentalist conclaves in a high-price Volvo or

BMV. Kirkpatrick Sale, the "neo-Luddite neo-leader", will never be able to elevate Ted Kaczynski to a trendy,

new rôle-model status; a real case of trying to fashion a silken purse out of a sow's ear. Sale has noted a

"Luddistic strain" in such countercultural idols as Aldous Huxley, Herbert Marcuse, Paul Goodman; in

contemporary figures Jeremy Rifkin, Fritjof Capra et al.[14] Despite Kaczynski's apparent ability to comfortably

wear a Tweed jacket over his prison-orange jumpsuit, he is still the cow-licked, uncool nerd with a potential

slide-rule peeping out of his pocket ... not a ready-for-prime-time candidate at radically-chic private gatherings, or politically-correct public appearances among the rich and famous. For Theodore John Kaczynski is not a neo-anything, but became a true-blue Luddite amidst long, lonely periods of silence and solitude. He walked the walk and lived the Luddite life. But somewhere along life's path the Unabom[b]er stumbled psychically, and became a Luddite of a different stripe: One who killed imagined enemies --nonetheless real people-- from afar, employing an (albeit home-made) intricate technology he professed to eschew.

Afterword

It has been said that a man may be known by the books he reads. Ted Kaczynski had more than 150 books among the personal items found by the FBI. Some of the titles were: Les Miserables, Asimov's Guide to the Bible, Growing Up Absurd: Problems of Youth in the Organized System[15]; works by Shakespeare and Thackeray.[16]

<u>NOTES</u>

1. David Johnston, 'Ex-Professor Is Seized in Montana as Suspect in the Unabom Attacks,' <u>The New York Times</u>, 4 April 1996, p.A-1.

2. Theodore John Kaczynski, 'Industrial Society and Its Future.' 232 paragraphs, 68pp. Written in conjunction with the Freedom Club who appeared to be anarchist Luddites rather than mystical Greens. Eg. Mention of "Gaia" only once throughout.

3. William Kittredge and Anick Smith, eds. <u>The Last Best Place: A Montana Anthology</u> (Seattle and London:University of Washington Press, 1995). NB: Montana as "The Last Best Place" for Big Government - hating private militias has been much in the U.S. national news during 1995-1996. See William Kittredge, 'The War for Montana's Soul', <u>Newsweek</u>, 15 April 1996; and his <u>Who Owns the West?</u> (San Francisco: Mercury House, 1996).

4. David Johnston, <u>The New York Times</u>, pp.A-1, ff.

5. Richard Pérez-Peña, 'A Man Known to Few, and a Mystery to Many,' <u>The New York Times</u>, 4 April 1996, p.A-14.

6. 'U.S. Detains Ex-Professor as a Suspect in Bombings," <u>The New York Times</u>, 4 April 1996, p.A-14.

7. 'Probing the Mind of a Killer," <u>Newsweek</u>, 15 April 1996, p.35.

8. <u>Ibid.</u>, p.39.

9. Ray Archer, 'Is the Unabomber a left-wing eco-nut?' <u>Peninsula Daily News</u>, 30 April 1996, p.A-6. Cf. Unabom[b]er's alleged radical-<u>liberalism</u> in articles by Brent Bozell, Thomas Sowell, Cal Thomas.

10. <u>Ibid.</u>, p.6.

11. Joe Klein, 'The Unabomer and the Left, <u>Newsweek</u>, 22 April 1996, p.39.

12. 'The End of the Road', <u>Newsweek</u>, 15 April 1996, pp.36-37.

13. Jeff Jacoby, 'Who's Responsible for the Unabomber?', <u>Peninsula Daily News</u>, 25 April 1996, p.A-10.

14. Kirkpatrick Sale, <u>Rebels against the Future: The Luddites and Their War on the Industrial Revolution</u> (Reading, Mass.:Addison-Wesley Publishing Company, 1996), pp.18-19, 254-255. Author's note: Sale has even spotted a "Luddistic strain" in Thorstein Veblen (!), a man John Kenneth Galbraith has described as a "patron saint of technocracy." See Appendix G.

15. Kevin Johnson, <u>USA Today</u>, 'Tools, Weapons Among Items in Kaczynski's Cabin', 16 April 1996, p.3A.

16. John Kifner, 'A Loner "Not that Remarkable"', <u>The New York Times</u>, 4 April 1996, ff.

Bibliography

1. Kaczynski, Theodore John. 'Industrial Society and Its Future,' (n.d.).

2. Roszak, Theodore. The Making of a Counter Culture. Anchor Books, Doubleday & Company, Inc., Garden City, N.Y., 1969.

3. Sale, Kirkpatrick. Rebels against the Future. Addison-Wesley Publishing Company, Reading, Mass., 1996 ed.

Appendix K

Scientific Ideal: Albert Einstein, Ontological Deist

In the Introduction to the 1962 edition of The Universe and Doctor Einstein by Lincoln Barnett,

Glenn T. Seaborg, then-chairman of the Atomic Energy Commission, wrote:

"He [Man] may not realize that Relativity, over and above its scientific import, comprises a major
philosophical system which augments and illumines the reflections of the great epistemologists -- Locke,
Berkeley, and Hume. Consequently he [Man] has very little notion of the vast, arcane, and mysteriously
ordered universe in which he dwells."[1]

The reader will recall that Dr. Seaborg appeared on the 1992 "List of Honorary Sponsors" of the

globalist World Constitution and Parliamentary Association (WCPA), closely examined in the previous chapter

of this work.[2] Other WCPA "Honorary Sponsors" on the list included Archbishop Desmond Tutu, comedic

actor Ed Asner, and documelodrama director Oliver Stone.[3] (After all the intervening years since 1962, Dr.

Seaborg still ranked in the liberal élite three decades later.) Even before Einstein died in 1955, the American

"Old-line" Left had held him up as a liberal paragon of secular/scientistic virtue. The mantra one has been

forced to hear, during the last half-century, is "All Things Are Relative" ... over and over and over again.

Indeed, modern "situational ethics" have been mistakenly lifted from Einstein's Theory of Relativity, and then

been built on the sand-(corner) stone of Relativism. In fact, "Relativity" itself is a scientific misnomer. On

the centennial of Einstein's birth in 1979, British biographer Nigel Calder maintained that...

"...Einstein is often said to have held that 'all things are relative.' He did not. 'Relativity' is ... a
thoroughly bad name for the theory. Einstein considered calling it the opposite: 'invariance theory.' He
discovered what was 'absolute' and reliable despite the apparent confusions, illusions, and contradictions
produced by relative motions or the actions of gravity. The chief merit of the name "relativity" is in reminding
us that a scientist is unavoidably a participant in the system he is studying. Einstein gave 'the observer' his
proper status in modern science."[4]

The Theory of Relativity hit the world like a post-war bomb when it was proven true on 29 May 1919.

On that date, photographs of a solar eclipse showed that starlight is not straight but curves when passing close

to the sun. Einstein's concept of bended space -- hence Relativity -- had been indubitably confirmed.[5] But

this brought on a commensurate philosophical counter-query: If the Theory of Relativity negated absolutes

of space and time, what about absolutes of morality and metaphysics? Relativity quickly became confused in

the public mind with Relativism, causing the conundrum present to this day. Historian Paul Johnson has averred that no-one was more distressed by social misunderstanding of Relativity/Relativism than Einstein himself. Scientifically speaking, Einstein had merely substituted a physical absolute, i.e., the velocity of light, for the metaphysical absolutes of space and time.[6] Moreover the post-World War I 1920s was a relativistic era anyway, with Western society "already questioning traditional certitudes."[7] Einstein, a self-described socialist, signed a manifesto in 1955, along with Bertrand Russell and many other scholars and scientists to ban any further development of nuclear weapons.[7] (This was Einstein's last public act before he died that same year.) Einstein thus identified himself with the anti-war Left, seeming to justify public suspicions of his political, cultural, and religious relativism.[8]

Forty years and more after his death, worship of Albert Einstein persists by Old-line and New Left, who think they see in the deceased physicist a muted testimony to secular humanism. But although the political Einstein allied himself -- frivolously and foolishly at times, in this writer's opinion -- with some questionable causes and outré leaders, Einstein personally... "exhibited a religious urge, without engaging in any religion. His wisecracks about God, the 'Old One', reflected a deep reverence for Nature."[9] Spiritless scientist Carl Sagan credited Einstein for more than "a deep reverence for nature" than did British biographer Nigel Calder. Sagan wrote in Broca's Brain that "Einstein's religious beliefs were very genuine, and "[i]n matters of religion, Einstein thought more deeply than many others and was repeatedly misunderstood."[10] Sagan quoted Einstein as having said "'God does not play dice with the cosmos.... God is subtle but not malicious.'"[11] But, according to Sagan, Einstein's conventional Judaism came to an abrupt end at age twelve: "'Through the reading of popular scientific books I [Einstein] soon reached the conviction that much of the stories of the Bible could not be true'"....[12] So what did Albert Einstein, the adult-physicist, believe?

During the 1930s in Europe, Einstein's theories were widely reviled, with Hitler's Nazi Germany officially repudiating the "Jewish" Theory of Relativity. In 1929 on the occasion of Einstein's initial visit to the United States, Cardinal O'Connell of Boston -- supported by the Vatican -- declared that Relativity produced "'universal doubt about God and [H]is creation'"[13], and warned that Relativity "cloaked the ghostly apparition of atheism."[14] At this, an alarmed New York rabbi sent Einstein a telegram: "Do you believe in God?" Einstein had cabled back: "I believe in Spinoza's God who reveals himself in the harmony of all being [that exists], but not in a God who concerns himself with the fate and action[s] of men."[15]

Baruch Spinoza (1632-1677) was a Dutch Jewish philosopher-metaphysicist of Portuguese Sephardi ancestry. An early heretic, Spinoza questioned both Judaism and Christianity and was excommunicated by the Amsterdam rabbinate in 1656. Spinoza was deeply influenced by the mediaeval Jewish mystical philosophy of Kabbala, and maintained that the Old Testament prophets were only significant morally, not philosophically; their factual beliefs were appropriate only in their own time. Spinoza completed writing the Ethica in 1675; his Tractatus Theologico-Politicus (1670) was denounced as "forged in hell by a renegade Jew and the devil." Spinoza, a lens-grinder by trade, died of consumption and inhalation of glass-dust in 1677. Later materialistic Marxists were inspired by Spinozan psychology, while rejecting Spinozan metaphysics.[16] In his final commentary on Kabbala, Dr. Erich Bischoff stated in (about) 1910:

"It represents ... a peculiar monism .... Concerning magic, it had considerable influence on various superstitions and occult movements.... [I]t is a very interesting subject ... much hampered by the mysterious manner of presentation and the many magical and mystical references....[17]
"Spinoza had monistic doctrine similar to that in Kabbala."[18]

This, then, was "Spinoza's God" -- a god of Kabbalistic pantheism. Was this Einstein's God too?

Albert Einstein has answered:

"My religion consists of a humble admiration of the illimitable superior spirit who reveals himself in the slight details we are able to perceive with our frail and feeble minds. That deeply emotional conviction of the presence of a superior reasoning power, which is revealed in the incomprehensible universe, forms my idea of God."[19]

NOTES

1.   Lincoln Barnett, <u>The Universe and Doctor Einstein</u> (New York:Time Incorporated, 1962) p.2.

2.   Chapter 2, note no. 272.

3.   Gary Kah, 'Part Two -- the WCPA', <u>En Route to Global Occupation</u> (Lafayette, La.:Huntington House, 1992), Exhibits N3-N6.

4.   Nigel Calder, <u>Einstein's Universe</u> (New York, N.Y.:Greenwich House, 1982), p.2.

5.   Nancy R. Pearcey and Charles B. Thaxton, <u>The Soul of Science</u> (Wheaton, Ill.:Crossway Books, 1994), p.165.

6.   <u>Ibid.</u>, pp.165-166. Taken from Paul Johnson, <u>Modern Times: The World from the Twenties to the Eighties</u> (New York:Harper and Row, 1983), pp.1-4,5.

7.   Op.cit., Nancy R. Pearcey and Charles B. Thaxton, p.165.

8.   Nigel Calder, pp.139-140. See also Carl Sagan, <u>Broca's Brain: Reflections on the Romance of Science</u> (New York:Ballantine Books, 1980 ed.), pp.36-37.

9.   Op.cit., Nigel Calder, p.138.

10.   Op.cit., Carl Sagan, p.35.

11.   <u>Ibid.</u>, p.35.

12.   <u>Ibid.</u>, p.29.

13.   Op.cit., Nigel Calder, p.138.

14.   Op.cit., Carl Sagan, p.35.

15.   <u>Ibid.</u>; cf. Calder, p.138.

16.   'Micropaedia', Vol.11 (Chicago, Ill.:<u>Encyclopaedia Brittanica, Inc.</u>, 1990, 15th ed.) pp.99-101.

17.   Dr. Erich Bischoff, ed., <u>The Kabbala: An Introduction to Jewish Mysticism and Its Secret Doctrine</u> (York Beach, Me.: Samuel Weiser, Inc., 1995 ed.), note no. 205, p.68. Orig. published in Germany, ca. 1910.

18.   <u>Ibid.</u>, p.23.

19.   Quoted by Lincoln Barnett, p.101.

Bibliography

1. Barnett, Lincoln. <u>The Universe and Doctor Einstein</u>. Time Incorporated, New York, 1962. (Orig. published in 1948.)

2. Bischoff, Dr. Erich, ed. <u>The Kabbala</u>. Samuel Weiser, Inc., York Beach, Me., 1995 ed. (Orig. published in Germany, ca. 1910.)

3. Calder, Nigel. <u>Einstein's Universe</u>. Greenwich House, New York, N.Y. 1982. (Orig. published in U.K., 1979.)

Appendix L

E.T.s in the New Age: Magonians Interpenetrating Space-Time?[1]

".... So in an age when traditional religions have been under withering fire from science, it is not natural to wrap up the old gods and demons in scientific raiment and call them aliens?"
-Carl Sagan, The Demon-Haunted World, 1995

During a 1972 debate on UFOs (Unidentified Flying Objects), Cornell scientist-celebrity Dr. Carl Sagan observed that "unfulfilled religious needs" were responsible for the UFO phenomenon.[2] Almost a quarter century later the debate - and furore - continues unabated. The difference is that UFOlogy by the 1990s has become a recognised, established religious cult. Dr. Jacques Vallée, the real-life model for the French scientist-character in Steven Spielberg's "Close Encounters of the Third Kind," is arguably the world's leading UFOlogy expert. He has confirmed that "'We are dealing here with the next form of religion, with a new spiritual movement.'"[3] In the mid-1990s, the Western mainstream culture is in the throes of a simultaneous ETIs (Extra-Terrestrial Intelligences) obsession and an Angels craze. These have been seen in certain sectors as related phenomena.

Jacques Vallée has informed us that, throughout history, the E.T. Visitors sighted have "'consistently received (or provided) their own explanation within the framework of each [mundane] culture.'"[4] In other words, the Aliens encountered have inevitably conformed to what we humans have wanted -- or feared -- them to be. Godfrey Daniels in Planet 21 has added that, "Modern mythology having shifted from the magical to the scientific, it's only logical that the visitors would pose as scientifically advanced beings from space."[5] But Jacques Vallée doesn't believe that Aliens are beings from space; Carl Sagan doesn't believe that Aliens are angels from heaven (or demons from hell). In fact, Sagan has agreed with Vallée, saying that UFOs are "'of distinctly terrestrial origin.'"[6] Vallée has written that he thinks: (1) UFOs are real physical objects, 2) but are not extra-terrestrial in the usual sense; (3) rather are from an undiscovered level of reality or consciousness; (4) a level independent of man but closely tied to the earth, (5) with its own "relationship to cosmic forces."[7]

Unlike Sagan, however, Vallée definitely believes in a "psychic component" in the UFO phenomenon, and that so-called Alien contactees have indeed tripped the "delicate levers of the collective unconscious." If segments of that unconsciousness can be made (consciously) manifest outside the body (through cracks in space-time), the range of hypotheses for the existence of ETIs/UFOs can be expanded virtually <u>ad infinitum</u>. Vallée has asked, "Are we dealing ... with a parallel universe, another dimension, where there are human[oid] races living, and where we may go ... never to return to the present?"[8] Vallée, as stated, also believes that a UFO is a real physical object, with mass, inertia, volume, and physical parameters; serving as "a window into another reality .... a window toward undiscovered dimensions of our own environment."[9] In concluding <u>Dimensions: A Casebook of Alien Contact</u>, Vallée emphatically states that the UFO phenomenon "<u>represents evidence for other dimensions beyond spacetime</u>; the UFOs may not come from ordinary [outer] space, but from a <u>multiverse</u> which is all around us...."[10]

There is another hypothesis as to the exact identity of the ETIs, but it entails a spiritual component in the UFO phenomenon. That spiritual component is perceived as the spirit of daemonic evil by evangelical Christians and other people of monotheistic faith. These are the "certain sectors" previously referred to as equating UFOlogy with the Angels craze. Both Aliens and Angels are viewed as wise, benign, supernatural rescuers who have come to save Earth and Humankind for the approaching New Age of Aquarius. As other New Age religions, UFOlogy and Angelology are passively-received, values-free, non-judgmental, and unsoteriological. UFOlogy, which pretends to no Judaeo-Christian roots, has all the ear-marks of an occult sect. Kurt Koch, the renowned Christian theologian and daemonologist-exorcist, explained UFOlogy's occultic connections more than a decade ago (1986):

"The whole manner of communication between UFO's and contact persons proceeds in thousands of cases, according to occult rules. Frequently telepathy is the means of transferring messages. The UFO people also communicate by automatic writing, by use of the ouija board while in trance. All the spiritualistic rules of the game are practiced; levitation, teletransport, apports, telekinesis, pschokinesis, materializations, astral traveling and many more. UFO manifestations all arise from the same demonic morass."[11]

The numerous and proliferating UFO cults and societies vary from Ashtar Command to Urantia, with the Church of Scientology -- founded by the deceased, once-enigmatic L. Ron Hubbard ("Dianetics") -- being the most (in)famous.[12] Christian physician and cardiologist Maurice Rawlings is also an expert on near-death-experience (NDE), and reported in 1993 that "some well-known NDE researchers" were spiritualising UFOs, correlating The Light, seen by UFO observers and those experiencing near-death, as one and the same.

Indeed, some of these NDE researchers have developed the devilish idea of combining UFOs with NDEs, to form the combined category of "Extraordinary Encounters" (EEs); engendering a whole New Age potential for psychospiritual after-effects. According to Kenneth Ring, of the Omega Project, in the new revelation of EEs "We are experiencing the first bursts of a ... self-renewing power for the healing of the earth, with millennial energies that have been liberated through direct contact with the transcendental order."[13] The Omega Project believes that a "Planetary Overmind" operates behind the transcendental order "directing the psychospiritual preparation and evolution of Mankind toward ....[the] Omega[n] [Brave New World].[14] Professor Ring elaborated further, that UFO and NDE psychospiritual contacts act as agents of the Planetary Overmind for "deconstruction" of human belief systems, cultures, and even evolution. The synergy of fused UFOs and NDEs (the EEs) will transform the human body, mind, and soul into the New Age Man, Homo noeticus. Ring ventured that the Extraordinary Encounters might "presage the shamanizing of modern humanity."[15]

If the above sounds familiar to the reader, it should be: We are back where we left off in Chapter 2, Part I, with the sylphs of the air and sprites of the earth. But we've journeyed this far, to UFOs in the New Age, and we're not turning back. The momentary return to terrestrial spirits comes as a result of Kenneth Ring's reference to "the shamanizing of modern humanity." Jacques Vallée's main thesis has been that supernatural contacts since time memorial -- "Greco-Roman tales of sky chariots, Celtic stories of elves and fairies [The Little People] abducting children and mutilating animals, Joseph Smith's alleged heavenly visions, even apparitions of the Virgin Mary"[16] -- exactly parallel the earthly contacts of "close encounters" with UFOs and ETIs. That UFOlogy/E.T. worship now qualifies as a bona fide religious creed does not surprise this writer. The enveloping and devouring New Age movement is like a great, syncretistic octopus gathering in its tentacles all belief systems, save the strict monotheisms: Orthodox Judaism, evangelical Christianity, fundamentalist Islam. Along with New Age expansion, the concept of local gods and resident spirits has gained ground world-wide during the "shamanizing of modern humanity" in the 1990s. Jacques Vallée has commented:

"The most interesting theory put forth by [Walter] Evans-Wentz [American Celtic folklorist during the early 20th century] is a further development of the observation that ancient gods are continued under new names as myths evolve from civilization to civilization. Could it be, he asked, that every land has its own psychic and telluric forces, contributing to the appearance of certain spirit entities, regarded by human beings as gods and goddesses?"[17]

The question should also be asked: Could those spirit entities be the omnipresent and ubiquitous daemons in Holy Scripture? The evangelical Christian would certainly think so! Those spirit entities may be likened to an infernal troupe of travelling actors on an eternal mediaeval Magical Tour. They are Morris dancers and Mystery players who are forever changing masques and costumes ... but these actors are always those same old daemons; appearing whenever and wherever they will, from cracks in space-time out of the multiverse. Throughout space-time they have appeared as "Shining Beings" (et al.) to accomplish all their mischief. In the 1990s, the "Shining Beings" are being sighted as Aquarian Angels and New Age Aliens.

NOTES

1. Saint Agobard, Archbishop of Lyons, France (779-840 A.D.), referred to outer space-time (the parallel universe) as <u>Magonia</u>; its interdimensional denizens as <u>Magonians</u>. St. Agobard was the author of <u>De Grandine et Tonitruis</u> ("Of Hail and Thunder"). This early work on UFOs and ETIs was revised and reprinted a millennium after his death, in 1841, by Imprimerie de Demoulin, Ronet et Sibuet, Quai St. Antoine, Lyon, France. From Vallée, <u>Dimensions</u>, pp.15,63.

2. Carl Sagan, 'UFOs: The Extraterrestrial and Other Hypotheses', <u>UFOs -- A Scientific Debate</u>, eds. Carl Sagan, Thornton Page (New York:Norton, 1972), p.272. Quoted in William M. Alnor, <u>UFOs in the New Age</u> (Grand Rapids, Mich.:Baker Book House, 1993 ed.), pp.14-15.

3. Godfrey Daniels, <u>Planet 21</u>, 11-24 October 1995, p.13.

4. Op.cit., Jacques Vallée. <u>Ibid.</u>, p.13.

5. Op cit., Godfrey Daniels. <u>Ibid.</u>, p.13.

6. Carl Sagan, 'What's really Going On?', <u>Parade Magazine</u>, 7 March 1993, p.6. Quoted by Maurice S. Rawlings, M.D., <u>To Hell and Back</u> (Nashville, Tenn.:Thomas Nelson Publishers, 1993), p.221.

7. Jacques Vallée, <u>Dimensions: A Casebook of Alien Contact</u> (New York:Ballantine Books, 1989), p. xvii, Introduction.

8. <u>Ibid.</u>, pp.143,ff.

9. <u>Ibid.</u>, pp.202-203.

10. <u>Ibid.</u>, p.253.

11. Kurt E. Koch, 'E. Supplement: UFO', <u>Occult ABC</u> (Grand Rapids, Mich.:Kregel Publications, 1986), p.341. Translated from the German by Michael Freeman.

12. <u>Texe Marrs Book of New Age Cults & Religions</u>, Living Truth Publishers (Austin, Tex.:1990), pp.286-290, 321-323, 330-331.

13. Kenneth Ring, <u>The Omega Project</u> (New York:William Morrow and Company, 1992), p.236. Cited by William S. Rawlings, M.D., p.220.

14. Op.cit., Rawlings, p.220.

15. <u>Ibid.</u>, p.221. Op.cit., Ring, <u>passim</u>.

16. Op.cit., Godfrey Daniels, <u>Planet 21</u>, p.13.

17. Jacques Vallée, 'Shining Beings', <u>Dimensions</u>, p.185.

Bibliography

1. Alnor, William M. <u>UFOs in the New Age</u>. Baker Book House, Grand Rapids, Mich. 1993 ed.

2. Fowles, John. <u>A Maggot</u>. New American Library, New York, 1986.

3. Vallée, Jacques. <u>Dimensions: A Casebook of Alien Contact</u>. Ballantine Books, New York, 1989.

Appendix M

"Liberal" labels as opposed to "conservative" labels:

e.g. 1. Labels applied by Theodore Roszak, author of ...Counter Culture[1] (1969)

Historic/cultural figure	Roszak's label
Brown, Norman O.	Apocalyptic Body Mysticism
Goodman, Paul	Gestalt-therapy Anarchism
Leary, Timothy	Occult Narcissism
Marcuse, Herbert	Freudian Marxism
Mills, C. Wright	New Left Sociology
Shaw, George Bernard	[Atheistic] Vitalism
Watts, Alan	Zen-based Psychotherapy

e.g. 2. Labels applied by C.D. Bay-Hansen, author of FutureFish... (1996)

Historic/cultural figure	Bay-Hansen's label
Capra, Fritjof	Taoist Quantum Physics
Carson, Rachel	Buddhistic Environmentalism
Clarke, Arthur C.	Astronomic Monism
Einstein, Albert	Ontological Deism
Marx, Wesley	Sierra Club Ecologism
Rifkin, Jeremy	New Age Geosophism
Sagan, Carl	Romantic Scientism
Spinoza, Baruch	Kabbalistic Pantheism

[1] Source: Theodore Roszak, The Making of a Counter Culture [Reflections on the technocratic society and its youthful opposition] (Garden City, N.Y.:Anchor Books, Doubleday & Company, Inc., 1969). See pp. 56, 64, 140, 167.

Appendix N

Afterdeath: Carl Sagan and Olam Haba[1]
(A Messianic Cautionary Tale)

"Reb Azrielke: 'Only he who has wandered from the straight path seeks out others.'"
-- S. Ansky, The Dybbuk: Between Two Worlds

"It is a fearful thing to fall into the hands of the living God."
-- Hebrews 10:31, Holy Bible, New King James Version

The brilliant astrophysicist Carl Edward Sagan (1934-1996) seemed to have a rational answer to every perplexing question. The articulate and personable "science popularizer" even had a naturalistic explanation for near-death experience (NDE) and out-of-body-experience (OBE). Simply put, this writer would characterise the good doctor's considered opinion on NDE/OBE as "The Strange Amniotic World of Carl Sagan" (the original title of Appendix N). For Sagan sincerely believed the NDE/OBE to be merely foetal/infantile memory of birth-pang trauma. In Broca's Brain, he brushed off Judaeo-Christian assertions that NDEs/OBEs were real visions of the olam haba, the world to come. In response, Sagan wrote:

"The only alternative [to the Judaeo-Christian view], as far as I can see, is that [e]very human being, without exception, has already shared an experience like that of those travelers who return from the land of death: the sensation of flight; the emergence from darkness into light; an experience in which ... a heroic figure can be dimly perceived, bathed in radiance and glory. There is only one common experience that matches this description. It is called birth."[2]

According to Dr. Carl Sagan, then, the NDE/OBE case is closed. A few pages earlier, Sagan described the post-NDE/OBE:

"And then he awoke ... he [as exemplar] had been resuscitated at the last possible moment ... [His] heart had stopped ... he had died. [He] was certain that he had died, and that he had been vouchsafed a glimpse of life after death and a confirmation of Judaeo-Christian theory."[3]

But what of the actual NDE/OBE itself; "he" [the exemplar] at the very door of death? Sagan dealt with that, too, in his own inimitable style:

"The operation was a success, but just as the anaesthesia was wearing off his heart went into fibrillation and he died. It seemed to him that he had somehow left his body and was able to look down upon it.... He regarded his body ... from a great height, it seemed -- and continued a kind of upward journey.... And then he was being illuminated from a distance, flooded with light. He entered a kind of radiant kingdom and there, just ahead of him, he could make out in silhouette, magnificently lit from behind, a great godlike figure whom he was now effortlessly approaching. [He] strained to make out His face...."[4]

It is at this juncture that the writer begs the reader's indulgence. If Carl Sagan's far-fetched hypothesis of the NDE/OBE, as being but a recall of the birth drama, may be noised abroad -- why not a Judaeo-Christian theory certainly as credible? But this gets personal, ad hominem. Let us conclude this as a messianic cautionary tale, with Carl Sagan as "he" (the exemplar). It is 20 December 1996, the day of Sagan's death.

...."[Carl] strained to make out His face." Was it that of Albert Einstein? Or perhaps it was that of Menachem Mendel Schneerson, the late, beloved rebbe of the Lubavitcher sect headquartered in Brooklyn, New York? Or was it that of the meshiach, the anointed one of G _ d? Surely not! Carl had heard about Him during his childhood. By now, Carl was getting close to the shining godlike figure, and was able to identify His face as that of a bearded young man of about thirty-three years of age ... with piercing but soft brown eyes; as Carl, Himself a Jew. Suddenly Carl Sagan's supernatural eyes widened in horror, his handsome face a mask of fear and loathing as he recognised who He was....

The moral: "But the natural man receiveth not the things of the Spirit of God: for they are foolishness unto him: neither can he know them, because they are spiritually discerned."

-- I Corinthians 2:14, Holy Bible, King James Version

NOTES

1. Or <u>olam chava</u> (Hebrew), "the world to come."

2. Carl Sagan, <u>Broca's Brain: Reflections on the Romance of Science</u> (New York:Ballantine Books, Inc., 1980), pp.356-357.

3. <u>Ibid.</u>, p.354.

4. <u>Ibid.</u>, p.354.

Bibliography

1. Ansky, S. (Shloyme Z. Rappaport). <u>The Dybbuk: Between Two Worlds</u>. Regnery Gateway, Inc., Washington, D.C., 1978 ed. Translated from the Yiddish by S. Morris Engel. (A play first performed 1920 in Warsaw, Poland, 30 days after Ansky's death as a tribute).

2. Unterman, Alan. <u>Dictionary of Jewish Lore and Legend</u>. Thames and Hudson Ltd., London (U.K.), 1991.

Appendix O

<u>Darwin; Darwinismus, and Neo-Darwinism</u>

"Newton banished God from nature, Darwin banished [H]im from life, Freud drove [H]im from the last fastness, the Soul. It was all latent in Newton, in Descartes, in Galileo; mechanism would conquer all, once it had conquered nature, for man's body was sprung from nature and his mind from his body."
-- Critic Gerald Heard quoted by Jacques Barzun in <u>Darwin, Marx, Wagner,</u> 1941

"Copernicus displaced us from the centre of the universe, Darwin closed Eden, showing that we are apes with shrews for ancestors and cabbages for cousins. Freud pointed out that we are not our own masters even in our own heads.... Modern genetics showed that we share over 98 percent of our genes with chimpanzees."
--Galen Strawson, <u>London Times Literary Supplement,</u> 1996

In late 1996, this writer saw a bumper-sticker which warmed his heart during a cold winter: The Christian fish (Greek, <u>ichthys</u>) swallowing a Darwinian amphibian, whole (along with feet). In early 1997, the writer read a very funny novel, <u>The Darwin Conspiracy,</u> by James Scott Bell.[1] But between the hilarious passages, Bell dealt effectively with the extremely grave issues of evolutionism-as-religion versus Judaeo-- Christian beliefs. Bell offered a recent incident as exemplar:

...."In late 1993, a biology professor at San Francisco State University, Dean Kenyon, was ordered silenced for pointing out flaws in the Darwinian view and evidence for intelligent design. Kenyon, a world-class scientist and recognized expert on chemical evolutionary theory, had come to the conclusion that the Darwinian model was baseless. When Kenyon challenged the threat to his academic freedom, he was yanked from teaching biology classes and reassigned to innocuous lab work."[2]

What immediately came to this writer's mind was--how had evolutionism become established as the Darwinian state religion, wherein "heretics" (like Dean Kenyon) were burned at the pc 90s academic stake? Who really was Charles Darwin anyway? Briefly told, Charles Robert Darwin was born a Shropshire lad on 12 February 1809, and died 19 April 1882. He produced two world-changing books, <u>On the Origin of Species</u> (1859) and <u>The Descent of Man</u> (1871). As a young man, Charles Darwin embarked aboard the H.M.S. <u>Beagle</u> (1831), sailing to far-away places including South America and many Pacific islands. Of interest to us, was Darwin's preoccupation with the formation of atolls and the taxonomy of barnacles. (See <u>Pollicipes polymerus</u> and <u>Balanus nubilis,</u> both Darwin, 1851.) To Christian determinists such as this writer, Charles Darwin is a historically significant biologist whose works are both informative and interesting to read. But Charles Darwin, possessed of no personal animus against Christianity, would, with time, become the eponymous "founder" of Darwinism; the unofficial state religion of the post-Christian West.

Thus Darwinism, along with its concurrent unholy stable-mate, Marxism (and Marxismus, neo-Marxism), jointly exhaled the musty stench of 19th century political (dialectic materialism) and religious (scientific materialism) death deep into our atheistic twentieth century; a deathly stench that may last well into the twenty-first. Darwinismus, so called by 19th century German intellectuals, is defined by the Encyclopedia Britannica as a "theory of evolutionary mechanism as an explanation of organic change." In neo-Darwinism, on the basis of twentieth century newer knowledge, "classical" Darwinism has been purged of lingering attachment to the Lamarckian theory of inheritance of acquired characteristics. Modern neo-Darwinism preaches that scientism can now better distinguish between non-inheritable bodily variation, and variation of a genuinely inheritable kind.[3]

As a student at Seattle Pacific University during the late 1970s, this writer was taught that the four great anti-Christs of history were Darwin, Marx, Nietzsche, and Freud. John Scott Bell, in his end notes of The Darwin Conspiracy, identified the "most influential atheists" as Nietzsche, Freud, and Thomas H. Huxley, the last known in his time as "Darwin's bulldog".[4] Huxley, of course, regarded Darwinism as a weapon to destroy Christianity.[5] Otherwise, Bell's offenders look remarkably similar to those of the crusty Christian history teacher's at SPU. Phillip E. Johnson, the eminent author of Darwin on Trial, called Bell's novel "... a mischievous book, and a very funny one, which makes some shrewd points in the course of telling a fantastic story. I enjoyed it immensely!"[6] (This writer did too.) But in the light of 1990s scientific-incorrectness as thought-crime, Darwin, Darwinismus, and neo-Darwinism are deadly serious issues.

Jacques Barzun's Darwin, Marx, Wagner was a fine perspective--first published in 1941--from which to properly place Charles Darwin in historical context.[7] Here, the writer learned, that it was at England's Metaphysical Society where "'Archbishop [arch-atheist Thomas H.] Huxley'" first coined the word "'agnostic'"; it was Herbert Spencer from whom Charles Darwin borrowed the phrase "'survival of the fittest'";[8] and that it was not Charles Darwin who began theorising on macro-evolution--that distinction belonged to Erasmus Darwin, Charles Darwin's grandfather, and others.[9] But evolutionism had to have a name and Charles Darwin became its epononym. Natural selection's appeal to both scientists and laymen was immediate: 1) It had the persuasiveness of gradualism; (2) it was automatic, entirely ridding man of the religious will of a Creator, or the (Lamarckian) will of His creatures; and (3) natural selection paralleled in nature what was happening in late nineteenth century society--Prussian militarism, ruthless robber-baron competition, the "eat or be eaten" of Erasmus Darwin.[10] Despite all the problems of scientific acceptance that evolutionism was to face, the Darwinist paradigm was here to stay. For Darwinism, in addition to the three reasons listed above for the short-run, in the longer run acted as a "test case for freedom of scientific inquiry" (i.e., unrestricted, unlimited freedom for scientists), and (it) satisfied the first requirement of a religion by "subsuming all phenomena under one cause." Surmised Jacques Barzun, "The scientific quest and the religious wish, both striving for unity, were thus fulfilled at one stroke".[11]

The uses of Darwinism are what we are experiencing today, especially during these pc 1990s. Barzun observed that materialism itself does not arise from any scientific or historical method, but emanates from the philosophy concealed in the use by the proponents of said method. It is there, summarised Barzun, that Darwinism..."can justly be accused of destroying faith and morality--not Darwin and his book, but the entire movement from which he sprang and to which he supplied impetus and a name."[12] Charles Darwin didn't invent a "dog eat dog" world, but he did transform political science forever. Both national [ethnic] and political [class] war (under the cloak of Darwinismus or Marxismus) became "the symbol, the image, the inducement, the reason, and the language of all human doings on the planet."[13]

Miami [Florida]-based syndicated columnist-comedian, Dave Barry, has referred to a National Science Foundation survey, conducted in 1996, which showed that the average U.S. citizen doesn't understand basic scientific principles.[14] The survey didn't disappoint Barry; as he wrote, "This is, after all, a nation that has produced tournament bass fishing and the Home Shopping Channel; we should be shocked that the average American still knows how to walk erect."[15]

Dave Barry's mild satire, however, proves that Jacques Barzun, writing more than fifty years ago, was prescient: "[T]he public holds to a touching belief in the absolute unanimity of science. Encouraged in dogmatic habits by the words of popularizers [i.e., the late Carl Sagan], it accepts what 'science [eg., evolutionism] says' or trust that 'we now know'... as if some agency existed for creating agreement among the workers of a particular age or ascertaining their consensus"[16]....This is probably even more true in the 1990s than it was a half century ago.

As a scruffy schoolboy at Deerfield, Massachusetts, from 1959-1963, this writer watched "Inherit the Wind" (1960, directed by Stanley Kramer), a Hollywood version of the Bible-versus-science J. T. Scopes "monkey trial" set in 1925 Tennessee. Even though the movie ended with the "triumphant" Clarence Darrow's (Spencer Tracy) hand on the Book, "Inherit the Wind" made the William Jennings Bryan (Fredric March) character look like a blow-hard Bible-thumping buffoon, and Christian creation-science as a complete fraud. More than thirty-five years later, special creation-science is still treated as scurrilous by Hollywood, the mass-media at large, and "the scientific community". This writer, an impressionable teenager in 1960, still recalls the feeling of fear and foreboding on viewing "Inherit the Wind."

Among those leading the charge against Darwinist evolutionism during the 1990s, has been Phillip E. Johnson, former law clerk to U.S. Chief Justice Earl Warren and professor of law (for more than twenty years) at U. Cal. Berkeley. The critics--and critiques--of Darwinism seem to be proliferating in the 1990s, but Johnson's Darwin on Trial (1991) is still definitive.[17] To counter-macro-evolutionism and neo-Darwinism, Johnson has employed an empirical dissecting knife to do so:

1. The Fossil Problem. Johnson opened his case most effectively by citing Darwin asking in 1859, "[W]hy, if species have descended from other species by insensibly fine gradations, do we not everywhere see innumerable transitional forms? Why is not all nature in confusion instead of the species being, as we see the, well defined?"[18] Why not indeed?

2. Archaeopterix. The discovery of Archaeopterix, the ancient bird with certain pronounced reptilian features, convinced many in "the scientific community" of sufficient fossil confirmation to justify macro-evolutionism.[19] In 1985, though, two respected scientists, Sir Fred Hoyle and Chandra Wickramasinghe, protested that the Archaeopterix fossil was bogus. But the British Museum, having paid handsomely for the fossil, disagreed.[20] (James Scott Bell, author of The Darwin Conspiracy, made the point that even if Archaeopterix were the real McCoy., it would hardly prove descent through modification--no other fossils lead to or came from it; thus Archaeopterix cannot be considered an example of transformation.)[21]

Moreover, Phillip Johnson referred to a 1990 review article by a Peter Wellnhofer, a "recognized authority', who admitted the impossibility in determining whether Archaeopterix was the actual ancestor of modern birds...or not. Wellnhofer concluded that..."this correlation is not of major importance...[as Archaeopterix specimens] provide clues as to how birds evolved....[and because] they are documents without which the idea of evolution would not be as powerful!"[22] Despite this supposedly Darwinist-supportive

evidence, the scientific jury is still out in 1996-7 on Archaeopterix.[23]

      3. Punctuated Equilibrium. (Johnson has told us that this is known as "punk eek' to the irreverent.) This theory was formulated by a 1970s revisit to fossil records by Stephen Jay Gould, Niles Eldredge and Steven Stanley to basically address an evolutionary embarrassment: The fossil record in the 1970s (and today after all that fossil hunting) looked very similar to that of 1859 (The Origin of Species).[24] The Gould-Eldredge theory of "punctuated equilibrium" postulated that gradual transitions have not occurred because evolution takes place in sudden--"punctuated"--leaps. (James Scott Bell has wryly commented that "punctuated equilibrium" is yet another article of evolutionary "faith", i.e., no one can explain the mechanism of these leaps--the how--or why they happen.)[25] Steven Stanley summed up, after a palaeontological analysis of the (ca. five million year-old) Bighorn Basin in Wyoming: "[T]he fossil record does not convincingly document a single transition from one species to another."[26]

Charles Darwin at the very outset wanted to accomplish for biology what contemporaneous lawyer-geologist Charles Lyell (1797-1875) had done for geology; namely to explain the great changes over time in gradual, uniform stages--natural forces still seen to be working in the present. But the saltations (systemic macro-mutations)--the sudden leaps--of the "punctuated equilibria" espoused by Gould and Eldredge, flew in the face of Charles Darwin and indeed in the faces of most scientist.[27] No matter; Stephen Jay Gould and Niles Eldredge have always included their theory under the Darwinist rubric.[28] As Phillip E. Johnson tersely stated, "Darwinism [has] apparently passed the fossil test, but only because it was not allowed to fail."[29] Darwinism in our time has become the Fact of Evolution.

There are many reasons to refute macro-evolutionism, both scientific (chemical, molecular) and religious (moral, ethical), and the myth is perpetuated by familiar-face neo-Darwinists such as Isaac Asimov, Stephen Jay Gould, Richard Leakey, Ashley Montagu et al. They, and the myth, are strongly supported by the fourth estate and the academy. Why is this so? Because Darwinist evolutionism has become a credo, an article of evolutionary "faith." Phillip E. Johnson has wrapped it all up:

    ...."As the creation myth of scientific naturalism, Darwinism plays an indispensable ideological role in the war against fundamentalism. For that reason, the scientific organizations are devoted to protecting Darwinism rather than testing it, and the rules of scientific investigation have been shaped to help them succeed."[30]

NOTES

1. Vision House Publishers, Inc., Gresham, Ore., 1995.

2. Ibid., p.151. NB: This writer attended SFSU for half a semester in 1974. SFSU was a terrifying place, despite the heroic efforts of S.I. Hayakawa.

3. Jean-Baptist[e] [Pierre Antoine de Monet] Lamarck (1744-1829).Pioneering French biologist and fore-runner of Charles Darwin. Despite his achievements, Lamarck died blind and in poverty. "Lamarckianism" was coined in 1802.

4. James Scott Bell, p.267.

5. Ibid., p.271.

6. Ibid., back cover.

7. Anchor Books, Doubleday & Company, Inc., New York, 1958 ed.

8. Ibid., pp.35,37,45-46.

9   .Ibid., p.55. Eg., Alfred, Lord Tennyson: "Nature red in   tooth and claw."

10. Ibid., pp.57-58.

11. Ibid., p.65.

12. Ibid., p.91.

13. Ibid., p.92.

14. Dave Barry, 'A page from Scientific (Illiterate) American; Peninsula Daily News, 7 July 1996, p.A-8.

15. Ibid.., p.A-8.

16. Jacques Barzun, p.122.

17. Phillip E. Johnson, Darwin on Trial (Downers Grove, Ill.: InterVarsity Press, 1993 ed.)

18. Ibid., p.46. Darwin quotation from the first edition of The Origin of Species (Penguin Library edition, 1982), p.133, ff.

19. Ibid., p.49.

20. James Scott Bell, p.271.

21. Ibid., p.271.

22. Phillip E. Johnson, pp.80-81. Brackets this writer's.

23. 'Scientists voice doubt birds, dinosaurs of same feather,' Peninsula Daily News, 17 November 1996, p.C-5.

NOTES (con't)

24. Phillip E. Johnson, p.50.

25. James Scott Bell, p.270.

26. Phillip E. Johnson, p.51.

27. Ibid., pp.33,32. This writer's emphasis.

28. Ibid., p.61.

29. Ibid., p.48.

30. Op.cit., p.155.

Bibliography

1. Barzun, Jacques. Darwin, Marx, Wagner: Critique of a Heritage. Anchor Books, Doubleday & Company, Inc., New York, 1958 ed. Copyright 1941.

2. Bell, James Scott. The Darwin Conspiracy. Vision House Publishers, Inc., Gresham, Ore., 1995. (A novel).

3. Johnson, Phillip E. Darwin on Trial. InterVarsity Press, Downers Grove, Ill., 1993 ed.

Scientists Who Have Rejected Darwinism

"Evolutionary humanism is...emerging as the new system of thought and belief concerned with our destiny. Man is a natural phenomenon produced by the evolutionary process...."

— Blurb on dust-jacket of The Humanist Frame (London: Allen & Unwin, 1965), Julian Huxley, ed.

Scientists who have rejected Darwinism:

1. Erik Nordenskiöld, biology

2. Sir Fred Hoyle, astronomy/mathematics

3. Chandra Wickramasinghe, astronomy/mathematics

4. H. S. Lipson, physics

5. W. R. Thompson, entomology

        ___ In   Alan Hayward

6. George Smoot, astronomy

7. Leon Lederman, physics

8. Frank Tipler, physics

        ___ In Carl Sagan

9. Michael Behe, biochemistry

10. Dean Kenyon, biology

11. Charles Thaxton, chemistry

12. Michael Denton, biochemistry

13. Robert Kaita, plasma - physics

14. Siegfried Scherer, taxonomy/molecular biology

        ___ In Human Events

Appendix P (concl'd.)

<u>Scientists Who Have Rejected Darwinism</u>

15.   Kurt Wise, palaeontology/geology

16.   Russell Humphreys, power generation

17.   John Baumgardner, geophysics

_____ In <u>Newsweek</u>

18.   Robert C. Newman, astrophysics

19.   Robert Selvendran, biochemistry

20.   Randall J. Fish, nuclear physics

21.   Col. James B. Irwin, Apollo 15 NASA astronaut

22.   Col. Jack Lousma, Skylab-3 NASA astronaut

_____ In Barret And Fisher

<u>Sources</u>

1.   Barret, Eric And David Fisher, eds. <u>Scientists Who Believe</u>. Moody Press, Chicago, 1984.

2.   Hayward, Alan. <u>Creation and Evolution</u>. Bethany House Publishers, Minneapolis, Minn., 1995 ed.

3.   Sagan, Carl. <u>The Demon - Haunted World</u>. Random House, New York, 1995.

4.   <u>Human Events</u> and <u>Newsweek</u> magazines.

If you enjoyed this book, please look for its companion volume
on the Trafford Publishing Website:

<u>FutureFish in Century 21: The North Pacific Fisheries Tackle
Asian Markets, the Can-Am Salmon Treaty,
and Micronesian Seas (1997-2001)</u>

Coming soon at

www.trafford.com

ISBN 155212411-8

9 781552 124116